HANDBOOK

CYCLE 3

Schola Rosa: Co-op & Home Curriculum

Author: Alecia J. Rolling

Contributors and Co-Editors:

Kenneth J. Rolling and T. Matthew Meyer

First Edition

MW01131773

No part of this publication may be reproduced in whole or in part, or stored in a retrieval system, or transmitted in any form or by any means, electronic, mechanical, photocopying, recording, or otherwise, without written permission of the publisher. For information regarding permission, write to The Rolling Acres School, Attn: Schola Rosa, P.O. Box 3, Lake Benton, MN 56149 or scholarosa@gmail.com.

Cover Art Credit:

"Der Schulspaziergang" 1872 "Von Anker bis Zünd, Die Kunst im jungen Bundesstaat 1848 - 1900", Kunsthaus Zürich

Copyright @ 2016 The Rolling Acres School, LLC.

All Rights Reserved.

ISBN-13: 978-1986760607
ISBN-10: 198676060X

AD GLORIAM DEI

Table of Contents

Foreword

Schola Rosa: Co-op & Home has been a work of the Rolling Family since 2012 as a response to the increasing requests to create a program for PreK – 6th Grade that prepares students for the Rolling Acres School Online Academy, that promotes a rigorous Catholic and Classical education, and that inspires families to be involved in their local parish life and Catholic communities. With this mission, *Schola Rosa: Co-op & Home Curriculum* has become much more than just another curriculum --- it is building faith-centered communities.

We humbly ask you to pray for the Rolling Family and for Schola Rosa and Rolling Acres School staff as you use this curriculum throughout the year. May God bless your efforts and ours as we seek to educate our children.

To find out more about Schola Rosa programs, visit www.scholarosa.com and find a co-op community near you.

i

Training

❖ This section takes you through a series of tips for understanding how to use the handbook, how to set your schedule, and how to create a learning environment conducive to the *Schola Rosa: Co-op & Home Curriculum.*

How to Use the Handbook

Every Unit in the online suite contains a Handbook to guide you throughout the unit in finding your materials and planning your week. This Cycle Handbook contains each unit handbook printed in one place. Be sure to listen to the Training Lessons # 1, #2, and #3 in the online suite to understand how to use the Handbook.

You might be wondering why a "Handbook"? Well, putting seven grades on two sheets of paper was no easy task, and it certainly involved some creative maneuvering. For example, there is a short abbreviation key that you will want to learn for locating materials quickly. You will also see that the details of lessons are in the online suite and/or in printables rather than in the Handbook. Having abbreviations and saving details for the printables allow you to have all your students' lesson plans on a couple of planner pages at a glance. As you sit down and learn how to use the Handbook, pay close attention to those abbreviations, which you will most often need for your family.

How to Set your Schedule

There is no way around it; scheduling your homeschool around several children at different ages is a logistical feat of wonder and awesomeness. Indeed, this is perhaps the greatest challenge of homeschooling: *How do I work in enough time with each student?* To this end we have provided both co-op families and just-home families some advice.

If you are in a co-op, the most logistically difficult tasks are taken care of on your co-op day. That said, you might wonder how to schedule teaching the subjects in your home the rest of the week. Here is a suggested schedule that has worked for many families over the years.

Sample Schedule for At-Home after Co-op
1. 9:00 am Start with "assembly" just like at co-op; prayers, hymn, virtue, memory work
2. 9:20 am Do a Letter Book page with your Pre-K to 1st grade students (you can make extra letter books by using the pages provided in the online suite; this is a good review for your K-1st graders!) Have older students working on their subjects and reporting to you when they finish an assignment.
3. 9:35 am Math! Give a brief instruction to each student and have each student working on his own math activity. Each student should wait his turn before asking you a question or before showing you completed work. This is an exercise in courtesy and patience.
4. 9:50 am Park or P.E. (If you have older students, allow them to entertain the little ones while you check over their work.)
5. 10:30 am Snack and Science Discussion
6. 11:00 am Work on Language Lesson and History Stories/Activities
7. 12:00 pm Lunch and Religion Discussion

8. 1:00 pm Phonics and Writing while littlest ones nap; be available for older students who have questions or need to show you work. Work on Latin/Greek.

If you are NOT in a co-op and you are JUST HOME, you might be wondering how you are supposed to complete all the Day 1 tasks in one day. We recommend that you space these tasks throughout the week to make clean-up and completion easier on the whole family. Here is a suggested schedule for your "Just Home" family, but feel free to alter it to your family's needs.

Schedule for JUST HOME
- 9:00 am Start with "assembly" (prayers, hymn, virtue, memory work).
- 9:20 am Do a Letter Book page with your Pre-K to 1st grade students Have older students working on their subjects and reporting to you when they finish an assignment.
- 9:35 am Math! Give a brief instruction to each student and have each student working on his own math activity. Each student should wait his turn before asking you a question or before showing you completed work. This is an exercise in courtesy and patience.
- 9:50 am Park or P.E. (If you have older students, allow them to do exercises and games with the little ones while you check over their work.)
- 10:30 am Snack and Science Discussion
- 11:00 am Work on Language Lesson and History Stories/Activities
   - Day 1: Add an introduction to each subject, activities for history, science, and religion
   - Day 2: Complete Art.
   - Day 3: Complete Music.
   - Day 4: Complete Preschool Craft.
- 12:00 pm Lunch and Religion
- 1:00 pm Phonics and Writing while littlest ones nap; be available for older students who have questions or need to show you work. Work on Latin/Greek and do an activity especially geared towards these older kids!

> Spacing the "BIG" Co-op Day activities throughout your week may help your family; however, some families have had success putting all the activities on one day. Feel free to test both and see which works best for your family.

As you continue to look through the Handbook, consider where lessons and activities will best fit into your family's overall schedule and make a PLAN. Regardless of the schedule you choose, it is having a plan and being prepared that will make the greatest difference in helping your week flow smoothly.

How to Create a Learning Environment

There are some basic strategies that can be followed in the home for making learning easier for your children.

For starters, you can target those activities that disable attention spans and encumber the ability to focus by instituting the following family rules:

1. No Television
2. No Video Games
3. No Movies

Training

Secondly, you can target those activities which build solidarity in your home and amongst your family members by establishing the following activities as a rule:

1. **Put a Message on Your Phone.** Communicate to others that you are homeschooling and are not available between the hours of x and x, but will return the phone call as soon as you are able. One, this tells people that homeschooling is a serious job, and two, that your job as a homeschooling mother should be honored.

2. **Family Supper Time is Protected** ~ Make meal time in the evenings a chance for discussion and togetherness, not even answering the phone or text messaging during this time. Give each child and adult a chance to report on the day and bring up questions that involve the entire family.

3. **Family Time is *Family Time*!** Activities such as playing ball outside, going on a walk, playing at the playground, playing board games, singing beside the fire, reading together, and so on involve your children in your life and help them know that you care about sharing the good things of life with them – together. This also communicates that you care about their *souls,* about their development as human beings.

4. **Sundays are Sacred** – Make them special for your family by spending quality time together doing wholesome things that build family, community, and prayer life. Find ideas at www.scholarosa.com under the title "Keeping Sundays Holy Series."

Homeschooling is truly an adventure for us all, and we hope that you have great success this year! Contact us at scholarosa@gmail.com if you have any curricular questions that cannot be answered by your local director.

Training

RENAISSANCE ARTISTS, MUSICIANS, & SCHOLARS

UNIT CHECKLIST

PREP FOR HOME

- ☐ Print and read this Handbook
- ☐ Read the Overview
- ☐ Review the Planner; do the following:
    - o Locate and review all Lessons and Activities in the Subject Folders (SF)
    - o Locate and review all readings and assignments in the Subject Folders (SF), Digital Library (DL), and Hard Copies (HC)
    - o Note and gather needed supplies for the unit
- ☐ Read the Virtue Lesson
- ☐ Email or call R.A.S. if you have questions or technical difficulty.

PREP FOR CO-OP

- ☐ Print your "Co-op Job Sheet" and prep for your job
- ☐ Make sure your child is ready for his or her presentation if assigned to present
- ☐ Gather maps, notebooks, prayer sheet, and other supplies the night or morning before the co-op meets.
- ☐ Gather students' assignments the night or morning before the co-op meets
- ☐ Listen to the Memory Work on the way!

PREP FOR UPCOMING WEEKS — <u>LOOK AHEAD AT UNITS 2–4</u>

- ☐ Make advanced purchases, as necessary
- ☐ Begin to gather books and materials

> Know your abbreviations to know where lessons, activities, and books can be found.

PLANNER ABBREVIATION KEY

DL	Digital Library (in course suite)
SF	Subject Folder (in course suite)
HC	Hard Copy
PLL	*Primary Language Lessons* (book)
ILL	*Intermediate Language Lessons* (book)
RS4K	*Real Science 4 Kids* (book)
I-CAT	*Illustrated Catechism* (book)
OHF-1	*Our Holy Faith, Book 1* (book)
OHF-2	*Our Holy Faith, Book 2* (book)
OHF-4	*Our Holy Faith, Book 4* (book)
OHF-1-TM	*Our Holy Faith, Book 1, Teacher's Manual* (book)

OVERVIEW

Common Topics (All students PreK to 6th)

Virtue:	Love
Hymn:	Tantum Ergo
Prayers:	Angelus, Pater Noster, Ave Maria, Gloria Patri
History:	Renaissance Artists, Musicians, and Scholars
Science:	Atoms

History Themes

"Historical Themes" summarizes the point of the unit's history lessons. To understand why there is a particular historical topic in a unit, simply read this.

We begin Unit 1 with a return to the Christian Age to be reminded of the greatness that is inherited by the Renaissance from the Middle Ages. We covered such great preachers as St. Dominic and churchmen like St. Thomas à Becket in Cycle 2, but we did not read much about the scholars, artists, and musicians of the 13th and 14th centuries, so we will not only learn about the early Renaissance figures, now, but those from the High Middle Ages, as well. It is a common misconception that it was not until the Renaissance that experimental science, art, and music developed, but what we learned in The Christian Age is that those genres blossomed in the medieval period and their fruits were born in the Renaissance. One might make the argument that what is considered beautiful and good in the Renaissance had its making in the medieval period, and indeed some refer to the period 1050-1450 as the High Middle Ages. This week we will learn about those fruits in scholarship, art, and music as we begin our studies of the Renaissance (1300-1600), focusing on the first period between 1300 and 1400.

For Pre-K through 6th grade, our focus is on what is good, true, and beautiful from these time periods. We will do this despite the fact that many of the issues and movements of modernity are things befitting of a critical attitude. A focused critique is left for 7th-12th graders, though some more mature readings are provided for parents. May God bless your studies this year!

Who were "scientists"?

This section is for parents. It offers brief explanations of the topics of the week to help you review history quickly and to give you tools in your toolbox for talking to older students.

Today we have a very specific definition of this term, which does not match up to the medieval or renaissance idea. One aspect of our goal for K-6th grade students this week is to resist the tendency to assert that "science" *began* in the Renaissance and to resist using the word "scientist" to describe the scholars of this period. The Latin word *scientia* simply means "knowledge", so anyone who sought knowledge was scientist, i.e. a "seeker of knowledge."

OVERVIEW

"Science" was not some separate field or set of fields to be studied outside the other categories of knowing. All learned persons who sought Truth experimented and measured or were familiar with that type of learning to some degree, yet they did not call themselves "scientists." It is Modern historians, then, who have put the label "scientist" on many great figures in history, thereby forcing them into a category inconsistent with the reality of their lives. These men and women were not "scientists;" they were seekers of Truth who were artists, musicians, mathematicians, astronomers, historians, philosophers, etc. They tried to use all their faculties and powers to learn the true, the good, and the beautiful. For this reason Schola Rosa does not emphasize "Great Scientists" when looking at the Renaissance; instead, we will refer to these learned men, to these 'seekers of Truth,' as *scholars*, underscoring their connection with the schools that were so central to learning in the high middle ages.

Art

Our goal for K-6th grade students this week is for them to see that art was not suddenly invented in the Renaissance. If students have completed Cycles 1 and 2, this will already stand out for them. What we want students to see is that the artists of this period continued the tradition they learned while experimenting with new techniques discovered in artwork found from the Classical Period. They were not inventing, but rediscovering beautiful techniques from the past.

A common misconception of these artists is that they were not Christian or that they were portraying pagan scenes as a way of "breaking free" from the Church. What we find in Renaissance art is a deep meditation on the metaphysical nature of man, freedom, and salvation. What is needed beyond Man's Intellect? Grace and Revelation. What is the result of man relying upon his own nature and powers? Sin and misery. Some paintings, true, stepped over the line of decency, but these did not meet a ready welcome by all. For example even Botticelli burned some of his paintings after hearing a Sermon by the Dominican Friar Savonarola.

Music

The beautiful polyphonic music of the Church flows from the Gregorian tradition of the Middle Ages. Many authors have argued that this was the pinnacle of Church liturgical music, pulling human thought toward God in his lofty heights.

There were some important instruments created in this period, for example, the viol, which allowed a greater variety of music. With the stability provided after the medieval Christianization and culturalization of Europe, musical composers became more and more widespread, working both for Church and King. By the time we get to the Early Modern period, we have such famous composers as Bach and Mozart.

OVERVIEW

This is a splendid period in music, this Renaissance, so try to take the time to listen to the sounds of the period.

How to Apply History to Everyday Life

Use the Virtue Guide this week to meditate on the theological virtue of Charity (or Love). Think about the call of each of us to remain in union with the One, Holy, Catholic, and Apostolic Church and what that means for each of us in our thoughts and actions with our neighbors. Can we just walk out of our local parish when something goes wrong, never to return again? Can we just banish a heretic, never to receive him back after reconciliation? This is a great difficulty, and we will see the challenge come soon enough in the Reformation.

"How to Apply History to Everyday Life" is for parents. It offers reflections on how to apply the historical lessons daily life.

Do I forgive the sinner? Do I instruct the ignorant? Do I practice the spiritual works of mercy? Do I feed the poor? Do I clothe the naked? Do I practice the corporal works of mercy? Do I pray for my enemy as well as my neighbor?

Important People, Events, and Places to Know (Potential Student Presentations)

❖ Boticelli (died ca. 1445), Girolamo Savonarola (1452-1498), Michelangelo (1475-1564), Raphael (1483-1520), Leonardo da Vinci (1452-1519), Albert the Great (1206-1280), Roger Bacon (1214-1294), Thomas Bradwardine (1290-1349), Jean Buridan (1300-1358), Giovanni di Casali (died 1375), Roman Llull (1232-1315), John Peckham (1230-1292), Richard of Wallingford (1292-1336), Nicolaus Copernicus (1473-1543)

❖ Saints (1300-1400 A.D.)

- St. Roch (1327)
- St. Elizabeth of Portugal (1236)
- St. Bridget of Sweden (1373)
- St. Andrew Corsini (1373)
- St. Conrad of Piacenza (1351)

- St. Noyburga (1313)
- St. Nicholas of Tolentino (1306)
- Bl. Raymond of Capua (1399)
- St. Flora of Beaulieu (1347)
- St. Gertrude the Great (1302)
- Bl. Urban V (1370)

Each week there are historical presentations in the 4th-6th grade class. If your student is scheduled to present, you may look here for quick topics.

OVERVIEW

Additional Project Ideas

- Renaissance Artists Flipbook
- Music Flipbook
- Scientia Flipbook
- Mastercopy of the Mona Lisa
- Perspective drawing of the Last Supper by da Vinci
- Sculpture study of Michelangelo's David or Pieta.

Week of _____   *Liturgical Theme & Colors* _____

Family Challenge-Task
Goals

_____

_____

_____

Reminders

_____

_____

_____

PRESCHOOL

	Music	Art, Reading, Religion	Virtue
Co-op	See "Music" heading below	Do craft **PreK Lesson A** (SF)	Review Virtue A-B (SF); practice "virtue training"
Day 2-4	See "Music" heading below	Do **Letter Book A-B** (SF); do **coloring pages** (SF); read & drill I-CAT, p. 5 (HC)	Review Virtue A-B (SF); practice "virtue training"

KINDERGARTEN – 6TH GRADE

ART

	K-6th Grade
Co-op	Do **All Lesson A** (SF).
Day 2-4	Review **All Lesson A** (SF) and do home follow-up.

CCM

	K-6th Grade
Co-op	Unit 1
Day 2-4	Listen to Unit 1 every day

HISTORY

	K-1st Grades	2nd-3rd Grades	4th-6th Grades
Co-op	Do **K-1 Lesson A** (SF).	Do **2-3 Lesson A** (SF).	Do **4-6 Lesson A** (SF).
Day 2	Read *Knights of Art* (DL) this week; Choose and do reading (or other project) from "Extras" (SF); draw a picture inspired by the readings	Read *Knights of Art* (DL) this week; Choose and do reading (or other project) from "Extras" (SF); draw a picture inspired by the readings	Read *Knights of Art* (DL); Choose and do readings (or other projects) from "Extras" (SF); begin writing **4-6 Activity A** (SF); listen to Polyphonic Music (DL).
Day 3	Continue readings; listen to Polyphonic Music (SF); do coloring page (SF).	Do online **2-3 Activity A** (SF); continue readings; listen to Polyphonic Music (SF); do coloring page (SF).	Read "Bellarmine ~ Doctor of the Church" (DL); do map **4-6 Activity B** (SF)
Day 4	Continue readings; Imagine & Draw a scene from the reading.	Continue readings; Imagine & Draw a scene from the reading	Do timeline **4-6 Activity C** (SF).

LANGUAGE ARTS

Co-op	Complete **K-1 Lesson A** (SF).	Complete **2-3 Lesson A** (SF); do **2-3 Activity B** (SF).	Complete **4-6 Lesson A** (SF); begin **4-6 Activity A** (SF).
Day 2	Review **K-1 Lesson A** (SF)	Review **2-3 Lesson A** (SF); continue **2-3 Activity A** (SF).	Review **4-6 Lesson A** (SF); continue **4-6 Activity A** (SF)
Day 3	Do pre-cursive copywork **K-1 Activity A** (SF).	Do cursive copywork **2-3 Activity B** (SF).	Complete first draft in **4-6 Activity A** (SF).
Day 4	Do narration and illustration **K-1 Activity B** (SF)	Do composition and illustration **2-3 Activity C** (SF)	Complete final draft in **4-6 Activity A** (SF).

LATIN/GREEK

Co-op	Practice Tantum Ergo (SF)	Practice Tantum Ergo (SF); do *Greek Primer* 1.1–4 (SF)	Practice Tantum Ergo (SF); do *Reading Greek* 1.1–2 (SF)
Day 2	Listen to CCM Unit 1 Latin prayer	Listen to CCM Unit 1 Latin prayer; do *Greek Primer* 1.5	Listen to CCM Unit 1 Latin prayer; do *Reading Greek* 1.3–4 (SF)
Day 3	Practice all the *Schola Rosa* Latin assembly prayers!	Practice all the *Schola Rosa* Latin assembly prayers!; do *Greek Primer* 1.5 (SF)	Practice all the *Schola Rosa* Latin assembly prayers!; do *Reading Greek* 1.4 (SF)
Day 4	Listen to Tantum Ergo video (SF); Sing along!	Listen to Tantum Ergo video (SF); Sing along!; finish *Greek Primer* Unit 1 (SF)	Listen to Tantum Ergo video (SF); Sing along!; finish *Reading Greek* Unit 1 (SF) and review/check work

MATH

	Level A	Level B	Level C
Co-op	None	None	None
Day 2-4	See *Ray's Primary*, Mastery Chart~ Do next lesson (DL)	See *Ray's Intellectual*, Mastery Chart~ Do next lesson (DL)	See *Ray's Practical*, Mastery Chart~ Do next lesson (DL)

MUSIC

	K-6th Grade
Co-op	Review **All Lesson A** (SF). Use audio files to
Day 2-4	sing along with: Hymn of the Week (Latin SF); Exercises Group 1 and Agnus Dei (DL). See addendum to Lesson for 2nd year additions.

READING

	Primer (pre-reader)	Reader
None		None
See *McGuffey's Eclectic Primer*, "Mastery Chart"~ Do next lesson (DL)		See *McGuffey's Eclectic Readers,* "Mastery Chart" ~ Do next lesson (DL)

RELIGION — *Liturgical Feast lessons can be moved to correspond to their dates – simply adjust the schedule accordingly*

	K-1st Grades	2nd-3rd Grades	4th-6th Grades
Co-op	Begin **K-1 Lesson A** (SF).	Begin **2-3 Lesson A** (SF). Drill Q & A.	Begin **4-6 Lesson A** (SF). Drill Q & A.
Day 2	Complete **K-1 Lesson A** (SF).	Review/complete **2-3 Lesson A** (SF). Drill Q & A.	Review/complete **4-6 Lesson A** (SF). Drill Q & A.
Day 3	Complete **K-1 Lesson B** (SF).	Review/complete **2-3 Lesson A** (SF). Drill Q & A.	Select activity(ies) from the "Let Us Work Together" section OHF-4, pp. 10-11.
Day 4	Complete **K-1 Lesson C** (SF).	Review/complete **2-3 Lesson A** (SF). Drill Q & A.	Select activity(ies) from the "Let Us Work Together" section OHF-4, pp. 10-11

SCIENCE

Co-op	Complete observation and discussion **K-1 Lesson A** (SF).	Complete observation and discussion **2-3 Lesson A** (SF).	Complete observation and discussion **4-6 Lesson A** (SF).
Day 2	Read Chapter 1 and 4, *The Wonder Book of Chemistry* (DL).	Read Chapter 1 and 4, *The Wonder Book of Chemistry* (DL).	RS4K *Elementary Chemistry Grades K-4* 1.1-5 & Experiment 1 (HC). Continue journaling **4-6 Lesson A** (SF).
Day 3	Do worksheet **K-1 Activity A** (SF).	Do worksheet **2-3 Activity A** (SF).	Do worksheet **4-6 Activity A** (SF); Continue journaling **4-6 Lesson A** (SF).
Day 4	Do drawing **K-1 Activity B** (SF); if possible, go on a nature walk.	Do drawing **2-3 Activity B** (SF); if possible, go on a nature walk.	Watch video (SF); Continue journaling **4-6 Lesson A** (SF); Do hands-on **4-6 Activity B** (SF).

VIRTUE

	K-6th Grades
Field	Do **All Virtue Lesson A – Love** (SF)
Day 2-4	Practice "virtue training"

CYCLE III
UNIT 2

EXPLORATION
& OTTOMAN EMPIRE

UNIT CHECKLIST

PREP FOR HOME

- ☐ Print and read this Handbook
- ☐ Read the Overview
- ☐ Review the Planner; do the following:
  - o Locate and review all Lessons and Activities in the Subject Folders (SF)
  - o Locate and review all readings and assignments in the Subject Folders (SF), Digital Library (DL), and Hard Copies (HC)
  - o Note and gather needed supplies for the unit
- ☐ Read the Virtue Lesson
- ☐ Email or call R.A.S. if you have questions or technical difficulty.

PREP FOR CO-OP

- ☐ Print your "Co-op Job Sheet" and prep for your job
- ☐ Make sure your child is ready for his or her presentation if assigned to present
- ☐ Gather maps, notebooks, prayer sheet, and other supplies the night or morning before the co-op meets.
- ☐ Gather students' assignments the night or morning before the co-op meets
- ☐ Listen to the Memory Work on the way!

PREP FOR UPCOMING WEEKS – <u>LOOK AHEAD AT UNITS 5</u>

- ☐ Make advanced purchases, as necessary
- ☐ Begin to gather books and materials

PLANNER ABBREVIATION KEY

DL	Digital Library (in course suite)
SF	Subject Folder (in course suite)
HC	Hard Copy
PLL	*Primary Language Lessons* (book)
ILL	*Intermediate Language Lessons* (book)
RS4K	*Real Science 4 Kids* (book)
I-CAT	*Illustrated Catechism* (book)
OHF-1	*Our Holy Faith, Book 1* (book)
OHF-2	*Our Holy Faith, Book 2* (book)
OHF-4	*Our Holy Faith, Book 4* (book)
OHF-1-TM	*Our Holy Faith, Book 1, Teacher's Manual* (book)

OVERVIEW

Common Topics (All students PreK to 6th)

Virtue:	Hope & Courage
Hymn:	Tantum Ergo
Prayers:	Angelus, Pater Noster, Ave Maria, Gloria Patri
History:	Exploration & Ottoman Empire
Science:	Elements

History Themes

According to the *Compendium of Church History,* the 15th century was the century of genuine reformation within the Church. "The great Schism of the West was ended, but the evils which it had wrought in the Church were still present. The Papacy, which had suffered most, preserved its faith intact; it enforced the reformatory statutes of the Councils of Constance and Basle; it sent legates throughout Europe to reform and elevate monastic life; it labored earnestly to bring about the reunion of the schismatic Greeks; it alone of all the European powers strove to defend Christendom against the military genius of Mohammedanism" (*Compendium,* 114). The crowning achievement of the Church during this period is considered the holiness and contribution of Her Saints. With that in mind, a focus is placed upon the study of the lives of those holy persons this week.

Most history books place a focus on the age of exploration when the 15th century is reached. This we will certainly not neglect! What we try to keep in context this week is (1) what is happening on the European continent in the Church and (2) what is going on overseas as explorers discover. It is fun to learn about the discoveries of new lands and new peoples, and we are able to see God's plan at work, too, as Catholics moved into new territories.

Common Myths about the 15th Century

1. *Myth ~ Everyone believed the earth was flat before Columbus.* We learned in Unit 1 that many scholars of the previous centuries believed the world to be a sphere. Even scholars from the ancient and classical periods argued for a round earth. This myth was spread during the 19th century to emphasize falsely the superiority of the modern age over those "barbaric and uncivilized" ages before.

2. *Myth ~ The Popes were evil.* A couple of Popes during the century just before this were indeed worldly and politically ambitious. The position had become a political one sought by rich families, and the papacy had become in many ways an Italian princedom, partly out of necessity to protect Vatican City from destruction and partly out of ambition. The Councils of the 14th Century addressed the problem, however, and it is in the 15th century that we begin to see a genuine age of reform. Though, there were setbacks, such as can be seen with the Borgian popes at the end of the 15th Century. As in the Middle Ages, Councils were called to correct errors and to reform the Church, so that after the passing of the Lutheran revolt, the Church has been repeatedly blessed with many wise and holy leaders.

3. *Myth ~ Galileo invented modern science.* We learned in Unit 1 that scholars for centuries before the Renaissance were busy learning about the world empirically and experimentally, and that these scholars did not divorce "science" from the other faculties.

4. *Myth ~ All the great humanist thinkers were secularists and against authority.* We learned in Unit 1 that many of these great humanist thinkers were Catholics and sought to create beauty for the Church. These thinkers also sought Truth within the Teachings of the Church and sought to reconcile what sometimes seemed to be false dichotomies between Church Teaching and what was observed in the world. They believed the Truth to be One, so they then sought explanation and sought to research all the more. Many of these thinkers were supporters of monarchy as well as Church authority. The few, e.g. Machiavelli, who espoused secularism and despotism have unfortunately become the "heroes" of the modern age.

Important Councils

- The Council of Constance (1414) healed the divisions caused by schismatical anti-popes and condemned the errors of Huss and Wickliffe.

- The Council of Florence (1438) affected a short-lived reunion between the churches of the East and West.

How to Apply History to Everyday Life

Our Mission. During the period of Exploration, we see examples of hope and courage. Both laity and religious ventured to travel far from their homelands in the name of discovery and salvation. We also see peoples fleeing their homelands to escape persecution of one kind or another. So, on the one hand, people *chose* to leave; and, on the other hand, people *were forced* to leave. In either event, we might reflect on the hope they must have had when leaving that they would find good opportunities wherever they might come and on the courage they must have had to brave the wild seas and the unknown consequences.

Are we ready to be hopeful in the face of unknown circumstances? Or do we despair and lose hope? Do we accept the necessities that confront us with the patience of the Blessed Mother who in her late pregnancy must needs travel to Bethlehem and deliver her baby in a stable? Do we accept God's guidance with the courage of David as he is led to Goliath?

We might also reflect on the marriage of hope and courage creating the fruit of fortitude. May we consider own virtue this week and how to improve upon it.

OVERVIEW

Important People, Events, and Places to Know (Potential Student Presentations)

- ❖ St. John Nepomucen, St. Catherine of Sienna, St. Elizabeth of Portugal, St. Catherine of Sweden, St. Vincent Ferrer, St. John Capistran, St. Casimur, St. Rita of Cassia, St. Frances of Paula, Christopher Columbus, Ferdinand, Isabella, Portugal, Sienna, Sweden, Cassia, Poland, St. Joan of Arc, Hundred Years' War, The Wars of the Roses (1455-1485), Vladimir I of Kiev
- ❖ Saints

    - St. John Nepomucen
    - St. Catherine of Sienna
    - St. Elizabeth of Portugal
    - St. Catherine of Sweden
    - St. Vincent Ferrer

    - St. John Capistran
    - St. Casimur
    - St. Rita of Cassia
    - St. Frances of Paula

Additional Project Ideas

- "Explorers of North America" *History Pockets* (4th-6th Grade)

OVERVIEW

PLANNER ~ Unit 2 (Co-op)

Week of _____   *Liturgical Theme & Colors* _____

Family Challenge-Task
Goals _____

_____

_____

Reminders _____

_____

_____

PRESCHOOL

	Music	Art, Reading, Religion	Virtue
Co-op	See "Music" heading below	Do craft **PreK Lesson A** (SF)	Review Virtue C-D (SF); practice "virtue training"
Day 2-4	See "Music" heading below	Do **Letter Book C-D** (SF); do **coloring pages** (SF); read & drill I-CAT, p. 5 (HC)	Review Virtue C-D (SF); practice "virtue training"

KINDERGARTEN – 6ᵀᴴ GRADE

ART   **CCM**

	K-6ᵗʰ Grade		K-6ᵗʰ Grade
Co-op	Do **All Lesson A** (SF).	Unit 2	
Day 2-4	Review **All Lesson A** (SF) and do home follow-up.	Listen to Unit 2 every day	

HISTORY

	K-1ˢᵗ Grades	2ⁿᵈ-3ʳᵈ Grades	4ᵗʰ-6ᵗʰ Grades
Co-op	Do craft **K-1 Lesson A** (SF).	Do History Pocket **2-3 Lesson A** (SF).	Do discussion **4-6 Lesson A** (SF).
Day 2	Read *Columbus* by D'Aulaire (HC) this week; Choose and do reading (or other project) from "Extras" (SF); draw a picture inspired by the readings	Read *Columbus* by D'Aulaire (HC) this week; Choose and do reading (or other project) from "Extras" (SF); draw a picture inspired by the readings	Read *The Discovery of New Worlds* (DL); Choose and do readings (or other projects) from "Extras" (SF); begin writing **4-6 Activity A** (SF).
Day 3	Continue readings; do coloring page (SF).	Do online **2-3 Activity A** (SF); continue readings; do coloring page (SF).	Continue readings; do map **4-6 Activity B** (SF)
Day 4	Continue readings; Imagine & Draw a scene from the reading.	Continue readings; Imagine & Draw a scene from the reading	Finish readings and **4-6 Activity A**; do timeline **4-6 Activity C** (SF).

LANGUAGE ARTS

	K-1ˢᵗ Grades	2ⁿᵈ-3ʳᵈ Grades	4ᵗʰ-6ᵗʰ Grades
Co-op	Complete **K-1 Lesson A** (SF).	Complete **2-3 Lesson A** (SF); do **2-3 Activity A** (SF).	Complete **4-6 Lesson A** (SF); begin **4-6 Activity A** (SF).
Day 2	Review **K-1 Lesson A** (SF); Ask your student to describe the picture.	Review **2-3 Lesson A** (SF); continue **2-3 Activity A** (SF).	Review **4-6 Lesson A** (SF); continue **4-6 Activity A** (SF)
Day 3	Do pre-cursive copywork **K-1 Activity A** (SF).	Do cursive copywork **2-3 Activity B** (SF).	Complete first draft in **4-6 Activity A** (SF).
Day 4	Do narration and illustration **K-1 Activity B** (SF)	Do composition and illustration **2-3 Activity C** (SF)	Complete final draft in **4-6 Activity A** (SF).

LATIN/GREEK

	K-1ˢᵗ Grades	2ⁿᵈ-3ʳᵈ Grades	4ᵗʰ-6ᵗʰ Grades
Co-op	Practice Tantum Ergo (SF)	Practice Tantum Ergo (SF); do *Greek Primer* 2.1–4 (SF)	Practice Tantum Ergo (SF); do *Reading Greek* 2.1–2 (SF)
Day 2	Listen to CCM Unit 2 Latin prayer	Listen to CCM Unit 2 Latin prayer; do *Greek Primer* 2.5	Listen to CCM Unit 2 Latin prayer; do *Reading Greek* 2.3–4 (SF)
Day 3	Practice all the *Schola Rosa* Latin assembly prayers!	Practice all the *Schola Rosa* Latin assembly prayers!; do *Greek Primer* 2.5 (SF)	Practice all the *Schola Rosa* Latin assembly prayers!; do *Reading Greek* 2.4 (SF)
Day 4	Listen to Tantum Ergo video (SF); Sing along!	Listen to Tantum Ergo video (SF); Sing along!; finish *Greek Primer* Unit 2 (SF)	Listen to Tantum Ergo video (SF); Sing along!; finish *Reading Greek* Unit 2 (SF) and review/check work

MATH

	Level A	Level B	Level C
Co-op	None	None	None
Day 2-4	See *Ray's Primary*, Mastery Chart~ Do next lesson (DL)	See *Ray's Intellectual*, Mastery Chart~ Do next lesson (DL)	See *Ray's Practical*, Mastery Chart~ Do next lesson (DL)

MUSIC

	K-6th Grade
Co-op Day 2-4	Review **All Lesson A** (SF). Use audio files to sing along with: Hymn of the Week (Latin SF); Exercises Group 1 and Agnus Dei (DL). See addendum to Lesson for 2nd year additions.

READING

	Primer (pre-reader)	Reader
Co-op	None	None
	See *McGuffey's Eclectic Primer*, "Mastery Chart"~ Do next lesson (DL)	See *McGuffey's Eclectic Readers,* "Mastery Chart" ~ Do next lesson (DL)

RELIGION — *Liturgical Feast lessons can be moved to correspond to their dates – simply adjust the schedule accordingly*

	K-1st Grades	2nd-3rd Grades	4th-6th Grades
Co-op	Begin **K-1 Lesson A** (SF).	Begin **2-3 Lesson A** (SF). Drill Q & A.	Begin **4-6 Lesson A** (SF). Drill Q & A.
Day 2	Complete **K-1 Lesson A** (SF).	Review/complete **2-3 Lesson A** (SF). Drill Q & A.	Review/complete **4-6 Lesson A** (SF). Drill Q & A.
Day 3	Complete **K-1 Lesson B** (SF).	Review/complete **2-3 Lesson A** (SF). Drill Q & A.	Select activity(ies) from the "Let Us Work Together" section OHF-4, pp. 19-20.
Day 4	Complete **K-1 Lesson C** (SF).	Review/complete **2-3 Lesson A** (SF). Drill Q & A.	Select activity(ies) from the "Let Us Work Together" section OHF-4, pp. 19-20.

SCIENCE

Co-op	Complete observation and discussion **K-1 Lesson A** (SF).	Complete observation and discussion **2-3 Lesson A** (SF).	Complete observation and discussion **4-6 Lesson A** (SF).
Day 2	Read Chapters 6, 7, and 13 of *The Wonder Book of Chemistry)* (DL); Review **K-1 Lesson A** (SF)	Read Chapters 6, 7, and 13 of *The Wonder Book of Chemistry)* (DL); Review **2-3 Lesson A** (SF)	Read Chapters 6, 7, and 13 of *The Wonder Book of Chemistry)* (DL); Review **4-6 Lesson A** (SF)
Day 3	Learn fun facts **K-1 Activity A** (SF)	Learn fun facts **2-3 Activity A** (SF)	Do **4-6 Activity A** (SF); continue journaling **4-6 Lesson A** (SF)
Day 4	Do drawing **K-1 Activity B** (SF); if possible, go on a nature walk.	Do drawing **2-3 Activity B** (SF); if possible, go on a nature walk.	Watch video (SF); Continue journaling **4-6 Lesson A** (SF); Do hands-on **4-6 Activity B** (SF).

VIRTUE

	K-6th Grades
Field	**Do All Virtue Lesson A – Hope & Courage** (SF)
Day 2-4	Practice "virtue training"

THE PRINTING PRESS

The Reformation in the 16th Century A.D.

UNIT CHECKLIST

PREP FOR HOME

- ☐ Print and read this Handbook
- ☐ Read the Overview
- ☐ Review the Planner; do the following:
    - o Locate and review all Lessons and Activities in the Subject Folders (SF)
    - o Locate and review all readings and assignments in the Subject Folders (SF), Digital Library (DL), and Hard Copies (HC)
    - o Note and gather needed supplies for the unit
- ☐ Read the Virtue Lesson
- ☐ Email or call R.A.S. if you have questions or technical difficulty.

PREP FOR CO-OP

- ☐ Print your "Co-op Job Sheet" and prep for your job
- ☐ Make sure your child is ready for his or her presentation if assigned to present
- ☐ Gather maps, notebooks, prayer sheet, and other supplies the night or morning before the co-op meets.
- ☐ Gather students' assignments the night or morning before the co-op meets
- ☐ Listen to the Memory Work on the way!

PREP FOR UPCOMING WEEKS — <u>LOOK AHEAD AT UNITS 6</u>

- ☐ Make advanced purchases, as necessary
- ☐ Begin to gather books and materials

PLANNER ABBREVIATION KEY	
DL	Digital Library (in course suite)
SF	Subject Folder (in course suite)
HC	Hard Copy
PLL	*Primary Language Lessons* (book)
ILL	*Intermediate Language Lessons* (book)
RS4K	*Real Science 4 Kids* (book)
I-CAT	*Illustrated Catechism* (book)
OHF-1	*Our Holy Faith, Book 1* (book)
OHF-2	*Our Holy Faith, Book 2* (book)
OHF-4	*Our Holy Faith, Book 4* (book)
OHF-1-TM	*Our Holy Faith, Book 1, Teacher's Manual* (book)

OVERVIEW

Common Topics (All students PreK to 6th)

Virtue:	Purity & Modesty
Hymn:	Tantum Ergo
Prayers:	Angelus, Pater Noster, Ave Maria, Gloria Patri
History:	The Printing Press (Reformation in the 16th Century A.D.)
Science:	Atomic Number & Atomic Weight

History Themes

According to the *Compendium of Church History:* "The opening decades of the sixteenth century witnessed a revolt which, ere the century was little more than half over, had torn all the Teutonic nations from the unity of the Church, and had spread a spirit of rebellion against all authority. This movement, erroneously styled the "Reformation," had its origin in Germany." This is a sensitive topic for young souls to tackle, and thus this issue is saved for the older grades and for home discussion. Please see the history textbook recommendations for appropriate sections on the reformation.

The younger students, K-3rd Grade, will focus on the Age of the Printing Press. 4th-6th Grade students will also discuss this topic at co-op. On the one hand, the press allowed the wonderful spread of literature and knowledge in the form of books and made reading easier and available to more people. On the other hand, the press also allowed the easy spread of ideas that negatively affected culture. Students will focus on the positive aspects of the printing press this week and enjoy hands-on activities to help them appreciate the value of this invention. In addition to our studies on the printing press, we will revisit some of the beloved fairy tales by Andrew Lang, since some of the earliest printed children's books were about these stories.

What were the causes and effects of Protestantism?

Read the *Compendium of Church History*, pp. 117-124 for helpful selections on this topic.

Important Councils, summaries from the *Compendium of Church History*

- The Fifth Council of Lateran (1512) decided that the authority of the Holy See is above that of a general council.

- The Council of Trent (1545) rejected and condemned the errors of the so-called reformers. This council brought forth a new life of sanctity, learning, and zeal in the Church, resulting in the establishment of religious orders for the promotion of Christian education and charity.

How to Apply History to Everyday Life

Our Mission. As Christians we are called to protect the purity and modesty of those around us, especially our own children. The printing press was certainly a great good; however, with such inventions, comes a responsibility, and modern tendencies have moved more and more toward a lack of discretion in what is printed and not printed. As parents, we attempt to guard the eyes and the ears of our children at every turn; and we should not neglect this duty when it comes to books.

Do we read or look at the pictures of books before we allow our children access to them? Do we allow our children to check out just any book from the library? Or do we supervise the library experience?

In regards to modesty, we usually think of how we dress. Do we help our children to dress modestly? Do we encourage our children to dress modestly not only for themselves but to protect the thoughts of others around them? Do we guard our own eyes against immodest pictures, such as billboards and advertisements? Do we guard our children's eyes?

Purity and Modesty have also to do with speech. Do we only speak purely? When someone else begins to tell an immodest story, do we ask them to stop? Or are we eager to hear gossip? Do we kindly remind our neighbor not to gossip? Not to share stories of indecency?

Important People, Events, and Places to Know (Potential Student Presentations)

❖ Johann von Gutenberg (1645-1698), Martin Luther's 95 Theses (1517), Pope Leo X (1513 becomes Pope), Excommunication of Martin Luther (1520), Conversion of Ignatius of Loyola (1521), Zwinglius' Anti-iconoclasm movement begins (1523), Melancthon, King Henry VIII (d. 1546), Pope Clement VII, Edward VI, Queen Mary restores the Church of England to the Catholic Church (1554), The Peace of Madrid (1526), Niccolò Machiavelli (d. 1527), St. John Fisher martyred (1534), St. Thomas More martyred (1535), John Calvin Exiled (1538), St. Francis Xavier Lands in India (1542), The Massacre of St. Bartholomew's Day (August 24, 1572), The Conversion of Henry IV (1593), The Edict of Nantes (1598)

❖ Saints of the Sixteenth Century

- Bl. Ladislaus of Gielniow (1505)
- Our Lady of Guadalupe (1531)
- St. John Fisher (1535)
- St. Jerome Emiliani (1537)
- St. Anthony Mary Zaccaria (1539)
- St. Angela Merici (1540)
- St. Cajetan (1547)
- St. John of God (1550)
- St. Francis Xavier (1552)

- St. Thomas Villanova (1555)
- St. Ignatius of Loyola (1556)
- St. Paul Miki (1597)
- St. Peter of Alcantara (1562)
- St. Stanislaus Kostka (1568)
- St. John of Avila (1569)
- Our Lady of the Rosary (1571)
- St. Pius V (1572)
- St. Francis Borgia (1572)
- St. Edmund Campion (1581)
- St. Louis Bertrand (1581)

- St. Teresa of Jesus (of Avila) (1582)
- St. Charles Borromeo (1584)
- St. Margaret Clitherow (1586)
- St. Catherine de Ricci (1589)
- Bls. Edward Jones & Anthony Middleton (1590)
- St. Aloysius Gonzaga (1591)
- Bls. Ralph Milner & Roger Dickenson (1591)
- St. John of the Cross (1591)
- St. Paschal Baylon (1592)
- St. Philip Neri (1595)
- St. Peter Canisius (1597)
- The Forty Martyrs of England

Additional Project Ideas

- Allow your student to experiment with movable type this week based on what he or she learned in class. Can he or she make a book?
- Help your child make an "engraving" for his or her book.

OVERVIEW

Week of _____   *Liturgical Theme & Colors* _____

Family Challenge-Task
Goals

_____

_____

_____

Reminders _____

_____

PRESCHOOL

PRESCHOOL

	Music	Art, Reading, Religion	Virtue
Co-op	See "Music" heading below	Do craft **PreK Lesson A** (SF)	Review Virtue E-F (SF); practice "virtue training"
Day 2-4	See "Music" heading below	Do **Letter Book E-F** (SF); do **coloring pages** (SF); read & drill I-CAT, p. 7 (HC)	Review Virtue E-F (SF); practice "virtue training"

KINDERGARTEN – 6TH GRADE

ART   **CCM**

	K-6th Grade		K-6th Grade
Co-op	Do **All Lesson A** (SF).	Unit 3	
Day 2-4	Review **All Lesson A** (SF) and do home follow-up.	Listen to Unit 3 every day	

HISTORY

	K-1st Grades	2nd-3rd Grades	4th-6th Grades
Co-op	Do craft **K-1 Lesson A** (SF).	Do History Pocket **2-3 Lesson A** (SF).	Do discussion **4-6 Lesson A** (SF).
Day 2	Read *The Pied Piper of Hamlin* (DL) & *Red, Yellow, Blue Fairy Books* (HC or DL) this week; Choose and do reading (or other project) from "Extras" (SF); draw a picture inspired by the readings	Read *The Pied Piper of Hamlin* (DL) & *Red, Yellow, Blue Fairy Books* (HC or DL) this week; Choose and do reading (or other project) from "Extras" (SF); draw a picture inspired by the readings	Read *The Incunable Era, sections:* "The Gutenberg Press," "The First Book" and "The Art of Type" (SF); Choose and do readings (or other projects) from "Extras" (SF); begin writing **4-6 Activity A** (SF).
Day 3	Continue readings; do coloring page (SF).	Do online **2-3 Activity A** (SF); continue readings; do coloring page (SF).	Continue readings; do map **4-6 Activity B** (SF)
Day 4	Continue readings; Imagine & Draw a scene from the reading.	Continue readings; Imagine & Draw a scene from the reading	Finish readings and **4-6 Activity A**; do timeline **4-6 Activity C** (SF).

LANGUAGE ARTS

	K-1st Grades	2nd-3rd Grades	4th-6th Grades
Co-op	Complete **K-1 Lesson A** (SF).	Complete **2-3 Lesson A** (SF); do **2-3 Activity A** (SF).	Complete **4-6 Lesson A** (SF); begin **4-6 Activity A** (SF).
Day 2	Review **K-1 Lesson A** (SF); Ask your student to describe the picture.	Review **2-3 Lesson A** (SF); continue **2-3 Activity A** (SF).	Review **4-6 Lesson A** (SF); continue **4-6 Activity A** (SF)
Day 3	Do pre-cursive copywork **K-1 Activity A** (SF).	Do cursive copywork **2-3 Activity B** (SF).	Complete first draft in **4-6 Activity A** (SF).
Day 4	Do narration and illustration **K-1 Activity B** (SF)	Do composition and illustration **2-3 Activity C** (SF)	Complete final draft in **4-6 Activity A** (SF).

LATIN/GREEK

	K-1st Grades	2nd-3rd Grades	4th-6th Grades
Co-op	Practice Tantum Ergo (SF)	Practice Tantum Ergo (SF); do *Greek Primer* 3.1–4 (SF)	Practice Tantum Ergo (SF); do *Reading Greek* 3.1–2 (SF)
Day 2	Listen to CCM Unit 3 Latin prayer	Listen to CCM Unit 3 Latin prayer; do *Greek Primer* 3.5	Listen to CCM Unit 3 Latin prayer; do *Reading Greek* 3.3–4 (SF)
Day 3	Practice all the *Schola Rosa* Latin assembly prayers!	Practice all the *Schola Rosa* Latin assembly prayers!; do *Greek Primer* 3.5 (SF)	Practice all the *Schola Rosa* Latin assembly prayers!; do *Reading Greek* 3.4 (SF)
Day 4	Listen to Tantum Ergo video (SF); Sing along!	Listen to Tantum Ergo video (SF); Sing along!; finish *Greek Primer* Unit 3 (SF)	Listen to Tantum Ergo video (SF); Sing along!; finish *Reading Greek* Unit 3 (SF) and check work.

MATH

	Level A	Level B	Level C
Co-op	None	None	None
Day 2-4	See *Ray's Primary*, Mastery Chart~ Do next lesson (DL)	See *Ray's Intellectual*, Mastery Chart~ Do next lesson (DL)	See *Ray's Practical*, Mastery Chart~ Do next lesson (DL)

MUSIC

	K-6th Grade
Co-op Day 2-4	Review **All Lesson A** (SF). Use audio files to sing along with: Hymn of the Week (Latin SF); Exercises Group 1, Agnus Dei, Sanctus, Merrily We Roll Along (DL). See addendum to Lesson for 2nd year additions.

READING

	Primer (pre-reader)	Reader
	None	None
	See *McGuffey's Eclectic Primer*, "Mastery Chart"~ Do next lesson (DL)	See *McGuffey's Eclectic Readers*, "Mastery Chart" ~ Do next lesson (DL)

RELIGION — *Liturgical Feast lessons can be moved to correspond to their dates — simply adjust the schedule accordingly*

	K-1st Grades	2nd-3rd Grades	4th-6th Grades
Co-op	Begin **K-1 Lesson A** (SF).	Begin **2-3 Lesson A** (SF). Drill Q & A.	Begin **4-6 Lesson A** (SF). Drill Q & A.
Day 2	Complete **K-1 Lesson A** (SF).	Review/complete **2-3 Lesson A** (SF). Drill Q & A.	Review/complete **4-6 Lesson A** (SF). Drill Q & A.
Day 3	Complete **K-1 Lesson B** (SF).	Review/complete **2-3 Lesson A** (SF). Drill Q & A.	Select activity(ies) from the "Let Us Work Together" section OHF-4, pp. 23.
Day 4	Complete **K-1 Lesson C** (SF).	Review/complete **2-3 Lesson A** (SF). Drill Q & A.	Select activity(ies) from the "Let Us Work Together" section OHF-4, pp. 23

SCIENCE

Co-op	Complete observation and discussion **K-1 Lesson A** (SF).	Complete observation and discussion **2-3 Lesson A** (SF).	Complete observation and discussion **4-6 Lesson A** (SF).
Day 2	Read "Hydrogen" and "A Drop of Water" in *The Wonder Book of Chemistry* (DL); Review **K-1 Lesson A** (SF)	Read "Hydrogen" and "A Drop of Water" in *The Wonder Book of Chemistry* (DL); Review **2-3 Lesson A** (SF)	Review **4-6 Lesson A** (SF); read *RS4K Elementary Chemistry Grades* K-4, 2.1-4 & Experiment 2 (HC)
Day 3	Learn fun facts **K-1 Activity A** (SF)	Learn fun facts **2-3 Activity A** (SF)	Do **4-6 Activity A** (SF); do journaling **4-6 Activity B** (SF)
Day 4	Do drawing **K-1 Activity B** (SF); if possible, go on a nature walk.	Do drawing **2-3 Activity B** (SF); if possible, go on a nature walk.	Watch video (SF); Continue journaling **4-6 Lesson A** and **4-6 Activity B** (SF).

VIRTUE

	K-6th Grades
Field	Do **All Virtue Lesson A – Purity & Modesty** (SF)
Day 2-4	Practice "virtue training"

CYCLE III
UNIT 4

NAUTICAL ADVENTURE

UNIT CHECKLIST

PREP FOR HOME

- ☐ Print and read this Handbook
- ☐ Read the Overview
- ☐ Review the Planner; do the following:
    - o Locate and review all Lessons and Activities in the Subject Folders (SF)
    - o Locate and review all readings and assignments in the Subject Folders (SF), Digital Library (DL), and Hard Copies (HC)
    - o Note and gather needed supplies for the unit
- ☐ Read the Virtue Lesson
- ☐ Email or call R.A.S. if you have questions or technical difficulty.

PREP FOR CO-OP

- ☐ Print your "Co-op Job Sheet" and prep for your job
- ☐ Make sure your child is ready for his or her presentation if assigned to present
- ☐ Gather maps, notebooks, prayer sheet, and other supplies the night or morning before the co-op meets.
- ☐ Gather students' assignments the night or morning before the co-op meets
- ☐ Listen to the Memory Work on the way!

PREP FOR UPCOMING WEEKS — <u>LOOK AHEAD AT UNITS 7</u>

- ☐ Make advanced purchases, as necessary
- ☐ Begin to gather books and materials

PLANNER ABBREVIATION KEY

DL	Digital Library (in course suite)
SF	Subject Folder (in course suite)
HC	Hard Copy
PLL	*Primary Language Lessons* (book)
ILL	*Intermediate Language Lessons* (book)
RS4K	*Real Science 4 Kids* (book)
I-CAT	*Illustrated Catechism* (book)
OHF-1	*Our Holy Faith, Book 1* (book)
OHF-2	*Our Holy Faith, Book 2* (book)
OHF-4	*Our Holy Faith, Book 4* (book)
OHF-1-TM	*Our Holy Faith, Book 1, Teacher's Manual* (book)

OVERVIEW

Common Topics (All students PreK to 6ᵗʰ)

Virtue:	Faith
Hymn:	Tantum Ergo
Prayers:	Angelus, Pater Noster, Ave Maria, Gloria Patri
History:	Nautical Adventure
Science:	Review

History Themes

With Unit 4 we continue our study of the age of exploration. We hope to help students relate personally with the families who traveled during this time period by reading *The Swiss Family Robinson*. With the political and religious unrest on the continent, many families decided to move to the "new world," hoping for opportunity and a fresh start. Of course, with the migration of peoples throughout the new world, the Church concerned Herself with their Faith. Imagine how Catholic families kept their Faith and Tradition though thousands of miles away from a Church! Imagine the religious orders that followed in hopes of converting natives and administering to the needs of the faithful!

Religious Orders, summaries from the *Compendium of Church History*

1. Society of Jesus ~ founded by St. Ignatius of Loyola in 1540, gave the Church a number of men illustrious for their sanctity, zeal, and learning. This order delivered Europe from the errors and miseries of Protestantism, and sent missionaries to evangelize pagan lands.
2. The Capuchins ~ founded by Matthew Bassi in 1528, affected great good by their austere, holy lives.
3. The Oratorians ~ founded by Philip Neri, lent effective aid to the popes and bishops in carrying out the decrees of the Council of Trent by training good priests.
4. The Discalced Carmelites ~ reformed and regenerated by St. Teresa in 1562, have been the means of drawing down God's blessing on the Church by their cloistered lives of prayer and penance.

How to Apply History to Everyday Life

Our Mission. If we return to Unit 2 and consider the hope and courage that a family must have needed, we now reflect on the *faith* of such a family. Imagine a father and mother keeping track of Sundays throughout the year, though they are far away from civilization. Imagine keeping the Lord 's Day, though there is no Mass around to assist. Imagine a husband, wife, or child on death's bed without a priest to call. Imagine years without confession at all!

Now, we are at a place to reflect upon the faith and duty of a family to maintain Tradition. What would we have to do to maintain the Lord 's Day in such a situation?

OVERVIEW

Would we fail? Would we meet the challenge in humility? Would we pray every day for the Lord to send a priest? Would we continue to catechize our children? Would we remain true to the Nicene and Apostles' Creeds? Would we make sure our children memorize these creeds? Or would we revert and become pagans of old?

Important People, Events, and Places to Know (Potential Student Presentations)

❖ Elizabeth I becomes Queen of England (1558), St. Pius V becomes Pope (1559), Mary Queen of Scots returns to Scotland from France (1559), War begins between French Catholics and Huguenots (1562), St. Charles Borromeo consecrated archbishop of Milan (1563), Death of Michelangelo (1564), The Christian Fleet defeats the Turks at the Battle of Lepanto (1571), Execution of Mary Queen of Scots (1587), Death of Elizabeth I (1603)

❖ Saints of the Sixteenth Century

- Bl. Ladislaus of Gielniow (1505)
- Our Lady of Guadalupe (1531)
- St. John Fisher (1535)
- St. Jerome Emiliani (1537)
- St. Anthony Mary Zaccaria (1539)
- St. Angela Merici (1540)
- St. Cajetan (1547)
- St. John of God (1550)
- St. Francis Xavier (1552)
- St. Thomas Villanova (1555)
- St. Ignatius of Loyola (1556)
- St. Paul Miki (1597)
- St. Peter of Alcantara (1562)
- St. Stanislaus Kostka (1568)
- St. John of Avila (1569)
- Our Lady of the Rosary (1571)

- St. Pius V (1572)
- St. Francis Borgia (1572)
- St. Edmund Campion (1581)
- St. Louis Bertrand (1581)
- St. Teresa of Jesus (of Avila) (1582)
- St. Charles Borromeo (1584)
- St. Margaret Clitherow (1586)
- St. Catherine de Ricci (1589)
- Bls. Edward Jones & Anthony Middleton (1590)
- St. Aloysius Gonzaga (1591)
- Bls. Ralph Milner & Roger Dickenson (1591)
- St. John of the Cross (1591)
- St. Paschal Baylon (1592)
- St. Philip Neri (1595)
- St. Peter Canisius (1597)
- The Forty Martyrs of England

Additional Project Ideas

- Model Ships in a Bottle
- Paint a Seascape
- Visit a Naval Museum

Week of _____ *Liturgical Theme & Colors* _____

Family Challenge-Task
Goals
_____
_____
_____
_____

Reminders
_____
_____
_____

PRESCHOOL

	Music	Art, Reading, Religion	Virtue
Field	See "Music" heading below	Do craft **PreK Lesson A** (SF)	Practice "virtue training"
Day 2-4	See "Music" heading below	Review A-F (SF), review & drill I-CAT, p 7 (HC)	Practice "virtue training"

KINDERGARTEN – 6TH GRADE

ART   **CCM**

	K-6th Grade	K-6th Grade
Field	Review **All Lesson A** (SF), Units 1-3.	Unit 4.
Day 2-4	Do extra art task from home follow-up sections, if there is time.	Listen to Unit 4 every day

HISTORY

	K-1st Grades	2nd-3rd Grades	4th-6th Grades
Field	Read *The Swiss Family Robinson* (HC) this week.	Read *The Swiss Family Robinson* (HC) this week.	Read *The Swiss Family Robinson* (HC) this week.
Day 2	Choose and do reading (or other project) from "Extras" (SF); draw a picture inspired by the readings; *Glory Story CD*, Vol. VII, St. Martin de Porres	Choose and do reading (or other project) from "Extras" (SF); draw a picture inspired by the readings; *Glory Story CD*, Vol. VII, St. Martin de Porres	Choose and do readings (or other projects) from "Extras" (SF); *Glory Story CD*, Vol. VII, St. Martin de Porres
Day 3	Continue readings.	Continue readings.	Continue readings.
Day 4	Do coloring page (SF)	Do coloring page (SF)	Do timeline **4-6 Activity A** (SF).

LANGUAGE ARTS

Field	Complete **K-1 Lesson A** (SF).	Complete **2-3 Lesson A** (SF).	Complete **4-6 Lesson A** (SF); do **4-6 Activity A** (SF).
Day 2	Review **K-1 Lesson A** (SF); do **K-1 Activity A** (SF).	Review **2-3 Lesson A** (SF); do **2-3 Activity A** (SF).	Review **4-6 Lesson A** (SF); do **4-6 Activity B** (SF)
Day 3	Do pre-cursive copywork **K-1 Activity B** (SF).	Do cursive copywork **2-3 Activity B** (SF).	Complete first draft in **4-6 Activity B** (SF).
Day 4	Do narration and illustration **K-1 Activity C** (SF)	Do composition and illustration **2-3 Activity C** (SF)	Complete final draft in **4-6 Activity B** (SF).

LATIN/GREEK

Field	Practice Tantum Ergo (SF)	Practice Tantum Ergo (SF); do *Greek Primer* 4.1–3 (SF)	Practice Tantum Ergo (SF); do *Reading Greek* 4.1–2 (SF)
Day 2	Listen to CCM Unit 4 Latin prayer	Listen to CCM Unit 4 Latin prayer; do *Greek Primer* 4.4-5	Listen to CCM Unit 4 Latin prayer; do *Reading Greek* 4.3–4 (SF)
Day 3	Practice all the *Schola Rosa* Latin assembly prayers!	Practice all the *Schola Rosa* Latin assembly prayers!	Practice all the *Schola Rosa* Latin assembly prayers!
Day 4	Listen to Tantum Ergo video (SF); Sing along!	Listen to Tantum Ergo video (SF); Sing along!; finish *Greek Primer* Unit 4 (SF)	Listen to Tantum Ergo video (SF); Sing along!; finish *Reading Greek* Unit 4 (SF) and check work.

MATH

	Level A	Level B	Level C
Field	None	None	None
Day 2-4	See *Ray's Primary*, Mastery Chart~ Do next lesson (DL)	See *Ray's Intellectual*, Mastery Chart~ Do next lesson (DL)	See *Ray's Practical*, Mastery Chart~ Do next lesson (DL)

MUSIC

READING

	K-6th Grade		Primer (pre-reader)	Reader
Field	Use audio files to sing along with: Hymn of		None	None
Day 2-4	the Week (Latin SF); Exercises Group 1; Agnus Dei; Sanctus; Merrily We Roll Along (DL). See addendum to Lesson for 2nd year additions.		See *McGuffey's Eclectic Primer*, "Mastery Chart"~ Do next lesson (DL)	See *McGuffey's Eclectic Readers*, "Mastery Chart" ~ Do next lesson (DL)

RELIGION — *Liturgical Feast lessons can be moved to correspond to their dates – simply adjust the schedule accordingly*

	K-1st Grades	2nd-3rd Grades	4th-6th Grades
Field	Field Trip	Field Trip	Field Trip
Day 2	Review/complete **K-1 Lesson A** (SF).	Review/complete **2-3 Lesson A** (SF). Drill Q & A.	Review/complete **4-6 Lesson A** (SF). Drill Q & A.
Day 3	Begin **K-1 Lesson B** (SF).	Review/complete **2-3 Lesson A** (SF). Drill Q & A.	Complete activity(-ies) from the "Let Us Work Together" section OHF-4, pp. 28-29.
Day 4	Review/complete **K-1 Lesson B** (SF).	Review/complete **2-3 Lesson A** (SF). Drill Q & A.	Complete activity(ies) from the "Let Us Work Together" section OHF-4, pp. 28-29. Complete Unit I test, OHF-4, p. 30

SCIENCE

Field	Review Units 1-3 and complete any missing assignments.	Review Units 1-3and complete any missing assignments.	Review Units 1-3 and complete any missing assignments.
Day 2	Read other selections from *The Wonder Book of Chemistry* (DL).	Read other selections from *The Wonder Book of Chemistry* (DL).	Read other selections from *The Wonder Book of Chemistry* (DL).
Day 3	Complete any experiments or activities that were not completed in Units 1-3.	Complete any experiments or activities that were not completed in Units 1-3.	Complete any experiments or activities that were not completed in Units 1-3.
Day 4	Do drawings of your favorite atoms or molecules! Go on a nature walk and contemplate the small things.	Do drawings of your favorite atoms or molecules! Go on a nature walk and contemplate the small things.	Go on a nature walk with the family and update your journal if anything is not finished.

VIRTUE

	K-6th Grades
Field	Do **All Virtue Lesson A - Faith** (SF)
Day 2-4	Practice "virtue training"

CYCLE III
UNIT 5

SPANISH CONQUEST

UNIT CHECKLIST

PREP FOR HOME

- ☐ Print and read this Handbook
- ☐ Read the Overview
- ☐ Review the Planner; do the following:
  - ○ Locate and review all Lessons and Activities in the Subject Folders (SF)
  - ○ Locate and review all readings and assignments in the Subject Folders (SF), Digital Library (DL), and Hard Copies (HC)
  - ○ Note and gather needed supplies for the unit
- ☐ Read the Virtue Lesson
- ☐ Email or call R.A.S. if you have questions or technical difficulty.

PREP FOR CO-OP

- ☐ Print your "Co-op Job Sheet" and prep for your job
- ☐ Make sure your child is ready for his or her presentation if assigned to present
- ☐ Gather maps, notebooks, prayer sheet, and other supplies the night or morning before the co-op meets.
- ☐ Gather students' assignments the night or morning before the co-op meets
- ☐ Listen to the Memory Work on the way!

PREP FOR UPCOMING WEEKS — LOOK AHEAD AT UNITS 8

- ☐ Make advanced purchases, as necessary
- ☐ Begin to gather books and materials

PLANNER ABBREVIATION KEY	
DL	Digital Library (in course suite)
SF	Subject Folder (in course suite)
HC	Hard Copy
PLL	*Primary Language Lessons* (book)
ILL	*Intermediate Language Lessons* (book)
RS4K	*Real Science 4 Kids* (book)
I-CAT	*Illustrated Catechism* (book)
OHF-1	*Our Holy Faith, Book 1* (book)
OHF-2	*Our Holy Faith, Book 2* (book)
OHF-4	*Our Holy Faith, Book 4* (book)
OHF-1-TM	*Our Holy Faith, Book 1, Teacher's Manual* (book)

OVERVIEW

Common Topics (All students PreK to 6th)

Virtue:	Discipline
Hymn:	Ecce nomen Domini
Prayers:	Angelus, Pater Noster, Ave Maria, Gloria Patri
History:	Spanish Conquest
Science:	Endothermic vs. Exothermic Chemical Reactions

History Themes

During Unit 5 we remain in the 16th Century, focusing on the Spanish conquest of the New World. The K–3rd Graders will be reading a version of *Don Quixote* for levity and the 4th–6th Graders will be reading about Cortes and De Soto. This is a wonderful unit for going to the library and digging deeper! We will remain in the 16th Century until Unit 8 when we meet the Pilgrims.

How to Apply History to Everyday Life

Our Mission. We might consider this week the degree of self-discipline needed to travel on a boat for a long period of time. What would we need to regulate? — food and water. Would we control our bodily appetites to preserve ourselves and those around us? Would we be mindful of others and refrain from being loud? Would we seek to comfort the sick? Would we seek to comfort the mournful? Would we seek to be cheerful despite ourselves?

When arriving in the new country, would we continue the practices of self-discipline, mastered aboard the ship? Or would we be gluttons before guaranteeing a future harvest? Would we work hard with others to produce food and shelter? Would we work cheerfully despite ourselves? Would we seek to learn from native peoples? Or would we seek to take advantage of them?

Important People, Events, and Places to Know (Potential Student Presentations)

❖ Christopher Columbus lands at San Salvador (1492), Balboa discovers the Pacific (1513), Las Casas begins he defense of the Indians (1517), Cortes carries out the conquest of Mexico (1518-1521), Las Casas's colony fails; he becomes a Dominican (1522), Franciscan friars arrive in Mexico (1524), Verrazano lands in America (1524), Pizarro conquers Peru & Our Lady of Guadalupe appears to Juan Diego (1531), Hernando de Soto explores "Florida" & Francisco Vasquez de Coronado explores the Southwest (1539-1543), Martyrdom of Fray Juan Padilla (1542), Las Casas made bishop of Chiapas (1544), King Charles I orders an end to all conquests in Americas (1550), Founding of St. Augustine, Florida (1560), Foundation of the Florida and Georgia missions (1560-1655)

OVERVIEW

- ❖ Saints of the Sixteenth Century

  - o Bl. Ladislaus of Gielniow (1505)
  - o Our Lady of Guadalupe (1531)
  - o St. John Fisher (1535)
  - o St. Jerome Emiliani (1537)
  - o St. Anthony Mary Zaccaria (1539)
  - o St. Angela Merici (1540)
  - o St. Cajetan (1547)
  - o St. John of God (1550)
  - o St. Francis Xavier (1552)
  - o St. Thomas Villanova (1555)
  - o St. Ignatius of Loyola (1556)
  - o St. Paul Miki (1597)
  - o St. Peter of Alcantara (1562)
  - o St. Stanislaus Kostka (1568)
  - o St. John of Avila (1569)
  - o Our Lady of the Rosary (1571)
  - o St. Pius V (1572)
  - o St. Francis Borgia (1572)
  - o St. Edmund Campion (1581)
  - o St. Louis Bertrand (1581)
  - o St. Teresa of Jesus (of Avila) (1582)
  - o St. Charles Borromeo (1584)
  - o St. Margaret Clitherow (1586)
  - o St. Catherine de Ricci (1589)
  - o Bls. Edward Jones & Anthony Middleton (1590)
  - o St. Aloysius Gonzaga (1591)
  - o Bls. Ralph Milner & Roger Dickenson (1591)
  - o St. John of the Cross (1591)
  - o St. Paschal Baylon (1592)
  - o St. Philip Neri (1595)
  - o St. Peter Canisius (1597)
  - o The Forty Martyrs of England

Additional Project Ideas

- ❖ Build a replica Spanish Fort
- ❖ Make a Spanish hat
- ❖ Visit a Shrine to Our Lady of Guadalupe and pray for All Souls

Week of _____   *Liturgical Theme & Colors* _____

Family Challenge-Task
Goals _____

_____

_____

_____

Reminders _____

_____

_____

PRESCHOOL

	Music	Art, Reading, Religion	Virtue
Co-op	See "Music" heading below	Do craft **PreK Lesson A** (SF)	Review Virtue G-H (SF); practice "virtue training"
Day 2-4	See "Music" heading below	Do **Letter Book G-H** (SF); do **coloring pages** (SF); read & drill I-CAT, p. 9 (HC)	Review Virtue G-H (SF); practice "virtue training"

KINDERGARTEN – 6ᵀᴴ GRADE

ART   **CCM**

	K-6th Grade		K-6th Grade
Co-op	Do **All Lesson A** (SF).		Unit 5
Day 2-4	Review **All Lesson A** (SF) and do home follow-up.		Listen to Unit 5 every day

HISTORY

	K-1st Grades	2nd-3rd Grades	4th-6th Grades
Co-op	Do craft **K-1 Lesson A** (SF).	Do History Pocket **2-3 Lesson A** (SF).	Do discussion **4-6 Lesson A** (SF).
Day 2	Read *Stories from Don Quixote Written Anew for Children* (DL) this week; Choose and do reading (or other project) from "Extras" (SF); draw a picture inspired by the readings; *Glory Story CD*, Vol. 1, St. Juan Diego and Vol. X St. Rose of Lima	Read *Stories from Don Quixote Written Anew for Children* (DL) this week; Choose and do reading (or other project) from "Extras" (SF); draw a picture inspired by the readings; *Glory Story CD*, Vol. 1, St. Juan Diego and Vol. X St. Rose of Lima	Read *Hernando Cortes* and *Ferdinand de Soto* (DL) this week; Choose and do readings (or other projects) from "Extras" (SF); begin writing **4-6 Activity A** (SF); *Glory Story CD*, Vol. 1, St. Juan Diego and Vol. X St. Rose of Lima
Day 3	Continue readings; do coloring page (SF).	Do map **2-3 Activity A** (SF); continue readings; do coloring page (SF).	Continue readings; do map **4-6 Activity B** (SF)
Day 4	Continue readings; Imagine & Draw a scene from the reading.	Continue readings; Imagine & Draw a scene from the reading	Finish readings and **4-6 Activity A**; do timeline **4-6 Activity C** (SF).

LANGUAGE ARTS

Co-op	Complete **K-1 Lesson A** (SF).	Complete **2-3 Lesson A** (SF); do **2-3 Activity A** (SF).	Complete **4-6 Lesson A** (SF); begin **4-6 Activity A** (SF).
Day 2	Review **K-1 Lesson A** (SF); Ask your student to describe the picture.	Review **2-3 Lesson A** (SF); continue **2-3 Activity A** (SF).	Review **4-6 Lesson A** (SF); continue **4-6 Activity A** (SF)
Day 3	Do pre-cursive copywork **K-1 Activity A** (SF).	Do cursive copywork **2-3 Activity B** (SF).	Complete first draft in **4-6 Activity A** (SF).
Day 4	Do narration and illustration **K-1 Activity B** (SF)	Do composition and illustration **2-3 Activity C** (SF)	Complete final draft in **4-6 Activity A** (SF).

LATIN/GREEK

Co-op	Practice Ecce Nomen Domini! (SF)	Practice Ecce Nomen Domini! (SF); do *Greek Primer* 5.1–4 (SF)	Practice Ecce Nomen Domini! (SF); do *Reading Greek* 5.1–2 (SF)
Day 2	Listen to CCM Unit 5 Latin prayer	Listen to CCM Unit 5 Latin prayer; do *Greek Primer* 5.5	Listen to CCM Unit 5 Latin prayer; do *Reading Greek* 5.3–4 (SF)
Day 3	Practice all the *Schola Rosa* Latin assembly prayers!	Practice all the *Schola Rosa* Latin assembly prayers!	Practice all the *Schola Rosa* Latin assembly prayers!
Day 4	Listen to Ecce Nomen Domini! video (SF); Sing along!	Listen to Ecce Nomen Domini! (SF); *Greek Primer* Unit 5 (SF)	Listen to Ecce Nomen Domini! (SF); *Reading Greek* Unit 5 (SF)

MATH

	Level A	Level B	Level C
Co-op	None	None	None
Day 2-4	See *Ray's Primary*, Mastery Chart~ Do next lesson (DL)	See *Ray's Intellectual*, Mastery Chart~ Do next lesson (DL)	See *Ray's Practical*, Mastery Chart~ Do next lesson (DL)

MUSIC

	K-6th Grade
Co-op	Review **All Lesson A** (SF). Use audio files to sing along with: Hymn of the Week (Latin SF); Exercises Group 1 and 2, Scale Drills, Agnus Dei, Sanctus, and Merrily We Roll Along (DL). See addendum to Lesson for 2nd year additions.
Day 2-4	

READING

	Primer (pre-reader)	Reader
Co-op	None	None
Day 2-4	See *McGuffey's Eclectic Primer*, "Mastery Chart" ~ Do next lesson (DL)	See *McGuffey's Eclectic Readers*, "Mastery Chart" ~ Do next lesson (DL)

RELIGION — *Liturgical Feast lessons can be moved to correspond to their dates — simply adjust the schedule accordingly*

	K-1st Grades	2nd-3rd Grades	4th-6th Grades
Co-op	Begin **K-1 Lesson A** (SF).	Begin **2-3 Lesson A** (SF). Drill Q & A.	Begin **4-6 Lesson A** (SF). Drill Q & A.
Day 2	Complete **K-1 Lesson A** (SF).	Review/complete **2-3 Lesson A** (SF). Drill Q & A.	Review/complete **4-6 Lesson A** (SF). Drill Q & A.
Day 3	Complete **K-1 Lesson B** (SF).	Review/complete **2-3 Lesson A** (SF). Drill Q & A.	Select activity(ies) from the "Let Us Work Together" section OHF-4, pp. 42-43.
Day 4	Complete **K-1 Lesson C** (SF).	Review/complete **2-3 Lesson A** (SF). Drill Q & A.	Select activity(ies) from the "Let Us Work Together" section OHF-4, pp. 42-43.

SCIENCE

Co-op	Do **K-1 Lesson A** (SF).	Do **2-3 Lesson A** (SF).	Do **4-6 Lesson A** (SF).
Day 2	Read "The Slice of Toast" and "Burning Phosphorous" in *The Wonder Book of Chemistry* (DL); do experiment **K-1 Activity A** (SF)	Read "The Slice of Toast" and "Burning Phosphorous" in *The Wonder Book of Chemistry* (DL); do experiment **2-3 Activity A** (SF)	Do experiment **4-6 Activity A** (SF); read RS4K *Elementary Chemistry Grades K-4* 3.1-5
Day 3	Do observe and draw **K-1 Activity B** (SF)	Do observe and draw **2-3 Activity B** (SF)	Do journaling **4-6 Activity B** (SF)
Day 4	Go on a nature walk and do drawing **K-1 Activity C** (SF).	Go on a nature walk and do drawing **2-3 Activity C** (SF).	Go on a nature walk and continue **4-6 Activity B** (SF).

VIRTUE

	K-6th Grades
Field	Do **All Virtue Lesson A – Discipline** (SF)
Day 2-4	Practice "virtue training"

CYCLE III
UNIT 6

SHAKESPEARE

UNIT CHECKLIST

PREP FOR HOME

- ☐ Print and read this Handbook
- ☐ Read the Overview
- ☐ Review the Planner; do the following:
    - o Locate and review all Lessons and Activities in the Subject Folders (SF)
    - o Locate and review all readings and assignments in the Subject Folders (SF), Digital Library (DL), and Hard Copies (HC)
    - o Note and gather needed supplies for the unit
- ☐ Read the Virtue Lesson
- ☐ Email or call R.A.S. if you have questions or technical difficulty.

PREP FOR CO-OP

- ☐ Print your "Co-op Job Sheet" and prep for your job
- ☐ Make sure your child is ready for his or her presentation if assigned to present
- ☐ Gather maps, notebooks, prayer sheet, and other supplies the night or morning before the co-op meets.
- ☐ Gather students' assignments the night or morning before the co-op meets
- ☐ Listen to the Memory Work on the way!

PREP FOR UPCOMING WEEKS – <u>LOOK AHEAD AT UNITS 9</u>

- ☐ Make advanced purchases, as necessary
- ☐ Begin to gather books and materials

PLANNER ABBREVIATION KEY	
DL	Digital Library (in course suite)
SF	Subject Folder (in course suite)
HC	Hard Copy
PLL	*Primary Language Lessons* (book)
ILL	*Intermediate Language Lessons* (book)
RS4K	*Real Science 4 Kids* (book)
I-CAT	*Illustrated Catechism* (book)
OHF-1	*Our Holy Faith, Book 1* (book)
OHF-2	*Our Holy Faith, Book 2* (book)
OHF-4	*Our Holy Faith, Book 4* (book)
OHF-1-TM	*Our Holy Faith, Book 1, Teacher's Manual* (book)

OVERVIEW

Common Topics (All students PreK to 6th)

Virtue:	Obedience
Hymn:	Ecce nomen Domini
Prayers:	Angelus, Pater Noster, Ave Maria, Gloria Patri
History:	Shakespeare
Science:	Kinds of Chemical Reactions

History Themes

During Unit 6 we once again remain in the 16th Century, but we look toward a famous poet, playwright, and actor who has influenced the English language ever since: William Shakespeare. Arguably, he is the greatest English writer and dramatist who has ever written and acted. From him alone the English language gained thousands of new words, which he created from Latin, Greek, and French! Since he wrote thirty seven plays and over 154 sonnets, we will spend two units studying his contributions to Western society. We encourage you to read and listen to as many of Shakespeare's works as possible during the next two units.

How to Apply History to Everyday Life

Our Mission. Shakespeare has much to say about the disobedient and just rewards. Are we obedient to God's Commandments? Are we obedient to the commandments of the Church? Are we obedient to our parents? Do we require our children to be obedient to us? Do we honor our parents? Do we require our children to honor us? Do we punish our children for disobedience? Do we confess to a priest when we are disobedient to God or to our own parents? Are we obedient to our government when our government's requests are in accord with God's commandments? Do we stand up against government when it asks us to sin? Do we put our obedience to God above all other allegiances?

OVERVIEW

Important People, Events, and Places to Know (Potential Student Presentations)

- ❖ Saints of the Sixteenth Century
    - o Bl. Ladislaus of Gielniow (1505)
    - o Our Lady of Guadalupe (1531)
    - o St. John Fisher (1535)
    - o St. Jerome Emiliani (1537)
    - o St. Anthony Mary Zaccaria (1539)
    - o St. Angela Merici (1540)
    - o St. Cajetan (1547)
    - o St. John of God (1550)
    - o St. Francis Xavier (1552)
    - o St. Thomas Villanova (1555)
    - o St. Ignatius of Loyola (1556)
    - o St. Paul Miki (1597)
    - o St. Peter of Alcantara (1562)
    - o St. Stanislaus Kostka (1568)
    - o St. John of Avila (1569)
    - o Our Lady of the Rosary (1571)
    - o St. Pius V (1572)
    - o St. Francis Borgia (1572)
    - o St. Edmund Campion (1581)
    - o St. Louis Bertrand (1581)
    - o St. Teresa of Jesus (of Avila) (1582)
    - o St. Charles Borromeo (1584)
    - o St. Margaret Clitherow (1586)
    - o St. Catherine de Ricci (1589)
    - o Bls. Edward Jones & Anthony Middleton (1590)
    - o St. Aloysius Gonzaga (1591)
    - o Bls. Ralph Milner & Roger Dickenson (1591)
    - o St. John of the Cross (1591)
    - o St. Paschal Baylon (1592)
    - o St. Philip Neri (1595)
    - o St. Peter Canisius (1597)
    - o The Forty Martyrs of England

Additional Project Ideas

- ❖ Build a Globe replica
- ❖ Read a Shakespearean Sonnet or Play and perform it for the family
- ❖ Memorize a Sonnet
- ❖ Build a set for your plays!
- ❖ Have family play night this week!

PLANNER ~ Unit 6 (Co-op)

Week of _____ *Liturgical Theme & Colors* _____

Family Challenge-Task
Goals _____
_____
_____
_____

Reminders _____
_____
_____

PRESCHOOL

	Music	Art, Reading, Religion	Virtue
Co-op	See "Music" heading below	Do craft **PreK Lesson A** (SF)	Review Virtue I-J (SF); practice "virtue training"
Day 2-4	See "Music" heading below	Do **Letter Book I-J** (SF); do **coloring pages** (SF); read & drill I-CAT, p. 9 (HC)	Review Virtue I-J (SF); practice "virtue training"

KINDERGARTEN – 6TH GRADE

ART   **CCM**

	K-6th Grade	K-6th Grade
Co-op	Do **All Lesson A** (SF).	Unit 6
Day 2-4	Review **All Lesson A** (SF) and do home follow-up.	Listen to Unit 6 every day

HISTORY

	K-1st Grades	2nd-3rd Grades	4th-6th Grades
Co-op	Do dramatization **K-1 Lesson A** (SF).	Do dramatization **2-3 Lesson A** (SF).	Do discussion **4-6 Lesson A** (SF).
Day 2	Read *Tales from Shakespeare* by Lamb (HC; Audio in DL) this week; Choose and do reading (or other project) from "Extras" (SF); draw a picture inspired by the readings.	Read *Tales from Shakespeare* by Lamb (HC; Audio in DL) this week; Choose and do reading (or other project) from "Extras" (SF); draw a picture inspired by the readings.	Read *Comedy of Errors,* Acts I and II (HC or DL) this week; Choose and do readings (or other projects) from "Extras" (SF); begin writing **4-6 Activity A** (SF).
Day 3	Continue readings; do coloring page (SF).	Continue readings; do coloring page (SF).	Continue readings and **4-6 Activity A** (SF).
Day 4	Continue readings; Imagine & Draw a scene from the reading.	Continue readings; Imagine & Draw a scene from the reading	Finish readings and **4-6 Activity A;** add items to your timeline from Units 1-5.

LANGUAGE ARTS

Co-op	Complete **K-1 Lesson A** (SF).	Complete **2-3 Lesson A** (SF); do **2-3 Activity A** (SF).	Complete **4-6 Lesson A** (SF); begin **4-6 Activity A** (SF).
Day 2	Review **K-1 Lesson A** (SF); Ask your student to describe the picture.	Review **2-3 Lesson A** (SF); continue **2-3 Activity A** (SF).	Review **4-6 Lesson A** (SF); continue **4-6 Activity A** (SF)
Day 3	Do pre-cursive copywork **K-1 Activity A** (SF).	Do cursive copywork **2-3 Activity B** (SF).	Complete first draft in **4-6 Activity A** (SF).
Day 4	Do narration and illustration **K-1 Activity B** (SF)	Do composition and illustration **2-3 Activity C** (SF)	Complete final draft in **4-6 Activity A** (SF).

LATIN/GREEK

Co-op	Practice Ecce Nomen Domini! (SF)	Practice Ecce Nomen Domini! (SF); do *Greek Primer* 6.1–4 (SF)	Practice Ecce Nomen Domini! (SF); do *Reading Greek* 6.1–2 (SF)
Day 2	Listen to CCM Unit 6 Latin prayer	Listen to CCM Unit 6 Latin prayer; do *Greek Primer* 6.5	Listen to CCM Unit 6 Latin prayer; do *Reading Greek* 6.3–4 (SF)
Day 3	Practice all the *Schola Rosa* Latin assembly prayers!	Practice all the *Schola Rosa* Latin assembly prayers!	Practice all the *Schola Rosa* Latin assembly prayers!
Day 4	Listen to Ecce Nomen Domini! video (SF); Sing along!	Listen to Ecce Nomen Domini! video (SF); Sing along!; finish *Greek Primer* Unit 6 (SF)	Listen to Ecce Nomen Domini! video (SF); Sing along! Finish *Reading Greek* Unit 6 (SF) and check work.

MATH

	Level A	Level B	Level C
Co-op	None	None	None
Day 2-4	See *Ray's Primary*, Mastery Chart~ Do next lesson (DL)	See *Ray's Intellectual*, Mastery Chart~ Do next lesson (DL)	See *Ray's Practical*, Mastery Chart~ Do next lesson (DL)

MUSIC

	K-6th Grade
Co-op	Review **All Lesson A** (SF). Use audio files
Day 2-4	to sing along with: Hymn of the Week (Latin SF); Exercises Group 1 and 2, Scale Drills, Kyrie Eleison, Agnus Dei, Sanctus, and Merrily We Roll Along (DL). See addendum to Lesson for 2nd year additions.

READING

	Primer (pre-reader)	Reader
Co-op	None	None
Day 2-4	See *McGuffey's Eclectic Primer*, "Mastery Chart"~ Do next lesson (DL)	See *McGuffey's Eclectic Readers*, "Mastery Chart" ~ Do next lesson (DL)

RELIGION — *Liturgical Feast lessons can be moved to correspond to their dates — simply adjust the schedule accordingly*

	K-1st Grades	2nd-3rd Grades	4th-6th Grades
Co-op	Begin **K-1 Lesson A** (SF).	Begin **2-3 Lesson A** (SF). Drill Q & A.	Begin **4-6 Lesson A** (SF). Drill Q & A.
Day 2	Complete **K-1 Lesson A** (SF).	Review/complete **2-3 Lesson A** (SF). Drill Q & A.	Review/complete **4-6 Lesson A** (SF). Drill Q & A.
Day 3	Complete **K-1 Lesson B** (SF).	Review/complete **2-3 Lesson A** (SF). Drill Q & A.	Select activity(ies) from the "Let Us Work Together" section OHF-4, pp. 50-51.
Day 4	Complete **K-1 Lesson C** (SF).	Review/complete **2-3 Lesson A** (SF). Drill Q & A.	Select activity(ies) from the "Let Us Work Together" section OHF-4, pp. 50-51; do "Unit 2 Test," OHF-4, p. 52 (DL).

SCIENCE

Co-op	Do **K-1 Lesson A** (SF).	Do **2-3 Lesson A** (SF).	Do **4-6 Lesson A** (SF).
Day 2	Continue reading *The Wonder Book of Chemistry* (DL)	Continue reading *The Wonder Book of Chemistry* (DL)	Read RS4K *Elementary Chemistry Grades K-4* 3.6-8 & Experiment 3
Day 3	Do observe and draw **K-1 Activity A** (SF)	Do observe and draw **2-3 Activity A** (SF)	Do journaling **4-6 Activity A** (SF)
Day 4	Go on a nature walk and do drawing **K-1 Activity B** (SF).	Go on a nature walk and do drawing **2-3 Activity B** (SF).	Go on a nature walk and continue **4-6 Activity A** (SF).

VIRTUE

	K-6th Grades
Field	**Do All Virtue Lesson A – Obedience** (SF)
Day 2-4	Practice "virtue training"

CYCLE III
UNIT 7

SHAKESPEARE

UNIT CHECKLIST

PREP FOR HOME

- ☐ Print and read this Handbook
- ☐ Read the Overview
- ☐ Review the Planner; do the following:
  - o Locate and review all Lessons and Activities in the Subject Folders (SF)
  - o Locate and review all readings and assignments in the Subject Folders (SF), Digital Library (DL), and Hard Copies (HC)
  - o Note and gather needed supplies for the unit
- ☐ Read the Virtue Lesson
- ☐ Email or call R.A.S. if you have questions or technical difficulty.

PREP FOR CO-OP

- ☐ Print your "Co-op Job Sheet" and prep for your job
- ☐ Make sure your child is ready for his or her presentation if assigned to present
- ☐ Gather maps, notebooks, prayer sheet, and other supplies the night or morning before the co-op meets.
- ☐ Gather students' assignments the night or morning before the co-op meets
- ☐ Listen to the Memory Work on the way!

PREP FOR UPCOMING WEEKS — <u>LOOK AHEAD AT UNITS 10</u>

- ☐ Make advanced purchases, as necessary
- ☐ Begin to gather books and materials

PLANNER ABBREVIATION KEY

DL	Digital Library (in course suite)
SF	Subject Folder (in course suite)
HC	Hard Copy
PLL	*Primary Language Lessons* (book)
ILL	*Intermediate Language Lessons* (book)
RS4K	*Real Science 4 Kids* (book)
I-CAT	*Illustrated Catechism* (book)
OHF-1	*Our Holy Faith, Book 1* (book)
OHF-2	*Our Holy Faith, Book 2* (book)
OHF-4	*Our Holy Faith, Book 4* (book)
OHF-1-TM	*Our Holy Faith, Book 1, Teacher's Manual* (book)

OVERVIEW

Common Topics (All students PreK to 6th)

Virtue:	Justice
Hymn:	Ecce nomen Domini
Prayers:	Angelus, Pater Noster, Ave Maria, Gloria Patri
History:	Shakespeare
Science:	Acids & Bases

History Themes

We are continuing the Unit 6 theme this week: William Shakespeare.

How to Apply History to Everyday Life

Our Mission. Indeed, Shakespeare has much to say about the just and the unjust of the world. We might reflect upon the virtue of justice this week.

Do we do penance because we know it is just to do so? Do we go to confession because we know we have unjustly sinned against God and neighbor?

Do we seek to repay debts when we owe them? Do we sacrifice luxury to repay debt to others? Do we repay our neighbor's kind deed with another kind deed? Do we seek to treat our neighbor as we would treat ourselves?

Important People, Events, and Places to Know (Potential Student Presentations)

❖ Saints of the Sixteenth Century

- o Bl. Ladislaus of Gielniow (1505)
- o Our Lady of Guadalupe (1531)
- o St. John Fisher (1535)
- o St. Jerome Emiliani (1537)
- o St. Anthony Mary Zaccaria (1539)
- o St. Angela Merici (1540)
- o St. Cajetan (1547)
- o St. John of God (1550)
- o St. Francis Xavier (1552)
- o St. Thomas Villanova (1555)
- o St. Ignatius of Loyola (1556)
- o St. Paul Miki (1597)
- o St. Peter of Alcantara (1562)
- o St. Stanislaus Kostka (1568)
- o St. John of Avila (1569)
- o Our Lady of the Rosary (1571)
- o St. Pius V (1572)
- o St. Francis Borgia (1572)
- o St. Edmund Campion (1581)
- o St. Louis Bertrand (1581)
- o St. Teresa of Jesus (of Avila) (1582)
- o St. Charles Borromeo (1584)
- o St. Margaret Clitherow (1586)
- o St. Catherine de Ricci (1589)
- o Bls. Edward Jones & Anthony Middleton (1590)
- o St. Aloysius Gonzaga (1591)
- o Bls. Ralph Milner & Roger Dickenson (1591)

OVERVIEW

- ○ St. John of the Cross (1591)
- ○ St. Paschal Baylon (1592)
- ○ St. Philip Neri (1595)

- ○ St. Peter Canisius (1597)
- ○ The Forty Martyrs of England and Wales

Additional Project Ideas

- ❖ Read a Shakespearean Sonnet or Play and perform it for the family
- ❖ Memorize a Sonnet
- ❖ Build a set for your plays!
- ❖ Have family play night this week!

Week of _____   *Liturgical Theme & Colors* _____

Family Challenge-Task
Goals _____

_____

_____

_____

Reminders _____

_____

_____

PRESCHOOL

	Music	Art, Reading, Religion	Virtue
Co-op	See "Music" heading below	Do craft **PreK Lesson A** (SF)	Review Virtue K-L (SF); practice "virtue training"
Day 2-4	See "Music" heading below	Do **Letter Book K-L** (SF); do **coloring pages** (SF); read & drill I-CAT, p. 11 (HC)	Review Virtue K-L (SF); practice "virtue training"

KINDERGARTEN – 6TH GRADE

ART   **CCM**

	K-6th Grade		K-6th Grade
Co-op	Do **All Lesson A** (SF).	Co-op	Unit 7
Day 2-4	Review **All Lesson A** (SF) and do home follow-up.	Day 2-4	Listen to Unit 7 every day

HISTORY

	K-1st Grades	2nd-3rd Grades	4th-6th Grades
Co-op	Do narrative **K-1 Lesson A** (SF).	Do craft **2-3 Lesson A** (SF).	Do discussion **4-6 Lesson A** (SF).
Day 2	Read *Tales from Shakespeare* by Lamb (HC; Audio in DL) this week; Choose and do reading (or other project) from "Extras" (SF); draw a picture inspired by the readings.	Read *Tales from Shakespeare* by Lamb (HC; Audio in DL) this week; Choose and do reading (or other project) from "Extras" (SF); draw a picture inspired by the readings.	Read *Comedy of Errors,* Acts III-V (HC or DL) this week; Choose and do readings (or other projects) from "Extras" (SF); begin writing **4-6 Activity A** (SF).
Day 3	Continue readings; do coloring page (SF).	Continue readings; do coloring page (SF); do map **2-3 Activity A** (SF).	Continue readings and **4-6 Activity A** (SF); do map **4-6 Activity B** (SF).
Day 4	Continue readings; Imagine & Draw a scene from the reading.	Continue readings; Imagine & Draw a scene from the reading	Finish readings and **4-6 Activity A** (SF).

LANGUAGE ARTS

Co-op	Complete **K-1 Lesson A** (SF).	Complete **2-3 Lesson A** (SF); do **2-3 Activity A** (SF).	Complete **4-6 Lesson A** (SF); begin **4-6 Activity A** (SF).
Day 2	Review **K-1 Lesson A** (SF); Ask your student to describe the picture.	Review **2-3 Lesson A** (SF); continue **2-3 Activity A** (SF).	Review **4-6 Lesson A** (SF); continue **4-6 Activity A** (SF)
Day 3	Do pre-cursive copywork **K-1 Activity A** (SF).	Do cursive copywork **2-3 Activity B** (SF).	Complete first draft in **4-6 Activity A** (SF).
Day 4	Do narration and illustration **K-1 Activity B** (SF)	Do composition and illustration **2-3 Activity C** (SF)	Complete final draft in **4-6 Activity A** (SF).

LATIN/GREEK

Co-op	Practice Ecce Nomen Domini! (SF)	Practice Ecce Nomen Domini! (SF); do *Greek Primer* 7.1–4 (SF)	Practice Ecce Nomen Domini! (SF); do *Reading Greek* 7.1–2 (SF)
Day 2	Listen to CCM Unit 7 Latin prayer	Listen to CCM Unit 7 Latin prayer; do *Greek Primer* 7.5	Listen to CCM Unit 7 Latin prayer; do *Reading Greek* 7.3–4 (SF)
Day 3	Practice all the *Schola Rosa* Latin assembly prayers!	Practice all the *Schola Rosa* Latin assembly prayers!	Practice all the *Schola Rosa* Latin assembly prayers!
Day 4	Listen to Ecce Nomen Domini! video (SF); Sing along!	Listen to Ecce Nomen Domini! video (SF); Sing along!; finish *Greek Primer* Unit 7 (SF)	Listen to Ecce Nomen Domini! video (SF); Sing along! Finish *Reading Greek* Unit 7 (SF) and check work.

MATH

	Level A	Level B	Level C
Co-op	None	None	None
Day 2-4	See *Ray's Primary,* Mastery Chart~ Do next lesson (DL)	See *Ray's Intellectual,* Mastery Chart~ Do next lesson (DL)	See *Ray's Practical,* Mastery Chart~ Do next lesson (DL)

MUSIC

	K-6th Grade
Co-op	Review **All Lesson A** (SF). Use audio files to
Day 2-4	sing along with: Hymn of the Week (Latin SF); Exercises Group 1 and 2, Scale Drills, Ite Missa Est, Kyrie Eleison, Agnus Dei, Sanctus, Merrily We Roll Along; Oats, Peas, Beans, & Barley Grow (DL). See addendum to Lesson for 2nd year additions.

READING

	Primer (pre-reader)	Reader
Co-op	None	None
Day 2-4	See *McGuffey's Eclectic Primer*, "Mastery Chart" ~ Do next lesson (DL)	See *McGuffey's Eclectic Readers*, "Mastery Chart" ~ Do next lesson (DL)

RELIGION — *Liturgical Feast lessons can be moved to correspond to their dates — simply adjust the schedule accordingly*

	K-1st Grades	2nd-3rd Grades	4th-6th Grades
Co-op	Begin **K-1 Lesson A** (SF).	Begin **2-3 Lesson A** (SF). Drill Q & A.	Begin **4-6 Lesson A** (SF). Drill Q & A.
Day 2	Complete **K-1 Lesson A** (SF).	Review/complete **2-3 Lesson A** (SF). Drill Q & A.	Review/complete **4-6 Lesson A** (SF). Drill Q & A.
Day 3	Complete **K-1 Lesson B** (SF).	Review/complete **2-3 Lesson A** (SF). Drill Q & A.	Select activity(ies) from the "Let Us Work Together" section OHF-4, pp. 67-68.
Day 4	Complete **K-1 Lesson C** (SF).	Review/complete **2-3 Lesson A** (SF). Drill Q & A.	Select activity(ies) from the "Let Us Work Together" section OHF-4, pp. 67-68.

SCIENCE

Co-op	Do **K-1 Lesson A** (SF).	Do **2-3 Lesson A** (SF).	Do **4-6 Lesson A** (SF).
Day 2	Continue reading *The Wonder Book of Chemistry* (DL)	Continue reading *The Wonder Book of Chemistry* (DL)	Read RS4K *Elementary Chemistry Grades K-4* 4.1-5 & Experiment 4
Day 3	Do observe and draw **K-1 Activity A** (SF)	Do observe and draw **2-3 Activity A** (SF)	Do journaling **4-6 Activity A** (SF)
Day 4	Go on a nature walk and do drawing **K-1 Activity B** (SF).	Go on a nature walk and do drawing **2-3 Activity B** (SF).	Go on a nature walk and continue **4-6 Activity A** (SF).

VIRTUE

	K-6th Grades
Field	Do **All Virtue Lesson A – Justice** (SF)
Day 2-4	Practice "virtue training"

CYCLE III
UNIT 8

PILGRIMS COME TO AMERICA

UNIT CHECKLIST

PREP FOR HOME

- ☐ Print and read this Handbook
- ☐ Read the Overview
- ☐ Review the Planner; do the following:
    - o Locate and review all Lessons and Activities in the Subject Folders (SF)
    - o Locate and review all readings and assignments in the Subject Folders (SF), Digital Library (DL), and Hard Copies (HC)
    - o Note and gather needed supplies for the unit
- ☐ Read the Virtue Lesson
- ☐ Email or call R.A.S. if you have questions or technical difficulty.

PREP FOR CO-OP

- ☐ Print your "Co-op Job Sheet" and prep for your job
- ☐ Make sure your child is ready for his or her presentation if assigned to present
- ☐ Gather maps, notebooks, prayer sheet, and other supplies the night or morning before the co-op meets.
- ☐ Gather students' assignments the night or morning before the co-op meets
- ☐ Listen to the Memory Work on the way!

PREP FOR UPCOMING WEEKS — <u>LOOK AHEAD AT UNITS 11</u>

- ☐ Make advanced purchases, as necessary
- ☐ Begin to gather books and materials

PLANNER ABBREVIATION KEY

DL	Digital Library (in course suite)
SF	Subject Folder (in course suite)
HC	Hard Copy
PLL	*Primary Language Lessons* (book)
ILL	*Intermediate Language Lessons* (book)
RS4K	*Real Science 4 Kids* (book)
I-CAT	*Illustrated Catechism* (book)
OHF-1	*Our Holy Faith, Book 1* (book)
OHF-2	*Our Holy Faith, Book 2* (book)
OHF-4	*Our Holy Faith, Book 4* (book)
OHF-1-TM	*Our Holy Faith, Book 1, Teacher's Manual* (book)

OVERVIEW

Common Topics (All students PreK to 6th)

Virtue:	Temperance
Hymn:	Ecce nomen Domini
Prayers:	Angelus, Pater Noster, Ave Maria, Gloria Patri
History:	Pilgrims Come to America
Science:	Review

History Themes

With Unit 8 we enter the 17th Century, which the Sisters of Notre Dame in the *Compendium of Church History* called "The Century of Religious Agitation." They summarize the century as such: "Throughout the seventeenth century the Church had to struggle against absolutism and secularism in monarchies; Jansenism, Gallicanism, and Febronianism in religion. The Papacy was utterly ignored in concluding the Treaty of Westphalia, and in consequence the Church lost all influence in the affairs of State and political movements. Yet, while Louis XIV was setting aside the authority of Pope Alexander VII, by declaring "Gallican Liberties," and Germany was rent asunder by the Thirty Years' War, God raised up zealous missionaries to bring the light of the gospel to distant countries laid open by Catholic discoverers."

K-6th Graders will not focus on all the political scandals of this century, but simply on the settlement of America by looking at the Catholics who came to Maryland and the Pilgrims who came to Jamestown. It is important for us Catholics to understand that the Pilgrims were Puritans, or at least variants of Puritanism. According to the Catholic Encyclopedia, "One of the most picturesque incidents in the history of Puritanism and one of far reaching influence on subsequent American history was the departure of the "Pilgrim Fathers" — seventy-four English Puritans and twenty-eight women — who sailed from England in the May Flower and landed on Plymouth Rock, 25 December, 1620. There they founded a colony, representing both types, the Plymouth colony being Congregationalists, the Massachusetts Bay settlers, Presbyterians." As Catholics, we should perhaps put a greater focus on the missionaries who came before the pilgrims and also on the settlers of Maryland as the "Catholic Fathers of America." The next two units will provide your family with that opportunity, so alongside the study of pilgrims, be sure to read about the Saints listed in this overview!

Religious Orders, summaries from the *Compendium of Church History*

1. The Visitation Nuns ~ were founded by St. Jane Frances de Chantel, to carry on the work of Christian education
2. The Lazarists ~ were founded by St. Vincent de Paul to give missions
3. The Sisters of Charity ~ were founded by St. Vincent de Paul to protect and care for the sick and destitute.

4.   The Trappists ~ a branch of Cistercians, were founded by Bouthillièr de Rancé, to further by labor and prayer the welfare of the Church

5.   The Brothers of the Christian Schools ~ were founded by St. John Baptist de la Salle, for the education of youth

How to Apply History to Everyday Life

Our Mission. Temperance, or Moderation, is worth considering when reflecting upon Protestantism and Puritanism. On the one hand, we are not moderate or temperate when we reject authority that is legitimate—we are too proud and confident in our own judgment, perhaps. On the other hand, when we seem to be *pure* in one aspect, we might fail in another aspect. For example, we might seek to be *pure* ascetics and fast everyday in order to learn self-discipline and to pray more fervently. However, if we neglect to hear our neighbor's call for help and to feed him when he is hungry or to clothe him when he is naked, we have failed in charity. Temperance is the ability to temper or to moderate all virtues so that they are not at odds with one another.

Do we help our neighbor when he calls? Or do we make up excuses? Do we continue to seek to help that neighbor who never returns the favor? Or do we give up? Do we give up our cookie for the sake of our younger sibling? Do we willingly give of our possessions or do we covet? Do we praise our friends and enemies when they do well? Or are we envious?

Important People, Events, and Places to Know (Potential Student Presentations)

❖ John Cabot's first and second explorations of America (1497-1498), Henry VIII becomes king of England (1509), Henry VIII splits the Church of England from Rome (1535), Establishment of first and second Roanoke colonies (1585-1587), Death of Sir Francis Drake (1596), Founding of Jamestown (1607), Captain John Smith becomes governor of Jamestown (1608) and replaced as governor (1609), Henry Hudson discovers Hudson Bay and John Rolfe brings tobacco to Jamestown (1610), John Rolfe marries Pocahontas (1614), Death of Pocahontas (1617), Establishment of Salem colony (1628), Establishment of Massachusetts Bay Colony at Boston (1629), Establishment of St. Mary's, Maryland (1634), Establishment of Providence, Rhode Island Colony (1636), Establishment of Portsmouth, Rhode Island Colony (1638), Foundation of New York Colony (1660), Foundation of South Carolina Colony (1670)

OVERVIEW

- ❖ Saints of the Seventeenth Century

    - o St. Turibius of Mongrovejo (1606)
    - o St. Mary Magdalen de Pazzi (1607)
    - o St. Andrew Avellino (1608)
    - o St. Francis Caracciolo (1608)
    - o St. John Leonardi (1609)
    - o St. Francis Solano (1610)
    - o St. Camillus de Lellis (1614)
    - o St. Alphonsus Rodriguez (1617)
    - o St. Rose of Lima (1617)
    - o St. Lawrence of Brindisi (1619)
    - o Bl. John Sarkander (1620)
    - o St. Robert Bellarmine (1621)
    - o St. John Berchmans (1621)
    - o St. Fidelis of Sigmaringen (1622)
    - o St. Francis de Sales (1622)
    - o St. Josaphat (1623)
    - o St. Martin de Porres (1639)

    - o St. John Francis Regis (1640)
    - o St. Jane Frances de Chantel (1641)
    - o St. Joseph Calasanctius (1648)
    - o Sts. John de Brébeuf, Isaac Jogues, Priests and Companions (1642, 1646, 1648, 1649), the North American Martyrs
    - o St. Peter Claver (1654)
    - o St. Andrew Bobola (1657)
    - o St. Louise de Marillac (1660)
    - o St. Vincent de Paul (1660)
    - o St. Joseph Cupertino (1663)
    - o St. Kateri Tekakwitha (1680)
    - o St. John Eudes (1680)
    - o St. Oliver Plunket (1681)
    - o St. Claude de la Colombiere (1682)
    - o St. Margaret Mary Alacoque (1690)
    - o St. Gregory Barbarigo (1697)

Additional Project Ideas

- ❖ *History Pockets* lessons on the Pilgrims
- ❖ Create a "Magna Carta" for your home!
- ❖ Write a Thanksgiving Prayer for your home.
- ❖ Dry Corn on the Cob from the Fall Harvest and make popcorn
- ❖ Save seeds from the autumn plants for next spring! (Learn to farm like the Pilgrims!)

OVERVIEW

Week of _____ *Liturgical Theme & Colors* _____

Family Challenge-Task
Goals _____

_____

_____

_____

Reminders _____

_____

PRESCHOOL

	Music	Art, Reading, Religion	Virtue
Field	See "Music" heading below	Do craft **PreK Lesson A** (SF)	Practice "virtue training"
Day 2-4	See "Music" heading below	Review A-L (SF), review & drill I-CAT, p 11 (HC)	Practice "virtue training"

KINDERGARTEN – 6TH GRADE

ART   CCM

	K-6th Grade	K-6th Grade
Field	Review **All Lesson A** (SF), Units 5-7.	Unit 8.
Day 2-4	Do extra art task from home follow-up sections, if there is time.	Listen to Unit 8 every day

HISTORY

	K-1st Grades	2nd-3rd Grades	4th-6th Grades
Field	Read Selected Poetry from John Milton (DL) this week.	Read Selected Poetry from John Milton (DL) this week.	Read *Mayflower Compact* (DL) this week.
Day 2	Choose and do reading (or other project) from "Extras" (SF); draw a picture inspired by the readings	Choose and do reading (or other project) from "Extras" (SF); draw a picture inspired by the readings	Choose and do readings (or other projects) from "Extras" (SF);
Day 3	Continue readings.	Continue readings.	Continue readings.
Day 4	Do coloring page (SF)	Do coloring page (SF)	Do timeline **4-6 Activity A** (SF).

LANGUAGE ARTS

Field	Complete **K-1 Lesson A** (SF).	Complete **2-3 Lesson A** (SF).	Complete **4-6 Lesson A** (SF); do **4-6 Activity A** (SF).
Day 2	Review **K-1 Lesson A** (SF); describe the picture.	Review **2-3 Lesson A** (SF); do **2-3 Activity A** (SF).	Review **4-6 Lesson A** (SF); do **4-6 Activity B** (SF)
Day 3	Do pre-cursive copywork **K-1 Activity A** (SF).	Do cursive copywork **2-3 Activity B** (SF).	Complete first draft in **4-6 Activity B** (SF).
Day 4	Do narration and illustration **K-1 Activity B** (SF)	Do composition and illustration **2-3 Activity C** (SF)	Complete final draft in **4-6 Activity B** (SF).

LATIN/GREEK

Field	Practice Ecce Nomen Domini (SF)	Practice Ecce Nomen Domini (SF); do *Greek Primer* 8.1–3 (SF)	Practice Ecce Nomen Domini (SF); do *Reading Greek* 8.1–2 (SF)
Day 2	Listen to CCM Unit 8 Latin prayer	Listen to CCM Unit 8 Latin prayer; do *Greek Primer* 8.4-5	Listen to CCM Unit 8 Latin prayer; do *Reading Greek* 8.3-4 (SF)
Day 3	Practice all the *Schola Rosa* Latin assembly prayers!	Practice all the *Schola Rosa* Latin assembly prayers!	Practice all the *Schola Rosa* Latin assembly prayers!
Day 4	Listen to Ecce Nomen Domini video (SF); Sing along!	Listen to Ecce Nomen Domini video (SF); Sing along!; finish *Greek Primer* Unit 8 (SF)	Listen to Ecce Nomen Domini video (SF); Sing along!; finish *Reading Greek* Unit 8 (SF) and check work.

MATH

	Level A	Level B	Level C
Field	None	None	None
Day 2-4	See *Ray's Primary*, Mastery Chart~ Do next lesson (DL)	See *Ray's Intellectual*, Mastery Chart~ Do next lesson (DL)	See *Ray's Practical*, Mastery Chart~ Do next lesson (DL)

MUSIC

	K-6th Grade
Field	Use audio files to sing along with: Hymn of the Week (Latin SF); Exercises Group 1-2; Ite Missa Est, Agnus Dei; Sanctus; Merrily We Roll Along; Oats, Peas, Beans, & Barley Grow (DL). See addendum to Lesson for 2nd year additions.
Day 2-4	

READING

	Primer (pre-reader)	Reader
Field	None	None
Day 2-4	See *McGuffey's Eclectic Primer*, "Mastery Chart" ~ Do next lesson (DL)	See *McGuffey's Eclectic Readers*, "Mastery Chart" ~ Do next lesson (DL)

RELIGION — *Liturgical Feast lessons can be moved to correspond to their dates – simply adjust the schedule accordingly*

	K-1st Grades	2nd-3rd Grades	4th-6th Grades
Field	Field Trip	Field Trip	Field Trip
Day 2	Review/complete **K-1 Lesson A** (SF).	Review/complete **2-3 Lesson A** (SF). Drill Q & A.	Review/complete **4-6 Lesson A** (SF). Drill Q & A.
Day 3	Begin **K-1 Lesson B** (SF).	Review/complete **2-3 Lesson A** (SF). Drill Q & A.	Complete activity(-ies) from the "Let Us Work Together" section OHF-4, pp. 78-79.
Day 4	Review/complete **K-1 Lesson B** (SF).	Review/complete **2-3 Lesson A** (SF). Drill Q & A.	Complete activity(ies) from the "Let Us Work Together" section OHF-4, pp. 78-79.

SCIENCE

Field	Review Units 5-7 and complete any missing assignments.	Review Units 5-7 and complete any missing assignments.	Review Units 5-7 and complete any missing assignments.
Day 2	Read other selections from *The Wonder Book of Chemistry* (DL).	Read other selections from *The Wonder Book of Chemistry* (DL).	Read RS4K *Elementary Chemistry Grades K-4* 5.1-5 & Experiment 5
Day 3	Complete any experiments or activities that were not completed in Units 5-7.	Complete any experiments or activities that were not completed in Units 15-7.	Complete any experiments or activities that were not completed in Units 5-7.
Day 4	Do drawings of your favorite chemical reactions! Go on a nature walk and contemplate how things interact.	Do drawings of your favorite chemical reactions! Go on a nature walk and contemplate how things interact.	Go on a nature walk with the family and update your journal if anything is not finished.

VIRTUE

	K-6th Grades
Field	Do **All Virtue Lesson A – Temperance** (SF)
Day 2-4	Practice "virtue training"

CYCLE III
UNIT 9

PILGRIM LIFE
& NATIVE AMERICANS

UNIT CHECKLIST

PREP FOR HOME

- ☐ Print and read this Handbook
- ☐ Read the Overview
- ☐ Review the Planner; do the following:
  - ○ Locate and review all Lessons and Activities in the Subject Folders (SF)
  - ○ Locate and review all readings and assignments in the Subject Folders (SF), Digital Library (DL), and Hard Copies (HC)
  - ○ Note and gather needed supplies for the unit
- ☐ Read the Virtue Lesson
- ☐ Email or call R.A.S. if you have questions or technical difficulty.

PREP FOR CO-OP

- ☐ Print your "Co-op Job Sheet" and prep for your job
- ☐ Make sure your child is ready for his or her presentation if assigned to present
- ☐ Gather maps, notebooks, prayer sheet, and other supplies the night or morning before the co-op meets.
- ☐ Gather students' assignments the night or morning before the co-op meets
- ☐ Listen to the Memory Work on the way!

PREP FOR UPCOMING WEEKS — <u>LOOK AHEAD AT UNITS 12</u>

- ☐ Make advanced purchases, as necessary
- ☐ Begin to gather books and materials

PLANNER ABBREVIATION KEY	
DL	Digital Library (in course suite)
SF	Subject Folder (in course suite)
HC	Hard Copy
PLL	*Primary Language Lessons* (book)
ILL	*Intermediate Language Lessons* (book)
RS4K	*Real Science 4 Kids* (book)
I-CAT	*Illustrated Catechism* (book)
OHF-1	*Our Holy Faith, Book 1* (book)
OHF-2	*Our Holy Faith, Book 2* (book)
OHF-4	*Our Holy Faith, Book 4* (book)
OHF-1-TM	*Our Holy Faith, Book 1, Teacher's Manual* (book)

OVERVIEW

Common Topics (All students PreK to 6th)

Virtue:	Charity – Love of Neighbor
Hymn:	Lumen ad revelationem
Prayers:	Angelus, Pater Noster, Ave Maria, Gloria Patri
History:	Pilgrim Life & Native Americans
Science:	Separating Mixtures

History Themes

We continue our consideration of the themes introduced in Unit 8 studies in this unit. As a further means of considering human exploration and what it means to encounter foreign peoples we add an entertaining family read-aloud to the mix: *Gulliver's Travels* retold by John Lang for children.

How to Apply History to Everyday Life

Our Mission. When the Native Americans met the Pilgrims in an hour of need, they helped teach the pilgrims to grow food, though the Native Americans were considered "pagans." This example bespeaks the natural inclination of man to perform works of charity for his neighbor.

Do we seek to help our neighbor though there is no reward for us? Do we seek to help our enemy, though it might be our future downfall? Do we seek to clothe the naked, to feed the hungry, to give water to the thirsty? Do we bury the dead? Do we speak only good words about our friends and enemies? Or do we gossip and slander? Do we eagerly listen to gossip and slander about others? Or do we remind the speaker of the virtue of charity? Do we correct the sinner? Do we instruct the ignorant?

Important People, Events, and Places to Know (Potential Student Presentations)

- ❖ Destruction of Georgia missions (1680-1685), Founding of Pennsylvania Colony (1681), Joliet's voyage down the Mississippi (1681-1682), William III decrees that all Marylanders support the Church of England (1692), Destruction of the Apalachee (Florida) missions (1704), England and Scotland united as Great Britain (1707)
- ❖ Saints of the Seventeenth Century
  - St. Turibius of Mongrovejo (1606)
  - St. Mary Magdalen de Pazzi (1607)
  - St. Andrew Avellino (1608)
  - St. Francis Caracciolo (1608)
  - St. John Leonardi (1609)
  - St. Francis Solano (1610)
  - St. Camillus de Lellis (1614)
  - St. Alphonsus Rodriguez (1617)
  - St. Rose of Lima (1617)
  - St. Lawrence of Brindisi (1619)
  - Bl. John Sarkander (1620)
  - St. Robert Bellarmine (1621)

OVERVIEW

- St. John Berchmans (1621)
- St. Fidelis of Sigmaringen (1622)
- St. Francis de Sales (1622)
- St. Josaphat (1623)
- St. Martin de Porres (1639)
- St. John Francis Regis (1640)
- St. Jane Frances de Chantel (1641)
- St. Joseph Calasanctius (1648)
- Sts. John de Brébeuf, Isaac Jogues, Priests and Companions (1642, 1646, 1648, 1649), the North American Martyrs
- St. Peter Claver (1654)
- St. Andrew Bobola (1657)
- St. Louise de Marillac (1660)
- St. Vincent de Paul (1660)
- St. Joseph Cupertino (1663)
- St. Kateri Tekakwitha (1680)
- St. John Eudes (1680)
- St. Oliver Plunket (1681)
- St. Claude de la Colombiere (1682)

Additional Project Ideas

- *History Pockets* lessons on the Pilgrims
- Create a "Magna Carta" for your home!
- Write a Thanksgiving Prayer for your home.
- Dry Corn on the Cob from the Fall Harvest and make popcorn
- Save seeds from the autumn plants for next spring! (Learn to farm like the Pilgrims!)

Week of _____   *Liturgical Theme & Colors* _____

Family Challenge-Task
Goals _____

_____

_____

Reminders _____

_____

_____

PRESCHOOL

	Music	Art, Reading, Religion	Virtue
Co-op	See "Music" heading below	Do craft **PreK Lesson A** (SF)	Review Virtue M-N (SF); practice "virtue training"
Day 2-4	See "Music" heading below	Do **Letter Book M-N** (SF); do **coloring pages** (SF); read & drill I-CAT, p. 13 (HC)	Review Virtue M-N (SF); practice "virtue training"

KINDERGARTEN – 6TH GRADE

ART   **CCM**

	K-6th Grade		K-6th Grade
Co-op	Do **All Lesson A** (SF).		Unit 9
Day 2-4	Review **All Lesson A** (SF) and do home follow-up.		Listen to Unit 9 every day

HISTORY

	K-1st Grades	2nd-3rd Grades	4th-6th Grades
Co-op	Do craft **K-1 Lesson A** (SF).	Do History Pocket **2-3 Lesson A** (SF).	Do discussion **4-6 Lesson A** (SF).
Day 2	Read *Gulliver's Travels* by John Lang (DL) this week; Choose and do reading (or other project) from "Extras" (SF); draw a picture inspired by the readings.	Read *Gulliver's Travels* by John Lang (DL) this week; Choose and do reading (or other project) from "Extras" (SF); draw a picture inspired by the readings.	Read *Gulliver's Travels* by John Lang (DL) this week; Choose and do readings (or other projects) from "Extras" (SF); begin writing **4-6 Activity A** (SF).
Day 3	Continue readings; do coloring page (SF).	Continue readings; do coloring page (SF); do map **2-3 Activity A** (SF).	Continue readings and **4-6 Activity A** (SF); do map **4-6 Activity B** (SF).
Day 4	Continue readings; Imagine & Draw a scene from the reading.	Continue readings; Imagine & Draw a scene from the reading	Finish readings and **4-6 Activity A** (SF); do timeline **4-6 Activity C** (SF).

LANGUAGE ARTS

Co-op	Complete **K-1 Lesson A** (SF).	Complete **2-3 Lesson A** (SF); do **2-3 Activity A** (SF).	Complete **4-6 Lesson A** (SF); begin **4-6 Activity A** (SF).
Day 2	Review **K-1 Lesson A** (SF); Ask your student to describe the picture.	Review **2-3 Lesson A** (SF); continue **2-3 Activity A** (SF).	Review **4-6 Lesson A** (SF); continue **4-6 Activity A** (SF)
Day 3	Do pre-cursive copywork **K-1 Activity A** (SF).	Do cursive copywork **2-3 Activity B** (SF).	Complete first draft in **4-6 Activity A** (SF).
Day 4	Do narration and illustration **K-1 Activity B** (SF)	Do composition and illustration **2-3 Activity C** (SF)	Complete final draft in **4-6 Activity A** (SF).

LATIN/GREEK

Co-op	Practice Lumen ad Revelationem! (SF)	Practice Lumen ad Revelationem! (SF); do *Greek Primer* 9.1–4 (SF)	Practice Lumen ad Revelationem! (SF); do *Reading Greek* 9.1–2 (SF)
Day 2	Listen to CCM Unit 9 Latin prayer	Listen to CCM Unit 9 Latin prayer; do *Greek Primer* 9.5	Listen to CCM Unit 9 Latin prayer; do *Reading Greek* 9.3–4 (SF)
Day 3	Practice all the *Schola Rosa* Latin assembly prayers!	Practice all the *Schola Rosa* Latin assembly prayers!	Practice all the *Schola Rosa* Latin assembly prayers!
Day 4	Listen to Lumen ad Revelationem! video (SF); Sing along!	Listen to Lumen ad Revelationem! video (SF); Sing along!; finish *Greek Primer* Unit 9 (SF)	Listen to Lumen ad Revelationem! video (SF); Sing along! Finish *Reading Greek* Unit 9 (SF) and check work.

MATH

	Level A	Level B	Level C
Co-op	None	None	None
Day 2-4	See *Ray's Primary*, Mastery Chart~ Do next lesson (DL)	See *Ray's Intellectual*, Mastery Chart~ Do next lesson (DL)	See *Ray's Practical*, Mastery Chart~ Do next lesson (DL)

MUSIC

	K-6th Grade
Co-op	Review **All Lesson A** (SF). Use audio files to sing along with: Hymn of the Week (Latin SF); Exercises Group 1, 2, & 3; Scale Drills, Ite Missa Est, Kyrie Eleison, Agnus Dei, Sanctus, Merrily We Roll Along; Oats, Peas, Beans, & Barley Grow; Lightly Row (DL). See addendum to Lesson for 2nd year additions.
Day 2-4	

READING

	Primer (pre-reader)	Reader
	None	None
	See *McGuffey's Eclectic Primer*, "Mastery Chart" ~ Do next lesson (DL)	See *McGuffey's Eclectic Readers*, "Mastery Chart" ~ Do next lesson (DL)

RELIGION — *Liturgical Feast lessons can be moved to correspond to their dates — simply adjust the schedule accordingly*

	K-1st Grades	2nd-3rd Grades	4th-6th Grades
Co-op	Begin **K-1 Lesson A** (SF).	Begin **2-3 Lesson A** (SF). Drill Q & A.	Begin **4-6 Lesson A** (SF). Drill Q & A.
Day 2	Complete **K-1 Lesson A** (SF).	Review/complete **2-3 Lesson A** (SF). Drill Q & A.	Review/complete **4-6 Lesson A** (SF). Drill Q & A.
Day 3	Complete **K-1 Lesson B** (SF).	Review/complete **2-3 Lesson A** (SF). Drill Q & A.	Select activity(ies) from the "Let Us Work Together" section OHF-4, pp. 78-79.
Day 4	Complete **K-1 Lesson C** (SF).	Review/complete **2-3 Lesson A** (SF). Drill Q & A.	Select activity(ies) from the "Let Us Work Together" section OHF-4, pp. 78-79.

SCIENCE

Co-op	Do **K-1 Lesson A** (SF).	Do **2-3 Lesson A** (SF).	Do **4-6 Lesson A** (SF).
Day 2	Continue reading *The Wonder Book of Chemistry* (DL)	Continue reading *The Wonder Book of Chemistry* (DL)	Read RS4K *Elementary Chemistry Grades K-4* 6.1-6 & Experiment 6
Day 3	Do observe and draw **K-1 Activity A** (SF)	Do observe and draw **2-3 Activity A** (SF)	Do journaling **4-6 Activity A** (SF)
Day 4	Go on a nature walk and do drawing **K-1 Activity B** (SF).	Go on a nature walk and do drawing **2-3 Activity B** (SF).	Go on a nature walk and continue **4-6 Activity A** (SF).

VIRTUE

	K-6th Grades
Field	Do **All Virtue Lesson A – Charity** (SF)
Day 2-4	Practice "virtue training"

86

CYCLE III
UNIT 10

FRENCH EXPLORATION

&

THE FRENCH-INDIAN WAR

UNIT CHECKLIST

PREP FOR HOME

- ☐ Print and read this Handbook
- ☐ Read the Overview
- ☐ Review the Planner; do the following:
    - o Locate and review all Lessons and Activities in the Subject Folders (SF)
    - o Locate and review all readings and assignments in the Subject Folders (SF), Digital Library (DL), and Hard Copies (HC)
    - o Note and gather needed supplies for the unit
- ☐ Read the Virtue Lesson
- ☐ Email or call R.A.S. if you have questions or technical difficulty.

PREP FOR CO-OP

- ☐ Print your "Co-op Job Sheet" and prep for your job
- ☐ Make sure your child is ready for his or her presentation if assigned to present
- ☐ Gather maps, notebooks, prayer sheet, and other supplies the night or morning before the co-op meets.
- ☐ Gather students' assignments the night or morning before the co-op meets
- ☐ Listen to the Memory Work on the way!

PREP FOR UPCOMING WEEKS — <u>LOOK AHEAD AT UNITS 13</u>

- ☐ Make advanced purchases, as necessary
- ☐ Begin to gather books and materials

PLANNER ABBREVIATION KEY

DL	Digital Library (in course suite)
SF	Subject Folder (in course suite)
HC	Hard Copy
PLL	*Primary Language Lessons* (book)
ILL	*Intermediate Language Lessons* (book)
RS4K	*Real Science 4 Kids* (book)
I-CAT	*Illustrated Catechism* (book)
OHF-1	*Our Holy Faith, Book 1* (book)
OHF-2	*Our Holy Faith, Book 2* (book)
OHF-4	*Our Holy Faith, Book 4* (book)
OHF-1-TM	*Our Holy Faith, Book 1, Teacher's Manual* (book)

OVERVIEW

Common Topics (All students PreK to 6th)

Virtue:	Moderation
Hymn:	Lumen ad revelationem
Prayers:	Angelus, Pater Noster, Ave Maria, Gloria Patri
History:	French Exploration & The French-Indian War (1754-1763 A.D.)
Science:	States of Matter

History Themes

We briefly met the Native Americans in our units on the pilgrims, but with Unit 10 we begin to look at their situation more closely. This week we consider how the French encountered and treated the Native Americans in North America by looking at historical literature about this time period. We also study the conflicts between the British colonies and New France colonies by looking at the French and Indian War. We see in this war how the Native Americans were pulled into European struggles.

How to Apply History to Everyday Life

Our Mission. It is interesting to reflect upon the age of exploration and expansion in regards to moderation. Do we want too much? Do we always want more? Or are we satisfied with what we have now? Do we seek to work with others? Or do we plot to take advantage of others? Do we covet our neighbor's belongings? Or do we moderately admire our neighbor for his wealth? Do we envy our neighbor when things go well for him? Or are we glad of heart that things have gone well for him? Do we buy too much? Do we buy things we do not need? Or do we only buy what is needed for the family? Do we overindulge in good foods and good drinks? Or do we save such extravagances for feasts? Do we fast on fasting days of obligation? Do we abstain on those days appointed by the Church for abstinence? Do we moderate our luxuries during penitential seasons, such as Advent and Lent? Or do we allow secular society to dictate how and when we celebrate? Do we save our Christmas parties for the Christmas season? Do we save our Easter celebrations for the Easter octave? Do we follow the Church calendar or the secular calendar?

Important People, Events, and Places to Know (Potential Student Presentations)

❖ French and Indian War Begins (1755), Washington fights with Braddock at Fort Duquesne (1755), French capture British forts on Lake Ontario and Lake George, French Governor surrenders Montreal to the British (1760), Treaty of Paris ends French and Indian War (1763)

❖ Saints of the Eighteenth Century:

OVERVIEW

- St. Marguerite Bourgeoys (1700)
- St. John Baptist de la Salle (1719)
- St. John Baptist de Rossi (1764)
- The Blessed Martyrs of Compiègne (1794)
- St. Paul of the Cross (1775)
- St. Benedit Joseph Labre (1783)
- Bl. Junipero Serra (1784)
- St. Alphonsus Liguori (1787)

Additional Project Ideas

- Learn to make a bow and arrow for small game hunting.
- Learn to make your own pair of pants.
- Make a fur hat.
- Create a rabbit snare from saplings.
- Carve a fishhook out of wood.
- Go fishing!

Week of _____   *Liturgical Theme & Colors* _____

Family Challenge-Task
Goals _____

_____

_____

Reminders _____

_____

PRESCHOOL

	Music	Art, Reading, Religion	Virtue
Co-op	See "Music" heading below	Do craft **PreK Lesson A** (SF)	Review Virtue O-P (SF); practice "virtue training"
Day 2-4	See "Music" heading below	Do **Letter Book O-P** (SF); do **coloring pages** (SF); read & drill I-CAT, p. 13 (HC)	Review Virtue O-P (SF); practice "virtue training"

KINDERGARTEN – 6TH GRADE

ART   **CCM**

	K-6th Grade		K-6th Grade
Co-op	Do **All Lesson A** (SF).	Unit 10	
Day 2-4	Review **All Lesson A** (SF) and do home follow-up.	Listen to Unit 10 every day	

HISTORY

	K-1st Grades	2nd-3rd Grades	4th-6th Grades
Co-op	Do listen and draw **K-1 Lesson A** (SF).	Do History Pocket **2-3 Lesson A** (SF).	Do discussion **4-6 Lesson A** (SF).
Day 2	Read *The Sign of the Beaver* (HC) this week; Choose and do reading (or other project) from "Extras" (SF); draw a picture inspired by the readings.	Read *The Sign of the Beaver* (HC) this week; Choose and do reading (or other project) from "Extras" (SF); draw a picture inspired by the readings.	Read "Evangeline" (DL) this week; Choose and do readings (or other projects) from "Extras" (SF); begin writing **4-6 Activity A** (SF).
Day 3	Continue readings; do coloring page (SF).	Continue readings; do coloring page (SF); do map **2-3 Activity A** (SF).	Continue readings and **4-6 Activity A** (SF); do map **4-6 Activity B** (SF).
Day 4	Continue readings; Imagine & Draw a scene from the reading.	Continue readings; Imagine & Draw a scene from the reading	Finish readings and **4-6 Activity A** (SF); do timeline **4-6 Activity C** (SF).

LANGUAGE ARTS

Co-op	Complete **K-1 Lesson A** (SF).	Complete **2-3 Lesson A** (SF); do **2-3 Activity A** (SF).	Complete **4-6 Lesson A** (SF); begin **4-6 Activity A** (SF).
Day 2	Review **K-1 Lesson A** (SF); Ask your student to describe the picture.	Review **2-3 Lesson A** (SF); continue **2-3 Activity A** (SF).	Review **4-6 Lesson A** (SF); continue **4-6 Activity A** (SF)
Day 3	Do pre-cursive copywork **K-1 Activity A** (SF).	Do cursive copywork **2-3 Activity B** (SF).	Complete first draft in **4-6 Activity A** (SF).
Day 4	Do narration and illustration **K-1 Activity B** (SF)	Do composition and illustration **2-3 Activity C** (SF)	Complete final draft in **4-6 Activity A** (SF).

LATIN/GREEK

Co-op	Practice Lumen ad Revelationem! (SF)	Practice Lumen ad Revelationem! (SF); do *Greek Primer* 10.1–4 (SF)	Practice Lumen ad Revelationem! (SF); do *Reading Greek* 10.1–2 (SF)
Day 2	Listen to CCM Unit 10 Latin prayer	Listen to CCM Unit 10 Latin prayer; do *Greek Primer* 10.5	Listen to CCM Unit 10 Latin prayer; do *Reading Greek* 10.3–4 (SF)
Day 3	Practice all the *Schola Rosa* Latin assembly prayers!	Practice all the *Schola Rosa* Latin assembly prayers!	Practice all the *Schola Rosa* Latin assembly prayers!
Day 4	Listen to Lumen ad Revelationem! video (SF); Sing along!	Listen to Lumen ad Revelationem! video (SF); Sing along!; finish *Greek Primer* Unit 10 (SF)	Listen to Lumen ad Revelationem! video (SF); Sing along! Finish *Reading Greek* Unit 10 (SF).

MATH

	Level A	Level B	Level C
Co-op	None	None	None
Day 2-4	See *Ray's Primary*, Mastery Chart~ Do next lesson (DL)	See *Ray's Intellectual*, Mastery Chart~ Do next lesson (DL)	See *Ray's Practical*, Mastery Chart~ Do next lesson (DL)

MUSIC

	K-6th Grade
Co-op	Review **All Lesson A** (SF). Use audio files to sing along with: Hymn of the Week (Latin SF); Exercises Group 1, 2, & 3; Scale Drills, Gloria, Ite Missa Est, Kyrie Eleison, Agnus Dei, Sanctus, Merrily We Roll Along; Oats, Peas, Beans, & Barley Grow; Lightly Row (DL). See addendum to Lesson for 2nd year additions.
Day 2-4	

READING

	Primer (pre-reader)	Reader
Co-op	None	None
Day 2-4	See *McGuffey's Eclectic Primer*, "Mastery Chart"~ Do next lesson (DL)	See *McGuffey's Eclectic Readers*, "Mastery Chart" ~ Do next lesson (DL)

RELIGION — *Liturgical Feast lessons can be moved to correspond to their dates – simply adjust the schedule accordingly*

	K-1st Grades	2nd-3rd Grades	4th-6th Grades
Co-op	Begin **K-1 Lesson A** (SF).	Begin **2-3 Lesson A** (SF). Drill Q & A.	Begin **4-6 Lesson A** (SF). Drill Q & A.
Day 2	Complete **K-1 Lesson A** (SF).	Review/complete **2-3 Lesson A** (SF). Drill Q & A.	Review/complete **4-6 Lesson A** (SF). Drill Q & A.
Day 3	Complete **K-1 Lesson B** (SF).	Review/complete **2-3 Lesson A** (SF). Drill Q & A.	Select activity(ies) from the "Let Us Work Together" section OHF-4, pp. 83-84.
Day 4	Complete **K-1 Lesson C** (SF).	Review/complete **2-3 Lesson A** (SF). Drill Q & A.	Select activity(ies) from the "Let Us Work Together" section OHF-4, pp. 83-84.

SCIENCE

Co-op	Complete observation and discussion **K-1 Lesson A** (SF)	Complete observation and discussion **2-3 Lesson A** (SF)	Complete observation and discussion **4-6 Lesson A** (SF)
Day 2	Continue reading *The Wonder Book of Chemistry* (DL)	Continue reading *The Wonder Book of Chemistry* (DL)	Read RS4K *Elementary Chemistry Grades K-4* (HC) 7.1-6 & Experiment 7
Day 3	Do worksheet **K-1 Activity A** (SF).	Do worksheet **2-3 Activity A** (SF).	Do journal **4-6 Activity A** (SF); Do worksheet **4-6 Activity B** (SF).
Day 4	Go on a nature walk and do drawing **K-1 Activity B** (SF).	Go on a nature walk and do drawing **2-3 Activity B** (SF).	Go on a nature walk and continue **4-6 Activity A** (SF).

VIRTUE

	K-6th Grades
Field	**Do All Virtue Lesson A – Moderation** (SF)
Day 2-4	Practice "virtue training"

CYCLE III
UNIT 11

AMERICAN REVOLUTION

UNIT CHECKLIST

PREP FOR HOME

- ☐ Print and read this Handbook

  (NOTE: To minimize print cost, you may wish to omit either the Unit or Subject Planner, if you will use only one or the other.)

- ☐ Read the Overview
- ☐ Review the Planner; do the following:
  - o Locate and review all Lessons and Activities in the Subject Folders (SF)
  - o Locate and review all readings and assignments in the Subject Folders (SF), Digital Library (DL), and Hard Copies (HC)
  - o Note and gather needed supplies for the unit
- ☐ Read the Virtue Lesson
- ☐ Email or call R.A.S. if you have questions or technical difficulty.

PREP FOR CO-OP

- ☐ Print your "Co-op Job Sheet" and prep for your job
- ☐ Make sure your child is ready for his or her presentation if assigned to present
- ☐ Gather maps, notebooks, prayer sheet, and other supplies the night or morning before the co-op meets.
- ☐ Gather students' assignments the night or morning before the co-op meets
- ☐ Listen to the Memory Work on the way!

PREP FOR UPCOMING WEEKS – <u>LOOK AHEAD AT UNITS 14</u>

- ☐ Make advanced purchases, as necessary
- ☐ Begin to gather books and materials

PLANNER ABBREVIATION KEY

DL	Digital Library (in course suite)
SF	Subject Folder (in course suite)
HC	Hard Copy
PLL	*Primary Language Lessons* (book)
ILL	*Intermediate Language Lessons* (book)
RS4K	*Real Science 4 Kids* (book)
I-CAT	*Illustrated Catechism* (book)
OHF-1	*Our Holy Faith, Book 1* (book)
OHF-2	*Our Holy Faith, Book 2* (book)
OHF-4	*Our Holy Faith, Book 4* (book)
OHF-1-TM	*Our Holy Faith, Book 1, Teacher's Manual* (book)

OVERVIEW

Common Topics (All students PreK to 6th)

Virtue:	Prudence
Hymn:	Lumen ad revelationem
Prayers:	Angelus, Pater Noster, Ave Maria, Gloria Patri
History:	American Revolution (1776-1783)
Science:	Law of Conservation of Energy & Types of Energy

History Themes

In Unit 11 we continue our investigation of the Native Americans and their interactions with the settlers. Younger students will read *The Song of Hiawatha* by Longfellow this week, and 4th-6th Graders will read novels by James Fennimore Cooper, who beautifully paints the portrait of the often sad plight of the Native American amongst the settlers.

We also enter into the 18th Century during this unit as we look at the events that led up to the American Revolution. The Sisters of Notre Dame have called this century the "Century of Free Thought," which sounds a positive title, and indeed in most history books we are led to believe so. Let us take a look at their *Compendium*'s summary of the age: "The self-styled philosophers of the eighteenth century were the next enemies the Church had to encounter. Their system was the natural and logical outcome of the religious upheaval of the sixteenth century. Man had cast off his allegiance to lawful authority, denied the right of the Church to be his guide, and set up his own private judgment as a beacon-light, and as a result he became a prey to the demon of free thought." Foreboding words are these, which ought to cause us to reconsider our own American History courses. Were Americans in the right to fight for independence? What was the true motivation behind the revolution? Was it a just war? As parents living in America, we ought to consider these questions quite seriously over the next several weeks.

More about Free Thought, from the *Compendium*

> *Free thought* had its origin in Protestant England, and was fostered by the writings of English skeptics who rejected the Bible, revelation, and Christianity and asserted the sufficiency of natural religion. These men were first called Deists or Rationalists. John Locke became the forerunner of materialism, and the substitution of Deism, Pantheism, and Atheism for Christianity went by the name of "Philosophy." About the middle of the eighteenth century a reaction set in against this skepticism, and most of the English free-thinkers retired into the secrecy of Freemasonry.

> *Freemasonry* had its first lodge, 1717, in London, whence it spread to every state of Europe, to North America, and to East India. In no country did the new philosophy have a more destructive influence than in France, under the leadership of the *Encyclopediss* to whom belong D'Alembert, Diderot, and Voltaire. Diderot had the supervision of an encyclopedia, a dictionary ostensibly devoted to the sciences, but in reality a blasphemous work. Voltaire for half a century did not cease to attack the

Catholic Church. Rousseau was the author of a work called *Social Contract* aimed at all government and rights of private ownership. As head of the *Socialists* he denied all authority to religion and state.

Suppression of the Society of Jesus. The great obstacle to the growth of Philosophism was the zeal of the Society of Jesus. These religious therefore became the target for the enemies of the Church, who knew no rest until the ruin of their powerful foe was accomplished. The conspiracy of the ministers Pompal of Portugal, Aranda of Spain, Tannucci of Naples, supported by Voltaire and the Jansenists in France, brought pressure to bear on the Holy See. The Sovereign Pontiff had to choose between two evils: the suppression of the Society of Jesus or the desertion of the Church by the Catholic rulers of Europe. Clement XIV chose the former alternative, and reluctantly signed the brief for the suppression in 1773, protesting that he did so only for the sake of peace in the Church. The Jesuits obeyed, and had it not been for the protection of the Protestant King, Frederick of Prussia, and the schismatic Empress, Catherine of Russia, they would have ceased to exist as an Order. These two sovereigns obtained from the Pope permission for the Jesuits to continue in their dominions as if the suppression had not taken place.

How to Apply History to Everyday Life

Our Mission. For reading on the virtue of prudence, we highly recommend you read the article posted in the "Handbook Supplements" folder.

Important People, Events, and Places to Know (Potential Student Presentations)

❖ Saints of the Eighteenth Century:

- St. Marguerite Bourgeoys (1700)
- St. John Baptist de la Salle (1719)
- St. John Baptist de Rossi (1764)
- The Blessed Martyrs of Compiègne (1794)
- St. Paul of the Cross (1775)
- St. Benedit Joseph Labre (1783)
- Bl. Junipero Serra (1784)
- St. Alphonsus Liguori (1787)

Additional Project Ideas

- Write a "Pamphlet" with an "Agenda" for conquering the messy build-up in your home!
- Write a "Farmer's Almanac" for your Home.
- Re-enact the Boston Tea Party
- Write a letter from the King of Great Britain asking the Americans not to cross the Mountains for fear of war with the Native Americans
- Write a letter from your Mother asking you not to cross your sister's threshold lest you enter to war with the Natives

Week of _____   *Liturgical Theme & Colors* _____

Family Challenge-Task
Goals _____

_____

_____

_____

Reminders _____

_____

_____

PRESCHOOL

	Music	Art, Reading, Religion	Virtue
Co-op	See "Music" heading below	Do craft **PreK Lesson A** (SF)	Review Virtue Q-R (SF); practice "virtue training"
Day 2-4	See "Music" heading below	Do **Letter Book Q-R** (SF); do **coloring pages** (SF); read & drill I-CAT, p. 14 (HC)	Review Virtue Q-R (SF); practice "virtue training"

KINDERGARTEN – 6TH GRADE

ART   CCM

	K-6th Grade		K-6th Grade
Co-op	Do **All Lesson A** (SF).		Unit 11
Day 2-4	Review **All Lesson A** (SF) and do home follow-up.		Listen to Unit 11 every day

HISTORY

	K-1st Grades	2nd-3rd Grades	4th-6th Grades
Co-op	Do dramatization **K-1 Lesson A** (SF)	Do History Pocket **2-3 Lesson A** (SF).	Do discussion **4-6 Lesson A** (SF).
Day 2	Read *Song of Hiawatha* (DL) this week; Choose and do reading (or other project) from "Extras" (SF); draw a picture inspired by the readings.	Read *Song of Hiawatha* (DL) this week; Choose and do reading (or other project) from "Extras" (SF); draw a picture inspired by the readings.	Read *The Deerslayer, The Pathfinder,* OR *The Last of the Mohicans* (HC or DL) this week; Choose and do readings (or other projects) from "Extras" (SF); begin writing **4-6 Activity A** (SF).
Day 3	Continue readings; do coloring page (SF).	do coloring page (SF); do map **2-3 Activity A** (SF).	Continue readings; do map **4-6 Activity B** (SF).
Day 4	Continue readings; Imagine & Draw.	Continue readings; Imagine & Draw.	Finish readings and **4-6 Activity A** (SF); add other items to timeline from Units 8-10

LANGUAGE ARTS

	K-1st Grades	2nd-3rd Grades	4th-6th Grades
Co-op	Complete **K-1 Lesson A** (SF).	Complete **2-3 Lesson A** (SF); do **2-3 Activity A** (SF).	Complete **4-6 Lesson A** (SF); begin **4-6 Activity A** (SF).
Day 2	Review **K-1 Lesson A** (SF); Ask your student to describe the picture.	Review **2-3 Lesson A** (SF); continue **2-3 Activity A** (SF).	Review **4-6 Lesson A** (SF); Begin **4-6 Activity B** (SF)
Day 3	Do pre-cursive copywork **K-1 Activity A** (SF).	Do cursive copywork **2-3 Activity B** (SF).	Complete first draft in **4-6 Activity B** (SF).
Day 4	Do narration and illustration **K-1 Activity B** (SF)	Do composition and illustration **2-3 Activity C** (SF)	Complete final draft in **4-6 Activity B** (SF).

LATIN/GREEK

	K-1st Grades	2nd-3rd Grades	4th-6th Grades
Co-op	Practice Lumen ad Revelationem! (SF)	Practice Lumen ad Revelationem! (SF); do *Greek Primer* 11.1–4 (SF)	Practice Lumen ad Revelationem! (SF); do *Reading Greek* 11.1–2 (SF)
Day 2	Listen to CCM Unit 11 Latin prayer	Listen to CCM Unit 11 Latin prayer; do *Greek Primer* 11.5	Listen to CCM Unit 11 Latin prayer; do *Reading Greek* 11.3–4 (SF)
Day 3	Practice all the *Schola Rosa* Latin assembly prayers!	Practice all the *Schola Rosa* Latin assembly prayers!	Practice all the *Schola Rosa* Latin assembly prayers!
Day 4	Listen to Lumen ad Revelationem! video (SF); Sing along!	Listen to Lumen ad Revelationem! video (SF); Sing along!; finish *Greek Primer* Unit 11 (SF)	Listen to Lumen ad Revelationem! video (SF); Sing along! Finish *Reading Greek* Unit 11 (SF).

MATH

	Level A	Level B	Level C
Co-op	None	None	None
Day 2-4	See *Ray's Primary*, Mastery Chart~ Do next lesson (DL)	See *Ray's Intellectual*, Mastery Chart~ Do next lesson (DL)	See *Ray's Practical*, Mastery Chart~ Do next lesson (DL)

MUSIC

READING

	K-6th Grade	Primer (pre-reader)	Reader
Co-op	Review **All Lesson A** (SF). Use audio files	None	None
Day 2-4	to sing along with: Hymn of the Week (Latin SF); Exercises Group 1, 2, & 3; Scale Drills, Gloria, Ite Missa Est, Kyrie Eleison, Agnus Dei, Sanctus, Merrily We Roll Along; Oats, Peas, Beans, & Barley Grow; Lightly Row; Aura Lee (DL). See addendum to Lesson for 2nd year additions.	See *McGuffey's Eclectic Primer*, "Mastery Chart"~ Do next lesson (DL)	See *McGuffey's Eclectic Readers*, "Mastery Chart" ~ Do next lesson (DL)

RELIGION — *Liturgical Feast lessons can be moved to correspond to their dates – simply adjust the schedule accordingly*

	K-1st Grades	2nd-3rd Grades	4th-6th Grades
Co-op	Begin **K-1 Lesson A** (SF).	Begin **2-3 Lesson A** (SF). Drill Q & A.	Begin **4-6 Lesson A** (SF). Drill Q & A.
Day 2	Complete **K-1 Lesson A** (SF).	Review/complete **2-3 Lesson A** (SF). Drill Q & A.	Review/complete **4-6 Lesson A** (SF). Drill Q & A.
Day 3	Complete **K-1 Lesson B** (SF).	Review/complete **2-3 Lesson A** (SF). Drill Q & A.	Select activity(ies) from the "Let Us Work Together" section OHF-4, pp. 97-99.
Day 4	Complete **K-1 Lesson C** (SF).	Review/complete **2-3 Lesson A** (SF). Drill Q & A.	Select activity(ies) from the "Let Us Work Together" section OHF-4, pp. 97-99.

SCIENCE

Co-op	Complete observation and discussion **K-1 Lesson A** (SF)	Complete observation and discussion **2-3 Lesson A** (SF)	Complete observation and discussion **4-6 Lesson A** (SF)
Day 2	Continue reading *The Wonder Book of Chemistry* (DL)	Continue reading *The Wonder Book of Chemistry* (DL)	Read RS4K *Elementary Chemistry Grades K-4* (HC) 8.1-4 & Experiment 8
Day 3	Do hands-on **K-1 Activity A** (SF).	Do hands-on **2-3 Activity A** (SF).	Do journal **4-6 Activity A** (SF); Do hands-on **4-6 Activity B** (SF).
Day 4	Go on a nature walk and do drawing **K-1 Activity B** (SF).	Go on a nature walk and do drawing **2-3 Activity B** (SF).	Go on a nature walk and continue **4-6 Activity A** (SF).

VIRTUE

	K-6th Grades
Field	Do **All Virtue Lesson A – Prudence** (SF)
Day 2-4	Practice "virtue training"

CYCLE III
UNIT 12

AMERICAN REVOLUTION

CONTINUED

UNIT CHECKLIST

PREP FOR HOME

- ☐ Print and read this Handbook
- ☐ Read the Overview
- ☐ Review the Planner; do the following:
    - o Locate and review all Lessons and Activities in the Subject Folders (SF)
    - o Locate and review all readings and assignments in the Subject Folders (SF), Digital Library (DL), and Hard Copies (HC)
    - o Note and gather needed supplies for the unit
- ☐ Read the Virtue Lesson
- ☐ Email or call R.A.S. if you have questions or technical difficulty.

PREP FOR CO-OP

- ☐ Print your "Co-op Job Sheet" and prep for your job
- ☐ Make sure your child is ready for his or her presentation if assigned to present
- ☐ Gather maps, notebooks, prayer sheet, and other supplies the night or morning before the co-op meets.
- ☐ Gather students' assignments the night or morning before the co-op meets
- ☐ Listen to the Memory Work on the way!

PREP FOR UPCOMING WEEKS — <u>LOOK AHEAD AT UNITS 15</u>

- ☐ Make advanced purchases, as necessary
- ☐ Begin to gather books and materials

PLANNER ABBREVIATION KEY

DL	Digital Library (in course suite)
SF	Subject Folder (in course suite)
HC	Hard Copy
PLL	*Primary Language Lessons* (book)
ILL	*Intermediate Language Lessons* (book)
RS4K	*Real Science 4 Kids* (book)
I-CAT	*Illustrated Catechism* (book)
OHF-1	*Our Holy Faith, Book 1* (book)
OHF-2	*Our Holy Faith, Book 2* (book)
OHF-4	*Our Holy Faith, Book 4* (book)
OHF-1-TM	*Our Holy Faith, Book 1, Teacher's Manual* (book)

OVERVIEW

Common Topics (All students PreK to 6th)

Virtue:	Gratitude
Hymn:	Lumen ad revelationem
Prayers:	Angelus, Pater Noster, Ave Maria, Gloria Patri
History:	American Revolution—Continued
Science:	Review

History Themes

In Unit 12 we continue to read about the American Revolution and its events and consequences.

Religious Orders, summaries from the *Compendium of Church History*

1. The Redemptorists ~ were founded by St. Alphonsus Ligouri in 1732, to serve as "missionaries for the poorest and most neglected sheep" of Christ's flock.
2. The Ladies of the Sacred Heart ~ were founded by Blessed Sophie Barat, to provide for the education of girls of the upper class.
3. The Sisters of Notre Dame ~ were founded by Blessed Julie Billiart, to instruct the children of the poor.

How to Apply History to Everyday Life

Our Mission. Despite all the bad news in the world, we are able to be free of worry. "The Lord is my shepherd; I shall not want." "Though I walk through the valley of the shadow of death, I shall fear no evil." One way we can practice being free of the world is with the virtue of gratitude. Are we thankful for what we have when we have it? Or are we like the Hebrews in the desert, always asking for more? Do we look to see God's Grace even in the worst of times, hoping and having faith in His Will? Do we teach our children to find ways of being thankful? Do we say "Thank You" to others when they give a gift or offer a kind deed? Do we teach our children to say "Thank You" likewise? Do we actively promote the virtue of gratitude in our home?

Important People, Events, and Places to Know (Potential Student Presentations)

❖ Founding of New Orleans (1717), George II becomes King of Great Britain (1727), Birth of George Washington (1732), Establishment of Georgia Colony (1733), Parliament presses the Stamp Act for the colonies & Sons of Liberty protest Stamp Act (1765), Townshend Acts passed (1767), Massachusetts Assembly dissolved (1768), Parliament repeals Townshend Acts, keeps tax on tea & Boston Massacre (1770), Boston Tea Party (1773), Parliament passes Boston Port Act & First Continental Congress meets (1774), Battle of Lexington and Concord – American Revolution

OVERVIEW

begins (1775), Battle of Bunker Hill, Daniel Boone cuts the Wilderness Road to Kentucky

❖ Saints of the Eighteenth Century:

- St. Marguerite Bourgeoys (1700)
- St. John Baptist de la Salle (1719)
- St. John Baptist de Rossi (1764)
- The Blessed Martyrs of Compiègne (1794)
- St. Paul of the Cross (1775)
- St. Benedit Joseph Labre (1783)
- Bl. Junipero Serra (1784)
- St. Alphonsus Liguori (1787)

Additional Project Ideas

- Write a "Declaration of Independence" to you mother from your 4 year old sibling who was justly put into Time-Out
- Paint a picture of the Surrender of General Cornwallis to General Washington ~ Who is in the front?

Week of _____   *Liturgical Theme & Colors* _____

*Family Challenge-Task
Goals*

_____

_____

_____

Reminders

_____

_____

PRESCHOOL

	Music	Art, Reading, Religion	Virtue
Day 1	See "Music" heading below	Do craft **PreK Lesson A** (SF).	Practice "virtue training"
Day 2-4	See "Music" heading below	Review Letters A-F (SF), review & drill I-CAT, p. 15 (HC)	Practice "virtue training"

KINDERGARTEN – 6TH GRADE

ART   **CCM**

	K-6th Grade	K-6th Grade
Day 1	Review Units 9-11	Unit 12
Day 2-4	Review Units 9-11; do an extra art task from the home follow-up section, if there is time.	Listen to Unit 12 every day

HISTORY

	K-1st Grades	2nd-3rd Grades	4th-6th Grades
Day 1	Read *Great Americans for Little Americans* (DL) this week.	Read *Great Americans for Little Americans* (DL) this week.	Read *Four Great Americans* (DL) this week.
Day 2	Choose and do reading (or other project) from "Extras" (SF); draw a picture inspired by the readings	Choose and do reading (or other project) from "Extras" (SF); draw a picture inspired by the readings	Choose and do readings (or other projects) from "Extras" (SF); begin **4-6 Activity A** (SF).
Day 3	Continue readings; do coloring page (SF)	Continue readings; do map **2-3 Activity A** (SF)	Continue readings.
Day 4	Imagine & draw a scene from the reading.	Imagine & draw a scene from the reading.	Do timeline **4-6 Activity B** (SF); finish **4-6 Activity A** (SF) and readings.

LANGUAGE ARTS

	K-1st Grades	2nd-3rd Grades	4th-6th Grades
Day 1	Complete **K-1 Lesson A** (SF).	Complete **2-3 Lesson A** (SF).	Complete **4-6 Lesson A** (SF).
Day 2	Review **K-1 Lesson A** (SF); do **K-1 Activity A** (SF).	Review **2-3 Lesson A** (SF); do **2-3 Activity A** (SF).	Review **4-6 Lesson A** (SF); do **4-6 Activity A** (SF)
Day 3	Do pre-cursive copywork **K-1 Activity B** (SF).	Do cursive copywork **2-3 Activity B** (SF).	Complete first draft in **4-6 Activity A** (SF).
Day 4	Do narration and illustration **K-1 Activity C** (SF)	Do composition and illustration **2-3 Activity C** (SF)	Complete final draft in **4-6 Activity A** (SF).

LATIN/GREEK

	K-1st Grades	2nd-3rd Grades	4th-6th Grades
Day 1	Practice Lumen ad Revelationem (SF)	Practice Lumen ad Revelationem (SF); do *Greek Primer* 12.1–4 (SF)	Practice Lumen ad Revelationem (SF); do *Reading Greek* 12.1–2 (SF)
Day 2	Listen to CCM Unit 12 Latin prayer	Listen to CCM Unit 12 Latin prayer; do *Greek Primer* 12.5	Listen to CCM Unit 12 Latin prayer; do *Reading Greek* 12.3–4 (SF)
Day 3	Practice all the *Schola Rosa* Latin assembly prayers!	Practice all the *Schola Rosa* Latin assembly prayers!	Practice all the *Schola Rosa* Latin assembly prayers!
Day 4	Listen to Lumen ad Revelationem video (SF); Sing along!	Listen to Lumen ad Revelationem video (SF); Sing along!; finish *Greek Primer* Unit 12 (SF)	Listen to Lumen ad Revelationem video (SF); Sing along!; finish *Reading Greek* Unit 12 (SF) and review/check work

MATH

	Level A	Level B	Level C
Day 1	None	None	None
Day 2-4	See *Ray's Primary*, Mastery Chart~ Do next lesson (DL)	See *Ray's Intellectual*, Mastery Chart~ Do next lesson (DL)	See *Ray's Practical*, Mastery Chart~ Do next lesson (DL)

MUSIC

	K-6th Grade
Day 1	Use audio files to sing along with: Hymn of
Day 2-4	the Week (Latin SF); Exercises Group 1, 2, & 3; Gloria; ite missa est; Kyrie; Agnus Dei; Sanctus; Merrily We Roll Along; Oats, Peas, Beans & Barley Grow; Lightly Row; Aura Lee (DL). See addendum to last Lesson for 2nd year additions.

READING

	Primer (pre-reader)	Reader
	None	None
	See *McGuffey's Eclectic Primer*, "Mastery Chart"~ Do next lesson (DL)	See *McGuffey's Eclectic Readers*, "Mastery Chart" ~ Do next lesson (DL)

RELIGION — *Liturgical Feast lessons can be moved to correspond to their dates – simply adjust the schedule accordingly*

	K-1st Grades	2nd-3rd Grades	4th-6th Grades
Day 1	Begin **K-1 Lesson A** (SF).	Review lessons for Units 1-5; discuss themes; drill Q & A	Begin **4-6 Lesson A** (SF); Drill Q & A.
Day 2	Complete **K-1 Lesson A** (SF).	Review lessons for Units 1-5; discuss themes; drill Q & A	Review/complete **4-6 Lesson A** (SF); Drill Q & A.
Day 3	Complete **K-1 Lesson B** (SF).	Review lessons for Units 1-5; discuss themes; drill Q & A	Select activity(ies) from the "Let Us Work Together Section OHF-4, pp. 97-99.
Day 4	Complete **K-1 Lesson C** (SF).	Review lessons for Units 1-5; discuss themes; drill Q & A	Select activity(ies) from the "Let Us Work Together Section OHF-4, pp. 97-99.

SCIENCE

Day 1	Review Memory Work Q & A for Units 9-11 (DL).	Review Memory Work Q & A for Units 9-11 (DL).	Review Memory Work Q & A for Units 9-11 (DL).
Day 2	Check out books on "Kinetic Energy" from your local library (HC).	Check out books on "Kinetic Energy" from your local library (HC).	Check out books on "Kinetic Energy" from your local library (HC).
Day 3	Complete any experiments or activities that were not completed in Units 9-11.	Complete any experiments or activities that were not completed in Units 9-11.	Complete any experiments or activities that were not completed in Units 9-11.
Day 4	Draw pictures on a nature walk that remind you of lessons learned this week.	Draw pictures on a nature walk that remind you of lessons learned this week.	Draw pictures on a nature walk that remind you of lessons learned this week.

VIRTUE

	K-6th Grades
Day 1	Do **All Virtue Lesson A – Gratitude** (SF)
Day 2-4	Practice "virtue training"

CYCLE III
UNIT 13

SCIENTIFIC REVOLUTION

UNIT CHECKLIST

PREP FOR HOME

- ☐ Print and read this Handbook
- ☐ Read the Overview
- ☐ Review the Planner; do the following:
    - o Locate and review all Lessons and Activities in the Subject Folders (SF)
    - o Locate and review all readings and assignments in the Subject Folders (SF), Digital Library (DL), and Hard Copies (HC)
    - o Note and gather needed supplies for the unit
- ☐ Read the Virtue Lesson
- ☐ Email or call R.A.S. if you have questions or technical difficulty.

PREP FOR CO-OP

- ☐ Print your "Co-op Job Sheet" and prep for your job
- ☐ Make sure your child is ready for his or her presentation if assigned to present
- ☐ Gather maps, notebooks, prayer sheet, and other supplies the night or morning before the co-op meets.
- ☐ Gather students' assignments the night or morning before the co-op meets
- ☐ Listen to the Memory Work on the way!

PREP FOR UPCOMING WEEKS – <u>LOOK AHEAD AT UNITS 16</u>

- ☐ Make advanced purchases, as necessary
- ☐ Begin to gather books and materials

PLANNER ABBREVIATION KEY

DL	Digital Library (in course suite)
SF	Subject Folder (in course suite)
HC	Hard Copy
PLL	*Primary Language Lessons* (book)
ILL	*Intermediate Language Lessons* (book)
RS4K	*Real Science 4 Kids* (book)
I-CAT	*Illustrated Catechism* (book)
OHF-1	*Our Holy Faith, Book 1* (book)
OHF-2	*Our Holy Faith, Book 2* (book)
OHF-4	*Our Holy Faith, Book 4* (book)
OHF-1-TM	*Our Holy Faith, Book 1, Teacher's Manual* (book)

OVERVIEW

Common Topics (All students PreK to 6th)

Virtue:	Humility
Hymn:	Review
Prayers:	Angelus, Pater Noster, Ave Maria, Gloria Patri
History:	Scientific Revolution (16th-18th centuries A.D.)
Science:	Chemistry Investigation ~ Baking!

History Themes

We end the fall semester with a Unit study on the Scientific Revolution; this lasted from approximately the 16th to 18th centuries (though it continues today in a certain sense). This is meant to be a particularly fun unit! Enjoy learning about the inventions and the inventors, but be careful not to paint too great a picture of any inventor as a "great" or "hero," for this period of history is marked by many a great deed done by many a poor soul. We may praise the invention without necessarily praising the whole person of the inventor.

How to Apply History to Everyday Life

Our Mission. Perhaps, one of the saddest consequences to come out of the Protestant revolts, the various political revolutions, and the "free-thought" philosophy is an arrogance or pride in the human person's ability that goes far beyond the Renaissance appreciation for human accomplishment with God's Grace. We find a lonely individualism and an arrogant intellectualism that are divorced from the virtue of humility. How do we break free from that custom that pervades even modern American society?

Ask ourselves. Do we humbly present our works? Do we acknowledge that God has given us a talent or ability? Do we praise God when we do good works? Do we praise God to others and thank Him when others praise you or your work? Do you humbly ask God to bless your work and your study before beginning? Do you pray to God during your work, begging for continued guidance as you work? Do you thank Him when you are finished with your work and pray humbly that this work is in accord with His Will? Fear of the Lord is a Christian virtue and in all works of all kinds we might fear that we fail God's plan; therefore, do we beg Him for knowledge, understanding, and truth, and for whatever virtues and graces we might need along the way.

Important People, Events, and Places to Know (Potential Student Presentations)

* Declaration of Independence (1776), Battles of Trenton and Princeton (1776), Battle of Brandywine Creek (1777), Articles of Confederation approved by Congress (1777),

OVERVIEW

Cornwallis surrenders to Washington (1781), Treaty of Paris – end of American Revolution (1783)

❖ Saints of the Eighteenth Century:

- St. Marguerite Bourgeoys (1700)
- St. John Baptist de la Salle (1719)
- St. John Baptist de Rossi (1764)
- The Blessed Martyrs of Compiègne (1794)

- St. Paul of the Cross (1775)
- St. Benedit Joseph Labre (1783)
- Bl. Junipero Serra (1784)
- St. Alphonsus Liguori (1787)

Additional Project Ideas

- Invent something and try to build it!
- Take a part an old machine and try to figure out how it works.
- Read about an invention; then, try to make it with just the description.

Week of .... *Liturgical Theme & Colors* ....

Family Challenge-Task
Goals ....

....

....

Reminders ....

....

....

PRESCHOOL

	Music	Art, Reading, Religion	Virtue
Day 1	See "Music" heading below	Do craft **PreK Lesson A** (SF).	Practice "virtue training"
Day 2-4	See "Music" heading below	Review Letters G-L (SF), review & drill I-CAT, p. 17 (HC)	Practice "virtue training"

KINDERGARTEN – 6TH GRADE

ART   CCM

	K-6th Grade	K-6th Grade
Day 1	Review Units 1-11	Unit 13
Day 2-4	Review Units 1-11; do an extra art task from the home follow-up section, if there is time.	Listen to Unit 13 every day

HISTORY

	K-1st Grades	2nd-3rd Grades	4th-6th Grades
Day 1	Read *America First* (DL) and listen to music by Mozart (SF) this week.	Read *America First* (DL) and listen to music by Mozart (SF) this week.	Read *America First* (DL) and listen to music by Mozart (SF) this week.
Day 2	Choose and do reading (or other project) from "Extras" (SF); draw a picture inspired by the readings	Choose and do reading (or other project) from "Extras" (SF); draw a picture inspired by the readings	Choose and do readings (or other projects) from "Extras" (SF); begin **4-6 Activity A** (SF).
Day 3	Continue readings; do coloring page (SF)	Continue readings.	Continue readings.
Day 4	Imagine & draw a scene from the reading.	Imagine & draw a scene from the reading.	Do timeline **4-6 Activity B** (SF); finish **4-6 Activity A** (SF) and readings.

LANGUAGE ARTS

Day 1	Complete **K-1 Lesson A** (SF).	Complete **2-3 Lesson A** (SF).	Complete **4-6 Lesson A** (SF).
Day 2	Review **K-1 Lesson A** (SF); do **K-1 Activity A** (SF).	Review **2-3 Lesson A** (SF); do **2-3 Activity A** (SF).	Review **4-6 Lesson A** (SF); do **4-6 Activity A** (SF)
Day 3	Do pre-cursive copywork **K-1 Activity B** (SF).	Do cursive copywork **2-3 Activity B** (SF).	Complete first draft in **4-6 Activity A** (SF).
Day 4	Do narration and illustration **K-1 Activity C** (SF)	Do composition and illustration **2-3 Activity C** (SF)	Complete final draft in **4-6 Activity A** (SF).

LATIN/GREEK

Day 1	Practice Lumen ad Revelationem (SF)	Practice Lumen ad Revelationem (SF); do *Greek Primer* 13.1–4 (SF)	Practice Lumen ad Revelationem (SF); do *Reading Greek* 13.1–2 (SF)
Day 2	Listen to CCM Unit 13 Latin prayer	Listen to CCM Unit 13 Latin prayer; do *Greek Primer* 13.5	Listen to CCM Unit 13 Latin prayer; do *Reading Greek* 13.3–4 (SF)
Day 3	Practice all the *Schola Rosa* Latin assembly prayers!	Practice all the *Schola Rosa* Latin assembly prayers!	Practice all the *Schola Rosa* Latin assembly prayers!
Day 4	Listen to Lumen ad Revelationem video (SF); Sing along!	Listen to Lumen ad Revelationem video (SF); Sing along!; finish *Greek Primer* Unit 13 (SF)	Listen to Lumen ad Revelationem video (SF); Sing along!; finish *Reading Greek* Unit 13 (SF) and review/check work

MATH

	Level A	Level B	Level C
Day 1	None	None	None
Day 2-4	See *Ray's Primary*, Mastery Chart~ Do next lesson (DL)	See *Ray's Intellectual*, Mastery Chart~ Do next lesson (DL)	See *Ray's Practical*, Mastery Chart~ Do next lesson (DL)

MUSIC   READING

	K-6th Grade	Primer (pre-reader)	Reader
Day 1	Use audio files to sing along with: Hymn of the Week (Latin SF); Exercises Group 1, 2, & 3; Gloria; ite missa est; Kyrie; Agnus Dei; Sanctus; Merrily We Roll Along; Oats, Peas, Beans & Barley Grow; Lightly Row; Aura Lee (DL). See addendum to last Lesson for 2nd year additions.	None	None
Day 2-4		See *McGuffey's Eclectic Primer*, "Mastery Chart" ~ Do next lesson (DL)	See *McGuffey's Eclectic Readers*, "Mastery Chart" ~ Do next lesson (DL)

RELIGION — *Liturgical Feast lessons can be moved to correspond to their dates — simply adjust the schedule accordingly*

	K-1st Grades	2nd-3rd Grades	4th-6th Grades
Day 1	Begin **K-1 Lesson A** (SF).	Review lessons for Units 1-5; discuss themes; drill Q & A	Begin **4-6 Lesson A** (SF); Drill Q & A.
Day 2	Complete **K-1 Lesson A** (SF).	Review lessons for Units 1-5; discuss themes; drill Q & A	Review/complete **4-6 Lesson A** (SF); Drill Q & A.
Day 3	Complete **K-1 Lesson B** (SF).	Review lessons for Units 1-5; discuss themes; drill Q & A	Select activity(ies) from the "Let Us Work Together Section OHF-4, pp. 103-104.
Day 4	Complete **K-1 Lesson C** (SF).	Review lessons for Units 1-5; discuss themes; drill Q & A	Select activity(ies) from the "Let Us Work Together Section OHF-4, pp. 103-104.

SCIENCE

Day 1	Review Memory Work Q & A for Units 1-11 (DL).	Review Memory Work Q & A for Units 1-11 (DL).	Review Memory Work Q & A for Units 1-11 (DL).
Day 2	Do **All Lesson A** (SF).	Do **All Lesson A** (SF).	Do **All Lesson A** (SF).
Day 3	Complete any experiments or activities that were not completed in Units 1-11.	Complete any experiments or activities that were not completed in Units 1-11.	Complete any experiments or activities that were not completed in Units 1-11.
Day 4	Go ahead and try a different recipe from **All Lesson A!**	Go ahead and try a different recipe from **All Lesson A!**	Go ahead and try a different recipe from **All Lesson A!**

VIRTUE

	K-6th Grades
Day 1	Do **All Virtue Lesson A – Humility** (SF)
Day 2-4	Practice "virtue training"

CYCLE III
UNIT 14

REVIEW

UNIT CHECKLIST

PREP FOR HOME

- ☐ Print and read this Handbook
- ☐ Read the Overview
- ☐ Review the Planner; do the following:
    - o Locate and review all Lessons and Activities in the Subject Folders (SF)
    - o Locate and review all readings and assignments in the Subject Folders (SF), Digital Library (DL), and Hard Copies (HC)
    - o Note and gather needed supplies for the unit
- ☐ Read the Virtue Lesson
- ☐ Email or call R.A.S. if you have questions or technical difficulty.

PREP FOR CO-OP

- ☐ Print your "Co-op Job Sheet" and prep for your job
- ☐ Make sure your child is ready for his or her presentation if assigned to present
- ☐ Gather maps, notebooks, prayer sheet, and other supplies the night or morning before the co-op meets.
- ☐ Gather students' assignments the night or morning before the co-op meets
- ☐ Listen to the Memory Work on the way!

PREP FOR UPCOMING WEEKS — <u>LOOK AHEAD AT UNITS 17</u>

- ☐ Make advanced purchases, as necessary
- ☐ Begin to gather books and materials

PLANNER ABBREVIATION KEY	
DL	Digital Library (in course suite)
SF	Subject Folder (in course suite)
HC	Hard Copy
PLL	*Primary Language Lessons* (book)
ILL	*Intermediate Language Lessons* (book)
RS4K	*Real Science 4 Kids* (book)
I-CAT	*Illustrated Catechism* (book)
OHF-1	*Our Holy Faith, Book 1* (book)
OHF-2	*Our Holy Faith, Book 2* (book)
OHF-4	*Our Holy Faith, Book 4* (book)
OHF-1-TM	*Our Holy Faith, Book 1, Teacher's Manual* (book)

OVERVIEW

Common Topics (All students PreK to 6th)

Virtue: Review
Hymn: Review
Prayers: Angelus, Pater Noster, Ave Maria, Gloria Patri
History: Review
Science: Review

History Themes

This is a review week for all subjects. Please review Units 1-13.

How to Apply History to Everyday Life

Our Mission. It is a tough thing to consider, even reconsider, one's national patronage. It is especially difficult as a Christian to consider one's home country in light of history. Is our country culturally Catholic? Is it Christian? Did America ever represent core Christian values? Who were the Deists? Do we call them Christians? What influence did they have on the American Revolution and the establishment of American government? What were Catholic voices saying before the American Revolution? What were Catholic voices saying during and after the revolution? These are questions we ought to consider as we live in today's American culture. What are we to think? What should we be saying in the public square—at work and at home? How do we vote? And more importantly how should we live, if we wish to truly stand with Christ before all others? How does a Christian live in a pluralistic society?

Important People, Events, and Places to Know (Potential Student Presentations)

❖ Review your Timeline activities.
❖ Review the Saints.

Additional Project Ideas

❖ Complete any projects that you found interesting but did not have time to finish in Units 1-13.

Week of _____   *Liturgical Theme & Colors* _____

Family Challenge-Task

Goals _____

_____

_____

Reminders _____

_____

PRESCHOOL

	Music	Art, Reading, Religion	Virtue
Day 1	See "Music" heading below	Do craft **PreK Lesson A** (SF).	Practice "virtue training"
Day 2-4	See "Music" heading below	Review Letters M-R (SF), review & drill I-CAT, p. 17 (HC)	Practice "virtue training"

KINDERGARTEN – 6TH GRADE

ART   **CCM**

	K-6th Grade	K-6th Grade
Day 1	Review Units 1-11	Unit 14
Day 2-4	Review Units 1-11; do an extra art task from the home follow-up section, if there is time.	Listen to Unit 14 every day

HISTORY

	K-1st Grades	2nd-3rd Grades	4th-6th Grades
Day 1	Complete any unfished readings from Units 1-13 this week.	Complete any unfished readings from Units 1-13 this week.	Complete any unfished readings from Units 1-13 this week.
Day 2	Choose and do reading (or other project) from "Extras" (SF); draw a picture inspired by the readings	Choose and do reading (or other project) from "Extras" (SF); draw a picture inspired by the readings	Choose and do readings (or other projects) from "Extras" (SF).
Day 3	Continue readings; do coloring page (SF)	Continue readings.	Continue readings.
Day 4	Imagine & draw a scene from the reading.	Imagine & draw a scene from the reading.	Finish readings; Imagine & draw your favorite scene from a reading.

LANGUAGE ARTS

Day 1	Complete **K-1 Lesson A** (SF).	Complete **2-3 Lesson A** (SF).	Complete **4-6 Lesson A** (SF).
Day 2	Review **K-1 Lesson A** (SF).	Review **2-3 Lesson A** (SF); do **2-3 Activity A** (SF).	Review **4-6 Lesson A** (SF); do **4-6 Activity A** (SF)
Day 3	Do pre-cursive copywork **K-1 Activity A** (SF).	Do cursive copywork **2-3 Activity B** (SF).	Complete first draft in **4-6 Activity A** (SF).
Day 4	Review **K-1 Lesson A** (SF).	Do composition and illustration **2-3 Activity C** (SF)	Complete final draft in **4-6 Activity A** (SF).

LATIN/GREEK

Day 1	Practice all hymns from Units 1-13 (SF)	Practice all hymns from Units 1-13 (SF); start *Greek Primer*, Unit 14 review (SF).	Practice all hymns from Units 1-13 (SF)do *Reading Greek* Unit 14, review (SF)
Day 2	Listen to CCM Unit 14 Latin prayer	Listen to CCM Unit 14 Latin prayer; continue Greek review.	Listen to CCM Unit 14 Latin prayer; continue Greek review.
Day 3	Practice all the *Schola Rosa* Latin assembly prayers!	Practice all the *Schola Rosa* Latin assembly prayers!	Practice all the *Schola Rosa* Latin assembly prayers!
Day 4	Listen to Lumen ad Revelationem video (SF); Sing along!	Listen to Lumen ad Revelationem video (SF); Sing along!; finish *Greek Primer* Unit 14, review (SF).	Listen to Lumen ad Revelationem video (SF); Sing along!; finish *Reading Greek* Unit 14, review (SF).

MATH

	Level A	Level B	Level C
Day 1	None	None	None
Day 2-4	See *Ray's Primary*, Mastery Chart~ Do next lesson (DL)	See *Ray's Intellectual*, Mastery Chart~ Do next lesson (DL)	See *Ray's Practical*, Mastery Chart~ Do next lesson (DL)

MUSIC

	K-6th Grade
Day 1	Use audio files to sing along with: Hymn of
Day 2-4	the Week (Latin SF); Exercises Group 1, 2, & 3; Gloria; ite missa est; Kyrie; Agnus Dei; Sanctus; Merrily We Roll Along; Oats, Peas, Beans & Barley Grow; Lightly Row; Aura Lee (DL). See addendum to last Lesson for 2nd year additions.

READING

	Primer (pre-reader)	Reader
Day 1	None	None
Day 2-4	See *McGuffey's Eclectic Primer*, "Mastery Chart" ~ Do next lesson (DL)	See *McGuffey's Eclectic Readers*, "Mastery Chart" ~ Do next lesson (DL)

RELIGION — *Liturgical Feast lessons can be moved to correspond to their dates – simply adjust the schedule accordingly*

	K-1st Grades	2nd-3rd Grades	4th-6th Grades
Day 1	Begin **K-1 Lesson A** (SF).	Review lessons for Units 6–12; discuss themes; drill Q & A	Begin **4-6 Lesson A** (SF); Drill Q & A.
Day 2	Complete **K-1 Lesson A** (SF).	Review lessons for Units 6–12; discuss themes; drill Q & A	Review/complete **4-6 Lesson A** (SF); Drill Q & A.
Day 3	Complete **K-1 Lesson B** (SF).	Review lessons for Units 6–12; discuss themes; drill Q & A	Select activity(ies) from the "Let Us Work Together Section OHF-4, pp. 110-111.
Day 4	Complete **K-1 Lesson C** (SF).	Review lessons for Units 6–12; discuss themes; drill Q & A	Select activity(ies) from the "Let Us Work Together Section OHF-4, pp. 110-111; Take "Unit 3 Test,"OHF-4, p. 112.

SCIENCE

Day 1	Listen to CCM Science Memory Work (DL) 1 item at a time. Ask students what they can tell you about each item.	Listen to CCM Science Memory Work (DL) 1 item at a time. Ask students what they can tell you about each item.	Listen to CCM Science Memory Work 1 (DL) item at a time. Ask students what they can tell you about each item.
Day 2	Organize notebooks before the break. Make sure all lessons and activities are in the correct order.	Organize notebooks before the break. Make sure all lessons and activities are in the correct order.	Organize notebooks before the break. Make sure all lessons and activities are in the correct order.
Day 3	Complete any missing assignments for your student's notebook.	Complete any missing assignments for your student's notebook.	Complete any missing assignments for your student's notebook.
Day 4	Spend the day singing memory work and enjoying looking at your neat notebooks. Show off to Dad!	Spend the day singing memory work and enjoying looking at your neat notebooks. Show off to Dad!	Spend the day singing memory work and enjoying looking at your neat notebooks. Show off to Dad!

VIRTUE

	K-6th Grades
Day 1	Review All Virtues, Units 1-13 (SF)
Day 2-4	Practice "virtue training"

CYCLE III
UNIT 15

REVIEW

UNIT CHECKLIST

PREP FOR HOME

- ☐ Print and read this Handbook
- ☐ Read the Overview
- ☐ Review the Planner; do the following:
    - o Locate and review all Lessons and Activities in the Subject Folders (SF)
    - o Locate and review all readings and assignments in the Subject Folders (SF), Digital Library (DL), and Hard Copies (HC)
    - o Note and gather needed supplies for the unit
- ☐ Read the Virtue Lesson
- ☐ Email or call R.A.S. if you have questions or technical difficulty.

PREP FOR CO-OP

- ☐ Print your "Co-op Job Sheet" and prep for your job
- ☐ Make sure your child is ready for his or her presentation if assigned to present
- ☐ Gather maps, notebooks, prayer sheet, and other supplies the night or morning before the co-op meets.
- ☐ Gather students' assignments the night or morning before the co-op meets
- ☐ Listen to the Memory Work on the way!

PREP FOR UPCOMING WEEKS — <u>LOOK AHEAD AT UNITS 16-18</u>

- ☐ Make advanced purchases, as necessary
- ☐ Begin to gather books and materials

PLANNER ABBREVIATION KEY

DL	Digital Library (in course suite)
SF	Subject Folder (in course suite)
HC	Hard Copy
PLL	*Primary Language Lessons* (book)
ILL	*Intermediate Language Lessons* (book)
RS4K	*Real Science 4 Kids* (book)
I-CAT	*Illustrated Catechism* (book)
OHF-1	*Our Holy Faith, Book 1* (book)
OHF-2	*Our Holy Faith, Book 2* (book)
OHF-4	*Our Holy Faith, Book 4* (book)
OHF-1-TM	*Our Holy Faith, Book 1, Teacher's Manual* (book)

OVERVIEW

Common Topics (All students PreK to 6th)

Virtue:	Piety
Hymn:	Parce Domine
Prayers:	Angelus, Pater Noster, Ave Maria, Gloria Patri
History:	Review
Science:	Magnetism

History Themes

This is a review week for History. Please review Units 1-14.

How to Apply History to Everyday Life

Piety. The beginning of a new year is a time for reflection. We spend time reflecting upon our life during the past year and we set goals in order to improve in virtue. It is a good thing to use this time to think about piety, and to make it our goal to be more pious throughout the upcoming year. Piety involves a devotion and sincere loyalty to our faith, our family, and our locality. We must be devoted to the Tradition handed down from the fathers of our faith, and there are many ways in which we can create a culture in our home that is devoted to this faith. Likewise to our family we must show similar devotion, being faithful to fulfill our obligations as parents and as sons and daughters. Piety also beckons us to be devoted to our locality, realizing that we are in debt to those who have helped build the places in which we reside. We are Americans, or maybe more accurately, Virginians, Nebraskans, Texans, Californians, etc.; but we are also members of local communities. The place where we live, where our parents lived, and where their parents lived have formed us, and we owe those ancestors and communities, not only gratitude and respect, but a desire to maintain and pass down that which they have given us. Being pious is understanding the weight of history upon us, especially with regards to our communities. We must always consider what it means to be devoted and loyal to our community and to our history. Consider how you can teach your children to value their community, and to connect with its history.

Important People, Events, and Places to Know (Potential Student Presentations)

❖ Review your Timeline activities.
❖ Review the Saints.

OVERVIEW

Additional Project Ideas

- ❖ Complete any projects that you found interesting but did not have time to finish in Units 1-15.

PLANNER ~ Unit 15 (Home)

Week of _____ *Liturgical Theme & Colors* _____

Family Challenge-Task
Goals _____

_____

_____

Reminders _____

PRESCHOOL

	Music	Art, Reading, Religion	Virtue
Day 1	Review all hymns (SF-Latin)	Do craft **PreK Lesson A** (SF)	Review Virtue A-D (SF); practice "virtue training"
Day 2-4	Review all hymns (SF-Latin)	Review Letters A-D (SF), review and drill I-CAT, p. 1-3 (HC)	Review Virtue A-D (SF); practice "virtue training"

KINDERGARTEN – 6TH GRADE

ART   **CCM**

	K-6th Grade	K-6th Grade
Day 1	Review Units 1-3	Unit 15
Day 2-4	Review Units 1-3; do an extra art task from the home follow-up section, if there is time.	Listen to Unit 15 every day

HISTORY

	K-1st Grades	2nd-3rd Grades	4th-6th Grades
Day 1	Review any story(ies) from Units 1–13; draw a picture of your favorite story	Review any story(ies) from Units 1–13; draw a picture of your favorite story	Review any story(ies) from Units 1–13; draw a picture of your favorite story
Day 2	Review any story(ies) from Units 1–13; choose a story and act it out.	Review any story(ies) from Units 1–13; choose a story and act it out.	Review any story(ies) from Units 1–13; choose a story and act it out.
Day 3	Review any story(ies) from Units 1–13; choose a story and act it out.	Review any story(ies) from Units 1–13; do map **2-3 Activity A** (SF)	Review any story(ies) from Units 1–13; do map **4-6 Activity A** (SF).
Day 4	Do Family Quiz **All Activity A Bowl** (SF)	Do Family Quiz **All Activity A Bowl** (SF)	Do Family Quiz **All Activity A Bowl** (SF)

LANGUAGE ARTS

Day 1	Complete **K-1 Lesson A** (SF).	Complete **2-3 Lesson A** (SF).	Complete **4-6 Lesson A** (SF).
Day 2	Review **K-1 Lesson A** (SF); do **K-1 Activity A** (SF).	Review **2-3 Lesson A** (SF); do **2-3 Activity A** (SF).	Review **4-6 Lesson A** (SF); do **4-6 Activity A** (SF)
Day 3	Do pre-cursive copywork **K-1 Activity B** (SF).	Do cursive copywork **2-3 Activity B** (SF).	Complete first draft in **4-6 Activity A** (SF).
Day 4	Do narration and illustration **K-1 Activity C** (SF)	Do composition and illustration **2-3 Activity C** (SF)	Complete final draft in **4-6 Activity A** (SF).

LATIN/GREEK

Day 1	Practice Parce Domine! (SF)	Practice Parce Domine! (SF); start *Greek Primer* Unit 15 review (SF)	Practice Parce Domine! (SF); start *Reading Greek* Unit 15 review (SF)
Day 2	Listen to CCM Unit 15 Latin prayer	Listen to CCM Unit 15 Latin prayer; continue *Greek Primer* Unit 15 review	Listen to CCM Unit 15 Latin prayer; continue *Reading Greek* Unit 15 review (SF)
Day 3	Practice all the *Schola Rosa* Latin assembly prayers!	Practice all the *Schola Rosa* Latin assembly prayers!; continue *Greek Primer* Unit 15 review	Practice all the *Schola Rosa* Latin assembly prayers!; continue *Reading Greek* Unit 15 review (SF)
Day 4	Listen to Parce Domine video (SF); Sing along!	Listen to Parce Domine video (SF); Sing along!; finish *Greek Primer* Unit 15 (SF)	Listen to Parce Domine video (SF); Sing along!; finish *Reading Greek* Unit 15 (SF) and review/check work

MATH

	Level A	Level B	Level C
Day 1	None	None	None
Day 2-4	See *Ray's Primary*, Mastery Chart~ Do next lesson (DL)	See *Ray's Intellectual*, Mastery Chart~ Do next lesson (DL)	See *Ray's Practical*, Mastery Chart~ Do next lesson (DL)

MUSIC

	K-6th Grade
Day 1	Use audio files to sing along with: Hymn of the Week (Latin SF); Exercises Group 1, 2, & 3; Gloria; ite missa est; Kyrie; Agnus Dei; Sanctus; Merrily We Roll Along; Oats, Peas, Beans & Barley Grow; Lightly Row; Aura Lee (DL). See addendum to last Lesson for 2nd year additions.
Day 2-4	

READING

	Primer (pre-reader)	Reader
Day 1	None	None
Day 2-4	See *McGuffey's Eclectic Primer*, "Mastery Chart" ~ Do next lesson (DL)	See *McGuffey's Eclectic Readers*, "Mastery Chart" ~ Do next lesson (DL)

RELIGION — *Liturgical Feast lessons can be moved to correspond to their dates — simply adjust the schedule accordingly*

	K-1st Grades	2nd-3rd Grades	4th-6th Grades
Day 1	Do a liturgical feast lesson from OHF-4, Ch. 16 (SF), read aloud and discuss.	Do a liturgical feast lesson from OHF-4, Ch. 16 (SF), read aloud and discuss.	Do a liturgical feast lesson from OHF-4, Ch. 16 (SF), read and discuss.
Day 2	Review and drill lessons from OHF-1, covered during units 1-3	Review and drill Q & A from OHF-2, covered during units 1-3	Review and drill Q& A from OHF-4, covered during units 1-3
Day 3	Do a liturgical feast lesson from OHF-4, Ch. 16 (SF), read and discuss.	Do a liturgical feast lesson from OHF-4, Ch. 16 (SF), read and discuss.	Do a liturgical feast lesson from OHF-4, Ch. 16 (SF), read and discuss.
Day 4	Select and adapt "Things-to-do" activity from end of OHF-4, Ch. 16 (SF)	Select "Things-to-do" activity from end of OHF-4, Ch. 16 (SF)	Select "Things-to-do" activity from end of OHF-4, Ch. 16 (SF)

SCIENCE

Day 1	Complete **All Lesson A** (SF).	Complete **All Lesson A** (SF).	Complete **All Lesson A** (SF).
Day 2	Complete online **K-1 Activity A** (SF).	Complete online **2-3 Activity A** (SF).	Complete online **4-6 Activity A** (SF).
Day 3	Complete drawing **K-1 Activity B** (SF).	Complete drawing **2-3 Activity B** (SF).	Complete writing and drawing **4-6 Activity B** (SF). Work on nature journaling from **All Lesson A** (SF).
Day 4	Complete free-time experiment **K-1 Activity C** (SF).	Complete free-time experiment **2-3 Activity C** (SF).	Complete library research and writing **4-6 Activity C** (SF).

VIRTUE

	K-6th Grades
Day 1	Do **All Virtue Lesson A - Piety** (SF)
Day 2-4	Practice "virtue training"

CYCLE III
UNIT 16

ENLIGHTENMENT

VS. CONSERVATISM

&

FRENCH REVOLUTION

UNIT CHECKLIST

PREP FOR HOME

- ☐ Print and read this Handbook
- ☐ Read the Overview
- ☐ Review the Planner; do the following:
    - o Locate and review all Lessons and Activities in the Subject Folders (SF)
    - o Locate and review all readings and assignments in the Subject Folders (SF), Digital Library (DL), and Hard Copies (HC)
    - o Note and gather needed supplies for the unit
- ☐ Read the Virtue Lesson
- ☐ Email or call R.A.S. if you have questions or technical difficulty.

PREP FOR CO-OP

- ☐ Print your "Co-op Job Sheet" and prep for your job
- ☐ Make sure your child is ready for his or her presentation if assigned to present
- ☐ Gather maps, notebooks, prayer sheet, and other supplies the night or morning before the co-op meets.
- ☐ Gather students' assignments the night or morning before the co-op meets
- ☐ Listen to the Memory Work on the way!

PREP FOR UPCOMING WEEKS – <u>LOOK AHEAD AT UNIT 19</u>

- ☐ Make advanced purchases, as necessary
- ☐ Begin to gather books and materials

PLANNER ABBREVIATION KEY	
DL	Digital Library (in course suite)
SF	Subject Folder (in course suite)
HC	Hard Copy
PLL	*Primary Language Lessons* (book)
ILL	*Intermediate Language Lessons* (book)
RS4K	*Real Science 4 Kids* (book)
I-CAT	*Illustrated Catechism* (book)
OHF-1	*Our Holy Faith, Book 1* (book)
OHF-2	*Our Holy Faith, Book 2* (book)
OHF-4	*Our Holy Faith, Book 4* (book)
OHF-1-TM	*Our Holy Faith, Book 1, Teacher's Manual* (book)

OVERVIEW

Common Topics (All students PreK to 6th)

Virtue:	Patriotism
Hymn:	Parce Domine
Prayers:	Signum Crucis, Angelus, Pater Noster, Ave Maria, Gloria Patri
History:	Enlightenment vs. Conservatism & French Revolution (1789-1799)
Science:	Magnetism

History Themes

In Unit 16 we wade into the turbulent waters of the 18th century, where the forces of progress—the belief that all social, political, and moral problems can be conquered by the limitless possibility of human reason—collide with the foundation of the Christian West. This period of the European Enlightenment followed by the French Revolution was a rejection of the Christian heritage of Europe in favor for a new religion, that of Progress. Peter Kreeft aptly comments about the Enlightenment that "[t]he term is ironic; for spiritually the eighteenth century was the darkest ever. Scientism and rationalism replaced faith; the human heart narrowed and hardened in conformity with its own gods, the inventions of its own hands" (*Spiritual History 101: How Did We Get to the Edge?*). Likewise, Christopher Dawson notes that "the French Enlightenment was, in fact, the last of the great European heresies, and its appeal to Reason was in itself an act of faith which admitted no criticism. Even materialists ... shared the Deist belief in the transcendence of Reason and the inevitability of intellectual and moral progress, though there was nothing in their premises to warrant such assumptions" (*Progress & Religion: An Historical Inquiry*). However, not all Europeans embraced such folly; men such as Edmund Burke resisted the pull of progress and criticized the intellectual trends of the time. They gave birth to a Conservatism that attempted to maintain a connection to the treasures of Christendom and Western Civilization.

How to Apply History to Everyday Life

Our Mission. We must approach this period in history with much care. So many of the evils of the modern age were born out of the Enlightenment. A critical evaluation of the 18th century reveals the danger in believing in progress for the sake of progress as our contemporary culture does. Sadly, an ardent faith in man's ability to solve the social, political, and moral issues of today is pervasive. We must ask ourselves, "Do I believe that today's social, political, and moral problems can be solved by human reason, by legislation, by government intervention, or by social institutions?" "Is our faith in God, or in man?" "Do we trust God to redeem mankind, or do we believe that man will solve all his problems, redeeming himself?" "Do we connect our lives with the treasures of our Christian heritage, recognizing the influence of the Enlightenment upon modern American culture?" As Peter Kreeft notes, our culture has divided the head (reason) from the heart (will), and instead of being a united whole, people are either unhealthily devoted to reason or sentimentality, above all other things. We must not separate our heads, and the ability for us to know the truth, form our hearts, and the ability for us to practice the truth. Take time this week to read *Spiritual History 101: How Did We Get to the Edge*. Think about how we can contribute to the creation of a new age that connects to historical Christendom.

Important People, Events, and Places to Know (Potential Student Presentations)

❖ French Revolution: Edmund Burke (1729–1797); Louis XVI marries Marie Antoinette (1770); Louis XVI becomes King of France (1774); Meeting of the Estates General (1789); Tennis Court Oath (1789); Storming of the Bastille (1789); Declaration of the Rights of Man and Citizen (1789); Execution of Louis XVI (1793); The Committee of Public Safety takes over the revolution (1793); Reign of Terror (1793); Execution of Marie Antoinette (1794); The Thermidorian Reaction (1794); The Directory comes to power in France (1795); Napoleon elected as First Consul of the Consulate (1799); Napoleonic Code (1804); Napoleon invades Russia (1812); Napoloen exiled to Elba (1814); Napoleon escapes from Elba and begins his Hundred Days campaign (1815); Battle of Waterloo (1815); Napoleon exiled to St. Helena (1815)

❖ Saints of the late Eighteenth Century:

- Alphonsus Ligouri, C. Ss.R. (d. 1787)
- Mary Frances of the Five Wounds of Jesus, F.M.M. (1791)
- John-Michael Langevin (d. 1793)
- Frances de Croissy (d. 1794)
- John Baptist Souzy and 63 companions (d.1794)
- Madeleine Brideau (d. 1794)
- Madeleine Lidoine (d. 1794)
- Marie Claude Brard (d. 1794)
- Marie Croissy (d. 1794)
- Marie Dufour (d. 1794)
- Marie Hanisset (d. 1794)
- Marie Meunier (d. 1794)
- Marie Trezelle (d. 1794)

Additional Project Ideas

- Write a mini biography of Edmund Burke or François-René de Chateaubriand.
- Compare the French, English, and American Revolutions.
- Make a meal of French food.
- Read about Edmund Burke's criticism of the French Revolution.
- Make a series of maps that show Napoleon's conquest of Europe.
- Create daily edition of a newspaper that would have been published in Great Britain during the French Revolution.
  - Make a model of Versailles or the Notre Dame.

PLANNER ~ Unit 16 (Home)

Week of _____   *Liturgical Theme & Colors* _____

Family Challenge-Task
Goals _____

_____

_____

Reminders _____

_____

_____

PRESCHOOL

	Music	Art, Reading, Religion	Virtue
Day 1	Review all hymns (SF-Latin)	Do craft **PreK Lesson A** (SF)	Review Virtue E-H (SF); practice "virtue training"
Day 2-4	Review all hymns (SF-Latin)	Review Letters E-H (SF), review and drill I-CAT, p. 5-9 (HC)	Review Virtue E-H (SF); practice "virtue training"

KINDERGARTEN – 6TH GRADE

ART   **CCM**

	K-6th Grade	K-6th Grade
Day 1	Review Units 5-7	Unit 16
Day 2-4	Review Units 5-7; do an extra art task from the home follow-up section, if there is time.	Listen to Unit 16 every day

139

HISTORY

	K-1st Grades	2nd-3rd Grades	4th-6th Grades
Day 1	Read *Stories from Wagner* (DL)	Read *Stories from Wagner* (DL)	Read from *The Story of Napoleon* (DL).
Day 2	Continue *Stories from Wagner* (DL). Choose and do reading (or other project) from "Extras"	Continue *Stories from Wagner* (DL). Choose and do reading (or other project) from	Continue *The Story of Napoleon* (DL). Choose and do readings (or other projects) from
Day 3	Continue *Stories from Wagner* (DL). Do coloring page (SF)	Continue *Stories from Wagner* (DL). Do map **2-3 Activity A** (SF)	Continue *The Story of Napoleon* (DL). Do map **4-6 Activity A** (SF)
Day 4	Continue *Stories from Wagner* (DL). Create "popsicle puppets" and act out one of the readings (see SF for instructions).	Continue *Stories from Wagner* (DL). Create "popsicle puppets" and act out one of the readings (see SF for instructions).	Continue *The Story of Napoleon* (DL). Do timeline **4-6 Activity B (SF)**; summarize the reading this week and draw!

LANGUAGE ARTS

Day 1	Complete **K-1 Lesson A** (SF).	Complete **2-3 Lesson A** (SF).	Complete **4-6 Lesson A** (SF).
Day 2	Review **K-1 Lesson A** (SF); do **K-1 Activity A** (SF).	Review **2-3 Lesson A** (SF); do **2-3 Activity A** (SF).	Review **4-6 Lesson A** (SF); do **4-6 Activity A** (SF)
Day 3	Do pre-cursive copywork **K-1 Activity B** (SF).	Do cursive copywork **2-3 Activity B** (SF).	Complete first draft in **4-6 Activity A** (SF).
Day 4	Do narration and illustration **K-1 Activity C** (SF)	Do composition and illustration **2-3 Activity C** (SF)	Complete final draft in **4-6 Activity A** (SF).

LATIN/GREEK

Day 1	Practice Parce Domine! (SF)	Practice Parce Domine! (SF); do *Greek Primer* 16.1–4 (SF)	Practice Parce Domine! (SF); do *Reading Greek* 16.1–2 (SF)
Day 2	Listen to CCM Unit 16 Latin prayer	Listen to CCM Unit 16 Latin prayer; do *Greek Primer* 16.5	Listen to CCM Unit 16 Latin prayer; do *Reading Greek* 16.3–4 (SF)
Day 3	Practice all the *Schola Rosa* Latin assembly prayers!	Practice all the *Schola Rosa* Latin assembly prayers!; do *Greek Primer* 16.5 (SF)	Practice all the *Schola Rosa* Latin assembly prayers!; do *Reading Greek* 16.4 (SF)
Day 4	Listen to Parce Domine video (SF); Sing along!	Listen to Parce Domine video (SF); Sing along!; finish *Greek Primer* Unit 16 (SF)	Listen to Parce Domine video (SF); Sing along!; finish *Reading Greek* Unit 16 (SF) and review/check work

MATH

	Level A	Level B	Level C
Day 1	None	None	None
Day 2-4	See *Ray's Primary*, Mastery Chart~ Do next lesson (DL)	See *Ray's Intellectual*, Mastery Chart~ Do next lesson (DL)	See *Ray's Practical*, Mastery Chart~ Do next lesson (DL)

MUSIC

	K-6th Grade
Day 1	Use audio files to sing along with: Hymn of the Week (Latin SF); Exercises Group 1, 2, & 3; Gloria; ite missa est; Kyrie; Agnus Dei; Sanctus; Merrily We Roll Along; Oats, Peas, Beans & Barley Grow; Lightly Row; Aura Lee (DL). See addendum to last Lesson for 2nd year additions.
Day 2-4	

READING

	Primer (pre-reader)	Reader
Day 1	None	None
Day 2-4	See *McGuffey's Eclectic Primer*, "Mastery Chart"~ Do next lesson (DL)	See *McGuffey's Eclectic Readers,* "Mastery Chart" ~ Do next lesson (DL)

RELIGION — *Liturgical Feast lessons can be moved to correspond to their dates – simply adjust the schedule accordingly*

	K-1st Grades	2nd-3rd Grades	4th-6th Grades
Day 1	Do a liturgical feast lesson from OHF-4, Ch. 16 (SF), read aloud and discuss.	Do a liturgical feast lesson from OHF-4, Ch. 16 (SF), read aloud and discuss.	Do a liturgical feast lesson from OHF-4, Ch. 16 (SF), read and discuss.
Day 2	Review and drill lessons from OHF-1, covered during units 4-6	Review and drill Q & A from OHF-2, covered during units 4-6	Review and drill Q& A from OHF-4, covered during units 4-6
Day 3	Do a liturgical feast lesson from OHF-4, Ch. 16 (SF), read and discuss.	Do a liturgical feast lesson from OHF-4, Ch. 16 (SF), read and discuss.	Do a liturgical feast lesson from OHF-4, Ch. 16 (SF), read and discuss.
Day 4	Select and adapt "Things-to-do" activity from end of OHF-4, Ch. 16 (SF)	Select "Things-to-do" activity from end of OHF-4, Ch. 16 (SF)	Select "Things-to-do" activity from end of OHF-4, Ch. 16 (SF)

SCIENCE

Day 1	Complete **All Lesson A** (SF).	Complete **All Lesson A** (SF).	Complete **All Lesson A** (SF).
Day 2	Complete online **K-1 Activity A** (SF).	Complete online **2-3 Activity A** (SF).	Complete online **4-6 Activity A** (SF).
Day 3	Complete drawing **K-1 Activity B** (SF).	Complete drawing **2-3 Activity B** (SF).	Complete writing and drawing **4-6 Activity B** (SF). Work on nature journaling from **All Lesson A** (SF).
Day 4	Complete free-time experiment **K-1 Activity C** (SF).	Complete free-time experiment **2-3 Activity C** (SF).	Complete library research and writing **4-6 Activity C** (SF).

VIRTUE

	K-6th Grades
Day 1	Do **All Virtue Lesson A – Patriotism** (SF)
Day 2-4	Practice "virtue training"

CYCLE III
UNIT 17

THE UNITED STATES CONSTITUTION

UNIT CHECKLIST

PREP FOR HOME

- ☐ Print and read this Handbook
- ☐ Read the Overview
- ☐ Review the Planner; do the following:
    - o Locate and review all Lessons and Activities in the Subject Folders (SF)
    - o Locate and review all readings and assignments in the Subject Folders (SF), Digital Library (DL), and Hard Copies (HC)
    - o Note and gather needed supplies for the unit
- ☐ Read the Virtue Lesson
- ☐ Email or call R.A.S. if you have questions or technical difficulty.

PREP FOR CO-OP

- ☐ Print your "Co-op Job Sheet" and prep for your job
- ☐ Make sure your child is ready for his or her presentation if assigned to present
- ☐ Gather maps, notebooks, prayer sheet, and other supplies the night or morning before the co-op meets.
- ☐ Gather students' assignments the night or morning before the co-op meets
- ☐ Listen to the Memory Work on the way!

PREP FOR UPCOMING WEEKS — <u>LOOK AHEAD AT UNIT 20</u>

- ☐ Make advanced purchases, as necessary
- ☐ Begin to gather books and materials

PLANNER ABBREVIATION KEY

DL	Digital Library (in course suite)
SF	Subject Folder (in course suite)
HC	Hard Copy
PLL	*Primary Language Lessons* (book)
ILL	*Intermediate Language Lessons* (book)
RS4K	*Real Science 4 Kids* (book)
I-CAT	*Illustrated Catechism* (book)
OHF-1	*Our Holy Faith, Book 1* (book)
OHF-2	*Our Holy Faith, Book 2* (book)
OHF-4	*Our Holy Faith, Book 4* (book)
OHF-1-TM	*Our Holy Faith, Book 1, Teacher's Manual* (book)

OVERVIEW

Common Topics (All students PreK to 6th)

Virtue:	Honesty
Hymn:	Parce Domine
Prayers:	Signum Crucis, Angelus, Pater Noster, Ave Maria, Gloria Patri
History:	The United States Constitution
Science:	Magnetism

History Themes

In Unit 17 we return to the narrative of the United States by studying the development of the Constitution. Our founding fathers, after the American Revolution, vigorously debated the philosophy and structure of the government to be assumed by the newly independent colonies. One central matter of discussion was the balance of power between the federal government and the states with the Federalists arguing for a stronger centralized government, and the Anti-federalists arguing against such system. Eventually, the argument of the Federalists came to be predominately accepted and the Constitution was ratified. Despite this debate, our founding fathers looked to the Christian heritage of the west, to classical antiquity, and to the European Enlightenment of the 18th century for inspiration. In the end it is important to note, as professor Claes Ryn points out, that "[f]or the framers of the U.S. Constitution no task seemed more important than to limit and tame power. The chief reason why they established a government of divided powers and checks and balances was their view of human nature, which was primarily Christian and classical. It seemed to them self-evident that human beings are morally cleft. They are potentially decent, even admirable, but also have darker inclinations that pose a great threat to themselves and others. Human beings cannot be trusted with unrestricted power. The constitutionalism of the framers assumed that the drive for power had to be contained first of all through the self-discipline of individuals, but corresponding external restraints, including constitutional checks, were necessary to protect the public" ("Idealism and the Constitution" http://www.theimaginativeconservative.org/2014/11/idealism-constitution.html).

How to Apply History to Everyday Life

Our Mission. It is important for us to remember Pope Leo XIII's letter, *Testem benevolentiae,* on the heresy of Americanism. His Holiness writes "[t]he underlying principle of these new opinions [Americanism] is that, in order to more easily attract those who differ from her, the Church should shape her teachings more in accord with the spirit of the age and relax some of her ancient severity and make some concessions to new opinions. Many think that these concessions should be made not only in regard to ways of living, but even in regard to doctrines which belong to the deposit of the faith. They contend that it would be opportune, in order to gain those who differ from us, to omit certain points of her teaching which are of lesser importance, and to tone down the meaning which the Church has always attached to them.

It does not need many words, beloved son, to prove the falsity of these ideas if the nature and origin of the doctrine which the Church proposes are recalled to mind. The Vatican Council [Vatican I] says concerning this point: "For the doctrine of faith which God has revealed has not been proposed, like a philosophical invention to be perfected by human ingenuity, but has been delivered as a divine deposit to the Spouse of Christ to be faithfully kept and infallibly declared. Hence that meaning of the sacred dogmas is perpetually to be retained which our Holy Mother, the Church, has once declared, nor is that meaning ever to be departed from under the pretense or pretext of a deeper comprehension of them" (*Constitutio de Fide Catholica*, Chapter iv http://www.ccel.org/ccel/schaff/creeds2.v.ii.i.html).

We must ask such questions of ourselves. Have we been relaxing the teachings of the church? Are we making concession to new opinions that are opposed to the Deposit of the Faith? Are we guilty of Americanism?

Important People, Events, and Places to Know (Potential Student Presentations)

❖ American Revolution begins (1775); Declaration of Independence (1776); Britain surrenders at Yorktown (1781); Articles of Confederation (1781); End of the American Revolution – Treaty of Paris (1783); Constitutional Convention (1787); Delaware, New Jersey, and Pennsylvania ratify the Constitution (1787); Connecticut, Georgia, Maryland, Massachusetts, New Hampshire, New York, South Carolina, and Virginia ratify the Constitution (1788); North Carolina ratifies the Constitution (1789); First presidential election (1789); George Washington is inaugurated as the 1st President of the United States (1789)

❖ Saints of the late Eighteenth Century:

- Alphonsus Ligouri, C. Ss.R. (d. 1787)
- Mary Frances of the Five Wounds of Jesus, F.M.M. (1791)
- John-Michael Langevin (d. 1793)
- Frances de Croissy (d. 1794)
- John Baptist Souzy and 63 companions (d.1794)

- Madeleine Brideau (d. 1794)
- Madeleine Lidoine (d. 1794)
- Marie Claude Brard (d. 1794)
- Marie Croissy (d. 1794)
- Marie Dufour (d. 1794)
- Marie Hanisset (d. 1794)
- Marie Meunier (d. 1794)
- Marie Trezelle (d. 1794)

OVERVIEW

Additional Project Ideas

- Write a constitution for your home and family.
- Create the first flag of the United States, and as many subsequent flags as you wish.
- Memorize the preamble of the Constitution of the United States.
- Have a family quiz bowl over the American Revolution and the adoption of the Constitution.
- Research early American food and make a meal.
- Write a mini-biography of one of the fathers of the Constitution (Jefferson, Adams, Hamilton, etc.)
- Paint a portrait of one of the framers of the Constitution (Jefferson, Adams, Hamilton, Franklin, Washington, etc.)

Week of _____ *Liturgical Theme & Colors* _____

Family Challenge-Task
Goals _____

_____

_____

_____

Reminders _____

_____

_____

PRESCHOOL

	Music	Art, Reading, Religion	Virtue
Day 1	Review all hymns (SF-Latin)	Do craft **PreK Lesson A** (SF)	Review Virtue I-L (SF); practice "virtue training"
Day 2-4	Review all hymns (SF-Latin)	Review Letters I-L (SF), review & drill I-CAT, p. 8-11 (HC)	Review Virtue I-L (SF); practice "virtue training"

KINDERGARTEN – 6TH GRADE

ART   **CCM**

	K-6th Grade	K-6th Grade
Day 1	Review Units 9-11	Unit 17
Day 2-4	Review Units 9-11; do an extra art task from the home follow-up section, if there is time.	Listen to Unit 17 every day

HISTORY

	K-1st Grades	2nd-3rd Grades	4th-6th Grades
Day 1	Read *Stories of America: From Conflict to Constitution, K-3rd* (DL)	Read *Stories of America: From Conflict to Constitution, K-3rd* (DL)	Read from *Stories of America: From Conflict to Constitution, 4th-6th* (DL).
Day 2	Continue *Stories of America, K-3rd* (DL). Choose and do reading (or other project) from "Extras" (SF); draw a picture inspired by the readings	Continue *Stories of America, K-3rd* (DL). Choose and do reading (or other project) from "Extras" (SF); draw a picture inspired by the readings	Continue *Stories of America, 4th-6th* (DL). Choose and do readings (or other projects) from "Extras" (SF)
Day 3	Continue *Stories of America, K-3rd* (DL). Do coloring page (SF)	Continue *Stories of America, K-3rd* (DL). Do map **2-3 Activity A** (SF)	Continue *Stories of America, 4th-6th* (DL). Do map **4-6 Activity A** (SF)
Day 4	Continue *Stories of America, K-3rd* (DL). Act out one of the readings (see SF for instructions).	Continue *Stories of America, K-3rd* (DL). Act out one of the readings (see SF for instructions).	Continue *Stories of America, 4th-6th* (DL). Do timeline **4-6 Activity B (SF)**; summarize the reading this week and draw!

LANGUAGE ARTS

	K-1st Grades	2nd-3rd Grades	4th-6th Grades
Day 1	Complete **K-1 Lesson A** (SF).	Complete **2-3 Lesson A** (SF).	Complete **4-6 Lesson A** (SF).
Day 2	Review **K-1 Lesson A** (SF); do **K-1 Activity A** (SF).	Review **2-3 Lesson A** (SF); do **2-3 Activity A** (SF).	Review **4-6 Lesson A** (SF); do **4-6 Activity A** (SF)
Day 3	Do pre-cursive copywork **K-1 Activity B** (SF).	Do cursive copywork **2-3 Activity B** (SF).	Complete first draft in **4-6 Activity A** (SF).
Day 4	Do narration and illustration **K-1 Activity C** (SF)	Do composition and illustration **2-3 Activity C** (SF)	Complete final draft in **4-6 Activity A** (SF).

LATIN/GREEK

	K-1st Grades	2nd-3rd Grades	4th-6th Grades
Day 1	Practice Parce Domine! (SF)	Practice Parce Domine! (SF); do *Greek Primer* 17.1–4 (SF)	Practice Parce Domine! (SF); do *Reading Greek* 17.1–2 (SF)
Day 2	Listen to CCM Unit 17 Latin prayer	Listen to CCM Unit 17 Latin prayer; do *Greek Primer* 17.5	Listen to CCM Unit 17 Latin prayer; do *Reading Greek* 17.3–4 (SF)
Day 3	Practice all the *Schola Rosa* Latin assembly prayers!	Practice all the *Schola Rosa* Latin assembly prayers!; do *Greek Primer* 17.5 (SF)	Practice all the *Schola Rosa* Latin assembly prayers!; do *Reading Greek* 17.4 (SF)
Day 4	Listen to Parce Domine video (SF); Sing along!	Listen to Parce Domine video (SF); Sing along!; finish *Greek Primer* Unit 17 (SF)	Listen to Parce Domine video (SF); Sing along!; finish *Reading Greek* Unit 17 (SF) and review/check work

MATH

	Level A	Level B	Level C
Day 1	None	None	None
Day 2-4	See *Ray's Primary*, Mastery Chart~ Do next lesson (DL)	See *Ray's Intellectual*, Mastery Chart~ Do next lesson (DL)	See *Ray's Practical*, Mastery Chart~ Do next lesson (DL)

MUSIC

	K-6th Grade
Day 1	Use audio files to sing along with: Hymn of
Day 2-4	the Week (Latin SF); Exercises Group 1, 2, & 3; Gloria; ite missa est; Kyrie; Agnus Dei; Sanctus; Merrily We Roll Along; Oats, Peas, Beans & Barley Grow; Lightly Row; Aura Lee (DL). See addendum to last Lesson for 2nd year additions.

READING

	Primer (pre-reader)	Reader
Day 1	None	None
Day 2-4	See *McGuffey's Eclectic Primer*, "Mastery Chart"~ Do next lesson (DL)	See *McGuffey's Eclectic Readers*, "Mastery Chart" ~ Do next lesson (DL)

RELIGION — *Liturgical Feast lessons can be moved to correspond to their dates — simply adjust the schedule accordingly*

	K-1st Grades	2nd-3rd Grades	4th-6th Grades
Day 1	Do a liturgical feast lesson from OHF-4, Ch. 16 (SF), read aloud and discuss.	Do a liturgical feast lesson from OHF-4, Ch. 16 (SF), read aloud and discuss.	Do a liturgical feast lesson from OHF-4, Ch. 16 (SF), read and discuss.
Day 2	Review and drill lessons from OHF-1, covered during units 7-10	Review and drill Q & A from OHF-2, covered during units 7-10	Review and drill Q & A from OHF-4, covered during unit 7-10
Day 3	Do a liturgical feast lesson from OHF-4, Ch. 16 (SF), read and discuss.	Do a liturgical feast lesson from OHF-4, Ch. 16 (SF), read and discuss.	Do a liturgical feast lesson from OHF-4, Ch. 16 (SF), read and discuss.
Day 4	Select and adapt "Things-to-do" activity from end of OHF-4, Ch. 16 (SF)	Select "Things-to-do" activity from end of OHF-4, Ch. 16 (SF)	Select "Things-to-do" activity from end of OHF-4, Ch. 16 (SF)

SCIENCE

Day 1	Complete **All Lesson A** (SF).	Complete **All Lesson A** (SF).	Complete **All Lesson A** (SF).
Day 2	Complete online **K-1 Activity A** (SF).	Complete online **2-3 Activity A** (SF).	Complete online **4-6 Activity A** (SF).
Day 3	Complete drawing **K-1 Activity B** (SF).	Complete drawing **2-3 Activity B** (SF).	Complete writing and drawing **4-6 Activity B** (SF). Work on nature journaling from **All Lesson A** (SF). Read *RS4K Focus on Elementary Physics* Chapter 8 and do Experiment 8.
Day 4	Complete free-time experiment **K-1 Activity C** (SF).	Complete free-time experiment **2-3 Activity C** (SF).	Complete library research and writing **4-6 Activity C** (SF).

VIRTUE

	K-6th Grades
Day 1	Do **All Virtue Lesson A – Honesty** (SF)
Day 2-4	Practice "virtue training"

CYCLE III
UNIT 18

THE UNITED STATES
CONSTITUTION

UNIT CHECKLIST

PREP FOR HOME

- ☐ Print and read this Handbook
- ☐ Read the Overview
- ☐ Review the Planner; do the following:
  - o Locate and review all Lessons and Activities in the Subject Folders (SF)
  - o Locate and review all readings and assignments in the Subject Folders (SF), Digital Library (DL), and Hard Copies (HC)
  - o Note and gather needed supplies for the unit
- ☐ Read the Virtue Lesson
- ☐ Email or call R.A.S. if you have questions or technical difficulty.

PREP FOR CO-OP

- ☐ Print your "Co-op Job Sheet" and prep for your job
- ☐ Make sure your child is ready for his or her presentation if assigned to present
- ☐ Gather maps, notebooks, prayer sheet, and other supplies the night or morning before the co-op meets.
- ☐ Gather students' assignments the night or morning before the co-op meets
- ☐ Listen to the Memory Work on the way!

PREP FOR UPCOMING WEEKS — <u>LOOK AHEAD AT UNIT 21</u>

- ☐ Make advanced purchases, as necessary
- ☐ Begin to gather books and materials

PLANNER ABBREVIATION KEY

DL	Digital Library (in course suite)
SF	Subject Folder (in course suite)
HC	Hard Copy
PLL	*Primary Language Lessons* (book)
ILL	*Intermediate Language Lessons* (book)
RS4K	*Real Science 4 Kids* (book)
I-CAT	*Illustrated Catechism* (book)
OHF-1	*Our Holy Faith, Book 1* (book)
OHF-2	*Our Holy Faith, Book 2* (book)
OHF-4	*Our Holy Faith, Book 4* (book)
OHF-1-TM	*Our Holy Faith, Book 1, Teacher's Manual* (book)

OVERVIEW

Common Topics (All students PreK to 6th)

Virtue:	Self-Discipline
Hymn:	Parce Domine
Prayers:	Signum Crucis, Angelus, Pater Noster, Ave Maria, Gloria Patri
History:	The United States Constitution
Science:	Review

History Themes

In Unit 18 we continue our study of the Constitution of the United States by specifically looking at the document itself. Quickly upon reading the document, we are confronted with the political innovations and ideals of our founding fathers, innovations and ideals such as liberty, popular sovereignty, the balance of power, checks and balances in government, and so on. The American framers of the Constitution, embracing such ideas, departed from their European heritage by adopting a form and function of government that was a departure from the monarchies and absolute states of Europe. Yet we can trace the thread of these political innovations back to Europe, to the political thinkers of the French Enlightenment and to classical antiquity, which reminds us that it is always necessary for us, as Americans, to remember our connection with the Old World and with Western Civilization.

How to Apply History to Everyday Life

Our Mission. Once again we must remember Pope Leo XIII's condemnation of Americanism. "The underlying principle of these new opinions [Americanism] is that, in order to more easily attract those who differ from her, the Church should shape her teachings more in accord with the spirit of the age and relax some of her ancient severity and make some concessions to new opinions. Many think that these concessions should be made not only in regard to ways of living, but even in regard to doctrines which belong to the deposit of the faith. They contend that it would be opportune, in order to gain those who differ from us, to omit certain points of her teaching which are of lesser importance, and to tone down the meaning which the Church has always attached to them.

It does not need many words, beloved son, to prove the falsity of these ideas if the nature and origin of the doctrine which the Church proposes are recalled to mind. The Vatican Council [Vatican I] says concerning this point: "For the doctrine of faith which God has revealed has not been proposed, like a philosophical invention to be perfected by human ingenuity, but has been delivered as a divine deposit to the Spouse of Christ to be faithfully kept and infallibly declared. Hence that meaning of the sacred dogmas is perpetually to be retained which our Holy Mother, the Church, has once declared, nor is that meaning ever to be departed from under the pretense or pretext of a deeper comprehension of them" (*Constitutio de Fide Catholica*, Chapter iv http://www.ccel.org/ccel/schaff/creeds2.v.ii.i.html).

Ask yourself if you are guilty of picking and choosing doctrines of the Church to believe or not believe, to follow or not to follow. Have you lessened any of the teachings of the Church because they are not consistent with the opinions today? Reflect upon your beliefs and actions regarding the hard teachings of Christ and His Church.

Important People, Events, and Places to Know (Potential Student Presentations)

❖ American Revolution begins (1775); Declaration of Independence (1776); Britain surrenders at Yorktown (1781); Articles of Confederation (1781); End of the American Revolution – Treaty of Paris (1783); Constitutional Convention (1787); Delaware, New Jersey, and Pennsylvania ratify the Constitution (1787); Connecticut, Georgia, Maryland, Massachusetts, New Hampshire, New York, South Carolina, and Virginia ratify the Constitution (1788); North Carolina ratifies the Constitution (1789); First presidential election (1789); George Washington is inaugurated as the 1st President of the United States (1789)

❖ Saints of the late Eighteenth Century:

- Alphonsus Ligouri, C. Ss.R. (d. 1787)
- Mary Frances of the Five Wounds of Jesus, F.M.M. (1791)
- John-Michael Langevin (d. 1793)
- Frances de Croissy (d. 1794)
- John Baptist Souzy and 63 companions (d.1794)

- Madeleine Brideau (d. 1794)
- Madeleine Lidoine (d. 1794)
- Marie Claude Brard (d. 1794)
- Marie Croissy (d. 1794)
- Marie Dufour (d. 1794)
- Marie Hanisset (d. 1794)
- Marie Meunier (d. 1794)
- Marie Trezelle (d. 1794)

Additional Project Ideas

- Memorize the preamble of the Constitution.
- Choose other activities from Constitutioncenter.org (http://constitutioncenter.org/constitution-day/constitution-day-resources)

Week of _____   Liturgical Theme & Colors _____

Family Challenge-Task
Goals _____

_____

_____

Reminders _____

_____

PRESCHOOL

	Music	Art, Reading, Religion	Virtue
Field	Review all hymns (SF-Latin)	Do craft **PreK Lesson A** (SF)	Review Virtue M-P (SF); practice "virtue training"
Day 2-4	Review all hymns (SF-Latin)	Review Letters M-P (SF), review & drill I-CAT, pp 12-17 (HC)	Review Virtue M-P (SF); practice "virtue training"

KINDERGARTEN – 6TH GRADE

ART   **CCM**

	K-6th Grade		K-6th Grade
Day 1	Review Units 1-11		Unit 18
Day 2-4	Review Units 1-11; do an extra art task from the home follow-up section, if there is time.		Listen to Unit 18 every day

HISTORY

	K-1st Grades	2nd-3rd Grades	4th-6th Grades
Field	Read *Constitution Explained* (DL)	Read *Constitution of the United States of America* (DL)	Read *Constitution of the United States of America* (DL).
Day 2	Choose and do reading (or other project) from "Extras" (SF); draw a picture inspired by the readings	Choose and do reading (or other project) from "Extras" (SF); draw a picture inspired by the readings	Choose and do readings (or other projects) from "Extras" (SF)
Day 3	Do Constitution **K-1 Activity A** (SF)	Do Constitution **2-3 Activity A** (SF)	Do Constitution **4-6 Activity A** (SF)
Day 4	Do coloring page (SF)	Do coloring page (SF)	Do Constitution **4-6 Activity B (SF)**; summarize the reading this week and draw!

LANGUAGE ARTS

Field	Complete **K-1 Lesson A** (SF).	Complete **2-3 Lesson A** (SF).	Complete **4-6 Lesson A** (SF).
Day 2	Review **K-1 Lesson A** (SF); do **K-1 Activity A** (SF).	Review **2-3 Lesson A** (SF); do **2-3 Activity A** (SF).	Review **4-6 Lesson A** (SF); do **4-6 Activity A** (SF)
Day 3	Do pre-cursive copywork **K-1 Activity B** (SF).	Do cursive copywork **2-3 Activity B** (SF).	Complete first draft in **4-6 Activity A** (SF).
Day 4	Do narration and illustration **K-1 Activity C** (SF)	Do composition and illustration **2-3 Activity C** (SF)	Complete final draft in **4-6 Activity A** (SF).

LATIN/GREEK

Field	Practice Parce Domine! (SF)	Practice Parce Domine! (SF); do *Greek Primer* 18.1–4 (SF)	Practice Parce Domine! (SF); do *Reading Greek* 18.1–2 (SF)
Day 2	Listen to CCM Unit 18 Latin prayer	Listen to CCM Unit 18 Latin prayer; do *Greek Primer* 18.5	Listen to CCM Unit 18 Latin prayer; do *Reading Greek* 18.3–4 (SF)
Day 3	Practice all the *Schola Rosa* Latin assembly prayers!	Practice all the *Schola Rosa* Latin assembly prayers!; do *Greek Primer* 18.5 (SF)	Practice all the *Schola Rosa* Latin assembly prayers!; do *Reading Greek* 18.4 (SF)
Day 4	Listen to Parce Domine video (SF); Sing along!	Listen to Parce Domine video (SF); Sing along!; finish *Greek Primer* Unit 18 (SF)	Listen to Parce Domine video (SF); Sing along!; finish *Reading Greek* Unit 18 (SF) and review/check work

MATH

	Level A	Level B	Level C
Field	None	None	None
Day 2-4	See *Ray's Primary*, Mastery Chart~ Do next lesson (DL)	See *Ray's Intellectual*, Mastery Chart~ Do next lesson (DL)	See *Ray's Practical*, Mastery Chart~ Do next lesson (DL)

MUSIC

	K-6th Grade
Field Day 2-4	Use audio files to sing along with: Hymn of the Week (Latin SF); Exercises Group 1, 2, & 3; Gloria; ite missa est; Kyrie; Agnus Dei; Sanctus; Merrily We Roll Along; Oats, Peas, Beans & Barley Grow; Lightly Row; Aura Lee (DL). See addendum to last Lesson for 2nd year additions.

READING

	Primer (pre-reader)	Reader
	None	None
	See *McGuffey's Eclectic Primer*, "Mastery Chart" ~ Do next lesson (DL)	See *McGuffey's Eclectic Readers*, "Mastery Chart" ~ Do next lesson (DL)

RELIGION — *Liturgical Feast lessons can be moved to correspond to their dates — simply adjust the schedule accordingly*

	K-1st Grades	2nd-3rd Grades	4th-6th Grades
Field	Do a liturgical feast lesson from OHF-4, Ch. 16 (SF), read aloud and discuss.	Do a liturgical feast lesson from OHF-4, Ch. 16 (SF), read aloud and discuss.	Do a liturgical feast lesson from OHF-4, Ch. 16 (SF), read and discuss.
Day 2	Review and drill lessons from OHF-1, covered during units 11-14	Review and drill Q & A from OHF-2, covered during units 11-14	Review and drill Q& A from OHF-4, covered during units 11-14
Day 3	Do a liturgical feast lesson from OHF-4, Ch. 16 (SF), read and discuss.	Do a liturgical feast lesson from OHF-4, Ch. 16 (SF), read and discuss.	Do a liturgical feast lesson from OHF-4, Ch. 16 (SF), read and discuss.
Day 4	Select and adapt "Things-to-do" activity from end of OHF-4, Ch. 16 (SF)	Select "Things-to-do" activity from end of OHF-4, Ch. 16 (SF)	Select "Things-to-do" activity from end of OHF-4, Ch. 16 (SF)

SCIENCE

Field	Review Units 15-18 and complete any missing assignments.	Review Units 15-18 and complete any missing assignments.	Review Units 15-18 and complete any missing assignments.
Day 2	Read selections from Fabre's *Story Book of Science* (DL).	Read selections from Fabre's *Story Book of Science* (DL).	Read selections from Fabre's *Story Book of Science* (DL).
Day 3	Complete free-time experiment **K-1 Activity A** (SF).	Complete free-time experiment **2-3 Activity A** (SF).	Complete free-time experiment **4-6 Activity A** (SF).
Day 4	Continue **K-1 Activity A** (SF).	Continue **2-3 Activity A** (SF).	Continue **4-6 Activity A** (SF).

VIRTUE

	K-6th Grades
Field	Do **All Virtue Lesson A – Piety** (SF)
Day 2-4	Practice "virtue training"

CYCLE III
UNIT 19

INDUSTRIAL REVOLUTION

UNIT CHECKLIST

PREP FOR HOME

- ☐ Print and read this Handbook
- ☐ Read the Overview
- ☐ Review the Planner; do the following:
    - o Locate and review all Lessons and Activities in the Subject Folders (SF)
    - o Locate and review all readings and assignments in the Subject Folders (SF), Digital Library (DL), and Hard Copies (HC)
    - o Note and gather needed supplies for the unit
- ☐ Read the Virtue Lesson
- ☐ Email or call R.A.S. if you have questions or technical difficulty.

PREP FOR CO-OP

- ☐ Print your "Co-op Job Sheet" and prep for your job
- ☐ Make sure your child is ready for his or her presentation if assigned to present
- ☐ Gather maps, notebooks, prayer sheet, and other supplies the night or morning before the co-op meets.
- ☐ Gather students' assignments the night or morning before the co-op meets
- ☐ Listen to the Memory Work on the way!

PREP FOR UPCOMING WEEKS — <u>LOOK AHEAD AT UNIT 21</u>

- ☐ Make advanced purchases, as necessary
- ☐ Begin to gather books and materials

PLANNER ABBREVIATION KEY

DL	Digital Library (in course suite)
SF	Subject Folder (in course suite)
HC	Hard Copy
PLL	*Primary Language Lessons* (book)
ILL	*Intermediate Language Lessons* (book)
RS4K	*Real Science 4 Kids* (book)
I-CAT	*Illustrated Catechism* (book)
OHF-1	*Our Holy Faith, Book 1* (book)
OHF-2	*Our Holy Faith, Book 2* (book)
OHF-4	*Our Holy Faith, Book 4* (book)
OHF-1-TM	*Our Holy Faith, Book 1, Teacher's Manual* (book)

OVERVIEW

Common Topics (All students PreK to 6th)

Virtue:	Forgiveness
Hymn:	Review
Prayers:	Signum Crucis, Angelus, Pater Noster, Ave Maria, Gloria Patri
History:	Industrial Revolution (1760-1840)
Science:	Thermal Energy

History Themes

In Unit 19 we look at the inventors and industry of the late 18th and early 19th centuries. This is a fun unit and a nice break from the more serious topics of this century. Unfortunately, the "fun" does not come without some degree of solemnity. As industry increases, especially in the North, we begin to see economic tensions rise between the industrial North and the agricultural South. This comes to a peak when we reach the Civil War unit.

For now, we shall be content to enjoy inventions of the age and to read two good books: *Black Beauty* (K-3rd Grade) and *Two Years before the Mast* (4th-6th Grade). Both novels provide characters who are robust in dimension and who can readily be identified with a vice or a virtue. Now that students have progressed in their understanding of virtues, these provide material for discerning the good from the bad. Both novels are also relatively contemporary with the century we are studying and provide glimpses into the ways of life during that time period.

How to Apply History to Everyday Life

Our Mission. This week we might reflect upon the necessity or non-necessity of industry. What did it gain the people? What did it cause them to lose? How did everyday life change? How would our own lives be different without the inventions that came from this time period? What would the world have been like without the telegraph? What would our lives be like without the cotton gin? What would the pace of life be like?

In addition, in our literary readings of the week, we might consider humbly and bravely the good examples from *Black Beauty*. This is a book wrought with virtue lessons, and we can certainly aim to learn them and to teach them to our children. *Two Years before the Mast* calls us to reflect on the simplicity of changing one's own lifestyle as a cure to illness. What would life be like without all the medical visits and bills?

Important People, Events, and Places to Know (Potential Student Presentations)

❖ Bill of Rights added to Constitution (1791); beginning of French Republic (1792); Eli Whitney invents cotton gin (1793); Founding of San Fernando, San Miguel, San Juan

Bautista, and San Jose Missions (1797); John Adams is President; Alien and Sedition Acts passed by Congress (1798); San Luis Rey Mission founded; Death of George Washinton (1799); Napoleon Bonaparte takes control of the French government; U.S. Capital becomes Washington, D.C. (1800); Thomas Jefferson is President; The Louisiana Purchase (1803)

❖ Saints of the late Nineteenth Century:

- St. Augustine Zhao Rong (1815)
- St. Andrew Dung-Lac & Companions (1820-1866)
- St. Julie Billiart (1816)
- St Elizabeth Ann Seton (1821)
- Our Lady of the Miraculous Medal (1830)
- St. Andrew Hubert Fournet (1834)
- Sts. Andrew Kim Tae-gon & Companions (1839-1867)
- St. Rose Philippine Duchesne (1852)
- St. Dominic Savio (1857)
- Our Lady of Lourdes (1858)
- St. John Vianney (1859)
- St. John Neumann (1860)
- St. Madeleine Sophie Barat (1865)
- St. Euphrasia Pelletier (1868)
- St. Peter Julian Eymard (1868)
- St. Anthony Mary Claret (1870)
- St. Catherine Laboure (1876)
- St. Charles Lwanga & Companions (1887)
- St. John Bosco (1888)
- St. Conrad (1894)
- St. Therese of Lisieux (1897)
- St. Sharbel Makhluf (1898)

Additional Project Ideas

- Create imitation inventions based on the inventions of this unit
- Write biographies of the inventors

Week of _____ *Liturgical Theme & Colors* _____

Family Challenge-Task
Goals _____

_____

_____

_____

Reminders _____

_____

_____

PRESCHOOL

	Music	Art, Reading, Religion	Virtue
Co-op	See "Music" heading below	Do craft **PreK Lesson A** (SF)	Review Virtue S-T (SF); practice "virtue training"
Day 2-4	See "Music" heading below	Do **Letter Book S-T** (SF); do **coloring pages** (SF); read & drill I-CAT, p. 19 (HC)	Review Virtue S-T (SF); practice "virtue training"

KINDERGARTEN – 6TH GRADE

ART   **CCM**

	K-6th Grade	K-6th Grade
Day 1	Do **All Lesson A** (SF).	Unit 19
Day 2-4	Review **All Lesson A** (SF); do home follow-up.	Listen to Unit 19 every day

HISTORY

	K-1st Grades	2nd-3rd Grades	4th-6th Grades
Co-op	Do **K-1 Lesson A** (SF).	Do **2-3 Lesson A** (SF).	Do **4-6 Lesson A** (SF).
Day 2	Read *Black Beauty* (DL) this week; Choose and do reading (or other project) from "Extras" (SF); draw a picture inspired by the readings	Read *Black Beauty* (DL) this week; Choose and do reading (or other project) from "Extras" (SF); draw a picture inspired by the readings	Read *Two Years Before the Mast* (DL); Choose and do readings (or other projects) from "Extras" (SF); Do writing **4-6 Activity A** (SF).
Day 3	Do hands-on **K-1 Activity A** (SF)	Do hands-on **2-3 Activity A** (SF)	Do map **4-6 Activity B** (SF).
Day 4	Do coloring page (SF)	Do coloring page (SF)	Do hands-on **4-6 Activity C (SF)**; summarize the reading this week and draw!

LANGUAGE ARTS

	K-1st Grades	2nd-3rd Grades	4th-6th Grades
Co-op	Complete **K-1 Lesson A** (SF).	Complete **2-3 Lesson A** (SF).	Complete **4-6 Lesson A** (SF).
Day 2	Review **K-1 Lesson A** (SF); do **K-1 Activity A** (SF).	Review **2-3 Lesson A** (SF); do **2-3 Activity A** (SF).	Review **4-6 Lesson A** (SF); do **4-6 Activity A** (SF)
Day 3	Do pre-cursive copywork **K-1 Activity B** (SF).	Do cursive copywork **2-3 Activity B** (SF).	Complete first draft in **4-6 Activity A** (SF).
Day 4	Do narration and illustration **K-1 Activity C** (SF)	Do composition and illustration **2-3 Activity C** (SF)	Complete final draft in **4-6 Activity A** (SF).

LATIN/GREEK

	K-1st Grades	2nd-3rd Grades	4th-6th Grades
Co-op	Practice Hosanna Filio David (SF)	Practice Hosanna Filio David (SF); do *Greek Primer* 19.1–4 (SF)	Practice Hosanna Filio David (SF); do *Reading Greek* 19.1–2 (SF)
Day 2	Listen to CCM Unit 19 Latin prayer	Listen to CCM Unit 19 Latin prayer; do *Greek Primer* 19.5	Listen to CCM Unit 19 Latin prayer; do *Reading Greek* 19.3–4 (SF)
Day 3	Practice all the *Schola Rosa* Latin assembly prayers!	Practice all the *Schola Rosa* Latin assembly prayers!; do *Greek Primer* 19.5 (SF)	Practice all the *Schola Rosa* Latin assembly prayers!; do *Reading Greek* 19.4 (SF)
Day 4	Listen to Hosanna Filio David video (SF); Sing along!	Listen to Hosanna Filio David video (SF); Sing along!; finish *Greek Primer* Unit 19 (SF)	Listen to Hosanna Filio David video (SF); Sing along!; finish *Reading Greek* Unit 19 (SF) and review/check work

MATH

	Level A	Level B	Level C
Co-op	None	None	None
Day 2-4	See *Ray's Primary*, Mastery Chart~ Do next lesson (DL)	See *Ray's Intellectual*, Mastery Chart~ Do next lesson (DL)	See *Ray's Practical*, Mastery Chart~ Do next lesson (DL)

MUSIC

	K-6th Grade
Co-op	Review **All Lesson A** (SF). Use audio files to sing along with: Hymn of the Week (Latin SF); Exercises Group 1, 2, 3, & 4; Gloria; ite missa est; Kyrie; Agnus Dei; Sanctus; Merrily We Roll Along; Oats, Peas, Beans & Barley Grow; Lightly Row; Aura Lee, Lavendar Blue (DL). See addendum to Lesson for 2nd year additions.
Day 2-4	

READING

	Primer (pre-reader)	Reader
Co-op	None	None
Day 2-4	See *McGuffey's Eclectic Primer*, "Mastery Chart"~ Do next lesson (DL)	See *McGuffey's Eclectic Readers*, "Mastery Chart" ~ Do next lesson (DL)

RELIGION — *Liturgical Feast lessons can be moved to correspond to their dates – simply adjust the schedule accordingly*

	K-1st Grades	2nd-3rd Grades	4th-6th Grades
Co-op	Begin **K-1 Lesson A** (SF).	Begin **2-3 Lesson A** (SF). Drill Q & A.	Begin **4-6 Lesson A** (SF). Drill Q & A.
Day 2	Review/complete **K-1 Lesson A** (SF).	Review/complete **2-3 Lesson A** (SF). Drill Q & A.	Review/complete **4-6 Lesson A** (SF). Drill Q & A.
Day 3	Begin **K-1 Lesson B** (SF).	Begin **2-3 Lesson B** (SF). Drill Q & A.	Select activity(ies) from the "Let Us Work Together" section OHF-4, pp. 198-199.
Day 4	Review/complete **K-1 Lesson B** (SF).	Review/complete **2-3 Lesson B** (SF). Drill Q & A.	Select activity(ies) from the "Let Us Work Together" section OHF-4, pp. 198-199

SCIENCE

Co-op	Do **K-1 Lesson A** (SF).	Do **2-3 Lesson A** (SF).	Do **4-6 Lesson A** (SF).
Day 2	Review **K-1 Lesson A** (SF); Read "Heat-Conduction" in *Secret of Everyday Things* (DL).	Review **2-3 Lesson A** (SF); Read "Heat-Conduction" in *Secret of Everyday Things* (DL).	Review **4-6 Lesson A** (SF); Read "Heat-Conduction" and "Heating" in *Secret of Everyday Things* (DL); do Nature Journal from **4-6 Lesson A** (SF). Read Ch. 5 *RS4K, Focus on Elementary Physics* and do Experiment 5.
Day 3	Complete free-time experiment **K-1 Activity A** (SF).	Complete free-time experiment **2-3 Activity A** (SF).	Complete free-time experiment **4-6 Activity A** (SF) and do **4-6 Activity B** (SF).
Day 4	Do drawing **K-1 Activity B** (SF); if possible, go on a nature walk.	Do description & illustration **2-3 Activity B** (SF); if possible, go on a nature walk.	Do library research **4-6 Activity C** (SF); if possible, go on a nature walk and do Nature Journaling.

VIRTUE

	K-6th Grades
Co-op	Do **All Virtue Lesson A – Forgiveness** (SF)
Day 2-4	Practice "virtue training"

CYCLE III
UNIT 20

WESTERN EXPANSION

UNIT CHECKLIST

PREP FOR HOME

- ☐ Print and read this Handbook
- ☐ Read the Overview
- ☐ Review the Planner; do the following:
    - o Locate and review all Lessons and Activities in the Subject Folders (SF)
    - o Locate and review all readings and assignments in the Subject Folders (SF), Digital Library (DL), and Hard Copies (HC)
    - o Note and gather needed supplies for the unit
- ☐ Read the Virtue Lesson
- ☐ Email or call R.A.S. if you have questions or technical difficulty.

PREP FOR CO-OP

- ☐ Print your "Co-op Job Sheet" and prep for your job
- ☐ Make sure your child is ready for his or her presentation if assigned to present
- ☐ Gather maps, notebooks, prayer sheet, and other supplies the night or morning before the co-op meets.
- ☐ Gather students' assignments the night or morning before the co-op meets
- ☐ Listen to the Memory Work on the way!

PREP FOR UPCOMING WEEKS — <u>LOOK AHEAD AT UNIT 21</u>

- ☐ Make advanced purchases, as necessary
- ☐ Begin to gather books and materials

PLANNER ABBREVIATION KEY

DL	Digital Library (in course suite)
SF	Subject Folder (in course suite)
HC	Hard Copy
PLL	*Primary Language Lessons* (book)
ILL	*Intermediate Language Lessons* (book)
RS4K	*Real Science 4 Kids* (book)
I-CAT	*Illustrated Catechism* (book)
OHF-1	*Our Holy Faith, Book 1* (book)
OHF-2	*Our Holy Faith, Book 2* (book)
OHF-4	*Our Holy Faith, Book 4* (book)
OHF-1-TM	*Our Holy Faith, Book 1, Teacher's Manual* (book)

OVERVIEW

Common Topics (All students PreK to 6th)

Virtue:	Compassion
Hymn:	Hosanna filio David
Prayers:	Signum Crucis, Angelus, Pater Noster, Ave Maria, Gloria Patri
History:	Western Expansion (19th Century)
Science:	Static and Current Electricity

History Themes

In Unit 20 we embark on the adventures of the West, perhaps one of the most romanticized and idealized periods in American history. What we know is that it was a period of conflict between the Native Americans and settlers, mixed with stories of friendship and massacre. The K-3rd Grade students will read the *Little House* books, written by Laura Ingalls Wilder, a settler herself. We find hints of tension in her books, but they allow the child to focus on the "good" of the period. 4th-6th Grade students having chosen the alternative reading of *Captains Courageous* find themselves with a 15 year old boy, son of a rich American entrepreneur, who is saved from drowning in the North Atlantic Ocean. We follow his plight until he is finally reunited with his mother. The contrast between the poor Ingalls family making its way West, sometimes retreating back East, and that of the young Harvey gives a glimpse into struggles suffered by early Americans.

How to Apply History to Everyday Life

Our Mission. As we read this week, we reflect on the struggles of past Americans. We might consider the massacres, both of Native Americans and of Settlers. Were Americans in the "right" to spread west? Did the Native Americans have rights to the land? Should we be proud of the way we settled the West? We recall that one of the contentious points between Great Britain and the Revolutionists was the question about settling beyond the Appalachian Mountains. Great Britain feared conflict with the Indians and did not wish to endanger the colonists. Was Great Britain correct on this point? We might reflect upon it.

On the other hand, what did the settlers offer and bring to the Native Americans? Did the Native Americans have "culture" that was civilized and noble? What did Christianity do for the Indian?

Important People, Events, and Places to Know (Potential Student Presentations)

❖ Aaron Burr kills Alexander Hamilton in duel (1804); Lewis and Clark set out on their expedition; Napoleon Bonaparte becomes emperor of France; Elizabeth Ann Seton becomes a Catholic (1805); Great Britain stopping American ships at sea; Lewis and

OVERVIEW

Clark return to St. Louis (1806); Battle between the HMS Leopard and the USS Chesapeake (1807); Revolution against Spain in Mexico (1810); battle between USS President and HMS Little Belt (1811); Elizabeth Ann Seton forms the Sisters of Charity (1812); U.S. declares war against Great Britain (1812); Battle of Lake Erie (1813); Napoleon Bonaparte gives up throne (1814); Treaty of Ghent, end of the war of 1812 (1814); Battle of New Orleans (1814); General Jackson invades Florida (1817)

❖ Saints of the late Nineteenth Century:

- St. Augustine Zhao Rong (1815)
- St. Andrew Dung-Lac & Companions (1820-1866)
- St. Julie Billiart (1816)
- St Elizabeth Ann Seton (1821)
- Our Lady of the Miraculous Medal (1830)
- St. Andrew Hubert Fournet (1834)
- Sts. Andrew Kim Tae-gon & Companions (1839-1867)
- St. Rose Philippine Duchesne (1852)
- St. Dominic Savio (1857)
- Our Lady of Lourdes (1858)
- St. John Vianney (1859)
- St. John Neumann (1860)
- St. Madeleine Sophie Barat (1865)
- St. Euphrasia Pelletier (1868)
- St. Peter Julian Eymard (1868)
- St. Anthony Mary Claret (1870)
- St. Catherine Laboure (1876)
- St. Charles Lwanga & Companions (1887)
- St. John Bosco (1888)
- St. Conrad (1894)
- St. Therese of Lisieux (1897)
- St. Sharbel Makhluf (1898)

Additional Project Ideas

- Visit a local museum.
- Map the Western Expansion of your own family (if you live in the West)
- Research a Native American tribe of the Plains

PLANNER ~ Unit 20 (Co-op)

Week of _____   *Liturgical Theme & Colors* _____

Family Challenge-Task
Goals _____

_____

_____

_____

Reminders _____

_____

_____

PRESCHOOL

	Music	Art, Reading, Religion	Virtue
Co-op	See "Music" heading below	Do craft **PreK Lesson A** (SF)	Review Virtue U-V (SF); practice "virtue training"
Day 2-4	See "Music" heading below	Do **Letter Book U-V** (SF); do **coloring pages** (SF); read & drill I-CAT, p. 21 (HC)	Review Virtue U-V (SF); practice "virtue training"

KINDERGARTEN – 6ᵀᴴ GRADE

ART   **CCM**

	K-6th Grade		K-6th Grade
Day 1	Do **All Lesson A** (SF)		Unit 20
Day 2-4	Review **All Lesson A** (SF); do home follow-up.		Listen to Unit 20 every day

HISTORY

	K-1st Grades	2nd-3rd Grades	4th-6th Grades
Co-op	Do **K-1 Lesson A** (SF).	Do **2-3 Lesson A** (SF).	Do **4-6 Lesson A** (SF).
Day 2	Read *Little House Books* (DL) 1-2 this week; Choose and do reading (or other project) from "Extras" (SF); draw a picture inspired by the readings	Read *Little House Books* (DL) 1-2 this week; Choose and do reading (or other project) from "Extras" (SF); draw a picture inspired by the readings	Read *Captains Courageous* (DL); Choose and do readings (or other projects) from "Extras" (SF); begin writing **4-6 Activity A** (SF).
Day 3	Do craft **K-1 Activity A** (SF)	Do map **2-3 Activity A** (SF)	Do map **4-6 Activity B** (SF)
Day 4	Do coloring page (SF)	Do craft **2-3 Activity B** (SF); Do coloring page (SF)	Do online **4-6 Activity C** (SF); summarize the reading this week and draw!

LANGUAGE ARTS

Co-op	Complete **K-1 Lesson A** (SF).	Complete **2-3 Lesson A** (SF).	Complete **4-6 Lesson A** (SF).
Day 2	Review **K-1 Lesson A** (SF); do **K-1 Activity A** (SF).	Review **2-3 Lesson A** (SF); do **2-3 Activity A** (SF).	Review **4-6 Lesson A** (SF); do **4-6 Activity A** (SF)
Day 3	Do pre-cursive copywork **K-1 Activity B** (SF).	Do cursive copywork **2-3 Activity B** (SF).	Complete first draft in **4-6 Activity A** (SF).
Day 4	Do narration and illustration **K-1 Activity C** (SF)	Do composition and illustration **2-3 Activity C** (SF)	Complete final draft in **4-6 Activity A** (SF).

LATIN/GREEK

Co-op	Practice Hosanna Filio David (SF)	Practice Hosanna Filio David (SF); do *Greek Primer* 20.1–4 (SF)	Practice Hosanna Filio David (SF); do *Reading Greek* 20.1–2 (SF)
Day 2	Listen to CCM Unit 20 Latin prayer	Listen to CCM Unit 20 Latin prayer; do *Greek Primer* 20.5	Listen to CCM Unit 20 Latin prayer; do *Reading Greek* 20.3–4 (SF)
Day 3	Practice all the *Schola Rosa* Latin assembly prayers!	Practice all the *Schola Rosa* Latin assembly prayers!; do *Greek Primer* 20.5 (SF)	Practice all the *Schola Rosa* Latin assembly prayers!; do *Reading Greek* 20.4 (SF)
Day 4	Listen to Hosanna Filio David video (SF); Sing along!	Listen to Hosanna Filio David video (SF); Sing along!; finish *Greek Primer* Unit 20 (SF)	Listen to Hosanna Filio David video (SF); Sing along!; finish *Reading Greek* Unit 20 (SF) and review/check work

MATH

	Level A	Level B	Level C
Co-op	None	None	None
Day 2-4	See *Ray's Primary*, Mastery Chart~ Do next lesson (DL)	See *Ray's Intellectual*, Mastery Chart~ Do next lesson (DL)	See *Ray's Practical*, Mastery Chart~ Do next lesson (DL)

MUSIC

	K-6th Grade
Co-op	Review **All Lesson A** (SF). Use audio files
Day 2-4	to sing along with: Hymn of the Week (Latin SF); Exercises Group 1, 2, 3, & 4; Gloria; ite missa est; Kyrie; Agnus Dei; Sanctus; Merrily We Roll Along; Oats, Peas, Beans & Barley Grow; Lightly Row; Aura Lee; Lavender Blue; Home on the Range (DL). See addendum to Lesson for 2nd year additions.

READING

	Primer (pre-reader)	Reader
Co-op	None	None
Day 2-4	See *McGuffey's Eclectic Primer*, "Mastery Chart" ~ Do next lesson (DL)	See *McGuffey's Eclectic Readers*, "Mastery Chart" ~ Do next lesson (DL)

RELIGION — *Liturgical Feast lessons can be moved to correspond to their dates — simply adjust the schedule accordingly*

	K-1st Grades	2nd-3rd Grades	4th-6th Grades
Co-op	Begin **K-1 Lesson A** (SF).	Begin **2-3 Lesson A** (SF). Drill Q & A.	Begin **4-6 Lesson A** (SF). Drill Q & A.
Day 2	Review/complete **K-1 Lesson A** (SF).	Review/complete **2-3 Lesson A** (SF). Drill Q & A.	Review/complete **4-6 Lesson A** (SF). Drill Q & A.
Day 3	Begin **K-1 Lesson B** (SF).	Begin **2-3 Lesson B** (SF). Drill Q & A.	Complete activity(-ies) from the "Let Us Work Together" section OHF-4, pp. 232-236.
Day 4	Review/complete **K-1 Lesson B** (SF).	Review/complete **2-3 Lesson B** (SF). Drill Q & A.	Complete activity(ies) from the "Let Us Work Together" section OHF-4, pp. 232-236.

SCIENCE

Co-op	Do **All Lesson A** (SF).	Do **All Lesson A** (SF).	Do **All Lesson A** (SF).
Day 2	Review **All Lesson A** (SF); Read Ch. 35-39 in *The Storybook of Science* (DL).	Review **All Lesson A** (SF); Read Ch. 35-39 in *The Storybook of Science* (DL).	Review **All Lesson A** (SF); Read Ch. 35-39 in *The Storybook of Science* (DL); do Nature Journal from **4-6 Lesson A** (SF). Read Ch. 6 *RS4K, Focus on Elementary Physics* and do Experiment 6.
Day 3	Complete free-time experiment **K-1 Activity A** (SF).	Complete free-time experiment **2-3 Activity A** (SF).	Complete free-time experiment **4-6 Activity A** (SF) and do **4-6 Activity B** (SF).
Day 4	Do drawing **K-1 Activity B** (SF); if possible, go on a nature walk.	Do description & illustration **2-3 Activity B** (SF); if possible, go on a nature walk.	Do library research **4-6 Activity C** (SF); if possible, go on a nature walk and do Nature Journaling.

VIRTUE

	K-6th Grades
Co-op	Do **All Virtue Lesson A – Compassion** (SF)
Day 2-4	Practice "virtue training"

CYCLE III
UNIT 21

WESTERN EXPANSION

UNIT CHECKLIST

PREP FOR HOME

☐ Print and read this Handbook

☐ Read the Overview

☐ Review the Planner; do the following:

    o Locate and review all Lessons and Activities in the Subject Folders (SF)

    o Locate and review all readings and assignments in the Subject Folders (SF), Digital Library (DL), and Hard Copies (HC)

    o Note and gather needed supplies for the unit

☐ Read the Virtue Lesson

☐ Email or call R.A.S. if you have questions or technical difficulty.

PREP FOR CO-OP

☐ Print your "Co-op Job Sheet" and prep for your job

☐ Make sure your child is ready for his or her presentation if assigned to present

☐ Gather maps, notebooks, prayer sheet, and other supplies the night or morning before the co-op meets.

☐ Gather students' assignments the night or morning before the co-op meets

☐ Listen to the Memory Work on the way!

PREP FOR UPCOMING WEEKS — <u>LOOK AHEAD AT UNIT 21</u>

☐ Make advanced purchases, as necessary

☐ Begin to gather books and materials

PLANNER ABBREVIATION KEY

DL	Digital Library (in course suite)
SF	Subject Folder (in course suite)
HC	Hard Copy
PLL	*Primary Language Lessons* (book)
ILL	*Intermediate Language Lessons* (book)
RS4K	*Real Science 4 Kids* (book)
I-CAT	*Illustrated Catechism* (book)
OHF-1	*Our Holy Faith, Book 1* (book)
OHF-2	*Our Holy Faith, Book 2* (book)
OHF-4	*Our Holy Faith, Book 4* (book)
OHF-1-TM	*Our Holy Faith, Book 1, Teacher's Manual* (book)

OVERVIEW

Common Topics (All students PreK to 6th)

Virtue:	Cheerfulness
Hymn:	Hosanna filio David
Prayers:	Signum Crucis, Angelus, Pater Noster, Ave Maria, Gloria Patri
History:	Western Expansion (19th Century)
Science:	Electricity & Magnetism

History Themes

In Unit 21 we continue our studies of Western Expansion begun in Unit 20. Our young students continue with the *Little House* books. In the 4th-6th Grade we introduce the lawlessness of the Plains and the Gold Rush with the book *Redskin and Cowboy: A Tale of the Western Plains.*

How to Apply History to Everyday Life

Our Mission. This week we consider a life without law, a life without rules. What would our day be like if we could not count on people to drive on the "right side" of the road? What would life be like if we could not leave our house for fear of someone else moving into it? What would life be like if the train stopped coming to town to deliver food? What would life be like if we had to depend on our neighbors and ourselves to keep criminals out of town? How would we behave differently toward our neighbor then?

As we reflect on this life, we might also consider the commandment "Love thy neighbor." Who is our neighbor? Is our neighbor always a friend? How do we behave toward our neighbor when lawlessness reigns? What do we learn from the Ingalls family about how to treat your neighbor? How does Ma "welcome" the Indians? How does Pa behave around the Indians?

Important People, Events, and Places to Know (Potential Student Presentations)

❖ Missouri Compromise (1820); John Quincy Adams elected president (1824); Jedediah Smith's expedition to California (1826); William Lloyd Garrison publishing the *Liberator* (1831); Jackson forms the Democratic party (1832); Black Hawk War; Sam Houston arrives in Texas; Samuel F.B. Morse invents the electric telegraph; First Americans settle in Oregon (1834); Cyrus McCormick patents his mechanical reaper; Seminole War under Osceola (1835); Cherokee "Trail of Tears" (1838); End of Seminole War (1842); Texas enters the Union (1845); Bear Flag Revolt (1846); U.S. declares war on Mexico; Elias Howe invents the sewing machine;

OVERVIEW

❖ Saints of the late Nineteenth Century:

- St. Augustine Zhao Rong (1815)
- St. Andrew Dung-Lac & Companions (1820-1866)
- St. Julie Billiart (1816)
- St Elizabeth Ann Seton (1821)
- Our Lady of the Miraculous Medal (1830)
- St. Andrew Hubert Fournet (1834)
- Sts. Andrew Kim Tae-gon & Companions (1839-1867)
- St. Rose Philippine Duchesne (1852)
- St. Dominic Savio (1857)
- Our Lady of Lourdes (1858)

- St. John Vianney (1859)
- St. John Neumann (1860)
- St. Madeleine Sophie Barat (1865)
- St. Euphrasia Pelletier (1868)
- St. Peter Julian Eymard (1868)
- St. Anthony Mary Claret (1870)
- St. Catherine Laboure (1876)
- St. Charles Lwanga & Companions (1887)
- St. John Bosco (1888)
- St. Conrad (1894)
- St. Therese of Lisieux (1897)
- St. Sharbel Makhluf (1898)

Additional Project Ideas

- Visit a local museum.
- Map the Western Expansion of your own family (if you live in the West)
- Research a Native American tribe of the Plains

Week of _____ *Liturgical Theme & Colors* _____

Family Challenge-Task
Goals _____

_____

_____

Reminders _____

_____

_____

_____

PRESCHOOL

	Music	Art, Reading, Religion	Virtue
Co-op	See "Music" heading below	Do craft **PreK Lesson A** (SF)	Review Virtue W-X (SF); practice "virtue training"
Day 2-4	See "Music" heading below	Do **Letter Book W-X** (SF); do **coloring pages** (SF); read & drill I-CAT, p. 23 (HC)	Review Virtue W-X (SF); practice "virtue training"

KINDERGARTEN – 6TH GRADE

ART   **CCM**

	K-6th Grade		K-6th Grade
Co-op	Do **All Lesson A** (SF).		Unit 21
Day 2-4	Review **All Lesson A** (SF) and do home follow-up.		Listen to Unit 21 every day

HISTORY

	K-1st Grades	2nd-3rd Grades	4th-6th Grades
Co-op	Do **K-1 Lesson A** (SF).	Do **2-3 Lesson A** (SF).	Do **4-6 Lesson A** (SF).
Day 2	Read *Little House Books* (DL) 3-4 this week; Choose and do reading (or other project) from "Extras" (SF); draw a picture inspired by the readings	Read *Little House Books* (DL) 3-4 this week; Choose and do reading (or other project) from "Extras" (SF); draw a picture inspired by the readings	Read *Redskin and Cowboy: A Tale of the Western Plains,* first half (DL); Choose and do readings (or other projects) from "Extras" (SF); begin writing **4-6 Activity A** (SF).
Day 3	Do craft **K-1 Activity A** (SF)	Do map **2-3 Activity A** (SF)	Do map **4-6 Activity B** (SF)
Day 4	Do coloring page (SF)	Do craft **2-3 Activity B**; Do coloring page (SF)	Do online **4-6 Activity C (SF)**; summarize the reading this week and draw!

LANGUAGE ARTS

	K-1st Grades	2nd-3rd Grades	4th-6th Grades
Co-op	Complete **K-1 Lesson A** (SF).	Complete **2-3 Lesson A** (SF).	Complete **4-6 Lesson A** (SF).
Day 2	Review **K-1 Lesson A** (SF); do **K-1 Activity A** (SF).	Review **2-3 Lesson A** (SF); do **2-3 Activity A** (SF).	Review **4-6 Lesson A** (SF); do **4-6 Activity A** (SF)
Day 3	Do pre-cursive copywork **K-1 Activity B** (SF).	Do cursive copywork **2-3 Activity B** (SF).	Complete first draft in **4-6 Activity A** (SF).
Day 4	Do narration and illustration **K-1 Activity C** (SF)	Do composition and illustration **2-3 Activity C** (SF)	Complete final draft in **4-6 Activity A** (SF).

LATIN/GREEK

	K-1st Grades	2nd-3rd Grades	4th-6th Grades
Co-op	Practice Hosanna Filio David (SF)	Practice Hosanna Filio David (SF); do *Greek Primer* 21.1–4 (SF)	Practice Hosanna Filio David (SF); do *Reading Greek* 21.1–2 (SF)
Day 2	Listen to CCM Unit 21 Latin prayer	Listen to CCM Unit 21 Latin prayer; do *Greek Primer* 21.5	Listen to CCM Unit 21 Latin prayer; do *Reading Greek* 21.3–4 (SF)
Day 3	Practice all the *Schola Rosa* Latin assembly prayers!	Practice all the *Schola Rosa* Latin assembly prayers!; do *Greek Primer* 21.5 (SF)	Practice all the *Schola Rosa* Latin assembly prayers!; do *Reading Greek* 21.4 (SF)
Day 4	Listen to Hosanna Filio David video (SF); Sing along!	Listen to Hosanna Filio David video (SF); Sing along!; finish *Greek Primer* Unit 21 (SF)	Listen to Hosanna Filio David video (SF); Sing along!; finish *Reading Greek* Unit 21 (SF) and review/check work

MATH

	Level A	Level B	Level C
Co-op	None	None	None
Day 2-4	See *Ray's Primary*, Mastery Chart~ Do next lesson (DL)	See *Ray's Intellectual*, Mastery Chart~ Do next lesson (DL)	See *Ray's Practical*, Mastery Chart~ Do next lesson (DL)

MUSIC

	K-6th Grade
Co-op	Review **All Lesson A** (SF). Use audio files to
Day 2-4	sing along with: Hymn of the Week (Latin SF); Exercises Group 1, 2, 3, & 4; Gloria; ite missa est; Kyrie; Agnus Dei; Sanctus; Credo; Merrily We Roll Along; Oats, Peas, Beans & Barley Grow; Lightly Row; Aura Lee; Lavender Blue; Home on the Range (DL). See addendum to Lesson for 2nd year additions.

READING

	Primer (pre-reader)	Reader
Co-op	None	None
	See *McGuffey's Eclectic Primer*, "Mastery Chart" ~ Do next lesson (DL)	See *McGuffey's Eclectic Readers*, "Mastery Chart" ~ Do next lesson (DL)

RELIGION — *Liturgical Feast lessons can be moved to correspond to their dates – simply adjust the schedule accordingly*

	K-1st Grades	2nd-3rd Grades	4th-6th Grades
Co-op	Begin **K-1 Lesson A** (SF).	Begin **2-3 Lesson A** (SF). Drill Q & A.	Begin **4-6 Lesson A** (SF). Drill Q & A.
Day 2	Review/complete **K-1 Lesson A** (SF).	Review/complete **2-3 Lesson A** (SF). Drill Q & A.	Review/complete **4-6 Lesson A** (SF). Drill Q & A.
Day 3	Begin **K-1 Lesson B** (SF).	Review/complete **2-3 Lesson A** (SF). Drill Q & A.	Complete activity(-ies) from the "Let Us Work Together" section OHf-4, pp. 232-236.
Day 4	Review/complete **K-1 Lesson B** (SF).	Review/complete **2-3 Lesson A** (SF). Drill Q & A.	Complete activity(ies) from the "Let Us Work Together" section OHf-4, pp. 232-236.

SCIENCE

Co-op	Do **All Lesson A** (SF).	Do **All Lesson A** (SF).	Do **All Lesson A** (SF).
Day 2	Review **All Lesson A** (SF); Choose and read a story or two from *The Storybook of Science* (DL).	Review **All Lesson A** (SF); Choose and read a story or two from *The Storybook of Science* (DL).	Review **All Lesson A** (SF); Choose and read a story or two from *The Storybook of Science* (DL); do Nature Journal from **4-6 Lesson A** (SF). Read Ch. 7 RS4K, *Focus on Elementary Physics* and do Experiment 7.
Day 3	Complete free-time experiment **K-1 Activity A** (SF).	Complete free-time experiment **2-3 Activity A** (SF).	Complete free-time experiment **4-6 Activity A** (SF) and do **4-6 Activity B** (SF).
Day 4	Do drawing **K-1 Activity B** (SF); if possible, go on a nature walk.	Do description & illustration **2-3 Activity B** (SF); if possible, go on a nature walk.	Do library research **4-6 Activity C** (SF); if possible, go on a nature walk and do Nature Journaling.

VIRTUE

	K-6th Grades
Field	Do **All Virtue Lesson A – Cheerfulness** (SF)
Day 2-4	Practice "virtue training"

CYCLE III
UNIT 22

GOLD RUSH

UNIT CHECKLIST

PREP FOR HOME

- ☐ Print and read this Handbook
- ☐ Read the Overview
- ☐ Review the Planner; do the following:
  - ○ Locate and review all Lessons and Activities in the Subject Folders (SF)
  - ○ Locate and review all readings and assignments in the Subject Folders (SF), Digital Library (DL), and Hard Copies (HC)
  - ○ Note and gather needed supplies for the unit
- ☐ Read the Virtue Lesson
- ☐ Email or call R.A.S. if you have questions or technical difficulty.

PREP FOR CO-OP

- ☐ Print your "Co-op Job Sheet" and prep for your job
- ☐ Make sure your child is ready for his or her presentation if assigned to present
- ☐ Gather maps, notebooks, prayer sheet, and other supplies the night or morning before the co-op meets.
- ☐ Gather students' assignments the night or morning before the co-op meets
- ☐ Listen to the Memory Work on the way!

PREP FOR UPCOMING WEEKS — <u>LOOK AHEAD AT UNIT 21</u>

- ☐ Make advanced purchases, as necessary
- ☐ Begin to gather books and materials

PLANNER ABBREVIATION KEY

DL	Digital Library (in course suite)
SF	Subject Folder (in course suite)
HC	Hard Copy
PLL	*Primary Language Lessons* (book)
ILL	*Intermediate Language Lessons* (book)
RS4K	*Real Science 4 Kids* (book)
I-CAT	*Illustrated Catechism* (book)
OHF-1	*Our Holy Faith, Book 1* (book)
OHF-2	*Our Holy Faith, Book 2* (book)
OHF-4	*Our Holy Faith, Book 4* (book)
OHF-1-TM	*Our Holy Faith, Book 1, Teacher's Manual* (book)

OVERVIEW

Common Topics (All students PreK to 6th)

Virtue:	Steadfastness
Hymn:	Hosanna filio David
Prayers:	Signum Crucis, Angelus, Pater Noster, Ave Maria, Gloria Patri
History:	Gold Rush
Science:	Review

History Themes

In Unit 22 we find ourselves focusing on the California and Klondike Gold Rushes. The K-3rd Grade students read *The Call of the Wild* as a literary introduction to the Klondike Gold Rush, and the 4th-6th Grade students continue to read *Redskin and Cowboy: A Tale of the Western Plains,* which includes descriptions of the California Gold Rush. Both are full of adventure and sorrow. We see in these books the ugliness of the time and of men full of greed. As we read these books, we also have our history textbook to guide us in understanding the historical context.

How to Apply History to Everyday Life

Our Mission. As we read this week we are called to reflect on the commandment "Covet not your neighbor's wife" and "Covet not your neighbor's goods." The stories of the Gold conquests are ridden with covetousness and greed. What is a life motivated by the desire for *more*? What happens to our characters? Do we find virtuous characters who choose another route?

Important People, Events, and Places to Know (Potential Student Presentations)

❖ Battle of Buena Vista (1847); Treaty of Guadalupe-Hidalgo (1848); End of the Mexican-American War; God discovered in California; Compromise of 1850; Father De Smet brings peace between the U.S. and Plains Indians (1851); Kansas-Nebraska Act passed (1854); Founding of the Republican Party; Dred Scott Decision (1856); Execution of John Brown (1859); Abraham Lincoln elected President (1860); South Carolina secedes from the Union; Death of Bishop Neumann (1860); Gulf states secede from the Union (1861)

❖ Saints of the late Nineteenth Century:

- St. Augustine Zhao Rong (1815)
- St. Andrew Dung-Lac & Companions (1820-1866)
- St. Julie Billiart (1816)

- St Elizabeth Ann Seton (1821)
- Our Lady of the Miraculous Medal (1830)
- St. Andrew Hubert Fournet (1834)

OVERVIEW

- Sts. Andrew Kim Tae-gon & Companions (1839-1867)
- St. Rose Philippine Duchesne (1852)
- St. Dominic Savio (1857)
- Our Lady of Lourdes (1858)
- St. John Vianney (1859)
- St. John Neumann (1860)
- St. Madeleine Sophie Barat (1865)
- St. Euphrasia Pelletier (1868)
- St. Peter Julian Eymard (1868)
- St. Anthony Mary Claret (1870)
- St. Catherine Laboure (1876)
- St. Charles Lwanga & Companions (1887)
- St. John Bosco (1888)
- St. Conrad (1894)
- St. Therese of Lisieux (1897)
- St. Sharbel Makhluf (1898)

Additional Project Ideas

- Pan for Gold!
- Map the California and Klondike Gold Rushes

PLANNER ~ Unit 22 (Field Trip)

Week of _____   *Liturgical Theme & Colors* _____

Family Challenge-Task
Goals _____

_____

_____

Reminders _____

_____

PRESCHOOL

	Music	Art, Reading, Religion	Virtue
Field	See "Music" heading below	Do craft **PreK Lesson A** (SF)	Review Virtues S-X (SF); practice "virtue training"
Day 2-4	See "Music" heading below	Review Letters S-X (SF), review & drill I-CAT, pp 19-23 (HC)	Review Virtues S-X (SF); practice "virtue training"

KINDERGARTEN – 6TH GRADE

ART   **CCM**

	K-6th Grade	K-6th Grade
Field	Review **All Lesson A** (SF), Units 19-21.	Unit 22.
Day 2-4	Do extra art task from home follow-up sections, if there is time.	Listen to Unit 22 every day

HISTORY

	K-1st Grades	2nd-3rd Grades	4th-6th Grades
Field	Read *The Call of the Wild* (DL).	Read *The Call of the Wild* (DL).	Read *Redskin and Cowboy: A Tale of the Western Plains*, second half (DL).
Day 2	Choose and do reading (or other project) from "Extras" (SF); draw a picture inspired by the readings;	Read *Little House Books* (DL) 1-2 this week; Choose and do reading (or other project) from "Extras" (SF); draw a picture inspired by the readings	Read *Redskin and Cowboy: A Tale of the Western Plains* (DL); Choose and do readings (or other projects) from "Extras" (SF); *Song of Bernadetta* (HC).
Day 3	Do hands-on **K-1 Activity A** (SF)	Do map **2-3 Activity A** (SF)	Do reading & discussion **4-6 Activity A** (SF)
Day 4	Do coloring page (SF)	Do hands-on **2-3 Activity B** (SF); Do coloring page (SF)	Do reading & discussion **4-6 Activity B (SF)**; summarize the reading this week and draw!

LANGUAGE ARTS

	K-1st Grades	2nd-3rd Grades	4th-6th Grades
Field	Complete **K-1 Lesson A** (SF).	Complete **2-3 Lesson A** (SF).	Complete **4-6 Lesson A** (SF).
Day 2	Review **K-1 Lesson A** (SF); do **K-1 Activity A** (SF).	Review **2-3 Lesson A** (SF); do **2-3 Activity A** (SF).	Review **4-6 Lesson A** (SF); do **4-6 Activity A** (SF)
Day 3	Do pre-cursive copywork **K-1 Activity B** (SF).	Do cursive copywork **2-3 Activity B** (SF).	Complete first draft in **4-6 Activity A** (SF).
Day 4	Do narration and illustration **K-1 Activity C** (SF)	Do composition and illustration **2-3 Activity C** (SF)	Complete final draft in **4-6 Activity A** (SF).

LATIN/GREEK

	K-1st Grades	2nd-3rd Grades	4th-6th Grades
Field	Practice Hosanna Filio David (SF)	Practice Hosanna Filio David (SF); do *Greek Primer* 22.1–4 (SF)	Practice Hosanna Filio David (SF); do *Reading Greek* 22.1–2 (SF)
Day 2	Listen to CCM Unit 22 Latin prayer	Listen to CCM Unit 22 Latin prayer; do *Greek Primer* 22.5	Listen to CCM Unit 22 Latin prayer; do *Reading Greek* 22.3–4 (SF)
Day 3	Practice all the *Schola Rosa* Latin assembly prayers!	Practice all the *Schola Rosa* Latin assembly prayers!; do *Greek Primer* 22.5 (SF)	Practice all the *Schola Rosa* Latin assembly prayers!; do *Reading Greek* 22.4 (SF)
Day 4	Listen to Hosanna Filio David video (SF); Sing along!	Listen to Hosanna Filio David video (SF); Sing along!; finish *Greek Primer* Unit 22 (SF)	Listen to Hosanna Filio David video (SF); Sing along!; finish *Reading Greek* Unit 22 (SF) and review/check work

MATH

	Level A	Level B	Level C
Field	None	None	None
Day 2-4	See *Ray's Primary*, Mastery Chart~ Do next lesson (DL)	See *Ray's Intellectual*, Mastery Chart~ Do next lesson (DL)	See *Ray's Practical*, Mastery Chart~ Do next lesson (DL)

MUSIC

	K-6th Grade
Field Day 2-4	Review **All Lesson A** (SF). Use audio files to sing along with: Hymn of the Week (Latin SF); Exercises Group 1, 2, 3, & 4; Gloria; ite missa est; Kyrie; Agnus Dei; Sanctus; Credo; Merrily We Roll Along; Oats, Peas, Beans & Barley Grow; Lightly Row; Aura Lee; Lavender Blue; Home on the Range (DL). See addendum to Lesson for 2nd year additions.

READING

	Primer (pre-reader)	Reader
Field	None	None
	See *McGuffey's Eclectic Primer*, "Mastery Chart"~ Do next lesson (DL)	See *McGuffey's Eclectic Readers*, "Mastery Chart" ~ Do next lesson (DL)

RELIGION — *Liturgical Feast lessons can be moved to correspond to their dates – simply adjust the schedule accordingly*

	K-1st Grades	2nd-3rd Grades	4th-6th Grades
Field	Begin **K-1 Lesson A** (SF).	Begin **2-3 Lesson A** (SF). Drill Q & A.	Begin **4-6 Lesson A** (SF). Drill Q & A.
Day 2	Review/complete **K-1 Lesson A** (SF).	Review/complete **2-3 Lesson A** (SF). Drill Q & A.	Review/complete **4-6 Lesson A** (SF). Drill Q & A.
Day 3	Begin **K-1 Lesson B** (SF).	Review/complete **2-3 Lesson A** (SF). Drill Q & A.	Complete activity(-ies) from the "Let Us Work Together" section OHF-4, pp. 232-236.
Day 4	Review/complete **K-1 Lesson B** (SF).	Review/complete **2-3 Lesson A** (SF). Drill Q & A.	Complete activity(ies) from the "Let Us Work Together" section OHF-4, pp. 232-236.

SCIENCE

Field	Review Units 19-22 and complete any missing assignments.	Review Units 19-22 and complete any missing assignments.	Review Units 19-22 and complete any missing assignments.
Day 2	Read selections from Fabre's *Story Book of Science* (DL).	Read selections from Fabre's *Story Book of Science* (DL).	Read selections from Fabre's *Story Book of Science* (DL).
Day 3	Complete free-time experiment **K-1 Activity A** (SF).	Complete free-time experiment **2-3 Activity A** (SF).	Complete free-time experiment **4-6 Activity A** (SF).
Day 4	Continue **K-1 Activity A** (SF).	Continue **2-3 Activity A** (SF).	Continue **4-6 Activity A** (SF).

VIRTUE

	K-6th Grades
Field	**Do All Virtue Lesson A – Steadfastness** (SF)
Day 2-4	Practice "virtue training"

CYCLE III
UNIT 23

CIVIL WAR
& RECONSTRUCTION

UNIT CHECKLIST

PREP FOR HOME

- ☐ Print and read this Handbook
- ☐ Read the Overview
- ☐ Review the Planner; do the following:
    - o Locate and review all Lessons and Activities in the Subject Folders (SF)
    - o Locate and review all readings and assignments in the Subject Folders (SF), Digital Library (DL), and Hard Copies (HC)
    - o Note and gather needed supplies for the unit
- ☐ Read the Virtue Lesson
- ☐ Email or call R.A.S. if you have questions or technical difficulty.

PREP FOR CO-OP

- ☐ Print your "Co-op Job Sheet" and prep for your job
- ☐ Make sure your child is ready for his or her presentation if assigned to present
- ☐ Gather maps, notebooks, prayer sheet, and other supplies the night or morning before the co-op meets.
- ☐ Gather students' assignments the night or morning before the co-op meets
- ☐ Listen to the Memory Work on the way!

PREP FOR UPCOMING WEEKS — <u>LOOK AHEAD AT UNIT 25</u>

- ☐ Make advanced purchases, as necessary
- ☐ Begin to gather books and materials

PLANNER ABBREVIATION KEY

DL	Digital Library (in course suite)
SF	Subject Folder (in course suite)
HC	Hard Copy
PLL	*Primary Language Lessons* (book)
ILL	*Intermediate Language Lessons* (book)
RS4K	*Real Science 4 Kids* (book)
I-CAT	*Illustrated Catechism* (book)
OHF-1	*Our Holy Faith, Book 1* (book)
OHF-2	*Our Holy Faith, Book 2* (book)
OHF-4	*Our Holy Faith, Book 4* (book)
OHF-1-TM	*Our Holy Faith, Book 1, Teacher's Manual* (book)

OVERVIEW

Common Topics (All students PreK to 6th)

Virtue:	Dependability
Hymn:	Ecce lignum
Prayers:	Signum Crucis, Angelus, Pater Noster, Ave Maria, Gloria Patri
History:	Civil War & Reconstruction (1861-1865)
Science:	Sound

History Themes

In Unit 23 students are introduced to the American Civil War, a war that was fought between families for many reasons, including slavery and economic tensions between Northern and Southern business interests. Our youngest students are not introduced to the political nuances of this period, but are instead brought to an awareness that this event happened and that it was tragic for both sides. K-3rd Grade students read Louisa May Alcott's novel *Little Women*, which is set during the Civil War. Their father is away at the war for much of the book. 4th-6th Grade students read either Henty's *With Lee in Virginia* or Louisa May Alcott's *Hospital Sketches*. Both of these novels contain graphic descriptions of the ugliness of the war and the suffering that was incurred by the soldiers and their families. Our goal of the K-6th Grade students is to help them sympathize with the families and persons of this time period as they consider how they would feel if such experiences happened in their lifetime.

How to Apply History to Everyday Life

The Church and the Civil War, from the Compendium of Church History (DL). The only part that the Church took in the Civil War was to pray that peace might be restored. Archbishop Kenrick of Baltimore ordered a prayer for peace to be said in the Mass and all religious communities to say the Litany of the Saints for the same end. The spirit and position of the Church was well explained in the pastoral letters of the Third Provincial Council of Cincinnati, May, 1861. "The Catholic Church," it proclaimed, "has carefully preserved her unity of spirit in the bond of peace, literally knowing no North, no South, no East, no West."

In 1861, Archbishop Hughes was called upon by the government to accept a mission of peace to Europe, and by his personal influence, kept France and Spain neutral in the struggle. The Catholic priest cheered and consoled the last moments of the dying soldier. Sisters of Charity, among whom Sister Anthony of Cincinnati was well-known figure, Sisters of St. Joseph, and Sisters of the Holy Cross proved themselves, "The Angels of the Battlefield." The rank and file of American Army were filled with Catholic officers and soldiers. Here could be mentioned the names of such officers as Sheridan, Meagher, Coppinger, and Corcoran in the North, and of Admiral Semmes

OVERVIEW

in the service of the South; while those of Fathers Scully, Corby, and Cooney add luster to the pages of history by their noble work as chaplains.

Important People, Events, and Places to Know (Potential Student Presentations)

- ❖ Abraham runs for Senate (1858); Abraham elected President (1860); South Caroline secedes from Union; Death of Bishop Neumann; Gulf States secede from Union (1861); Formation of the Confederate States; Jefferson Davis elected President of the Confederacy; Fall of Fort Sumter; Virginia and other border states secede; First Battle of Bull Run (Manassas); Battle of Shiloh (1862); Fall New Orleans; Robert E. Lee general of the Army of Northern Virginia; Battle of the Seven Days; Second Battle of Bull Run (Manassas); Battle of Sharpsburg (Antietam); Sioux Uprising in Minnesota; Battle of Fredericksburg; Congress and the Homestead Act; Congress approves transcontinental railroad; Emancipation Proclamation issued (1863); Battles of Chancellorsville, (death of Stonewall Jackson), Gettysburg, Vicksburg, Murfreesboro, Chickamauga, and Chattanooga; Grant becomes commander of the Federal Army (1864); Battles of Wilderness, Spotsylvania Courthouse, and Cold Harbor; Grant besieges Richmond; Battle of Peachtree Creek; General Sherman marches to the sea and reaches Savannah, Georgia; Sherman invades South Carolina, North Carolina(1865); Lee surrenders at Appomattox Court House; Lincoln Assassinated at Ford's Theatre; Amendment XIII added to Constitution and ends slavery.

- ❖ Saints of the late Nineteenth Century:

  - St. Augustine Zhao Rong (1815)
  - St. Andrew Dung-Lac & Companions (1820-1866)
  - St. Julie Billiart (1816)
  - St Elizabeth Ann Seton (1821)
  - Our Lady of the Miraculous Medal (1830)
  - St. Andrew Hubert Fournet (1834)
  - Sts. Andrew Kim Tae-gon & Companions (1839-1867)
  - St. Rose Philippine Duchesne (1852)
  - St. Dominic Savio (1857)
  - Our Lady of Lourdes (1858)
  - St. John Vianney (1859)

  - St. John Neumann (1860)
  - St. Madeleine Sophie Barat (1865)
  - St. Euphrasia Pelletier (1868)
  - St. Peter Julian Eymard (1868)
  - St. Anthony Mary Claret (1870)
  - St. Catherine Laboure (1876)
  - St. Charles Lwanga & Companions (1887)
  - St. John Bosco (1888)
  - St. Conrad (1894)
  - St. Therese of Lisieux (1897)
  - St. Sharbel Makhluf (1898)

OVERVIEW

Additional Project Ideas

- Visit a local museum.
- Map the famous battles of the Civil War
- Research the famous generals of the war

OVERVIEW

Week of _____   *Liturgical Theme & Colors* _____

Family Challenge-Task
Goals _____

_____

_____

Reminders _____

_____

_____

PRESCHOOL

	Music	Art, Reading, Religion	Virtue
Co-op	See "Music" heading below	Do craft **PreK Lesson A** (SF)	Review Virtue Y-Z (SF); practice "virtue training"
Day 2-4	See "Music" heading below	Do **Letter Book Y-Z** (SF); do **coloring pages** (SF); review & drill I-CAT, pp 23 (HC)	Review Virtue Y-Z (SF); practice "virtue training"

KINDERGARTEN – 6TH GRADE

ART   **CCM**

	K-6th Grade		K-6th Grade
Co-op	Do **All Lesson A** (SF).		Unit 23
Day 2-4	Review **All Lesson A** (SF) and do home follow-up.		Listen to Unit 23 every day

HISTORY

	K-1st Grades	2nd-3rd Grades	4th-6th Grades
Co-op	Do **K-1 Lesson A** (SF).	Do **2-3 Lesson A** (SF).	Do **4-6 Lesson A** (SF).
Day 2	Read *Little Women* (DL) this week; Choose and do reading (or other project) from "Extras" (SF); draw a picture inspired by the readings	Read *Little Women* (DL) this week; Choose and do reading (or other project) from "Extras" (SF); draw a picture inspired by the readings	Read *With Lee in Virginia* (DL) or *Hospital Sketches* (DL); Choose and do readings (or other projects) from "Extras" (SF); begin writing **4-6 Activity A** (SF).
Day 3	Do online **K-1 Activity A** (SF)	Do online **2-3 Activity A** (SF)	Do map **4-6 Activity B** (SF)
Day 4	Do coloring page (SF)	Do coloring page (SF)	Do timeline **4-6 Activity C** (SF); summarize the reading this week and draw!

LANGUAGE ARTS

Co-op	Complete **K-1 Lesson A** (SF).	Complete **2-3 Lesson A** (SF).	Complete **4-6 Lesson A** (SF).
Day 2	Review **K-1 Lesson A** (SF); do **K-1 Activity A** (SF).	Review **2-3 Lesson A** (SF); do **2-3 Activity A** (SF).	Review **4-6 Lesson A** (SF); do **4-6 Activity A** (SF)
Day 3	Do pre-cursive copywork **K-1 Activity B** (SF).	Do cursive copywork **2-3 Activity B** (SF).	Complete first draft in **4-6 Activity A** (SF).
Day 4	Do narration and illustration **K-1 Activity C** (SF)	Do composition and illustration **2-3 Activity C** (SF)	Complete final draft in **4-6 Activity A** (SF).

LATIN/GREEK

Co-op	Practice Ecce lignum (SF)	Practice Ecce lignum (SF); do *Greek Primer* 23.1-4 (SF)	Practice Ecce lignum (SF); do *Reading Greek* 23.1-2 (SF)
Day 2	Listen to CCM Unit 23 Latin prayer	Listen to CCM Unit 23 Latin prayer; do *Greek Primer* 21.5	Listen to CCM Unit 23 Latin prayer; do *Reading Greek* 23.3-4 (SF)
Day 3	Practice all the *Schola Rosa* Latin assembly prayers!	Practice all the *Schola Rosa* Latin assembly prayers!; do *Greek Primer* 23.5 (SF)	Practice all the *Schola Rosa* Latin assembly prayers!; do *Reading Greek* 23.4 (SF)
Day 4	Listen to Ecce lignum video (SF); Sing along!	Listen to Ecce lignum video (SF); Sing along!; finish *Greek Primer* Unit 23 (SF)	Listen to Ecce lignum video (SF); Sing along!; finish *Reading Greek* Unit 23 (SF) and review/check work

MATH

	Level A	Level B	Level C
Co-op	None	None	None
Day 2-4	See *Ray's Primary*, Mastery Chart~ Do next lesson (DL)	See *Ray's Intellectual*, Mastery Chart~ Do next lesson (DL)	See *Ray's Practical*, Mastery Chart~ Do next lesson (DL)

MUSIC

	K-6th Grade
Co-op	Review **All Lesson A** (SF). Use audio files to
Day 2-4	sing along with: Hymn of the Week (Latin SF); Exercises Group 1, 2, 3, 4, & 5; Gloria; ite missa est; Kyrie; Agnus Dei; Sanctus; Credo; Merrily We Roll Along; Oats, Peas, Beans & Barley Grow; Lightly Row; Aura Lee; Lavender Blue; Home on the Range (DL). See addendum to Lesson for 2nd year additions.

READING

	Primer (pre-reader)	Reader
	None	None
	See *McGuffey's Eclectic Primer*, "Mastery Chart" ~ Do next lesson (DL)	See *McGuffey's Eclectic Readers*, "Mastery Chart" ~ Do next lesson (DL)

RELIGION — *Liturgical Feast lessons can be moved to correspond to their dates – simply adjust the schedule accordingly*

	K-1st Grades	2nd-3rd Grades	4th-6th Grades
Co-op	Begin **K-1 Lesson A** (SF).	Begin **2-3 Lesson A** (SF). Drill Q & A.	Begin **4-6 Lesson A** (SF). Drill Q & A.
Day 2	Review/complete **K-1 Lesson A** (SF).	Review/complete **2-3 Lesson A** (SF). Drill Q & A.	Review/complete **4-6 Lesson A** (SF). Drill Q & A.
Day 3	Begin **K-1 Lesson B** (SF).	Review/complete **2-3 Lesson A** (SF). Drill Q & A.	Complete activity(-ies) from the "Let Us Work Together" section OHF-4, pp. 232-236.
Day 4	Review/complete **K-1 Lesson B** (SF).	Review/complete **2-3 Lesson A** (SF). Drill Q & A.	Complete activity(ies) from the "Let Us Work Together" section OHF-4, pp. 232-236.

SCIENCE

Co-op	Do **All Lesson A** (SF).	Do **All Lesson A** (SF).	Do **All Lesson A** (SF).
Day 2	Review **All Lesson A** (SF); Read "Sound" and "Sound Continued" in *Secret of Everyday Things* (DL). Complete experiment **K-1 Activity A** (SF).	Review **All Lesson A** (SF); Read "Sound" and "Sound Continued" in *Secret of Everyday Things* (DL). Complete experiment **2-3 Activity A** (SF).	Review **All Lesson A** (SF); Read "Sound" and "Sound Continued," in *Secret of Everyday Things* (DL); read "Velocity of Sound" in *Story Book of Science* (DL); do Nature Journal from **4-6 Lesson A** (SF).
Day 3	Complete experiment **K-1 Activity B** (SF).	Complete experiment **2-3 Activity A** (SF).	Complete experiment **4-6 Activity A** (SF) and do **4-6 Activity B** (SF).
Day 4	Do experiment **K-1 Activity C** (SF); if possible, go on a nature walk.	Do experiment **2-3 Activity C** (SF); if possible, go on a nature walk.	Do library research **4-6 Activity C** (SF); if possible, go on a nature walk and do Nature Journaling.

VIRTUE

	K-6th Grades
Field	Do **All Virtue Lesson A – Dependability** (SF)
Day 2-4	Practice "virtue training"

CYCLE III
UNIT 24

AGE OF INVENTION

UNIT CHECKLIST

PREP FOR HOME

☐ Print and read this Handbook

☐ Read the Overview

☐ Review the Planner; do the following:

  o Locate and review all Lessons and Activities in the Subject Folders (SF)

  o Locate and review all readings and assignments in the Subject Folders (SF), Digital Library (DL), and Hard Copies (HC)

  o Note and gather needed supplies for the unit

☐ Read the Virtue Lesson

☐ Email or call R.A.S. if you have questions or technical difficulty.

PREP FOR CO-OP

☐ Print your "Co-op Job Sheet" and prep for your job

☐ Make sure your child is ready for his or her presentation if assigned to present

☐ Gather maps, notebooks, prayer sheet, and other supplies the night or morning before the co-op meets.

☐ Gather students' assignments the night or morning before the co-op meets

☐ Listen to the Memory Work on the way!

PREP FOR UPCOMING WEEKS — LOOK AHEAD AT UNIT 26

☐ Make advanced purchases, as necessary

☐ Begin to gather books and materials

PLANNER ABBREVIATION KEY

DL	Digital Library (in course suite)
SF	Subject Folder (in course suite)
HC	Hard Copy
PLL	*Primary Language Lessons* (book)
ILL	*Intermediate Language Lessons* (book)
RS4K	*Real Science 4 Kids* (book)
I-CAT	*Illustrated Catechism* (book)
OHF-1	*Our Holy Faith, Book 1* (book)
OHF-2	*Our Holy Faith, Book 2* (book)
OHF-4	*Our Holy Faith, Book 4* (book)
OHF-1-TM	*Our Holy Faith, Book 1, Teacher's Manual* (book)

OVERVIEW

Common Topics (All students PreK to 6th)

Virtue:	Fear of God
Hymn:	Ecce lignum
Prayers:	Signum Crucis, Angelus, Pater Noster, Ave Maria, Gloria Patri
History:	Age of Invention (1860-1930)
Science:	Light & Matter

History Themes

In Unit 24 we do not completely abandon the Civil War, but make our way slowly from it. If you have chosen to read *Mother Seton and the Sisters of Charity* as a family, then you will find yourselves remaining in the Civil War period, focusing on the works of religious groups as they sought to care for both sides and to pray for peace.

Our other readings, *The Wind in the Willows* and *The Adventures of Huckleberry Finn,* are character studies from the decades just after the war. In the backdrop we find such modern inventions of the age as the steamboat and the motor car. The former novel by Kenneth Graham is a Scottish masterpiece; while, the novel by Twain has been called the "Great American Novel." We enjoy works from both Continents this week, and we reflect on the close relationship between American and European peoples into the twentieth century.

All seems at peace, but then we remember that there is Native American resistance still occurring amidst the Civil War and that the Battle of Little Big Horn is well after the war is finished. Workers are beginning to strike against corporations to obtain fair compensation and safer work environments, and African Americans gain the right to vote. This is not yet the country as we know it now.

How to Apply History to Everyday Life

Virtue. As we read this week, we might reflect on the virtues we have been learning throughout the year and how these virtues are exemplified by characters within our readings. We might also consider how the vices are exemplified. Not all characters are noble this week. In particular this week, we are learning "Fear of God." Do we find this virtue anywhere in our readings? Does God still have a *prominent* voice in the literature of the twentieth century? This will be a question that remains open as we finish up Cycle 3.

First Pope of the Twentieth Century, from the Compendium (DL). On August 4, 1903, Cardinal Sarto was proclaimed Pope under the title of Pius X. He set himself from the beginning "to renew all things in Christ." Some of his most important Encyclicals included --- The teaching of the Catechism; Church Music; Modernism; and The Laws of Christian Marriage. His principal works included: the formation of a Biblical

OVERVIEW

Commission; the codification of Canon Law; the arrangement and organization of the Roman Congregations.

Important People, Events, and Places to Know (Potential Student Presentations)

❖ Amendment XIV – equal rights promised; Fort Laramie peace conference with the Sioux (1868); Knights of Labor founded (1869); Amendment XV – blacks get right to vote; Death of Father De Smet (1873); Battle of Little Big Horn (1876); Geronimo goes on the warpath; Alexander Graham Bell invents the telephone; Thomas Edison invents light bulb (1879); Battle of Wounded Knee (1890)

❖ Some Saints of the Twentieth Century:

- St. Maria Goretti (1902)
- St. Pius X (1914)
- St. Christopher Magallanes & Companions (1915-1928)
- Our Lady of Fatima (1917)
- St. Frances Xavier Cabrini (1917)
- St. Raphaela Mary (1925)

- Bl. Philip Monarriz & Companions (1936)
- St. Andre Bessette (1937)
- St. Faustina Kowalska (1938)
- St. Maximillan Kolbe (1941)
- St. Teresa Benedicta of the Cross (Edith Stein) (1942)
- St. Josephine Bakhita (1947)

Additional Project Ideas

- Make a light bulb
- Research the Sioux and Apache conflicts

PLANNER ~ Unit 24 (Co-op)

Week of _____   *Liturgical Theme & Colors* _____

Family Challenge-Task
Goals _____

_____

_____

Reminders _____

_____

PRESCHOOL

	Music	Art, Reading, Religion	Virtue
Co-op	See "Music" heading below	Do craft **PreK Lesson A** (SF)	Practice "virtue training"
Day 2-4	See "Music" heading below	Do **Number Book 1-2** (SF); do **worksheets** (SF); review & drill I-CAT, pp 23 (HC)	Practice "virtue training"

KINDERGARTEN – 6TH GRADE

ART   **CCM**

	K-6th Grade		K-6th Grade
Co-op	Do **All Lesson A** (SF).		Unit 24
Day 2-4	Review **All Lesson A** (SF) and do home follow-up.		Listen to Unit 24 every day

HISTORY

	K-1ˢᵗ Grades	2ⁿᵈ-3ʳᵈ Grades	4ᵗʰ-6ᵗʰ Grades
Co-op	Do **K-1 Lesson A** (SF).	Do **2-3 Lesson A** (SF).	Do **4-6 Lesson A** (SF).
Day 2	Read *Wind in the Willows* (DL) this week; Choose and do reading (or other project) from "Extras" (SF); draw a picture inspired by the readings	Read *Wind in the Willows* (DL) this week; Choose and do reading (or other project) from "Extras" (SF); draw a picture inspired by the readings	Read *The Adventures of Huckleberry Finn* (DL); Choose and do readings (or other projects) from "Extras" (SF); begin writing **4-6 Activity A** (SF).
Day 3	Do online **K-1 Activity A** (SF); *Glory Story CD*, Vol. II, St. Therese	Do online **2-3 Activity A** (SF); *Glory Story CD*, Vol. II, St. Therese	Do map **4-6 Activity B** (SF); *Glory Story CD*, Vol. II, St. Therese
Day 4	Do coloring page (SF)	Do coloring page (SF)	Do timeline **4-6 Activity C** (SF); summarize the reading this week and draw!

LANGUAGE ARTS

Co-op	Complete **K-1 Lesson A** (SF).	Complete **2-3 Lesson A** (SF).	Complete **4-6 Lesson A** (SF).
Day 2	Review **K-1 Lesson A** (SF); do **K-1 Activity A** (SF).	Review **2-3 Lesson A** (SF); do **2-3 Activity A** (SF).	Review **4-6 Lesson A** (SF); do **4-6 Activity A** (SF)
Day 3	Do pre-cursive copywork **K-1 Activity B** (SF).	Do cursive copywork **2-3 Activity B** (SF).	Complete first draft in **4-6 Activity A** (SF).
Day 4	Do narration and illustration **K-1 Activity C** (SF)	Do composition and illustration **2-3 Activity C** (SF)	Complete final draft in **4-6 Activity A** (SF).

LATIN/GREEK

Co-op	Practice Ecce lignum (SF)	Practice Ecce lignum (SF); do *Greek Primer* 24.1–4 (SF)	Practice Ecce lignum (SF); do *Reading Greek* 24.1–2 (SF)
Day 2	Listen to CCM Unit 24 Latin prayer	Listen to CCM Unit 21 Latin prayer; do *Greek Primer* 24.5	Listen to CCM Unit 24 Latin prayer; do *Reading Greek* 24.3–4 (SF)
Day 3	Practice all the *Schola Rosa* Latin assembly prayers!	Practice all the *Schola Rosa* Latin assembly prayers!; do *Greek Primer* 24.5 (SF)	Practice all the *Schola Rosa* Latin assembly prayers!; do *Reading Greek* 24.4 (SF)
Day 4	Listen to Ecce lignum video (SF); Sing along!	Listen to Ecce lignum video (SF); Sing along!; finish *Greek Primer* Unit 24 (SF)	Listen to Ecce lignum video (SF); Sing along!; finish *Reading Greek* Unit 24 (SF) and review/check work

MATH

	Level A	Level B	Level C
Co-op	None	None	None
Day 2-4	See *Ray's Primary*, Mastery Chart~ Do next lesson (DL)	See *Ray's Intellectual*, Mastery Chart~ Do next lesson (DL)	See *Ray's Practical*, Mastery Chart~ Do next lesson (DL)

MUSIC

	K-6th Grade
Co-op	Review **All Lesson A** (SF). Use audio files to sing along with: Hymn of the Week (Latin SF); Exercises Group 1, 2, 3, 4, & 5; Gloria; ite missa est; Kyrie; Agnus Dei; Sanctus; Credo; Merrily We Roll Along; Oats, Peas, Beans & Barley Grow; Lightly Row; Aura Lee; Lavender Blue; Home on the Range (DL). See addendum to Lesson for 2nd year additions.
Day 2-4	

READING

	Primer (pre-reader)	Reader
Co-op	None	None
Day 2-4	See *McGuffey's Eclectic Primer*, "Mastery Chart" ~ Do next lesson (DL)	See *McGuffey's Eclectic Readers*, "Mastery Chart" ~ Do next lesson (DL)

RELIGION — *Liturgical Feast lessons can be moved to correspond to their dates — simply adjust the schedule accordingly*

	K-1st Grades	2nd-3rd Grades	4th-6th Grades
Co-op	Begin **K-1 Lesson A** (SF).	Begin **2-3 Lesson A** (SF). Drill Q & A.	Begin **4-6 Lesson A** (SF). Drill Q & A.
Day 2	Review/complete **K-1 Lesson A** (SF).	Review/complete **2-3 Lesson A** (SF). Drill Q & A.	Review/complete **4-6 Lesson A** (SF). Drill Q & A.
Day 3	Begin **K-1 Lesson B** (SF).	Review/complete **2-3 Lesson A** (SF). Drill Q & A.	Complete activity(-ies) from the "Let Us Work Together" section OHf-4, pp. 232-236.
Day 4	Review/complete **K-1 Lesson B** (SF).	Review/complete **2-3 Lesson A** (SF). Drill Q & A.	Complete activity(ies) from the "Let Us Work Together" section OHf-4, pp. 232-236.

SCIENCE

Co-op	Do **All Lesson A** (SF).	Do **All Lesson A** (SF).	Do **All Lesson A** (SF).
Day 2	Review **All Lesson A** (SF); Read "Light" in *Secret of Everyday Things* (DL).	Review **All Lesson A** (SF); Read "Light" in *Secret of Everyday Things* (DL).	Review **All Lesson A** (SF); Read "Light" in *Secret of Everyday Things* (DL); do Nature Journal from **4-6 Lesson A** (SF). Read Ch. 9 *RS4K, Focus on Elementary Physics* and do Experiment 9.
Day 3	Complete online **K-1 Activity A** (SF).	Complete online **2-3 Activity A** (SF).	Complete online experiment **4-6 Activity A** (SF) and do **4-6 Activity B** (SF).
Day 4	Do free-time experimenting in **All Lesson A** (SF); if possible, go on a nature walk.	Do free-time experimenting in **All Lesson A** (SF); if possible, go on a nature walk.	Do library research **4-6 Activity C** (SF); if possible, go on a nature walk and do Nature Journaling.

VIRTUE

	K-6th Grades
Field	Do **All Virtue Lesson A – Fear of God** (SF)
Day 2-4	Practice "virtue training"

**CYCLE III
UNIT 25**

WORLD WAR I

UNIT CHECKLIST

PREP FOR HOME

- ☐ Print and read this Handbook
- ☐ Read the Overview
- ☐ Review the Planner; do the following:
  - o Locate and review all Lessons and Activities in the Subject Folders (SF)
  - o Locate and review all readings and assignments in the Subject Folders (SF), Digital Library (DL), and Hard Copies (HC)
  - o Note and gather needed supplies for the unit
- ☐ Read the Virtue Lesson
- ☐ Email or call R.A.S. if you have questions or technical difficulty.

PREP FOR CO-OP

- ☐ Print your "Co-op Job Sheet" and prep for your job
- ☐ Make sure your child is ready for his or her presentation if assigned to present
- ☐ Gather maps, notebooks, prayer sheet, and other supplies the night or morning before the co-op meets.
- ☐ Gather students' assignments the night or morning before the co-op meets
- ☐ Listen to the Memory Work on the way!

PREP FOR UPCOMING WEEKS — <u>LOOK AHEAD AT UNIT 27</u>

- ☐ Make advanced purchases, as necessary
- ☐ Begin to gather books and materials

PLANNER ABBREVIATION KEY

DL	Digital Library (in course suite)
SF	Subject Folder (in course suite)
HC	Hard Copy
PLL	*Primary Language Lessons* (book)
ILL	*Intermediate Language Lessons* (book)
RS4K	*Real Science 4 Kids* (book)
I-CAT	*Illustrated Catechism* (book)
OHF-1	*Our Holy Faith, Book 1* (book)
OHF-2	*Our Holy Faith, Book 2* (book)
OHF-4	*Our Holy Faith, Book 4* (book)
OHF-1-TM	*Our Holy Faith, Book 1, Teacher's Manual* (book)

OVERVIEW

Common Topics (All students PreK to 6th)

Virtue:	Orderliness
Hymn:	Ecce lignum
Prayers:	Signum Crucis, Angelus, Pater Noster, Ave Maria, Gloria Patri
History:	World War I
Science:	Newton's First Law of Motion

History Themes

In Unit 25 our historical focus is on World War I. The older students will encounter a primary resource, a "story," written by Roland Usher who fought with the Allied Forces in the war. As he explains, he does not believe his story provides a full account or perhaps even a "fair" account, but it is the story as he understands it from his side. When reading his account, we are to put it in its context and understand it as one of the stories from one person among those millions who were in the war. To do proper justice to the time period, a similar reading from a German could be done, or even a book from an author of each country. Yet, even then, we would discover a multitude of nuances in perspective with the Great War. Usher writes that the sheer magnitude and scope of the war, though its battle movements were simple, make this war difficult to comprehend.

The younger students, who are perhaps not as ready to study great battles, especially battles which have less-than-clear causes, will be reading *The Chronicles of Narnia,* novels written by C.S. Lewis, who also lived through the war. The children we meet in the novels have been sent to live with a relative during the bombings of London. Though we are not studying the war formerly with these students, they are receiving a gentle introduction to its existence and being introduced to one of the most prolific Christian authors of the time period.

How to Apply History to Everyday Life

Heroes still Among Us. For Americans today the First World War seems very far away in our memory, but we still have veterans around us. They will not be here for much longer, but we may wish to ask them about the war if they are still around. If they are not, then perhaps their children are present and might remember stories from their mother or father. These, too, could be interviewed, allowing us to learn more about the war from our local relatives and friends. If you have no family around, you might visit the local nursing home to pay a visit to the elderly and to ask them about the war. Not only could they tell you about the First World War, but most likely about the Second as well.

Virtue. Orderliness is the virtue of this unit, and we might reflect upon this virtue as we consider the troops who went off to fight in World War I. Without obedience and without orderliness, many of the battles would have been quickly lost. Courage, too,

OVERVIEW

was a necessity --- courage to be obedient in the line of fire. As we consider this virtue, we may think about its necessity in times of emergency and immediacy.

Important People, Events, and Places to Know (Potential Student Presentations)

❖ King Wilhelm I proclaimed Kaiser over Prussian and German kingdoms (1871); France signs treaty to end Franco-Prussian War; Wilhelm II becomes Kaiser of Germany (1888); Nicolas is crowned Tsar Nicholas II of Russia (1894); Great Britain's Queen Victoria dies, who was related to almost all the ruling houses of Europe (1901); Russo-Japanese War results in defeat of Russia (1904-1905); "Bloody Sunday Massacre" in St. Petersburg, Russia; British launch first "dreadnought" class battleship (1906); Archduke Franz Ferdinand, heir to Austro-Hungarian Empire, and his wife assassinated in Sarajevo (1914); Emperor Franz Joseph of Austria-Hungary declares war on Servia; Russia, Serbia's ally, announces mobilization of armed forces; Germany mobilizes armed forces and declares war on Russia; German declares war on France; German declares war on neutral Belgium and invades; Britain declares war on Germany; Austria-Hungary declares war on Russia; Battle of the Frontiers.

❖ For more events of World War I, visit the PBS website here: http://www.pbs.org/greatwar/timeline/index.html

❖ Some Saints of the Twentieth Century:

- o St. Maria Goretti (1902)
- o St. Pius X (1914)
- o St. Christopher Magallanes & Companions (1915-1928)
- o Our Lady of Fatima (1917)
- o St. Frances Xavier Cabrini (1917)
- o St. Raphaela Mary (1925)

- o Bl. Philip Monarriz & Companions (1936)
- o St. Andre Bessette (1937)
- o St. Faustina Kowalska (1938)
- o St. Maximillan Kolbe (1941)
- o St. Teresa Benedicta of the Cross (Edith Stein) (1942)
- o St. Josephine Bakhita (1947)

Additional Project Ideas

- Play Battleship
- Re-enact battle movements on a model European landscape.
- Watch black and white films or view black and white photography from the period
- Visit a local World War I memorial and pray for the dead

Week of _____ *Liturgical Theme & Colors* _____

Family Challenge-Task
Goals

_____

_____

_____

Reminders

_____

_____

PRESCHOOL

	Music	Art, Reading, Religion	Virtue
Co-op	See "Music" heading below	Do craft **PreK Lesson A** (SF)	Practice "virtue training"
Day 2-4	See "Music" heading below	Do **Number Book 3-4** (SF); do **worksheets** (SF); review & drill I-CAT, pp 25 (HC)	Practice "virtue training"

KINDERGARTEN – 6TH GRADE

ART   **CCM**

	K-6th Grade	K-6th Grade
Co-op	Do **All Lesson A** (SF).	Unit 25
Day 2-4	Review **All Lesson A** (SF) and do home follow-up.	Listen to Unit 25 every day

HISTORY

	K-1st Grades	2nd-3rd Grades	4th-6th Grades
Co-op	Do **K-1 Lesson A** (SF).	Do **2-3 Lesson A** (SF).	Do **4-6 Lesson A** (SF).
Day 2	Read *The Chronicles of Narnia* (DL) this week; Choose and do reading (or other project) from "Extras" (SF); draw a picture inspired by the readings	Read *The Chronicles of Narnia* (DL) this week; Choose and do reading (or other project) from "Extras" (SF); draw a picture inspired by the readings	Read *The Story of the Great War* (DL); Choose and do readings (or other projects) from "Extras" (SF); begin writing **4-6 Activity A** (SF).
Day 3	Do craft **K-1 Activity A** (SF); *Glory Story CD,* Vol XIII, Secrets from Heaven	Do online **2-3 Activity A** (SF); *Glory Story CD,* Vol XIII, Secrets from Heaven	Do map **4-6 Activity B** (SF); *Glory Story CD,* Vol XIII, Secrets from Heaven
Day 4	Do coloring page (SF)	Do coloring page (SF)	Do timeline **4-6 Activity C** (SF); summarize the reading this week and draw!

LANGUAGE ARTS

Co-op	Complete **K-1 Lesson A** (SF).	Complete **2-3 Lesson A** (SF).	Complete **4-6 Lesson A** (SF).
Day 2	Review **K-1 Lesson A** (SF); do **K-1 Activity A** (SF).	Review **2-3 Lesson A** (SF); do **2-3 Activity A** (SF).	Review **4-6 Lesson A** (SF); do **4-6 Activity A** (SF)
Day 3	Do pre-cursive copywork **K-1 Activity B** (SF).	Do cursive copywork **2-3 Activity B** (SF).	Complete first draft in **4-6 Activity A** (SF).
Day 4	Do narration and illustration **K-1 Activity C** (SF)	Do composition and illustration **2-3 Activity C** (SF)	Complete final draft in **4-6 Activity A** (SF).

LATIN/GREEK

Co-op	Practice Ecce lignum (SF)	Practice Ecce lignum (SF); do *Greek Primer* 25.1–4 (SF)	Practice Ecce lignum (SF); do *Reading Greek* 25.1–2 (SF)
Day 2	Listen to CCM Unit 25 Latin prayer	Listen to CCM Unit 25 Latin prayer; do *Greek Primer* 25.5	Listen to CCM Unit 25 Latin prayer; do *Reading Greek* 25.3–4 (SF)
Day 3	Practice all the *Schola Rosa* Latin assembly prayers!	Practice all the *Schola Rosa* Latin assembly prayers!; do *Greek Primer* 25.5 (SF)	Practice all the *Schola Rosa* Latin assembly prayers!; do *Reading Greek* 25.4 (SF)
Day 4	Listen to Ecce lignum video (SF); Sing along!	Listen to Ecce lignum video (SF); Sing along!; finish *Greek Primer* Unit 25 (SF)	Listen to Ecce lignum video (SF); Sing along!; finish *Reading Greek* Unit 25 (SF) and review/check work

MATH

	Level A	Level B	Level C
Co-op	None	None	None
Day 2-4	See *Ray's Primary*, Mastery Chart~ Do next lesson (DL)	See *Ray's Intellectual*, Mastery Chart~ Do next lesson (DL)	See *Ray's Practical*, Mastery Chart~ Do next lesson (DL)

MUSIC

	K-6th Grade
Co-op	Review **All Lesson A** (SF). Use audio files
Day 2-4	to sing along with: Hymn of the Week (Latin SF); Exercises Group 1, 2, 3, 4, & 5; Gloria; ite missa est; Kyrie; Agnus Dei; Sanctus; Credo; Merrily We Roll Along; Oats, Peas, Beans & Barley Grow; Lightly Row; Aura Lee; Lavender Blue; Home on the Range (DL). See addendum to Lesson for 2nd year additions.

READING

	Primer (pre-reader)	Reader
Co-op	None	None
Day 2-4	See *McGuffey's Eclectic Primer*, "Mastery Chart" ~ Do next lesson (DL)	See *McGuffey's Eclectic Readers*, "Mastery Chart" ~ Do next lesson (DL)

RELIGION — *Liturgical Feast lessons can be moved to correspond to their dates — simply adjust the schedule accordingly*

	K-1st Grades	2nd-3rd Grades	4th-6th Grades
Co-op	Begin **K-1 Lesson A** (SF).	Begin **2-3 Lesson A** (SF). Drill Q & A.	Begin **4-6 Lesson A** (SF). Drill Q & A.
Day 2	Review/complete **K-1 Lesson A** (SF).	Review/complete **2-3 Lesson A** (SF). Drill Q & A.	Review/complete **4-6 Lesson A** (SF). Drill Q & A.
Day 3	Begin **K-1 Lesson B** (SF).	Review/complete **2-3 Lesson A** (SF). Drill Q & A.	Complete activity(-ies) from the "Let Us Work Together" section OHf-4, pp. 232-236.
Day 4	Review/complete **K-1 Lesson B** (SF).	Review/complete **2-3 Lesson A** (SF). Drill Q & A.	Complete activity(ies) from the "Let Us Work Together" section OHf-4, pp. 232-236.

SCIENCE

Co-op	Do **All Lesson A** (SF).	Do **All Lesson A** (SF).	Do **All Lesson A** (SF).
Day 2	Review **All Lesson A** (SF); Read "Locomotive" in *The Storybook of Science* (DL).	Review **All Lesson A** (SF); Read "Locomotive" in *The Storybook of Science* (DL).	Review **All Lesson A** (SF); Read "Locomotive" in *The Storybook of Science* (DL); do Nature Journal from **4-6 Lesson A** (SF). Read Ch. 1 *RS4K, Focus on Elementary Physics* and do Experiment 1.
Day 3	Complete free-time experiment **K-1 Activity A** (SF).	Complete free-time experiment **2-3 Activity A** (SF).	Complete free-time experiment **4-6 Activity A** (SF) and do **4-6 Activity B** (SF).
Day 4	Do drawing **K-1 Activity B** (SF); if possible, go on a nature walk.	Do description & illustration **2-3 Activity B** (SF); if possible, go on a nature walk.	Do library research **4-6 Activity C** (SF); if possible, go on a nature walk and do Nature Journaling.

VIRTUE

	K-6th Grades
Field	Do **All Virtue Lesson A – Orderliness** (SF)
Day 2-4	Practice "virtue training"

CYCLE III
UNIT 26

ROARING 20'S

&

THE GREAT DEPRESSION

UNIT CHECKLIST

PREP FOR HOME

- ☐ Print and read this Handbook
- ☐ Read the Overview
- ☐ Review the Planner; do the following:
    - o Locate and review all Lessons and Activities in the Subject Folders (SF)
    - o Locate and review all readings and assignments in the Subject Folders (SF), Digital Library (DL), and Hard Copies (HC)
    - o Note and gather needed supplies for the unit
- ☐ Read the Virtue Lesson
- ☐ Email or call R.A.S. if you have questions or technical difficulty.

PREP FOR CO-OP

- ☐ Print your "Co-op Job Sheet" and prep for your job
- ☐ Make sure your child is ready for his or her presentation if assigned to present
- ☐ Gather maps, notebooks, prayer sheet, and other supplies the night or morning before the co-op meets.
- ☐ Gather students' assignments the night or morning before the co-op meets
- ☐ Listen to the Memory Work on the way!

PREP FOR UPCOMING WEEKS – LOOK AHEAD AT UNIT 28

- ☐ Make advanced purchases, as necessary
- ☐ Begin to gather books and materials

PLANNER ABBREVIATION KEY

DL	Digital Library (in course suite)
SF	Subject Folder (in course suite)
HC	Hard Copy
PLL	*Primary Language Lessons* (book)
ILL	*Intermediate Language Lessons* (book)
RS4K	*Real Science 4 Kids* (book)
I-CAT	*Illustrated Catechism* (book)
OHF-1	*Our Holy Faith, Book 1* (book)
OHF-2	*Our Holy Faith, Book 2* (book)
OHF-4	*Our Holy Faith, Book 4* (book)
OHF-1-TM	*Our Holy Faith, Book 1, Teacher's Manual* (book)

OVERVIEW

Common Topics (All students PreK to 6ᵗʰ)

Virtue: Perseverance
Hymn: Ecce lignum
Prayers: Signum Crucis, Angelus, Pater Noster, Ave Maria, Gloria Patri
History: Roaring 20's & the Great Depression
Science: Review

History Themes

In Unit 26 students are introduced to the Roaring 20's and the Great Depression. One of the best ways to deepen students' understanding of this period is to complete photography studies. Simply visit your local library and check out books about this time period, making sure they are full of pictures! You can then practice using "primary sources" like we did in the Civil War unit. What do the photographs tell us?

For our reading, we are looking at an author contemporary with C.S. Lewis, G.K. Chesterton. He wrote a series of crime mysteries, which have been adapted for children --- *Father Brown Readers I* and *II*. These are only available as hardcopies and are not in the digital library. If you have not read the first reader, then you might consider having the whole family begin with I and save II for later. If your older students have already experienced I, then they may read II during this unit.

How to Apply History to Everyday Life

Roaring 20's and Great Depression. Americans have experienced "years of plenty" and the present generations have little to no memory of the Great Depression or what it is like to live through "tough times." This is a good unit for the family to consider what life would be like if another depression happened. How would the family cope? Is there a family garden already? What sorts of jobs would be available within the home? Do you have family or close friends nearby for extra help and for sharing of goods? What would be your community?

Virtue. Going along with the Great Depression is the virtue of perseverance. The families who lived through the Great Depression learned to eat little, store everything, and rely on their local resources. This took perseverance. There was no simply going to the grocer to buy what you needed. The grocer was perhaps out of business, or you had no money to buy food. You could not rely on buying seeds necessarily, but you would need to save seeds from your garden. In general the people in the cities had the hardest time, since they had come to rely on so many external resources – the bank, grocer, mechanic, bakery, butcher. They also did not have the funds or mobility to leave the city for a country life. We might then reflect upon the safety or risk of the location where we live.

OVERVIEW

Important People, Events, and Places to Know (Potential Student Presentations)

❖ For a wonderful resource on Great Depression events, see the PBS website here: http://www.pbs.org/wgbh/americanexperience/features/timeline/rails-timeline/

❖ Some Saints of the Twentieth Century:

- o St. Maria Goretti (1902)
- o St. Pius X (1914)
- o St. Christopher Magallanes & Companions (1915-1928)
- o Our Lady of Fatima (1917)
- o St. Frances Xavier Cabrini (1917)
- o St. Raphaela Mary (1925)
- o Bl. Philip Monarriz & Companions (1936)
- o St. Andre Bessette (1937)
- o St. Faustina Kowalska (1938)
- o St. Maximillan Kolbe (1941)
- o St. Teresa Benedicta of the Cross (Edith Stein) (1942)
- o St. Josephine Bakhita (1947)

Additional Project Ideas

- Live for a week as though you lived during the Great Depression – Without which commodities would you go? Would you travel away from home? What would you not buy that you usually buy during the week?
- Visit the tabernacle and pray for the homeless and hungry.

Week of _____   *Liturgical Theme & Colors* _____

Family Challenge-Task
Goals _____

_____

_____

Reminders _____

_____

_____

PRESCHOOL

	Music	Art, Reading, Religion	Virtue
Field	See "Music" heading below	Do craft **PreK Lesson A** (SF)	Practice "virtue training"
Day 2-4	See "Music" heading below	Review Y-Z and 1-4 (SF), review & drill I-CAT, pp 25 (HC)	Practice "virtue training"

KINDERGARTEN – 6TH GRADE

ART   **CCM**

	K-6th Grade	K-6th Grade
Field	Review **All Lesson A** (SF), Units 19-21.	Unit 26.
Day 2-4	Do extra art task from home follow-up sections, if there is time.	Listen to Unit 26 every day

HISTORY

	K-1st Grades	2nd-3rd Grades	4th-6th Grades
Field	Read *Father Brown Reader I* (HC).	Read *Father Brown Reader I* (HC).	Read *Father Brown Reader II* (HC).
Day 2	Choose and do reading (or other project) from "Extras" (SF); draw a picture inspired by the readings	Choose and do reading (or other project) from "Extras" (SF); draw a picture inspired by the readings	Choose and do readings (or other projects) from "Extras" (SF); Do reading & discussion **4-6 Activity A** (SF)
Day 3	Do music **K-1 Activity A** (SF); Glory Story CD, Vol. IX, Blessed Jose and Vol. II, St. Miguel.	Do reading **2-3 Activity A** (SF); Glory Story CD, Vol. IX, Blessed Jose and Vol. II, St. Miguel.	Do reading & writing **4-6 Activity B** (SF); Glory Story CD, Vol. IX, Blessed Jose and Vol. II, St. Miguel.
Day 4	Do coloring page (SF)	Do coloring page (SF)	Do timeline **4-6 Activity C** (SF); summarize the reading this week and draw!

LANGUAGE ARTS

Field	Complete **K-1 Lesson A** (SF).	Complete **2-3 Lesson A** (SF).	Complete **4-6 Lesson A** (SF).
Day 2	Review **K-1 Lesson A** (SF); do **K-1 Activity A** (SF).	Review **2-3 Lesson A** (SF); do **2-3 Activity A** (SF).	Review **4-6 Lesson A** (SF); do **4-6 Activity A** (SF)
Day 3	Do pre-cursive copywork **K-1 Activity B** (SF).	Do cursive copywork **2-3 Activity B** (SF).	Complete first draft in **4-6 Activity A** (SF).
Day 4	Do narration and illustration **K-1 Activity C** (SF)	Do composition and illustration **2-3 Activity C** (SF)	Complete final draft in **4-6 Activity A** (SF).

LATIN/GREEK

Field	Practice Ecce lignum (SF)	Practice Ecce lignum (SF); do *Greek Primer* 26.1–4 (SF)	Practice Ecce lignum (SF); do *Reading Greek* 26.1–2 (SF)
Day 2	Listen to CCM Unit 26 Latin prayer	Listen to CCM Unit 26 Latin prayer; do *Greek Primer* 26.5	Listen to CCM Unit 26 Latin prayer; do *Reading Greek* 26.3–4 (SF)
Day 3	Practice all the *Schola Rosa* Latin assembly prayers!	Practice all the *Schola Rosa* Latin assembly prayers!; do *Greek Primer* 26.5 (SF)	Practice all the *Schola Rosa* Latin assembly prayers!; do *Reading Greek* 26.4 (SF)
Day 4	Listen to Ecce lignum video (SF); Sing along!	Listen to Ecce lignum video (SF); Sing along!; finish *Greek Primer* Unit 26 (SF)	Listen to Ecce lignum video (SF); Sing along!; finish *Reading Greek* Unit 26 (SF) and review/check work

MATH

	Level A	Level B	Level C
Field	None	None	None
Day 2-4	See *Ray's Primary*, Mastery Chart~ Do next lesson (DL)	See *Ray's Intellectual*, Mastery Chart~ Do next lesson (DL)	See *Ray's Practical*, Mastery Chart~ Do next lesson (DL)

MUSIC

	K-6th Grade
Field	Use audio files to sing along with: Hymn of the Week (Latin SF); Exercises Group 1, 2, 3, 4, & 5; Gloria; ite missa est; Kyrie; Agnus Dei; Sanctus; Credo; Merrily We Roll Along; Oats, Peas, Beans & Barley Grow; Lightly Row; Aura Lee; Lavender Blue; Home on the Range (DL). See addendum to Lesson for 2nd year additions.
Day 2-4	

READING

	Primer (pre-reader)	Reader
Field	None	None
Day 2-4	See *McGuffey's Eclectic Primer*, "Mastery Chart" ~ Do next lesson (DL)	See *McGuffey's Eclectic Readers*, "Mastery Chart" ~ Do next lesson (DL)

RELIGION — *Liturgical Feast lessons can be moved to correspond to their dates — simply adjust the schedule accordingly*

	K-1st Grades	2nd-3rd Grades	4th-6th Grades
Field	Begin **K-1 Lesson A** (SF).	Begin **2-3 Lesson A** (SF). Drill Q & A.	Begin **4-6 Lesson A** (SF). Drill Q & A.
Day 2	Review/complete **K-1 Lesson A** (SF).	Review/complete **2-3 Lesson A** (SF). Drill Q & A.	Review/complete **4-6 Lesson A** (SF). Drill Q & A.
Day 3	Begin **K-1 Lesson B** (SF).	Review/complete **2-3 Lesson A** (SF). Drill Q & A.	Complete activity(-ies) from the "Let Us Work Together" section OHF-4, pp. 232-236.
Day 4	Review/complete **K-1 Lesson B** (SF).	Review/complete **2-3 Lesson A** (SF). Drill Q & A.	Complete activity(ies) from the "Let Us Work Together" section OHF-4, pp. 232-236.

SCIENCE

Field	Review Units 23-26 and complete any missing assignments.	Review Units 23-26 and complete any missing assignments.	Review Units 23-26 and complete any missing assignments.
Day 2	Read selections from Fabre's *The Secret of Everyday Things* (DL).	Read selections from Fabre's *The Secret of Everyday Things* (DL).	Read selections from Fabre's *The Secret of Everyday Things* (DL).
Day 3	Complete free-time experiment **K-1 Activity A** (SF).	Complete free-time experiment **2-3 Activity A** (SF).	Complete free-time experiment **4-6 Activity A** (SF).
Day 4	Continue **K-1 Activity A** (SF).	Continue **2-3 Activity A** (SF).	Continue **4-6 Activity A** (SF).

VIRTUE

	K-6th Grades
Field	Do **All Virtue Lesson A – Perseverance** (SF)
Day 2-4	Practice "virtue training"

CYCLE III
UNIT 27

WORLD WAR II

UNIT CHECKLIST

PREP FOR HOME

- ☐ Print and read this Handbook
- ☐ Read the Overview
- ☐ Review the Planner; do the following:
    - o Locate and review all Lessons and Activities in the Subject Folders (SF)
    - o Locate and review all readings and assignments in the Subject Folders (SF), Digital Library (DL), and Hard Copies (HC)
    - o Note and gather needed supplies for the unit
- ☐ Read the Virtue Lesson
- ☐ Email or call R.A.S. if you have questions or technical difficulty.

PREP FOR CO-OP

- ☐ Print your "Co-op Job Sheet" and prep for your job
- ☐ Make sure your child is ready for his or her presentation if assigned to present
- ☐ Gather maps, notebooks, prayer sheet, and other supplies the night or morning before the co-op meets.
- ☐ Gather students' assignments the night or morning before the co-op meets
- ☐ Listen to the Memory Work on the way!

PREP FOR UPCOMING WEEKS — <u>LOOK AHEAD AT UNIT 29</u>

- ☐ Make advanced purchases, as necessary
- ☐ Begin to gather books and materials

PLANNER ABBREVIATION KEY

DL	Digital Library (in course suite)
SF	Subject Folder (in course suite)
HC	Hard Copy
PLL	*Primary Language Lessons* (book)
ILL	*Intermediate Language Lessons* (book)
RS4K	*Real Science 4 Kids* (book)
I-CAT	*Illustrated Catechism* (book)
OHF-1	*Our Holy Faith, Book 1* (book)
OHF-2	*Our Holy Faith, Book 2* (book)
OHF-4	*Our Holy Faith, Book 4* (book)
OHF-1-TM	*Our Holy Faith, Book 1, Teacher's Manual* (book)

OVERVIEW

Common Topics (All students PreK to 6th)

Virtue:	Responsibility
Hymn:	Lumen Christi
Prayers:	Signum Crucis, Pater Noster, Ave Maria, Gloria Patri, Angelus
History:	World War II
Science:	Newton's Second Law of Motion

History Themes

In Unit 27 students are introduced to the Second World War. Twenty years after the signing of the Treatise of Versailles, Europe was once again at war. During the "Interwar" period, Europe witnessed the rise of totalitarian states in fascist Italy and Germany, and in the communist Soviet Union. Hitler's invasion of Poland on September 1, 1939 ignited the flame and quickly the world was engulfed in war. The United States, a long-time supporter of Great Britain, entered into the conflict after the bombing of Pearl Harbor on December 7, 1941.

World War II provides the family with an opportune time to discuss justice. The European theater, specifically, was a distinct struggle between good and evil, and it is an excellent example of a just war. In the *Catechism of the Catholic Church* (2309) the four conditions that must be met for a "legitimate defense by military force" are outlined as follows:

1. "the damage inflicted by the aggressor on the nation or community of nations must be lasting, grave, and certain;"
2. "all other means of putting an end to it must have been shown to be impractical or ineffective;"
3. "there must be serious prospects of success;"
4. "the use of arms must not produce evils and disorders graver than the evil to be eliminated. The power of modern means of destruction weighs very heavily in evaluating this condition."

It would be worthwhile, as a family, to review the Catechism's teaching about war (paragraphs 2307-2317), and to discuss with your students the justice of American intervention in the war in Europe. Interestingly the reading for this week is also about conflict and war. Younger students will begin reading *the Hobbit* by J.R.R. Tolkien, while the older ones are reading *The Lord of the Rings* also written by Tolkien. In these works of fiction, Tolkien explores justice in conflict and war. For the parent, these books provide excellent stories that teach the student profound truths about the Christian journey and the Christian's response to war.

OVERVIEW

How to Apply History to Everyday Life

World War II.   Understanding the philosophy of "just war" is a worthy pursuit, and the passages relating to war in the Catechism ought to be read and studied.   The probing questions about what the Christian ought to do in the face of war must be considered.   When should the Christian defend himself?   When should he defend his country?   When should a political state engage in war?   Are the present wars of the United States just?   In war what is the dignity of the human person?

Virtue.   The virtue of responsibility fits well with World War II.   What responsibility does a citizen have to his country?   What responsibility does a politician have to the state in war?   What responsibility does the state have towards its citizens in war?   As Gandalf states in *The Fellowship of the Ring,* despite the seeming terribleness of the times, "All we have to decide is what to do with the time that is given us."   How do we use our time responsibly?

Important People, Events, and Places to Know (Potential Student Presentations)

❖ German Invasion of Poland (1939); the Fall of France (1940); the Battle of Britain (1940); Pearl Harbor (1941); the Battle of Midway (1942); the Surrender of Japan (1945); the US invasion of Italy (1943); D-Day (1944); Battle of Stalingrad (1942-1943); Battle of the Bulge (1944); Dropping of the Atomic Bomb (1945); VE (Victory in Europe) Day (1945); Winston Churchill; Franklin Delano Roosevelt; Joseph Stalin; Benito Mussolini; Adolf Hitler

❖ Some Saints of the Twentieth Century:

- o St. Maria Goretti (1902)
- o St. Pius X (1914)
- o St. Christopher Magallanes & Companions (1915-1928)
- o Our Lady of Fatima (1917)
- o St. Frances Xavier Cabrini (1917)
- o St. Raphaela Mary (1925)

- o Bl. Philip Monarriz & Companions (1936)
- o St. Andre Bessette (1937)
- o St. Faustina Kowalska (1938)
- o St. Maximillan Kolbe (1941)
- o St. Teresa Benedicta of the Cross (Edith Stein) (1942)
- o St. Josephine Bakhita (1947)

Additional Project Ideas

- Research a Victory Garden and plant one!
- Act out a scene from the *Hobbit* or the *Lord of the Rings.* Make it a production by creating costumes and writing a script.

Week of _____   *Liturgical Theme & Colors* _____

Family Challenge-Task
Goals _____

_____

_____

_____

Reminders _____

_____

PRESCHOOL

	Music	Art, Reading, Religion	Virtue
Co-op	See "Music" heading below	Do craft **PreK Lesson A** (SF)	Practice "virtue training"
Day 2-4	See "Music" heading below	Do **Number Book 5-6** (SF); do **worksheets** (SF); review & drill I-CAT, pp 27 (HC)	Practice "virtue training"

KINDERGARTEN – 6TH GRADE

ART

	K-6th Grade
Co-op	Do **All Lesson A** (SF).
Day 2-4	Review **All Lesson A** (SF) and do home follow-up.

CCM

	K-6th Grade
Co-op	Unit 27
Day 2-4	Listen to Unit 27 every day

HISTORY

	K-1st Grades	2nd-3rd Grades	4th-6th Grades
Co-op	Do **K-1 Lesson A** (SF).	Do **2-3 Lesson A** (SF).	Read *The Lord of the Rings* (DL); Do **4-6 Lesson A** (SF).
Day 2	Read *The Hobbit* (HC) this week; Choose and do reading (or other project) from "Extras" (SF); draw a picture inspired by the readings	Read *The Hobbit* (DL) this week; Choose and do reading (or other project) from "Extras" (SF); draw a picture inspired by the readings	Continue *The Lord of the Rings* (DL); Choose and do readings (or other projects) from "Extras" (SF); begin writing **4-6 Activity A** (SF).
Day 3	Continue *The Hobbit* (HC); Do coloring page (SF); *Glory Story CD*, Vol. IV, St. Faustina & Vol. X, St. Maximilian	Continue *The Hobbit* (HC); Do map **2-3 Activity A** (SF); *Glory Story CD*, Vol. IV, St. Faustina & Vol. X, St. Maximilian	Continue *The Lord of the Rings* (DL); Do map **4-6 Activity B** (SF); *Glory Story CD*, Vol. IV, St. Faustina & Vol. X, St. Maximilian
Day 4	Continue *The Hobbit* (HC); Do coloring page (SF); summarize the reading this week and draw!	Continue *The Hobbit* (HC); Do coloring page (SF); summarize the reading this week and draw!	Continue *The Lord of the Rings* (DL); Do timeline **4-6 Activity C (SF)**; summarize the reading this week and draw!

LANGUAGE ARTS

Co-op	Complete **K-1 Lesson A** (SF).	Complete **2-3 Lesson A** (SF).	Complete **4-6 Lesson A** (SF).
Day 2	Review **K-1 Lesson A** (SF); do **K-1 Activity A** (SF).	Review **2-3 Lesson A** (SF); do **2-3 Activity A** (SF).	Review **4-6 Lesson A** (SF); do **4-6 Activity A** (SF)
Day 3	Do pre-cursive copywork **K-1 Activity B** (SF).	Do cursive copywork **2-3 Activity B** (SF).	Complete first draft in **4-6 Activity A** (SF).
Day 4	Do narration and illustration **K-1 Activity C** (SF)	Do composition and illustration **2-3 Activity C** (SF)	Complete final draft in **4-6 Activity A** (SF).

LATIN/GREEK

Co-op	Practice Lumen Christi (SF)	Practice Lumen Christi (SF); do *Greek Primer* 27.1–4 (SF)	Practice Lumen Christi (SF); do *Reading Greek* 27.1–2 (SF)
Day 2	Listen to CCM Unit 27 Latin prayer	Listen to CCM Unit 27 Latin prayer; do *Greek Primer* 27	Listen to CCM Unit 27 Latin prayer; do *Reading Greek* 27.3–4 (SF)
Day 3	Practice all the *Schola Rosa* Latin assembly prayers!	Practice all the *Schola Rosa* Latin assembly prayers!; do *Greek Primer* 27 (SF)	Practice all the *Schola Rosa* Latin assembly prayers!; do *Reading Greek* 27.4 (SF)
Day 4	Listen to Lumen Christi video (SF); Sing along!	Listen to Lumen Christi video (SF); *Greek Primer* Unit 27 (SF)	Listen to Lumen Christi video (SF); *Reading Greek* Unit 27 (SF)

MATH

	Level A	Level B	Level C
Co-op	None	None	None
Day 2-4	See *Ray's Primary*, Mastery Chart~ Do next lesson (DL)	See *Ray's Intellectual*, Mastery Chart~ Do next lesson (DL)	See *Ray's Practical*, Mastery Chart~ Do next lesson (DL)

MUSIC

	K-6th Grade
Co-op	Review **All Lesson A** (SF). Use audio files to sing along with: Hymn of the Week (Latin SF); Exercises Group 1, 2, 3, 4, & 5; Practice the songs selected by your music teacher for the end of the year performance (DL).
Day 2-4	

READING

Primer (pre-reader)	Reader
None	None
See *McGuffey's Eclectic Primer*, "Mastery Chart"~ Do next lesson (DL)	See *McGuffey's Eclectic Readers*, "Mastery Chart" ~ Do next lesson (DL)

RELIGION — *Liturgical Feast lessons can be moved to correspond to their dates — simply adjust the schedule accordingly*

	K-1st Grades	2nd-3rd Grades	4th-6th Grades
Co-op	Begin **K-1 Lesson A** (SF).	Begin **2-3 Lesson A** (SF). Drill Q & A.	Begin **4-6 Lesson A** (SF). Drill Q & A.
Day 2	Review/complete **K-1 Lesson A** (SF).	Review/complete **2-3 Lesson A** (SF). Drill Q & A.	Review/complete **4-6 Lesson A** (SF). Drill Q & A.
Day 3	Begin **K-1 Lesson B** (SF).	Review/complete **2-3 Lesson A** (SF). Drill Q & A.	Complete activity(-ies) from the "Let Us Work Together" section OHF-4, pp. 258-260.
Day 4	Review/complete **K-1 Lesson B** (SF).	Review/complete **2-3 Lesson A** (SF). Drill Q & A.	Complete activity(ies) from the "Let Us Work Together" section OHF-4, pp. 258-260.

SCIENCE

Co-op	Do **All Lesson A** (SF).	Do **All Lesson A** (SF).	Do **All Lesson A** (SF).
Day 2	Review **All Lesson A** (SF); Check out from the library books about Isaac Newton and his laws of motion.	Review **All Lesson A** (SF); Check out from the library books about Isaac Newton and his laws of motion.	Review **All Lesson A** (SF); Check out from the library books about Isaac Newton and his laws of motion; do Nature Journal from **4-6 Lesson A** (SF). Read Ch. 2 *RS4K, Focus on Elementary Physics* and do Experiment 2.
Day 3	Complete **K-1 Activity A** (SF).	Complete **2-3 Activity A** (SF).	Complete **4-6 Activity A** (SF) and do **4-6 Activity B** (SF).
Day 4	Do drawing **K-1 Activity B** (SF); if possible, go on a nature walk.	Do description & illustration **2-3 Activity B** (SF); if possible, go on a nature walk.	Do library research **4-6 Activity C** (SF); if possible, go on a nature walk and do Nature Journaling.

VIRTUE

	K-6th Grades
Field	Do **All Virtue Lesson A – Responsibility** (SF)
Day 2-4	Practice "virtue training"

CYCLE III
UNIT 28

RUSSIAN REVOLUTION

& THE COLD WAR

UNIT CHECKLIST

PREP FOR HOME

☐ Print and read this Handbook

☐ Read the Overview

☐ Review the Planner; do the following:

    ○ Locate and review all Lessons and Activities in the Subject Folders (SF)

    ○ Locate and review all readings and assignments in the Subject Folders (SF), Digital Library (DL), and Hard Copies (HC)

    ○ Note and gather needed supplies for the unit

☐ Read the Virtue Lesson

☐ Email or call R.A.S. if you have questions or technical difficulty.

PREP FOR CO-OP

☐ Print your "Co-op Job Sheet" and prep for your job

☐ Make sure your child is ready for his or her presentation if assigned to present

☐ Gather maps, notebooks, prayer sheet, and other supplies the night or morning before the co-op meets.

☐ Gather students' assignments the night or morning before the co-op meets

☐ Listen to the Memory Work on the way!

PREP FOR UPCOMING WEEKS — <u>LOOK AHEAD AT UNIT 30</u>

☐ Make advanced purchases, as necessary

☐ Begin to gather books and materials

PLANNER ABBREVIATION KEY

DL	Digital Library (in course suite)
SF	Subject Folder (in course suite)
HC	Hard Copy
PLL	*Primary Language Lessons* (book)
ILL	*Intermediate Language Lessons* (book)
RS4K	*Real Science 4 Kids* (book)
I-CAT	*Illustrated Catechism* (book)
OHF-1	*Our Holy Faith, Book 1* (book)
OHF-2	*Our Holy Faith, Book 2* (book)
OHF-4	*Our Holy Faith, Book 4* (book)
OHF-1-TM	*Our Holy Faith, Book 1, Teacher's Manual* (book)

OVERVIEW

Common Topics (All students PreK to 6th)

Virtue:	Temperance
Hymn:	Lumen Christi
Prayers:	Signum Crucis, Pater Noster, Ave Maria, Gloria Patri, Angelus
History:	Russian Revolution & the Cold War
Science:	Newton's Third Law of Motion

History Themes

In Unit 28 students are introduced to the Russian Revolution and the Cold War. During the February Revolution of 1917 the Russian Tsar, Nicholas II, was overthrown and a provisional government was established. Later that year, in October, the Bolsheviks (a Russian word meaning "majority") led by Vladimir Lenin, seized power from the provisional government and began to implement the transformation of Russia into a communist state. Lenin and the Bolsheviks brutally suppressed political opponents and anyone who dissented from their view. Peasants, politicians, aristocratic supporters of the Tsar, and Russian Orthodox priests were imprisoned or executed if they did not comply with the ruling powers. Through violence and civil war Russia was restructured into a communist state, the Soviet Union, with a totalitarian government. Christianity was outlawed and the state—the governmental structure of the Soviet Union—was deified.

Communism maintained a firm grip upon the Soviet Union through the period of the Cold War, which began at the end of the Second World War out of growing tensions between the Allies, namely the United States and the Soviet Union. Though this war never saw direct conflict between the U. S. and the Soviet Union, the two countries fought for the hearts and minds of peoples throughout the world, the one to allow free peoples to choose their own path, the other to bring all peoples under a single party state. The end of the Cold War first began in Poland, when the Polish people, stirred by the inspiration of Pope St. John Paul II, resisted communist forces. Their will inspired many other countries in the Soviet sphere to topple their local communist regimes and open the door to freedom. Often neglected in the history books, is the role that Christians played in the overthrow of communism. Many devout Christians earnestly prayed and sought to bring an end to the oppression. It is highly recommended that you read Barbara Elliot's article, "Why did the Berlin Wall Fall" (http://www.theimaginativeconservative.org/2014/11/berlin-wall-fall.html) about such souls.

The study of the Russian Revolution and the Cold War provides ample opportunities for students and parents to discuss how the Christian should act amidst persecution. The example of Pope St. John Paul II and his message of the dignity of all human persons can help us to understand the Christian's responsibility to act. Spend time this week reviewing

OVERVIEW

the life of Pope St. John Paul II, and the other brave souls who resisted the evils of communism.

How to Apply History to Everyday Life

Russian Revolution and the Cold War. Looking at the Russian Revolution and those countries locked behind the Iron Curtain of communism, the Christian should ask himself how he would act if he lived at such times. How ought the Christian resist a totalitarian state that seeks to impose its vision of the world, devoid of God, upon all of its citizens? How should the Christian respond to a government that is hostile to the truth of Christ? Should the Christian become involved in the freeing of oppressed peoples? What ideas are opposed to Christ in Western Civilization today? How are we confronting them and defending our children from them? What lessons can we learn from saints such as Pope John Paul II in his opposition of communism?

Virtue. Even though we may not yet be persecuted in this country for our beliefs, we are constantly assaulted by temptations to live intemperately. Our culture encourages the satisfaction of the bodily appetites, and it so often subordinates the mind to them. Practicing the virtue of temperance strengthens the will, and rightly orders the soul by placing the mind in control of the body.

Important People, Events, and Places to Know (Potential Student Presentations)

❖ Tsar Nicholas II (1868-1918); October Revolution (1917); Vladimir Lenin (1870-1924); *Bolshevik*; Leon Trotsky (1879-1940); Joseph Stalin (1878-1953); Potsdam Conference (1945); Winston Churchill (1874-1965); Franklin Delano Roosevelt (1888-1945); Harry Truman (1884-1972); Cold War (1945-1991); Berlin Airlift (1948-1949); Korean War (1950-1953); Berlin Wall (1961-1989); Cuban Missile Crisis (1962); Pope St. John Paul II (1920-2005); Margret Thatcher (1925-2013); Ronald Reagan (1911-2004); Mikhail Gorbachev (1931-present); Fall of the Soviet Union (1991)

❖ Some Saints of the Twentieth Century:

- St. Maria Goretti (1902)
- St. Pius X (1914)
- St. Christopher Magallanes & Companions (1915-1928)
- Our Lady of Fatima (1917)
- St. Frances Xavier Cabrini (1917)
- St. Raphaela Mary (1925)

- Bl. Philip Monarriz & Companions (1936)
- St. Andre Bessette (1937)
- St. Faustina Kowalska (1938)
- St. Maximillan Kolbe (1941)
- St. Teresa Benedicta of the Cross (Edith Stein) (1942)
- St. Josephine Bakhita (1947)

Additional Project Ideas

- Research the persecution of Christians in communist countries.

Week of _____ *Liturgical Theme & Colors* _____

Family Challenge-Task
Goals _____

_____

_____

Reminders _____

_____

_____

PRESCHOOL

	Music	Art, Reading, Religion	Virtue
Co-op	See "Music" heading below	Do craft **PreK Lesson A** (SF)	Practice "virtue training"
Day 2-4	See "Music" heading below	Do **Number Book 7-8** (SF); do **worksheets** (SF); review & drill I-CAT, pp 27 (HC)	Practice "virtue training"

KINDERGARTEN – 6TH GRADE

ART   **CCM**

	K-6th Grade	K-6th Grade
Co-op	Do **All Lesson A** (SF).	Unit 28
Day 2-4	Review **All Lesson A** (SF) and do home follow-up.	Listen to Unit 28 every day

HISTORY

	K-1st Grades	2nd-3rd Grades	4th-6th Grades
Co-op	Do **K-1 Lesson A** (SF).	Do **2-3 Lesson A** (SF).	Continue *The Lord of the Rings* (HC); Do **4-6 Lesson A** (SF)
Day 2	Read *Peter and the Wolf* (DL) this week; Choose and do reading (or other project) from "Extras" (SF); draw a picture inspired by the readings	Read *Peter and the Wolf* (DL) this week; Choose and do reading (or other project) from "Extras" (SF); draw a picture inspired by the readings	Read *Peter and the Wolf* (DL); Continue *The Lord of the Rings* (HC); Choose and do readings (or other projects) from "Extras" (SF); begin writing **4-6 Activity A** (SF).
Day 3	Do coloring page (SF)	Do coloring page (SF); do map **2-3 Activity A** (SF)	Continue *The Lord of the Rings* (HC); Do map **4-6 Activity B** (SF)
Day 4	Create "popsicle puppets" and act out one of the readings (see SF for instructions)	Create "popsicle puppets" and act out one of the readings (see SF for instructions)	Continue *The Lord of the Rings* (HC); Do timeline **4-6 Activity C (SF)**; summarize the reading this week and draw!

LANGUAGE ARTS

Co-op	Complete **K-1 Lesson A** (SF).	Complete **2-3 Lesson A** (SF).	Complete **4-6 Lesson A** (SF).
Day 2	Review **K-1 Lesson A** (SF); do **K-1 Activity A** (SF).	Review **2-3 Lesson A** (SF); do **2-3 Activity A** (SF).	Review **4-6 Lesson A** (SF); do **4-6 Activity A** (SF)
Day 3	Do pre-cursive copywork **K-1 Activity B** (SF).	Do cursive copywork **2-3 Activity B** (SF).	Complete first draft in **4-6 Activity A** (SF).
Day 4	Do narration and illustration **K-1 Activity C** (SF)	Do composition and illustration **2-3 Activity C** (SF)	Complete final draft in **4-6 Activity A** (SF).

LATIN/GREEK

Co-op	Practice Lumen Christi (SF)	Practice Lumen Christi (SF); do *Greek Primer* 28.1-4 (SF)	Practice Lumen Christi (SF); do *Reading Greek* 28.1-2 (SF)
Day 2	Listen to CCM Unit 28 Latin prayer	Listen to CCM Unit 28 Latin prayer; do *Greek Primer* 28	Listen to CCM Unit 28 Latin prayer; do *Reading Greek* 28.3-4 (SF)
Day 3	Practice all the *Schola Rosa* Latin assembly prayers!	Practice all the *Schola Rosa* Latin assembly prayers!; do *Greek Primer* 28 (SF)	Practice all the *Schola Rosa* Latin assembly prayers!; do *Reading Greek* 28.4 (SF)
Day 4	Listen to Lumen Christi video (SF); Sing along!	Listen to Lumen Christi video (SF); Sing along!; finish *Greek Primer* Unit 28 (SF)	Listen to Lumen Christi video (SF); Sing along!; finish *Reading Greek* Unit 28 (SF) and review/check work

MATH

	Level A	Level B	Level C
Co-op	None	None	None
Day 2-4	See *Ray's Primary*, Mastery Chart~ Do next lesson (DL)	See *Ray's Intellectual*, Mastery Chart~ Do next lesson (DL)	See *Ray's Practical*, Mastery Chart~ Do next lesson (DL)

MUSIC

	K-6th Grade
Co-op Day 2-4	Review **All Lesson A** (SF). Use audio files to sing along with: Hymn of the Week (Latin SF); Exercises Group 1, 2, 3, 4, & 5; Practice the songs selected by your music teacher for the end of the year performance (DL).

READING

	Primer (pre-reader)	Reader
Co-op	None	None
Day 2-4	See *McGuffey's Eclectic Primer*, "Mastery Chart" ~ Do next lesson (DL)	See *McGuffey's Eclectic Readers*, "Mastery Chart" ~ Do next lesson (DL)

RELIGION — *Liturgical Feast lessons can be moved to correspond to their dates – simply adjust the schedule accordingly*

	K-1st Grades	2nd-3rd Grades	4th-6th Grades
Co-op	Begin **K-1 Lesson A** (SF).	Begin **2-3 Lesson A** (SF). Drill Q & A.	Begin **4-6 Lesson A** (SF). Drill Q & A.
Day 2	Review/complete **K-1 Lesson A** (SF).	Review/complete **2-3 Lesson A** (SF). Drill Q & A.	Review/complete **4-6 Lesson A** (SF). Drill Q & A.
Day 3	Begin **K-1 Lesson B** (SF).	Review/complete **2-3 Lesson A** (SF). Drill Q & A.	Complete activity(-ies) from the "Let Us Work Together" section OHF-4, pp. 258-260.
Day 4	Review/complete **K-1 Lesson B** (SF).	Review/complete **2-3 Lesson A** (SF). Drill Q & A.	Complete activity(ies) from the "Let Us Work Together" section OHF-4, pp. 258-260.

SCIENCE

Co-op	Do **All Lesson A** (SF).	Do **All Lesson A** (SF).	Do **All Lesson A** (SF).
Day 2	Review **All Lesson A** (SF); Check out library books on Isaac Newton and his laws of motion.	Review **All Lesson A** (SF); Check out library books on Isaac Newton and his laws of motion.	Review **All Lesson A** (SF); Check out library books on Isaac Newton and his laws of motion; do Nature Journal from **4-6 Lesson A** (SF). Read Ch. 3 *RS4K, Focus on Elementary Physics* and do Experiment 3.
Day 3	Complete **K-1 Activity A** (SF).	Complete **2-3 Activity A** (SF).	Complete **4-6 Activity A** (SF) and do **4-6 Activity B** (SF).
Day 4	Do drawing **K-1 Activity B** (SF); if possible, go on a nature walk.	Do description & illustration **2-3 Activity B** (SF); if possible, go on a nature walk.	Do library research **4-6 Activity C** (SF); if possible, go on a nature walk and do Nature Journaling.

VIRTUE

	K-6th Grades
Field	Do **All Virtue Lesson A – Temperance** (SF)
Day 2-4	Practice "virtue training"

RIGHTS, TECHNOLOCIAL REVOLUTION, & THE CATHOLIC MOVEMENT

UNIT CHECKLIST

PREP FOR HOME

- ☐ Print and read this Handbook
- ☐ Read the Overview
- ☐ Review the Planner; do the following:
    - o Locate and review all Lessons and Activities in the Subject Folders (SF)
    - o Locate and review all readings and assignments in the Subject Folders (SF), Digital Library (DL), and Hard Copies (HC)
    - o Note and gather needed supplies for the unit
- ☐ Read the Virtue Lesson
- ☐ Email or call R.A.S. if you have questions or technical difficulty.

PREP FOR CO-OP

- ☐ Print your "Co-op Job Sheet" and prep for your job
- ☐ Make sure your child is ready for his or her presentation if assigned to present
- ☐ Gather maps, notebooks, prayer sheet, and other supplies the night or morning before the co-op meets.
- ☐ Gather students' assignments the night or morning before the co-op meets
- ☐ Listen to the Memory Work on the way!

PREP FOR UPCOMING WEEKS — LOOK AHEAD AT UNIT 30

- ☐ Make advanced purchases, as necessary
- ☐ Begin to gather books and materials

PLANNER ABBREVIATION KEY	
DL	Digital Library (in course suite)
SF	Subject Folder (in course suite)
HC	Hard Copy
PLL	*Primary Language Lessons* (book)
ILL	*Intermediate Language Lessons* (book)
RS4K	*Real Science 4 Kids* (book)
I-CAT	*Illustrated Catechism* (book)
OHF-1	*Our Holy Faith, Book 1* (book)
OHF-2	*Our Holy Faith, Book 2* (book)
OHF-4	*Our Holy Faith, Book 4* (book)
OHF-1-TM	*Our Holy Faith, Book 1, Teacher's Manual* (book)

OVERVIEW

Common Topics (All students PreK to 6th)

Virtue:	Generosity
Hymn:	Lumen Christi
Prayers:	Signum Crucis, Pater Noster, Ave Maria, Gloria Patri, Angelus
History:	Rights, Technological Revolution, and the Catholic Movement
Science:	Six Simple Machines

History Themes

In Unit 29 we conclude our study of the Modern age, and we are left with more questions than when we began. Western Civilization is progressing to some unknowable end, and it seems that culture is seeking progress solely for the sake of progress, which causes much alarm. Technology is changing at a rapid rate and more and more people are becoming completely addicted to its advancements, believing that it brings happiness. Culturally, technology is no longer a tool, a means to an end, as it once was. This explains our cultural craze to have the latest gadget. However, in the end, the pursuit of tech leaves people searching for the next great thing, always thirsty, but never satisfied.

The Western man at one point knew the end for which he and civilization was striving, but now society is confused. The West has lost sight of the true purpose of man. Its pursuit of happiness has become misguided. And yet hope is not lost. The Message of the Gospel is relevant and it reveals to this fallen world the Incarnate Christ, Who alone can re-create all things new. This unit is a good time not to despair, but to have hope. Hope in the Risen Christ and his power to transform souls. Let us all pray for the renewal of hearts and minds as we study the remainder of the 20th century.

The Church offers us answers to the problems of society today. The teachings about the dignity of the human person can bring much clarity to a confused culture that discards its elderly and murders its young. Spend time this week as a family reading the Catechism on the dignity of human persons (*CCC 1700-1869*). Perhaps one of the solutions to redirect the ship of civilization is the *Benedict Option*, where Christians separate themselves from mainstream secular society and form communities of authentic Christian culture in order to better engage with it (see Rod Dreher's article "The Benedict Option," http://www.theamericanconservative.com/articles/benedict-option/). This monastic model just might provide such a place for Christian culture to rediscover authentic culture and reinvigorate once again mainstream society.

How to Apply History to Everyday Life

Rights, Technological Revolution, and the Catholic Movement. Our culture today seems to be very concerned about the rights of individuals, but it often neglects to consider the dignity of the human person. People become upset when they feel that their rights have been disregarded or taken away, yet they often forget the dignity of their neighbor, the dignity of the elderly, the dignity of the unborn. We should always consider how we treat the people in our community. Do we help, as much as we can, in taking care of the spiritual and material needs of the poor? How can we treat our neighbors, those we are frequently in contact with, with dignity? How should our family deal with the rapid progress of technology? How do we establish authentic Christian culture in the place where we live? Should it be best for us to withdraw from mainstream secular culture?

Virtue. Practicing the virtue of generosity is another way in which we can provide for the needs of others. As the Catechism states, "The works of mercy are charitable actions by which we come to the aid of our neighbor in his spiritual and bodily necessities. Instructing, advising, consoling, comforting are spiritual works of mercy, as are forgiving and bearing wrongs patiently. The corporal works of mercy consist especially in feeding the hungry, sheltering the homeless, clothing the naked, visiting the sick and imprisoned, and burying the dead. Among all these, giving alms to the poor is one of the chief witnesses to fraternal charity: it is also a work of justice pleasing to God" (CCC 2447).

Important People, Events, and Places to Know (Potential Student Presentations)

❖ Humanae Vitae (1968); Second Vatican Council (1962-1965); Civil Rights Movement (1954-1968); Brown v. Board of Education (1954); Montgomery Bus Boycott (1955-1956); March on Washington (1963); Civil Rights Act of 1964; Dr. Martin Luther King Jr. (1929-1968); Malcolm X (1922-1965); Pope St. John Paul II (1920-2005); Vietnam War (1955-1975); Space Race (1955-1972); Roe v. Wade (1973); Mass production of personal computers (1977); Gulf War (1990-1991); 9/11 (2001); Israel becomes a state (1948); European Powers Decolonize Asia and Africa (1945-1960); Rise of militant Islam (ca. 1960 – present); invention of the "internet"; invention of the television
❖ Some Saints of the Twentieth Century:

- St. Maria Goretti (1902)
- St. Pius X (1914)
- St. Christopher Magallanes & Companions (1915-1928)
- Our Lady of Fatima (1917)
- St. Frances Xavier Cabrini (1917)
- St. Raphaela Mary (1925)
- Bl. Philip Monarriz & Companions (1936)
- St. Andre Bessette (1937)
- St. Faustina Kowalska (1938)
- St. Maximillan Kolbe (1941)
- St. Teresa Benedicta of the Cross (Edith Stein) (1942)
- St. Josephine Bakhita (1947)

Additional Project Ideas

- Take a week (or longer) break from all modern technology.

PLANNER ~ Unit 29 (Co-op)

Week of _____   *Liturgical Theme & Colors*_____

Family Challenge-Task Goals _____

_____

_____

Reminders _____

_____

_____

PRESCHOOL

	Music	Art, Reading, Religion	Virtue
Co-op	See "Music" heading below	Do craft **PreK Lesson A** (SF)	Practice "virtue training"
Day 2-4	See "Music" heading below	Do **Number Book 9-10** (SF); do **worksheets** (SF); review & drill I-CAT, pp 27 (HC)	Practice "virtue training"

KINDERGARTEN – 6TH GRADE

ART   **CCM**

	K-6th Grade		K-6th Grade
Co-op	Do **All Lesson A** (SF).		Unit 29
Day 2-4	Review **All Lesson A** (SF) and do home follow-up.		Listen to Unit 29 every day

HISTORY

	K-1st Grades	2nd-3rd Grades	4th-6th Grades
Co-op	Do **K-1 Lesson A** (SF).	Do **2-3 Lesson A** (SF).	Read *A.A. Milne's Winnie the Pooh* (HC); Do **4-6 Lesson A** (SF).
Day 2	Read *Angel in the Waters* (HC); Read *Beatrix Potter's Stories* (HC); Choose and do reading (or other project) from "Extras" (SF); draw a picture inspired by the readings; *Glory Story CD*, Vol. IV, Blessed Mother Teresa	Read *Angel in the Waters* (HC); Read *Beatrix Potter's Stories* (HC);Choose and do reading (or other project) from "Extras" (SF); draw a picture inspired by the readings; *Glory Story CD*, Vol. IV, Blessed Mother Teresa	Continue *A.A. Milne's Winnie the Pooh* (HC); Choose and do readings (or other projects) from "Extras" (SF); begin writing **4-6 Activity A** (SF); *Glory Story CD*, Vol. IV, Blessed Mother Teresa
Day 3	Continue *Beatrix Potter's Stories* (HC); Do coloring page (SF)	Continue *Beatrix Potter's Stories* (HC); Do map **2-3 Activity A** (SF); Do coloring page (SF);	Continue *A.A. Milne's Winnie the Pooh* (HC); Do map **4-6 Activity B** (SF)
Day 4	Continue *Beatrix Potter's Stories* (HC); Act out one of the readings (see SF for instructions)	Continue *Beatrix Potter's Stories* (HC); Act out one of the readings (see SF for instructions)	Continue *A.A. Milne's Winnie the Pooh* (HC); Do timeline **4-6 Activity C (SF)**; summarize the reading this week and draw!

LANGUAGE ARTS

Co-op	Complete **K-1 Lesson A** (SF).	Complete **2-3 Lesson A** (SF).	Complete **4-6 Lesson A** (SF).
Day 2	Review **K-1 Lesson A** (SF); do **K-1 Activity A** (SF).	Review **2-3 Lesson A** (SF); do **2-3 Activity A** (SF).	Review **4-6 Lesson A** (SF); do **4-6 Activity A** (SF)
Day 3	Do pre-cursive copywork **K-1 Activity B** (SF).	Do cursive copywork **2-3 Activity B** (SF).	Complete first draft in **4-6 Activity A** (SF).
Day 4	Do narration and illustration **K-1 Activity C** (SF)	Do composition and illustration **2-3 Activity C** (SF)	Complete final draft in **4-6 Activity A** (SF).

LATIN/GREEK

Co-op	Practice Lumen Christi (SF)	Practice Lumen Christi (SF); do *Greek Primer* 29.1–4 (SF)	Practice Lumen Christi (SF); do *Reading Greek* 28.1–2 (SF)
Day 2	Listen to CCM Unit 29 Latin prayer	Listen to CCM Unit 29 Latin prayer; do *Greek Primer* 29	Listen to CCM Unit 28 Latin prayer; do *Reading Greek* 28.3–4 (SF)
Day 3	Practice all the *Schola Rosa* Latin assembly prayers!	Practice all the *Schola Rosa* Latin assembly prayers!; do *Greek Primer* 29 (SF)	Practice all the *Schola Rosa* Latin assembly prayers!; do *Reading Greek* 28.4 (SF)
Day 4	Listen to Lumen Christi video (SF); Sing along!	Listen to Lumen Christi video (SF); Sing along!; finish *Greek Primer* Unit 29 (SF)	Listen to Lumen Christi video (SF); Sing along!; finish *Reading Greek* Unit 28 (SF) and check work

MATH

	Level A	Level B	Level C
Co-op	None	None	None
Day 2-4	See *Ray's Primary*, Mastery Chart~ Do next lesson (DL)	See *Ray's Intellectual*, Mastery Chart~ Do next lesson (DL)	See *Ray's Practical*, Mastery Chart~ Do next lesson (DL)

MUSIC

	K-6th Grade
Co-op Day 2-4	Review **All Lesson A** (SF). Use audio files to sing along with: Hymn of the Week (Latin SF); Exercises Group 1, 2, 3, 4, & 5; Practice the songs selected by your music teacher for the end of the year performance (DL).

READING

	Primer (pre-reader)	Reader
	None	None
	See *McGuffey's Eclectic Primer*, "Mastery Chart"~ Do next lesson (DL)	See *McGuffey's Eclectic Readers*, "Mastery Chart" ~ Do next lesson (DL)

RELIGION — *Liturgical Feast lessons can be moved to correspond to their dates – simply adjust the schedule accordingly*

	K-1st Grades	2nd-3rd Grades	4th-6th Grades
Co-op	Begin **K-1 Lesson A** (SF).	Begin **2-3 Lesson A** (SF). Drill Q & A.	Begin **4-6 Lesson A** (SF). Drill Q & A.
Day 2	Review/complete **K-1 Lesson A** (SF).	Review/complete **2-3 Lesson A** (SF). Drill Q & A.	Review/complete **4-6 Lesson A** (SF). Drill Q & A.
Day 3	Begin **K-1 Lesson B** (SF).	Review/complete **2-3 Lesson A** (SF). Drill Q & A.	Complete activity(-ies) from the "Let Us Work Together" section OHF-4, pp. 258-260.
Day 4	Review/complete **K-1 Lesson B** (SF).	Review/complete **2-3 Lesson A** (SF). Drill Q & A.	Complete activity(ies) from the "Let Us Work Together" section OHF-4, pp. 258-260.

SCIENCE

Co-op	Do **All Lesson A** (SF).	Do **All Lesson A** (SF).	Do **All Lesson A** (SF).
Day 2	Review **All Lesson A** (SF); Check out books on simple machines from your local library.	Review **All Lesson A** (SF); Check out books on simple machines from your local library.	Review **All Lesson A** (SF); Check out books on simple machines from your local library; do Nature Journal from **4-6 Lesson A** (SF). Read Ch. 4 *RS4K, Focus on Elementary Physics* and do Experiment 4.
Day 3	Complete **K-1 Activity A** (SF).	Complete **2-3 Activity A** (SF).	Complete **4-6 Activity A** (SF) and do **4-6 Activity B** (SF).
Day 4	Do drawing **K-1 Activity B** (SF); if possible, go on a nature walk.	Do description & illustration **2-3 Activity B** (SF); if possible, go on a nature walk.	Do library research **4-6 Activity C** (SF); if possible, go on a nature walk and do Nature Journaling.

VIRTUE

	K-6th Grades
Field	Do **All Virtue Lesson A –Generosity** (SF)
Day 2-4	Practice "virtue training"

CYCLE III
UNIT 30

REVIEW

UNIT CHECKLIST

PREP FOR HOME

- ☐ Print and read this Handbook
- ☐ Read the Overview
- ☐ Review the Planner; do the following:
  - ○ Locate and review all Lessons and Activities in the Subject Folders (SF)
  - ○ Locate and review all readings and assignments in the Subject Folders (SF), Digital Library (DL), and Hard Copies (HC)
  - ○ Note and gather needed supplies for the unit
- ☐ Read the Virtue Lesson
- ☐ Email or call R.A.S. if you have questions or technical difficulty.

PREP FOR CO-OP

- ☐ Print your "Co-op Job Sheet" and prep for your job
- ☐ Make sure your child is ready for his or her presentation if assigned to present
- ☐ Gather maps, notebooks, prayer sheet, and other supplies the night or morning before the co-op meets.
- ☐ Gather students' assignments the night or morning before the co-op meets
- ☐ Listen to the Memory Work on the way!

PREP FOR UPCOMING WEEKS — <u>Finis est!</u>

- ☐ Make advanced purchases, as necessary
- ☐ Begin to gather books and materials

PLANNER ABBREVIATION KEY	
DL	Digital Library (in course suite)
SF	Subject Folder (in course suite)
HC	Hard Copy
PLL	*Primary Language Lessons* (book)
ILL	*Intermediate Language Lessons* (book)
RS4K	*Real Science 4 Kids* (book)
I-CAT	*Illustrated Catechism* (book)
OHF-1	*Our Holy Faith, Book 1* (book)
OHF-2	*Our Holy Faith, Book 2* (book)
OHF-4	*Our Holy Faith, Book 4* (book)
OHF-1-TM	*Our Holy Faith, Book 1, Teacher's Manual* (book)

OVERVIEW

Common Topics (All students PreK to 6th)

Virtue:	Review
Hymn:	Lumen Christi
Prayers:	Signum Crucis, Pater Noster, Ave Maria, Gloria Patri, Angelus
History:	Review
Science:	Review

History Themes

This is a review week for History. Please review Units 16-30.

How to Apply History to Everyday Life

Review the virtues covered throughout the second semester and how they apply to the history units which you are reviewing.

Important People, Events, and Places to Know (Potential Student Presentations)

❖ Review your Timeline activities. Compile the entire year into a giant timeline!
❖ Review the Saints.

Additional Project Ideas

❖ Complete any projects that you found interesting but did not have time to finish in Units 16-30.

OVERVIEW

Week of _____   *Liturgical Theme & Colors* _____

Family Challenge-Task
Goals _____

_____

_____

Reminders _____

_____

_____

PRESCHOOL

	Music	Art, Reading, Religion	Virtue
Day 1	Review all hymns (SF-Latin)	Do craft **PreK Lesson A** (SF)	Practice "virtue training"
Day 2-4	Review all hymns (SF-Latin)	Review Numbers 1-10 (SF), review and drill I-CAT, p. 27 (HC)	Practice "virtue training"

KINDERGARTEN – 6TH GRADE

ART   **CCM**

	K-6th Grade	K-6th Grade
Day 1	Review Units 27-29	Unit 30
Day 2-4	Review Units 27-29; do an extra art task from the home follow-up section, if there is time.	Listen to Unit 30 every day

HISTORY

	K-1st Grades	2nd-3rd Grades	4th-6th Grades
Day 1	Review any story(ies) from Units 16-30; draw a picture of your favorite story	Review any story(ies) from Units 16-30; draw a picture of your favorite story	Review any story(ies) from Units 16-30; draw a picture of your favorite story
Day 2	Review any story(ies) from Units 16-30; choose a story and act it out; *Glory Story CD*, Vol. XI, Pope Saint John Paul II	Review any story(ies) from Units 16-30; choose a story and act it out; *Glory Story CD*, Vol. XI, Pope Saint John Paul II	Review any story(ies) from Units 16-30; choose a story and act it out; *Glory Story CD*, Vol. XI, Pope Saint John Paul II
Day 3	Review any story(ies) from Units 16-30; choose a story and act it out.	Review any story(ies) from Units 16-30; do map **2-3 Activity A** (SF)	Review any story(ies) from Units 16-30; do map **2-3 Activity A** (SF)
Day 4	Do **All Activity A** Family Quiz Bowl (SF)	Do **All Activity A** Family Quiz Bowl (SF)	Do **All Activity A** Family Quiz Bowl (SF)

LANGUAGE ARTS

Day 1	Complete **K-1 Lesson A** (SF).	Complete **2-3 Lesson A** (SF).	Complete **4-6 Lesson A** (SF).
Day 2	Review **K-1 Lesson A** (SF); do **K-1 Activity A** (SF).	Review **2-3 Lesson A** (SF); do **2-3 Activity A** (SF).	Review **4-6 Lesson A**; do **4-6 Activity A** (SF)
Day 3	Do pre-cursive copywork **K-1 Activity B** (SF).	Do cursive copywork **2-3 Activity B** (SF).	Continue **4-6 Lesson A**.
Day 4	Do narration and illustration **K-1 Activity C** (SF)	Do composition and illustration **2-3 Activity C** (SF)	Continue **4-6 Lesson A**.

LATIN/GREEK

Day 1	Practice Lumen Christi (SF)	Practice Lumen Christi (SF); do *Greek Primer* 30.1-4 (SF)	Practice Lumen Christi (SF); do *Reading Greek* 30.1-2 (SF)
Day 2	Listen to CCM Unit 30 Latin prayer	Listen to CCM Unit 30 Latin prayer; do *Greek Primer* 30	Listen to CCM Unit 30 Latin prayer; do *Reading Greek* 30.3-4 (SF)
Day 3	Practice all the *Schola Rosa* Latin assembly prayers!	Practice all the *Schola Rosa* Latin assembly prayers!; do *Greek Primer* 30 (SF)	Practice all the *Schola Rosa* Latin assembly prayers!; do *Reading Greek* 30.4 (SF)
Day 4	Listen to Lumen Christi video (SF); Sing along!	Listen to Lumen Christi video (SF); Sing along!; finish *Greek Primer* Unit 30 (SF)	Listen to Lumen Christi video (SF); Sing along!; finish *Reading Greek* Unit 30 (SF) and review/check work

MATH

	Level A	Level B	Level C
Day 1	None	None	None
Day 2-4	See *Ray's Primary*, Mastery Chart~ Do next lesson (DL)	See *Ray's Intellectual*, Mastery Chart~ Do next lesson (DL)	See *Ray's Practical*, Mastery Chart~ Do next lesson (DL)

MUSIC

	K-6th Grade
Day 1	Review **All Lesson A** (SF). Use audio files
Day 2-4	to sing along with: Hymn of the Week (Latin SF); Exercises Group 1, 2, 3, 4, & 5; Practice the songs selected by your music teacher for the end of the year performance (DL).

READING

	Primer (pre-reader)	Reader
Day 1	None	None
Day 2-4	See *McGuffey's Eclectic Primer*, "Mastery Chart" ~ Do next lesson (DL)	See *McGuffey's Eclectic Readers*, "Mastery Chart" ~ Do next lesson (DL)

RELIGION — *Liturgical Feast lessons can be moved to correspond to their dates – simply adjust the schedule accordingly*

	K-1st Grades	2nd-3rd Grades	4th-6th Grades
Day 1	Begin **K-1 Lesson A** (SF).	Begin **2-3 Lesson A** (SF). Drill Q & A.	Begin **4-6 Lesson A** (SF). Drill Q & A.
Day 2	Review/complete **K-1 Lesson A** (SF).	Review/complete **2-3 Lesson A** (SF). Drill Q & A.	Review/complete **4-6 Lesson A** (SF). Drill Q & A.
Day 3	Begin **K-1 Lesson B** (SF).	Review/complete **2-3 Lesson A** (SF). Drill Q & A.	Complete activity(-ies) from the "Let Us Work Together" section OHF-4, pp. 258-260.
Day 4	Review/complete **K-1 Lesson B** (SF).	Review/complete **2-3 Lesson A** (SF). Drill Q & A.	Complete activity(ies) from the "Let Us Work Together" section OHF-4, pp. 258-260.

SCIENCE

Day 1	Review CCM Science, Units 27-29.	Review CCM Science, Units 27-29.	Review CCM Science, Units 27-29.
Day 2	Gather readings and assignments and make sure all items are completed.	Gather readings and assignments and make sure all items are completed.	Gather readings and assignments and make sure all items are completed.
Day 3	Ask students to tell you their favorite science topic and activity of the year. Write it down.	Ask students to tell you their favorite science topic and activity of the year. Write it down.	Have students write a summary of their favorite science topic and activity this year.
Day 4	Finish reading anything left undone.	Finish reading anything left undone.	Finish reading anything left undone.

VIRTUE

	K-6th Grades
Day 1	Do **All Virtue Lesson A - Review**
Day 2-4	Practice "virtue training"

Preschool

- ❖ DL = in the Digital Library; HC = purchase the Hardcopy
- ❖ I-CAT = *Illustrated Catechism for Little Children* (HC); Catechism Q&A is from this resource.
- ❖ See Unit Handbooks for schedule of daily lessons and activities and their locations.

	Music	Art Goals	Reading Goals	Religion Goals	Virtue
Unit 1	Stretches & Posture	8 Basic Colors Watercolor Painting	**Read-Aloud:** *Alphabet of Saints* (HC) Letter Book A-B (DL) Poetry: "ABC" & "Burnie Bee" Sound-to-Letter Recognition Writing Coloring Pages A-B (DL)	**Catechism Q&A: God** (HC: I-CAT) **Read-Aloud:** *Alphabet of Mary* (HC) St. Agnus St. Bernadette Holy Name of Mary Watercolor	"Alphabet of Virtues," A-B
Unit 2	Breathing & Low-High Voices	Clay; Shapes: sphere, rectangle, cross	**Read-Aloud:** *Alphabet of Saints* (HC) Letter Book C-D (DL) Poetry: "Cross-Patch" & "Diddle, Diddle, Dumpling" Sound-to-Letter Recognition Writing Coloring Pages C-D (DL)	**Catechism Q&A: God** (HC: I-CAT) **Read-Aloud:** *A Tale of Three Trees* (HC) Exaltation of the Holy Cross St. Catherine of Sienna St. Dominic Make Clay Crucifixes	"Alphabet of Virtues," C-D
Unit 3	Voice Level & Sirens	8 Basic Colors Coloring in Line	**Read-Aloud:** *Alphabet of Saints* (HC) Letter Book E-F (DL) Poetry: "See, See" & "The Farmer" Sound-to-Letter Recognition Writing Coloring Pages E-F (DL)	**Catechism Q&A: The Blessed Trinity** (HC: I-CAT) **Read-Aloud:** *The Great Battle for Heaven* (HC) Color Cardboard Swords St. Michael St. Ermengild St. Francis Xavier	"Alphabet of Virtues," E-F
Unit	Review	Painting with Red	**Read-Aloud:** *Alphabet of Saints* (HC)	**Catechism Q&A: The Blessed Trinity**	Review

SCOPE & SEQUENCE

4			Review Letters A-F	(HC: I-CAT)	
Unit 5	Primary Vowels	Watercolor Painting 8 Basic Colors	**Read-Aloud:** *Alphabet of Saints* (HC) Letter Book G-H (DL) Poetry: "Georgy Porgy" & "Hot-Cross Buns" Sound-to-Letter Recognition Writing Coloring Pages G-H (DL)	**Catechism Q&A: The Holy Angels** (HC: I-CAT) **Read-Aloud:** *Angel in the Waters* (HC) Feast of the Guardian Angels Guardian Angel Craft St. George St. Hubert	"Alphabet of Virtues," G-H
Unit 6	Primary Vowels	Red, Blue, and Yellow Painting Birdhouses	**Read-Aloud:** *Alphabet of Saints* (HC) Letter Book I-J (DL) Poetry: "Rain" & "Jack" Sound-to-Letter Recognition Writing Coloring Pages I-J (DL)	**Catechism Q&A: The Holy Angels** (HC: I-CAT) **Read-Aloud:** *The Good Man of Assisi* (HC) Feast of St. Francis St. Isidore Ss. James and John	"Alphabet of Virtues," I-J
Unit 7	Tongue, Mouth, and Throat Posture	Cut and Paste	**Read-Aloud:** *Alphabet of Saints* (HC) Letter Book K-L (DL) Poetry: "Lock and Key" & "Little Boy Blue" Sound-to-Letter Recognition Writing Coloring Pages K-L (DL)	**Catechism Q&A: Man** (HC: I-CAT) **Read-Aloud:** *The Holy Rosary* (HC) Paper Bag Rosary St. Keyne St. Lucy Filippini	"Alphabet of Virtues," K-L
Unit	Review	Painting	**Read-Aloud:** *Alphabet*	**Catechism Q&A: Man**	Review

8		with Red and Blue	*of Saints* (HC) Review Letters A-L	(HC: I-CAT)	
Unit 9	Skips & Thirds	Pasting	**Read-Aloud:** *Alphabet of Saints* (HC) Letter Book M-N (DL) Poetry: "To Market" & "A Nick and a Nock" Sound-to-Letter Recognition Writing Coloring Pages M-N (DL)	**Catechism Q&A: Our Lord** (HC: I-CAT) **Read-Aloud:** *I Sing a Song of the Saints of God* (HC) Holy Saints Prayer Cloud Feast of All Saints Ss. Martha and Mary St. Nicholas of Myra	"Alphabet of Virtues," M-N
Unit 10	Fourths	Kneading	**Read-Aloud:** *Alphabet of Saints* (HC) Letter Book O-P (DL) Poetry: "Old Chairs to Mend" & "Polly and Sukey" Sound-to-Letter Recognition Writing Coloring Pages O-P (DL)	**Catechism Q&A: Our Lord** (HC: I-CAT) **Read-Aloud:** *A Story of Saint Elizabeth of Hungary* (HC) St. Elizabeth St. Odo St. Porcarius Bread for the Hungery	"Alphabet of Virtues," O-P
Unit 11	Tone Building	Cut and paste Paint	**Read-Aloud:** *Alphabet of Saints* (HC) Letter Book Q-R (DL) Poetry: "Q" & "Robin Redbreast" Sound-to-Letter Recognition Writing Coloring Pages Q-R (DL)	**Catechism Q&A: Our Lord** (HC: I-CAT) **Read-Aloud:** *Christmas is...*(HC) Advent St. Quentin St. Rumwald	"Alphabet of Virtues," Q-R
Unit	Review	Painting	**Read-Aloud:** *Alphabet*	**Catechism Q&A: Our**	Review

SCOPE & SEQUENCE

12		with Red and Yellow	*of Saints* (HC) Review	**Lord** (HC: I-CAT)	
Unit 13	Review	Painting with Blue and Yellow	**Read-Aloud:** *Alphabet of Saints* (HC)	**Catechism Q&A: Sin** (HC: I-CAT)	Review
Unit 14	Review	Painting with Red, Blue, and Yellow	**Read-Aloud:** *Alphabet of Saints* (HC)	**Catechism Q&A: Sin** (HC: I-CAT)	Review
Unit 15	Review	Cut and paste Using Form	**Read-Aloud:** *Alphabet of Saints* (HC)	Review Catechism Q&A: God Holy Family Craft	Review
Unit 16	Review	Textures Nature	**Read-Aloud:** *Alphabet of Saints* (HC)	Review Catechism Q&A: Trinity & Angels St. Agnes Craft Purity	Review
Unit 17	Review	Color, cut, and paste	**Read-Aloud:** *Alphabet of Saints* (HC) Retelling a Story with Puppets	Review Catechism Q&A: Angels & Man Conversion of St. Paul	Review
Unit 18	Review	Watercolor Painting Narrow and broad brush strokes	**Read-Aloud:** *Alphabet of Saints* (HC)	Review Catechism Q&A: Our Lord Presentation of Our Lord, Purification of Our Lady	Review
Unit 19	Fifths	Candle Making Color, texture, pliability	**Read-Aloud:** *Alphabet of Saints* (HC) Letter Book S-T Poetry: "The Seasons" & "This is the Way" Sound-to-Letter Recognition Writing Coloring Pages S-T (DL)	**Catechism Q&A: Confession** (HC: I-CAT) Presentation of Our Lord, Candlemas, Purification of Our Lady St. Sigfrid St. Theodore	"Alphabet of Virtues," S-T
Unit 20	Sixths	Colors, textures, nature; Cut and	**Read-Aloud:** *Alphabet of Saints* (HC) Letter Book U-V (DL) Poetry: "St.	**Catechism Q&A: Communion** (HC: I-CAT) **Read-Aloud:** *Our Lady*	"Alphabet of Virtues," U-V

		paste	Ursula" & "St. Victoria" Sound-to-Letter Recognition Writing Coloring Pages U-V (DL)	*of Lourdes* (HC) St. Bernadette Marian Grotto Craft St. Ursula St. Victoria	
Unit 21	Consonants	Cut and shape	**Read-Aloud:** *Alphabet of Saints* (HC) Letter Book W-X (DL) Poetry: "Whistle" & "Fox" Sound-to-Letter Recognition Writing Coloring Pages W-X (DL)	**Catechism Q&A: Communion** (HC: I-CAT) **Read-Aloud:** Scripture – St. Joseph St. Joseph Novena Craft St. Wenceslaus St. Xystus	"Alphabet of Virtues," W-X
Unit 22	Review	Primary and Secondary Colors; Color Wheel; Geometric Shape	**Read-Aloud:** *Alphabet of Saints* (HC) Review	Review Catechism Q&A: Confession & Communion	Review
Unit 23	Sevenths and Octaves	Sequence and Order	**Read-Aloud:** *Alphabet of Saints* (HC) Letter Book Y-Z (DL) Poetry: "Yippety, Yippety, Yip" & "Ziggy Zaphoon" Sound-to-Letter Recognition Writing Coloring Pages Y-Z (DL)	Review Catechism Q&A: Communion **Read-Aloud:** Stations of the Cross Cards Stations of the Cross Box St. Yves St. Zita	"Alphabet of Virtues," Y-Z
Unit 24	Legato	Stamping and Printmaking	**Read-Aloud:** *1 is One* (HC) Number Book 1-2 (DL) Poetry: "One" & "Two"	Review Catechism Q&A: Communion **Read-Aloud:** *Patrick: Patron Saint of Ireland* (HC)	Review

			Shape and Number Recognition Writing & Tracing Drawing	Trinity Shamrocks St. Patrick	
Unit 25	Half-Steps	Cutting curves Paste	**Read-Aloud:** *1 is One* (HC) Number Book 3-4 (DL) Poetry: "Three" & "Four" Shape and Number Recognition Writing & Tracing Drawing	**Catechism Q&A: Confirmation** (HC: I-CAT) **Read-Aloud:** *Song of the Swallows* (HC) Seven Sorrows of Mary	Review
Unit 26	Review	Shapes GeoBoard	**Read-Aloud:** *1 is One* (HC) Review	Review Catechism Q&A: Confirmation	Review
Unit 27	Performance Skills	Sequence and Order Cut and paste	**Read-Aloud:** *1 is One* (HC) Number Book 5-6 (DL) Poetry: "Five" & "Six" Shape and Number Recognition Writing & Tracing Drawing	**Catechism Q&A: Reward & Punishment** (HC: I-CAT) **Read-Aloud:** *Easter is for Me!* (HC) Easter Story	Review
Unit 28	Performance	Negative Space and Symmetry	**Read-Aloud:** *1 is One* (HC) Number Book 7-8 (DL) Poetry: "Seven" & "Eight" Shape and Number Recognition Writing & Tracing Drawing	Review Catechism Q&A: Reward & Punishment **Read-Aloud:** *Little Caterpillar that Finds Jesus* (HC) Host and Chalice Craft	Review

Unit 29	Performanc e	Paste, Drawing	**Read-Aloud:** *1 is One* (HC) Number Book 9-10 (DL) Poetry: "Nine" & "Ten" Shape and Number Recognition Writing & Tracing Drawing	Review Catechism Q&A: Reward & Punishment **Read-Aloud:** St. Mark's Gospel (HC) Macaroni Lions Craft	Review
Unit 30	Performanc e	Numbers, Counting, Cardboard Abacus	**Read-Aloud:** *1 is One* (HC) Review Numbers 1-10	Review Catechism Q&A: Reward & Punishment	Review

SCOPE & SEQUENCE

All Grades ~ SCOPE & SEQUENCE

Art

❖ Below you will find a list of the lessons, principles, skills, media, and home follow-ups for each unit of the cycle.

Unit 1	LESSON ~	Copperwork
	General Principle ~	Order
	Specific Skill ~	Foreground & Background
	Medium ~	Copper
	Home Follow-Up ~	Finish project
Unit 2	LESSON ~	Drawing the Human Form
	General Principle ~	Order
	Specific Skill ~	Shape
	Medium ~	Pencil & Charcoal
	Home Follow-Up ~	Finding Shapes in Nature
Unit 3	LESSON ~	Cross-Stitching
	General Principle ~	Order
	Specific Skill ~	Line
	Medium ~	Needle, Thread, & Canvas
	Home Follow-Up ~	Finish the Project
Unit 4	Review Principles, Skills, and Home Follow-ups, Units 1-3	
Unit 5	LESSON ~	Drawing Landscapes
	General Principle ~	Order
	Specific Skill ~	Depth
	Medium ~	Water Color Pencils
	Home Follow-Up ~	Finding the Principles in Art ~ Library Books
Units 6 – 7	LESSON ~	Oil Painting
	General Principle ~	Proportion
	Specific Skill ~	Primary & Secondary Colors
	Medium ~	Oil Paint
	Home Follow-Up ~	Finding the Principles in Art ~ Library Books
Unit 8	Review Principles, Skills, and Home Follow-ups, Units 1-7	
Unit 9	LESSON ~	Colored Pencil Nature Drawings
	General Principle ~	Proportion
	Specific Skill ~	Texture
	Medium ~	Colored Pencils
	Home Follow-Up ~	Imitate drawings by John James Audubon
Unit 10	LESSON ~	Colored Pencil Nature Drawings, Part 2
	General Principle ~	Proportion
	Specific Skill ~	Detail
	Medium ~	Colored Pencils
	Home Follow-Up ~	Imitate drawings by John James Audubon

Unit 11	LESSON ~	Architectural Sculpture
	General Principle ~	Proportion
	Specific Skill ~	Balance
	Medium ~	Wood & Clay
	Home Follow-Up ~	Finding the Principles in Art ~ Library Books
Units 12 – 18	Review Principles, Skills, and Home Follow-ups, Units 1-11	
Units 19 - 20	LESSON ~	Sewing a 9-Patch Block
	General Principle ~	Integrity
	Specific Skill ~	Function
	Medium ~	Textiles
	Home Follow-Up ~	Finding the Principles in Art ~ Around the Home
Unit 21	LESSON ~	Photography
	General Principle ~	Integrity
	Specific Skill ~	Composition
	Medium ~	Camera
	Home Follow-Up ~	Visit a Photography Museum and Discussion
Unit 22	Review Principles, Skills, and Home Follow-ups, Units 19-21	
Unit 23	LESSON ~	Photography
	General Principle ~	Integrity
	Specific Skill ~	Emphasis
	Medium ~	Camera
	Home Follow-Up ~ Discussion	Finding Principles in Art ~ Nature Walk &
Units 24 – 25	LESSON ~	Graphic Design, Part 1
	General Principle ~	Unity
	Specific Skill ~	Lay-out
	Medium ~	Pen & Ink
	Home Follow-Up ~	Finding the Principles in Art ~ Library Books
Unit 26	Review Principles, Skills, and Home Follow-ups, Units 19-25	
Unit 27	LESSON ~	Thaumatrope
	General Principle ~	Radiance
	Specific Skill ~	Visual Illusion
	Medium ~	Pen & Ink
	Home Follow-Up ~	Make more Thaumatropes
Unit 28	LESSON ~	Folioscope
	General Principle ~	Radiance
	Specific Skill ~	Movement
	Medium ~	Pen and Paper
	Home Follow-Up ~	Make more Folioscopes
Unit 29	Continuing Unit 28 with Advanced Folioscopes.	
Unit 30	Review	

Classically Catholic Memory – Schola Rosa

❖ Below you will find a list of the Memory Work, Maps, and Timeline Cards needed for each unit per grade range.

Unit 1	Unit 1 CCM – SR Memory Work Gamma, Map 1 ~ Continents & Oceans Timeline Cards 1 – 8
Unit 2	Unit 2 CCM – SR Memory Work Gamma, Map 2 ~ Canada Timeline Cards 9 – 16
Unit 3	Unit 3 CCM – SR Memory Work Gamma, Map 3 ~ United States of America Timeline Cards 17 – 24
Unit 4	Review Units 1-3 CCM – SR Memory Work Review Gamma Maps 1-2 Review Timeline Cards 1 – 24
Unit 5	Unit 5 CCM – SR Memory Work Gamma, Map 3 ~ United States of America Timeline Cards 25 – 32
Unit 6	Unit 6 CCM – SR Memory Work Gamma, Map 3 ~ United States of America Timeline Cards 33 – 40
Unit 7	Unit 7 CCM – SR Memory Work Gamma, Map 3 ~ United States of America Timeline Cards 41 – 48
Unit 8	Review Units 1-7 CCM – SR Memory Work Review Gamma Maps 1-3 Review Timeline Cards 1 – 48
Unit 9	Unit 9 CCM – SR Memory Work Gamma Map 4 ~ Central America Timeline Cards 49 – 56
Unit 10	Unit 10 CCM – SR Memory Work Gamma, Map 5 ~ Water Ways of Northern America Timeline Cards 57 – 64
Unit 11	Unit 11 CCM – SR Memory Work Gamma, Map 5 ~ Landmarks of Northern and Central America Timeline Cards 65 – 72
Unit 12	Review Units 1-11 CCM – SR Memory Work Review Gamma Maps 1-5 Review Timeline Cards 1 – 72

All Grades ~ SCOPE & SEQUENCE

Units 13 - 18	Review Units 1-11 CCM – SR Memory Work Review Gamma Maps 1-5 Review Timeline Cards 1 – 72
Unit 19	Unit 19 CCM – SR Memory Work Delta, Map 1 ~ Continents and Latitude/Longitude Marks Timeline Cards 73 – 80
Unit 20	Unit 20 CCM – SR Memory Work Delta, Map 2 ~ South American Rivers Timeline Cards 81 – 88
Unit 21	Unit 21 CCM – SR Memory Work Delta, Map 2 ~ South America Timeline Cards 89 – 96
Unit 22	Review Units 1-21 CCM – SR Memory Work Review Delta, Maps 1-2 Review Timeline Cards 1 – 96
Unit 23	Unit 23 CCM – SR Memory Work Delta, Map 2 ~ South America Timeline Cards 97 – 104
Unit 24	Unit 24 CCM – SR Memory Work Delta, Map 3 ~ Africa Timeline Cards 105 – 112
Unit 25	Unit 25 CCM – SR Memory Work Delta, Map 3 ~ Africa Timeline Cards 113 – 120
Unit 26	Review Units 1-25 CCM – SR Memory Work Review Maps 1-5 Review Timeline Cards 1 – 120
Unit 27	Unit 27 CCM – SR Memory Work Delta, Map 4 ~ Northern Africa and Arabia Timeline Cards 121 – 128
Unit 28	Unit 28 CCM – SR Memory Work Delta, Map 5 ~ Africa Timeline Cards 129 – 136
Unit 29	Unit 29 CCM – SR Memory Work Delta, Map 5 ~ Africa Timeline Cards 137 – 144
Unit 30	Review Units 1-29 CCM – SR Memory Work Review Gamma and Delta Maps 1-5 Review Timeline Cards 1 – 144

History

❖ Below you will find a list of the topics, books, lessons, and activities for each unit per grade range.
❖ DL = in Digital Library; HC = purchase Hardcopy; SF = provided in the subject folder
❖ See Unit Handbooks for schedule of daily lessons and activities and their locations.

Unit 1

	K – 1st Grade	2nd – 3rd Grade	4th – 6th Grade
Theme	The Renaissance		
Read-Aloud	*Knights of Art* by Steedman (DL) Polyphonic Music (SF)	*Knights of Art* by Steedman (DL) Polyphonic Music (SF)	*Knights of Art* by Steedman (DL) "Bellarmine ~ Doctor of the Church (DL) Polyphonic Music (SF)
Hands-on & Critical Engagement	Renaissance Artists Flipbook Coloring Pages Imagine & Draw	Renaissance Music Flipbook Map of Italy after the Peace of Lodi Coloring Pages Imagine and Draw	Discussion on Music Composition Map of Italy after the Peace of Lodi Timeline

Unit 2

	K – 1st Grade	2nd – 3rd Grade	4th – 6th Grade
Theme	Exploration and Ottoman Empire		
Read-Aloud	*Columbus* by D'Aulaire (HC)	*Columbus* by D'Aulaire (HC)	*The Discovery of New Worlds* by Synge (DL)
Hands-on & Critical Engagement	Make a Telescope Coloring Pages Imagine & Draw	History Pocket Map of European Explorers Coloring Pages Imagine and Draw	Discussion on Courage Composition Map of European Explorers of Lodi Timeline

Unit 3

	K – 1st Grade	2nd – 3rd Grade	4th – 6th Grade
Theme	The Printing Press		
Read-Aloud	*The Pied Piper of Hamlin* (DL) *Red, Yellow,* or *Blue Fairy Books* (HC or DL)	*The Pied Piper of Hamlin* (DL) *Red, Yellow,* or *Blue Fairy Books* (HC or DL)	"The Incurable Era" (SF) *Red, Yellow,* or *Blue Fairy Books* (HC or DL)
Hands-on & Critical Engagement	Moveable Type Letter Craft Coloring Pages Imagine & Draw	Moveable Type Letter Craft Map of Europe during the Renaissance Coloring Pages Imagine and Draw	Discussion on Technology Composition Map of Europe during the Renaissance Timeline

All Grades ~ SCOPE & SEQUENCE

Unit 4

	K – 1st Grade	2nd – 3rd Grade	4th – 6th Grade
Theme	Nautical Adventure		
Read-Aloud	*Featured Glory Story CD, Volume VII, Saint Martin de Porres (HC)*		
	The Swiss Family Robinson (HC)	*The Swiss Family Robinson* (HC)	*The Swiss Family Robinson* (HC)
Hands-on & Critical Engagement	Coloring Pages Imagine & Draw	Coloring Pages Imagine and Draw	Timeline

Unit 5

	K – 1st Grade	2nd – 3rd Grade	4th – 6th Grade
Theme	Spanish Conquest and Germanic Reformation		
Read-Aloud	*Featured Glory Story CD: Volume 1, Saint Juan Diego (HC) & Volume X, Saint Rose of Lima (HC)*		
	Stories of Don Quixote Written Anew for Children (DL)	*Stories of Don Quixote Written Anew for Children* (DL)	*Hernando Cortes* (DL) *Ferdinand de Soto* (DL)
Hands-on & Critical Engagement	Spanish Conquistador Helmet Coloring Pages Imagine & Draw	History Pocket Map of Colonies in the Americas Coloring Pages Imagine and Draw	Discussion on Cortes Map of Colonies in the Americas Composition Timeline

Unit 6

	K – 1st Grade	2nd – 3rd Grade	4th – 6th Grade
Theme	Shakespeare		
Read-Aloud	*Tales from Shakespeare* by Lamb (HC)	*Tales from Shakespeare* by Lamb (HC)	*Comedy of Errors, Acts I-II* (HC or DL)
Hands-on & Critical Engagement	Dramatize the Story Coloring Pages Imagine & Draw	Dramatize the Story Coloring Pages Imagine and Draw	Discussion on drama/comedy Composition

Unit 7

	K – 1st Grade	2nd – 3rd Grade	4th – 6th Grade
Theme	Shakespeare		
Read-Aloud	*Tales from Shakespeare* by Lamb (HC)	*Tales from Shakespeare* by Lamb (HC)	*Comedy of Errors, Acts III-V* (HC or DL)
Hands-on & Critical Engagement	Group Narrative Coloring Pages Imagine & Draw	Model Globe Theatre Map of the Continents Coloring Pages Imagine and Draw	Discussion Composition Map of the Continents

All Grades ~ SCOPE & SEQUENCE

Unit 8

	K – 1st Grade	2nd – 3rd Grade	4th – 6th Grade
Theme	Pilgrims Come to America		
Read-Aloud	Selected Poetry from John Milton (DL)	Selected Poetry from John Milton (DL)	*Mayflower Compact* (DL)
Hands-on & Critical Engagement	Coloring Pages Imagine & Draw	Coloring Pages Imagine and Draw	Timeline

Unit 9

	K – 1st Grade	2nd – 3rd Grade	4th – 6th Grade
Theme	Pilgrim Life and Native Americans		
Read-Aloud	*Gulliver's Travels* by John Lang (DL)	*Gulliver's Travels* by John Lang (DL)	*Gulliver's Travels* by John Lang (DL)
Hands-on & Critical Engagement	Popcorn Necklace Coloring Pages Imagine & Draw	History Pocket Map of Plymouth Colony Coloring Pages Imagine and Draw	Discussion on Exploration and Provincialism Composition Map of Plymouth Colony Timeline

Unit 10

	K – 1st Grade	2nd – 3rd Grade	4th – 6th Grade
Theme	French Exploration & French-Indian War		
Read-Aloud	*The Sign of the Beaver* (HC)	*The Sign of the Beaver* (HC)	*Evangeline* by Longfellow (DL)
Hands-on & Critical Engagement	Draw the Story Coloring Pages Imagine & Draw	History Pocket Map of North America 1750 Coloring Pages Imagine and Draw	Discussion on "Evangeline" Composition Map of North America 1750 Timeline

Unit 11

	K – 1st Grade	2nd – 3rd Grade	4th – 6th Grade
Theme	American Revolution		
Read-Aloud	*Song of Hiawatha* by Longfellow (DL)	*Song of Hiawatha* by Longfellow (DL)	*The Deerslayer, The Pathfinder,* or *The Last of the Mohicans* by Cooper (DL or HC)
Hands-on & Critical Engagement	Dramatize the Story Coloring Pages Imagine & Draw	History Pocket Map of British Territories Coloring Pages Imagine and Draw	Discussion on Native Americans Composition Map of British Territorial Growth 1775

All Grades ~ SCOPE & SEQUENCE

Unit 12

	K – 1st Grade	2nd – 3rd Grade	4th – 6th Grade
Theme	American Revolution		
Read-Aloud	*Great Americans for Little Americans* (DL)	*Great Americans for Little Americans* (DL)	*Four Great Americans* (DL)
Hands-on & Critical Engagement	Coloring Pages Imagine & Draw	Coloring Pages Imagine and Draw	Composition Timeline

Unit 13

	K – 1st Grade	2nd – 3rd Grade	4th – 6th Grade
Theme	Scientific Revolution		
Read-Aloud	*America First* (DL) Music by Mozart	*America First* (DL) Music by Mozart	*America First* (DL) Music by Mozart
Hands-on & Critical Engagement	Coloring Pages Imagine & Draw	Coloring Pages Imagine and Draw	Composition Timeline

Units 14 – 15

	K – 1st Grade	2nd – 3rd Grade	4th – 6th Grade
Theme	Review		
Read-Aloud	*n/a*	*n/a*	*n/a*
Hands-on & Critical Engagement	Finish incomplete assignments.	Finish incomplete assignments.	Finish incomplete assignments.

Unit 16

	K – 1st Grade	2nd – 3rd Grade	4th – 6th Grade
Theme	Enlightenment, Conservatism, and French Revolution		
Read-Aloud	*Stories from Wagner Told to the Children* (DL)	*Stories from Wagner Told to the Children* (DL)	*The Story of Napoleon* (DL)
Hands-on & Critical Engagement	Popsicle Puppets Coloring Pages Imagine & Draw	Popsicle Puppets Coloring Pages Imagine & Draw	Map of Europe 1792 Timeline

All Grades ~ SCOPE & SEQUENCE

Unit 17

	K – 1st Grade	2nd – 3rd Grade	4th – 6th Grade
Theme	United States Constitution		
Read-Aloud	*Stories of America: From Conflict to Constitution* (DL)	*Stories of America: From Conflict to Constitution* (DL)	*Stories of America: From Conflict to Constitution* (DL)
Hands-on & Critical Engagement	Act Out Coloring Pages Imagine & Draw	Act Out Map of the United States 1790 Coloring Pages Imagine & Draw	Map of the United States 1790 Timeline

Unit 18

	K – 1st Grade	2nd – 3rd Grade	4th – 6th Grade
Theme	United States Constitution		
Read-Aloud	*The Constitution Explained* (DL)	*The Constitution Explained* (DL)	*The Constitution of the United States* (DL)
Hands-on & Critical Engagement	Constitution Linked Craft Coloring Pages Imagine & Draw	Constitution Linked Craft Coloring Pages Imagine & Draw	Linked Activity on Bill of Rights Linked Activity on Amendments

Unit 19

	K – 1st Grade	2nd – 3rd Grade	4th – 6th Grade
Theme	Industrial Revolution		
Read-Aloud	*Black Beauty* (DL)	*Black Beauty* (DL)	*Two Years Before the Mast* (DL)
Hands-on & Critical Engagement	Telephone Craft Build a Telegraph Coloring Pages Imagine & Draw	Steamboat Craft Build a Telegraph Coloring Pages Imagine & Draw	Discussion on Sailors Composition Map of the Voyage of the Pilgrim Linked Activity on Road to Revolution

Unit 20

	K – 1st Grade	2nd – 3rd Grade	4th – 6th Grade
Theme	Western Expansion		
Read-Aloud	*Little House Books 1 and 2* (DL)	*Little House Books 1 and 2* (DL)	*Captains Courageous* (DL)
Hands-on & Critical Engagement	Covered Wagon Craft Linked Activities Coloring Pages Imagine & Draw	History Pocket Linked Map Activity Linked Craft Coloring Pages Imagine & Draw	Discussion on Frontiersmen and Merchants Linked Map Activity Linked Craft Composition

All Grades ~ SCOPE & SEQUENCE

Unit 21

	K – 1st Grade	2nd – 3rd Grade	4th – 6th Grade
Theme	Western Expansion		
Read-Aloud	*Little House Books 3 and 4* (DL)	*Little House Books 3 and 4* (DL)	*Redskin and Cowboy: A Tale of the Western Plains,* **first half** (DL)
Hands-on & Critical Engagement	Pioneer Town Craft Linked Activities Coloring Pages Imagine & Draw	History Pocket Linked Map Activity Linked Craft Coloring Pages Imagine & Draw	Discussion on Frontiersmen and Miners Linked Map Activity Linked Craft Composition

Unit 22

	K – 1st Grade	2nd – 3rd Grade	4th – 6th Grade
Theme	The Gold Rush		
Read-Aloud	*The Call of the Wild* (DL)	*The Call of the Wild* (DL)	*Redskin and Cowboy: A Tale of the Western Plains,* **second half** (DL) or *Song of Bernadetta* (HC)
Hands-on & Critical Engagement	Linked Klondike Activities Coloring Pages Imagine & Draw	Linked Klondike Activities Map of Routes to the Klondike Coloring Pages; Imagine & Draw	Linked Klondike Activities Linked Black Bart Activity

Unit 23

	K – 1st Grade	2nd – 3rd Grade	4th – 6th Grade
Theme	Civil War and Reconstruction		
Read-Aloud	*Little Women* (DL)	*Little Women* (DL)	*With Lee in Virginia* (DL) or *Hospital Sketches* (DL)
Hands-on & Critical Engagement	Civil War Soldier Puppets 3-D Photography Activity Coloring Pages Imagine & Draw	Drummer Boys Craft 3-D Photography Activity Coloring Pages Imagine & Draw	Discussion on Injured Soldiers and Nurses Animated Maps ~ Battles Timeline

All Grades ~ SCOPE & SEQUENCE

Unit 24

	K – 1st Grade	**2nd – 3rd Grade**	**4th – 6th Grade**
Theme	Age of Invention		
Read-Aloud	*Featured Glory Story CD: Volume II, Saint Therese of Lisieux (HC)*		
	Wind in the Willows (DL) or *Mother Seton and the Sisters of Charity* (HC)	*Wind in the Willows* (DL) or *Mother Seton and the Sisters of Charity* (HC)	*The Adventures of Huckleberry Finn* (D)
Hands-on & Critical Engagement	Automobiles Craft Wind in the Willows Linked Activities Coloring Pages Imagine & Draw	Automobiles Craft Wind in the Willows Linked Activities Coloring Pages Imagine & Draw	Discussion on Orphans Composition Map of Huckleberry Finn's Adventures Timeline

Unit 25

	K – 1st Grade	**2nd – 3rd Grade**	**4th – 6th Grade**
Theme	World War I		
Read-Aloud	*Featured Glory Story CD: Volume XIII, Secrets from Heaven, the Story of the Children of Fatima (HC)*		
	The Chronicles of Narnia ~ Prince Caspian (DL or HC)	*The Chronicles of Narnia ~ Prince Caspian* (DL or HC)	*The Story of the Great War* (DL)
Hands-on & Critical Engagement	Group Narrative Linked Narnia Activities Coloring Pages Imagine & Draw	Group Narrative Linked Narnia Activities Coloring Pages Imagine & Draw	Discussion on World War I Composition Map of World War I Timeline

Unit 26

	K – 1st Grade	**2nd – 3rd Grade**	**4th – 6th Grade**
Theme	Roaring 20's and the Great Depression		
Read-Aloud	*Featured Glory Story CD: Volume IX, Blessed Jose Sanchez del Rio & Volume II, Saint Miguel de la Mora (HC)*		
	Father Brown Reader I (HC)	*Father Brown Reader I* (HC)	*Father Brown Reader II* (HC)
Hands-on & Critical Engagement	Great Depression Music Coloring Pages Imagine & Draw	Linked Depression Activities Coloring Pages Imagine & Draw	Linked Activities Timeline

All Grades ~ SCOPE & SEQUENCE

Unit 27

	K – 1st Grade	2nd – 3rd Grade	4th – 6th Grade
Theme	World War II		
Read-Aloud	*Featured Glory Story CD: Volume IV, Saint Faustina Kowalska (HC) & Volume X, Saint Maximilian Kolbe (HC)*		
	The Hobbit (HC)	*The Hobbit* (HC)	*Lord of the Rings* (HC)
Hands-on & Critical Engagement	Draw the Story Coloring Pages Imagine & Draw	Draw the Story and Discussion Coloring Pages Imagine & Draw	Discussion on World War II Composition Map of World War II Timeline

Unit 28

	K – 1st Grade	2nd – 3rd Grade	4th – 6th Grade
Theme	Russian Revolution and the Cold War		
Read-Aloud	Sergei Prokofiev's "Peter and the Wolf" (HC-CD) *Peter and the Wolf* (HC)	Sergei Prokofiev's "Peter and the Wolf" (HC-CD) *Peter and the Wolf* (HC)	Sergei Prokofiev's "Peter and the Wolf" (HC-CD) *Lord of the Rings* (HC)
Hands-on & Critical Engagement	Dramatization of the Story Popsicle Puppets Coloring Pages Imagine & Draw	Dramatization of the Story Popsicle Puppets Map of the Cold War Coloring Pages Imagine & Draw	Discussion on history of the One Ring Composition Map of Cold War Timeline

Unit 29

	K – 1st Grade	2nd – 3rd Grade	4th – 6th Grade
Theme	Rights, Technological Revolution, and the Catholic Movement		
Read-Aloud	*Featured Glory Story CD: Volume IV, Blessed Mother Teresa of Calcutta (HC)*		
	"Angel in the Waters" (HC) Beatrix Potter's Stories (HC)	"Angel in the Waters" (HC) Beatrix Potter's Stories (HC)	*Winnie the Pooh* (HC)
Hands-on & Critical Engagement	Drawing the Story Act Out Coloring Pages Imagine & Draw	Drawing the Story Act Out Map of Modern Europe Coloring Pages Imagine & Draw	Discussion on Church's Teachings and the dignity of human persons Composition Map of Modern Europe Timeline

Unit 30

	K – 1st Grade	2nd – 3rd Grade	4th – 6th Grade
Theme	Review		
Read-Aloud	Featured Glory Story CD: Volume XI, Pope Saint John Paul II		
	n/a	n/a	n/a
Hands-on & Critical Engagement	Finish any incomplete assignments and organize notebooks.	Finish any incomplete assignments and organize notebooks.	Finish any incomplete assignments and organize notebooks.

Language Arts

❖ Below you will find a list of the lessons and activities for each unit per grade range.
❖ See Unit Handbooks for schedule of daily lessons and activities and their locations.

Unit 1

	K – 1st Grade	2nd – 3rd Grade	4th – 6th Grade
Foundation Lesson	Picture Study ~ "Pieta"	Memorization ~ "If I Knew"	Literature Study ~ Michael Angelo
Activities	Copywork ~ Poetry ~ "Bed in Summer" Narration & Illustration	Copywork ~ Poetry ~ "Bed in Summer" Composition & Illustration	Grammar & Composition ~ Pronouns and Antecedents

Unit 2

	K – 1st Grade	2nd – 3rd Grade	4th – 6th Grade
Foundation Lesson	Picture Study ~ "Christopher Columbus"	Grammar ~ *a* or *an*	Poetry Study ~ "Columbus"
Activities	Copywork ~ Poetry ~ "Bed in Summer" Narration & Illustration	Copywork ~ Poetry ~ "Bed in Summer" Composition & Illustration	Composition ~ Model Writing

Unit 3

	K – 1st Grade	2nd – 3rd Grade	4th – 6th Grade
Foundation Lesson	Picture Study ~ "Printers in the Workshop"	Grammar ~ Days of the Week	Literature Study ~ "The Invention of Printing"
Activities	Copywork ~ Poetry ~ "Bed in Summer" Narration & Illustration	Copywork ~ Poetry ~ "Bed in Summer" Composition & Illustration	Composition ~ Newspaper Articles

Unit 4

	K – 1st Grade	2nd – 3rd Grade	4th – 6th Grade
Foundation Lesson	Picture Study ~ "Dutch Boats in a Gale"	Conversation	Dictation
Activities	Copywork ~ Scripture ~ John 6: 51 Narration & Illustration	Grammar ~ Correct Use of Words Copywork ~ Scripture ~ John 6: 51 Composition & Illustration	Grammar & Composition ~ Proper Nouns

All Grades ~ SCOPE & SEQUENCE

Unit 5

	K – 1st Grade	2nd – 3rd Grade	4th – 6th Grade
Foundation Lesson	Picture Study ~ "Evangelization of Mexico"	Dictation & Grammar ~ *there* or *their*	Conversation
Activities	Copywork ~ Poetry ~ "The Months" Narration & Illustration	Copywork ~ Poetry ~ "The Months" Composition & Illustration	Grammar & Composition ~ Possessive Singular and Plural

Unit 6

	K – 1st Grade	2nd – 3rd Grade	4th – 6th Grade
Foundation Lesson	Picture Study ~ "Oberon, Titania, and Puck with Fairies"	Conversation	Poetry Study ~ "Down to Sleep"
Activities	Copywork ~ Poetry ~ "The Months" Narration & Illustration	Grammar ~ Adverbs Copywork ~ Poetry ~ "The Months" Composition & Illustration	Grammar ~ Common and Proper Nouns

Unit 7

	K – 1st Grade	2nd – 3rd Grade	4th – 6th Grade
Foundation Lesson	Picture Study ~ "Pity"	Discussion and Grammar ~ Commas	Picture Study ~ "The Breaking Wave"
Activities	Copywork ~ Poetry ~ "The Months" Narration & Illustration	Grammar ~ Adverbs Copywork ~ Poetry ~ "The Months" Composition & Illustration	Letter Writing ~ Business

Unit 8

	K – 1st Grade	2nd – 3rd Grade	4th – 6th Grade
Foundation Lesson	Picture Study ~ "Mayflower Compact"	Observation and Grammar ~ Proper Nouns	Conversation
Activities	Copywork ~ Scripture ~ John 11: 25 – 26 Narration & Illustration	Copywork ~ Scripture ~ John 11: 25 – 26 Composition & Illustration	Dictation and Composition

All Grades ~ SCOPE & SEQUENCE

Unit 9

	K – 1st Grade	2nd – 3rd Grade	4th – 6th Grade
Foundation Lesson	Picture Study ~ "Landing of the Pilgrims"	Poetry Study ~ "The Journey"	Literature Study
Activities	Copywork ~ Poetry ~ "The Months" Narration & Illustration	Copywork ~ Poetry ~ "The Months" Composition & Illustration	Composition & Grammar ~ Adjectives

Unit 10

	K – 1st Grade	2nd – 3rd Grade	4th – 6th Grade
Foundation Lesson	Picture Study ~ "Johnson Saving Dieskau"	Observation	Picture Study ~ The Horse Fair
Activities	Copywork ~ Poetry ~ "The Months" Narration & Illustration	Letter Writing ~ Thank you Copywork ~ Poetry ~ "The Months" Composition & Illustration	Literature Study and Model Writing

Unit 11

	K – 1st Grade	2nd – 3rd Grade	4th – 6th Grade
Foundation Lesson	Picture Study ~ "Boston Tea Party"	Grammar ~ Abbreviations	Poetry Study ~ "Landing of the Pilgrim Fathers"
Activities	Copywork ~ Poetry ~ "The Months" Narration & Illustration	Copywork ~ Poetry ~ "The Months" Composition & Illustration	Grammar ~ Adjectives and Important Grammar Terms

Unit 12

	K – 1st Grade	2nd – 3rd Grade	4th – 6th Grade
Foundation Lesson	Picture Study ~ "Surrender of General Cornwallis"	Grammar ~ Prepositions	Conversation
Activities	Copywork ~ Scripture ~ John 6: 48 Narration & Illustration	Copywork ~ Scripture ~ John 6: 48 Composition & Illustration	Conversation & Composition

All Grades ~ SCOPE & SEQUENCE

Unit 13

	K – 1st Grade	2nd – 3rd Grade	4th – 6th Grade
Foundation Lesson	Picture Study ~ "Experiments with Electrostatics"	Grammar ~ Dates	Dictation, Conversation, & Composition
Activities	Copywork ~ Scripture ~ John 10: 16 Narration & Illustration	Copywork ~ Scripture ~ John 10: 16 Composition & Illustration	Dictation, Conversation, & Composition

Unit 14

	K – 1st Grade	2nd – 3rd Grade	4th – 6th Grade
Foundation Lesson	Review	Review	Review
Activities	n/a	n/a	n/a

Unit 15

	K – 1st Grade	2nd – 3rd Grade	4th – 6th Grade
Foundation Lesson	Picture Study ~ "Betsy Ross 1777"	Grammar ~ Plural Nouns	Poetry Study and Verbs
Activities	Copywork ~ Poetry ~ "O Could We Always Live and Love" Narration & Illustration	Copywork ~ Poetry ~ "O Could We Always Live and Love" Composition & Illustration	Grammar ~ Verbs

Unit 16

	K – 1st Grade	2nd – 3rd Grade	4th – 6th Grade
Foundation Lesson	Picture Study ~ "Bonaparte Crossing the Grand Saint-Bernard Pass"	Letter Writing	Conversation
Activities	Copywork ~ Poetry ~ "O Could We Always Live and Love" Narration & Illustration	Reproduction and Grammar Copywork ~ Poetry ~ "O Could We Always Live and Love" Composition & Illustration	Poetry Study, Correct Use of Words, & Composition

All Grades ~ SCOPE & SEQUENCE

Unit 17

	K – 1st Grade	2nd – 3rd Grade	4th – 6th Grade
Foundation Lesson	Picture Study ~ "Signing of the Constitution"	Grammar ~ go, went, gone	Conversation
Activities	Copywork ~ Poetry ~ "O Could We Always Live and Love" Narration & Illustration	Reproduction and Grammar Copywork ~ Poetry ~ "O Could We Always Live and Love" Composition & Illustration	Grammar ~ Subjects and Predicates

Unit 18

	K – 1st Grade	2nd – 3rd Grade	4th – 6th Grade
Foundation Lesson	Picture Study ~ "Guericke Sulphur Globe"	Conversation	Conversation
Activities	Copywork ~ Poetry ~ "O Could We Always Live and Love" Narration & Illustration	Grammar ~ Contractions & Antonyms Copywork ~ Poetry ~ "O Could We Always Live and Love" Composition & Illustration	Grammar & Composition ~ Model Writing

Unit 19

	K – 1st Grade	2nd – 3rd Grade	4th – 6th Grade
Foundation Lesson	Picture Study ~ "Iron and Coal"	Picture Study ~ "Iron and Coal"	Grammar ~ Adverbs
Activities	Copywork ~ Poetry ~ "Stopping by Woods on Snowy Evening" Narration & Illustration	Grammar ~ Contractions & Antonyms Copywork ~ Poetry ~ "Stopping by Woods on Snowy Evening" Composition & Illustration	Grammar ~ Adverbs

Unit 20

	K – 1st Grade	2nd – 3rd Grade	4th – 6th Grade
Foundation Lesson	Picture Study ~ "The Chapel of the Virgin at Subiaco"	Picture Study ~ "The Chapel of the Virgin at Subiaco"	Composition ~ Advertisement
Activities	Copywork ~ Poetry ~ "Stopping by Woods on Snowy Evening" Oral Summary Narration & Illustration	Grammar ~ Contractions & Antonyms Copywork ~ Poetry ~ "Stopping by Woods on Snowy Evening" Composition & Illustration	Composition ~ Advertisement

All Grades ~ SCOPE & SEQUENCE

Unit 21

	K – 1st Grade	2nd – 3rd Grade	4th – 6th Grade
Foundation Lesson	Conversation	Conversation	Conversation
Activities	Copywork ~ Poetry ~ "Stopping by Woods on Snowy Evening" Oral Summary Narration & Illustration	Grammar ~ Writing Sentences Copywork ~ Poetry ~ "Stopping by Woods on Snowy Evening" Composition & Illustration	Composition & Grammar ~ Prepositions

Unit 22

	K – 1st Grade	2nd – 3rd Grade	4th – 6th Grade
Foundation Lesson	Observation	Observation	Poetry Study ~ "The Coming of Spring"
Activities	Copywork ~ Scripture ~ Luke 22: 28 – 30 Oral Summary Narration & Illustration	Memorization & Grammar ~ Irregular Verbs Copywork ~ Scripture ~ Luke 22: 28 – 30 Composition & Illustration	Composition & Grammar ~ *Whom*

Unit 23

	K – 1st Grade	2nd – 3rd Grade	4th – 6th Grade
Foundation Lesson	Picture Study ~ "Battle of Chickamauga"	Picture Study ~ "Battle of Chickamauga"	Literature Study
Activities	Copywork ~ Poetry ~ "The Pillar of the Cloud" Oral Summary Narration & Illustration	Memorization ~ "The Bluebird" Copywork ~ Poetry ~ "The Pillar of the Cloud" Composition & Illustration	Memorization & Poetry Study ~ "The Flag Goes By"

Unit 24

	K – 1st Grade	2nd – 3rd Grade	4th – 6th Grade
Foundation Lesson	Picture Study ~ "The Progress of the Century"	Picture Study ~ "The Progress of the Century"	Conversation
Activities	Copywork ~ Poetry ~ "The Song of Mr. Toad" Oral Summary Narration & Illustration	Grammar & Dictation ~ Direct Quotations Copywork ~ Poetry ~ "The Song of Mr. Toad" Composition & Illustration	Grammar ~ Interjections

All Grades ~ SCOPE & SEQUENCE

Unit 25

	K – 1st Grade	2nd – 3rd Grade	4th – 6th Grade
Foundation Lesson	Picture Study ~ "Together We Win"	Picture Study ~ "Together We Win"	Conversation
Activities	Copywork ~ Poetry ~ "The Song of Mr. Toad" Oral Summary Narration & Illustration	Composition ~ Finish the Story Copywork ~ Poetry ~ "The Song of Mr. Toad" Composition & Illustration	Dictation & Composition

Unit 26

	K – 1st Grade	2nd – 3rd Grade	4th – 6th Grade
Foundation Lesson	Picture Study ~ "Depression Photographs"	Conversation	Conversation
Activities	Copywork ~ Scripture ~ Matthew 9: 37 – 38 Oral Summary Narration & Illustration	Grammar ~ Demonstrative Pronouns Copywork ~ Scripture ~ Matthew 9: 37 – 38 Composition & Illustration	Composition & Grammar ~ Conjunctions

Unit 27

	K – 1st Grade	2nd – 3rd Grade	4th – 6th Grade
Foundation Lesson	Picture Study ~ "U.S. Navy Brewster F2A-3 Fighter"	Memorization ~ "The Sandman"	Grammar ~ Proper Nouns
Activities	Copywork ~ Poetry ~ "The Song of Mr. Toad" Oral Summary Narration & Illustration	Grammar ~ *hasn't* or *haven't* Copywork ~ Poetry ~ "The Song of Mr. Toad" Composition & Illustration	Letter Writing ~ Formal Invitations

Unit 28

	K – 1st Grade	2nd – 3rd Grade	4th – 6th Grade
Foundation Lesson	Picture Study ~ "Berlin Wall"	Grammar ~ Maxims and Proverbs	Conversation
Activities	Copywork ~ Poetry ~ "The Song of Mr. Toad" Oral Summary Narration & Illustration	Composition ~ Maxims and Proverbs Copywork ~ Poetry ~ "The Song of Mr. Toad" Composition & Illustration	Grammar & Poetry Study ~ "Daffodils"

All Grades ~ SCOPE & SEQUENCE

Unit 29

	K – 1st Grade	**2nd – 3rd Grade**	**4th – 6th Grade**
Foundation Lesson	Picture Study ~ "Earth from Space"	Picture Study ~ "Earth from Space"	Prose Study
Activities	Copywork ~ Poetry ~ "The Song of Mr. Toad" Oral Summary Narration & Illustration	Oral & Written Summary Copywork ~ Poetry ~ "The Song of Mr. Toad" Composition & Illustration	Composition

Unit 30

	K – 1st Grade	**2nd – 3rd Grade**	**4th – 6th Grade**
Foundation Lesson	Review	Review	Review
Activities	n/a	n/a	n/a

Latin/Greek

❖ Below you will find a list of the books and activities for each unit per grade range.
❖ SF = located as a printable in the Subject Folder of the unit
❖ See Unit Handbooks for schedule of daily lessons and activities and their locations.

Unit 1

	K – 1st Grade	2nd – 3rd Grade	4th – 6th Grade
Activities	n/a	*Greek Primer* (SF), Unit 1 The Letter α	*Reading Greek* (SF), Unit 1 α, β, γ
Memorization	CCM Unit 1 Prayer Tantum Ergo Hymn Assembly Prayers		

Unit 2

	K – 1st Grade	2nd – 3rd Grade	4th – 6th Grade
Activities	n/a	*Greek Primer* (SF), Unit 2 The Letter β	*Reading Greek* (SF), Unit 2 δ, ε, ζ
Memorization	CCM Unit 2 Prayer Tantum Ergo Hymn Assembly Prayers		

Unit 3

	K – 1st Grade	2nd – 3rd Grade	4th – 6th Grade
Activities	n/a	*Greek Primer* (SF), Unit 3 The Letter γ	*Reading Greek* (SF), Unit 3 η, θ, ι
Memorization	CCM Unit 3 Prayer Tantum Ergo Hymn Assembly Prayers		

Unit 4

	K – 1st Grade	2nd – 3rd Grade	4th – 6th Grade
Activities	n/a	*Greek Primer* (SF), Unit 4 The Letter δ	*Reading Greek* (SF), Unit 4 κ, λ, μ
Memorization	CCM Unit 4 Prayer Tantum Ergo Hymn Assembly Prayers		

All Grades ~ SCOPE & SEQUENCE

Unit 5

	K – 1st Grade	2nd – 3rd Grade	4th – 6th Grade
Activities	n/a	*Greek Primer* (SF), Unit 5 The Letter ε	*Reading Greek* (SF), Unit 5 ν, ξ, ο
Memorization	CCM Unit 5 Prayer Ecce Nomen Domini Hymn Assembly Prayers		

Unit 6

	K – 1st Grade	2nd – 3rd Grade	4th – 6th Grade
Activities	n/a	*Greek Primer* (SF), Unit 6 The Letter ζ	*Reading Greek* (SF), Unit 6 π, ρ, σ
Memorization	CCM Unit 6 Prayer Ecce Nomen Domini Hymn Assembly Prayers		

Unit 7

	K – 1st Grade	2nd – 3rd Grade	4th – 6th Grade
Activities	n/a	*Greek Primer* (SF), Unit 7 The Letter η	*Reading Greek* (SF), Unit 7 τ, υ, φ
Memorization	CCM Unit 7 Prayer Ecce Nomen Domini Hymn Assembly Prayers		

Unit 8

	K – 1st Grade	2nd – 3rd Grade	4th – 6th Grade
Activities	n/a	*Greek Primer* (SF), Unit 8 The Letter θ	*Reading Greek* (SF), Unit 8 χ, ψ, ω
Memorization	CCM Unit 8 Prayer Ecce Nomen Domini Hymn Assembly Prayers		

Unit 9

	K – 1st Grade	2nd – 3rd Grade	4th – 6th Grade
Activities	n/a	*Greek Primer* (SF), Unit 9 The Letter ι	*Reading Greek* (SF), Unit 9 The Greek Alphabet and Transliteration
Memorization	CCM Unit 9 Prayer Lumen ad Revelationem Hymn Assembly Prayers		

All Grades ~ SCOPE & SEQUENCE

Unit 10

	K – 1st Grade	2nd – 3rd Grade	4th – 6th Grade
Activities	n/a	*Greek Primer* (SF), Unit 10 The Letter κ	*Reading Greek* (SF), Unit 10 Transliteration and Reading
Memorization	CCM Unit 10 Prayer Lumen ad Revelationem Hymn Assembly Prayers		

Unit 11

	K – 1st Grade	2nd – 3rd Grade	4th – 6th Grade
Activities	n/a	*Greek Primer* (SF), Unit 11 The Letter λ	*Reading Greek* (SF), Unit 11 Transliteration and Reading
Memorization	CCM Unit 11 Prayer Lumen ad Revelationem Hymn Assembly Prayers		

Unit 12

	K – 1st Grade	2nd – 3rd Grade	4th – 6th Grade
Activities	n/a	*Greek Primer* (SF), Unit 12 The Letter μ	*Reading Greek* (SF), Unit 12 Transliteration and Reading
Memorization	CCM Unit 12 Prayer Lumen ad Revelationem Hymn Assembly Prayers		

Unit 13

	K – 1st Grade	2nd – 3rd Grade	4th – 6th Grade
Activities	n/a	*Greek Primer* (SF), Unit 13 The Letter ν	*Reading Greek* (SF), Unit 13 Transliteration and Reading
Memorization	CCM Unit 13 Prayer Lumen ad Revelationem Hymn Assembly Prayers		

Unit 14

	K – 1st Grade	2nd – 3rd Grade	4th – 6th Grade
Activities	n/a	*Greek Primer* (SF), Unit 14 α through ν	*Reading Greek* (SF), Unit 14 Transliteration and Reading
Memorization	CCM Unit 14 Prayer Lumen ad Revelationem Hymn Assembly Prayers		

All Grades ~ SCOPE & SEQUENCE

Unit 15

	K – 1st Grade	2nd – 3rd Grade	4th – 6th Grade
Activities	n/a	*Greek Primer* (SF), Unit 15 α through ν	*Reading Greek* (SF), Unit 15 Transliteration and Reading
Memorization		CCM Unit 15 Prayer Parce Domine Hymn Assembly Prayers	

Unit 16

	K – 1st Grade	2nd – 3rd Grade	4th – 6th Grade
Activities	n/a	*Greek Primer* (SF), Unit 16 The Letter ξ	*Reading Greek* (SF), Unit 16 Transliteration and Reading
Memorization		CCM Unit 16 Prayer Parce Domine Hymn Assembly Prayers	

Unit 17

	K – 1st Grade	2nd – 3rd Grade	4th – 6th Grade
Activities	n/a	*Greek Primer* (SF), Unit 17 The Letter o	*Reading Greek* (SF), Unit 17 Transliteration and Reading
Memorization		CCM Unit 17 Prayer Parce Domine Hymn Assembly Prayers	

Unit 18

	K – 1st Grade	2nd – 3rd Grade	4th – 6th Grade
Activities	n/a	*Greek Primer* (SF), Unit 18 The Letter π	*Reading Greek* (SF), Unit 18 Transliteration and Reading
Memorization		CCM Unit 18 Prayer Parce Domine Hymn Assembly Prayers	

Unit 19

	K – 1st Grade	2nd – 3rd Grade	4th – 6th Grade
Activities	n/a	*Greek Primer* (SF), Unit 19 The Letter ρ	*Reading Greek* (SF), Unit 19 Transliteration and Reading
Memorization		CCM Unit 19 Prayer Hosanna Filio David Hymn Assembly Prayers	

All Grades ~ SCOPE & SEQUENCE

Unit 20

	K – 1st Grade	2nd – 3rd Grade	4th – 6th Grade
Activities	n/a	*Greek Primer* (SF), Unit 20 The Letter σ	*Reading Greek* (SF), Unit 20 Transliteration and Reading
Memorization	CCM Unit 20 Prayer Hosanna Filio David Hymn Assembly Prayers		

Unit 21

	K – 1st Grade	2nd – 3rd Grade	4th – 6th Grade
Activities	n/a	*Greek Primer* (SF), Unit 21 The Letter τ	*Reading Greek* (SF), Unit 21 Transliteration and Reading
Memorization	CCM Unit 21 Prayer Hosanna Filio David Hymn Assembly Prayers		

Unit 22

	K – 1st Grade	2nd – 3rd Grade	4th – 6th Grade
Activities	n/a	*Greek Primer* (SF), Unit 22 The Letter υ	*Reading Greek* (SF), Unit 22 Transliteration and Reading
Memorization	CCM Unit 22 Prayer Hosanna Filio David Hymn Assembly Prayers		

Unit 23

	K – 1st Grade	2nd – 3rd Grade	4th – 6th Grade
Activities	n/a	*Greek Primer* (SF), Unit 23 The Letter φ	*Reading Greek* (SF), Unit 23 Transliteration and Reading
Memorization	CCM Unit 23 Prayer Ecce lignum Hymn Assembly Prayers		

Unit 24

	K – 1st Grade	2nd – 3rd Grade	4th – 6th Grade
Activities	n/a	*Greek Primer* (SF), Unit 24 The Letter χ	*Reading Greek* (SF), Unit 24 Transliteration and Reading
Memorization	CCM Unit 24 Prayer Ecce lignum Hymn Assembly Prayers		

All Grades ~ SCOPE & SEQUENCE

Unit 25

	K – 1st Grade	2nd – 3rd Grade	4th – 6th Grade
Activities	n/a	*Greek Primer* (SF), Unit 25 The Letter χ	*Reading Greek* (SF), Unit 25 Transliteration and Reading
Memorization	CCM Unit 25 Prayer Ecce lignum Hymn Assembly Prayers		

Unit 26

	K – 1st Grade	2nd – 3rd Grade	4th – 6th Grade
Activities	n/a	*Greek Primer* (SF), Unit 26 The Letter ω	*Reading Greek* (SF), Unit 26 Transliteration and Reading
Memorization	CCM Unit 26 Prayer Ecce lignum Hymn Assembly Prayers		

Unit 27

	K – 1st Grade	2nd – 3rd Grade	4th – 6th Grade
Activities	n/a	*Greek Primer* (SF), Unit 27 Transliteration	*Reading Greek* (SF), Unit 27 Transliteration and Reading
Memorization	CCM Unit 27 Prayer Lumen Christi Hymn Assembly Prayers		

Unit 28

	K – 1st Grade	2nd – 3rd Grade	4th – 6th Grade
Activities	n/a	*Greek Primer* (SF), Unit 28 Transliteration	*Reading Greek* (SF), Unit 28 Transliteration and Reading
Memorization	CCM Unit 28 Prayer Lumen Christi Hymn Assembly Prayers		

Unit 29

	K – 1st Grade	2nd – 3rd Grade	4th – 6th Grade
Activities	n/a	*Greek Primer* (SF), Unit 29 Transliteration	*Reading Greek* (SF), Unit 29 Transliteration and Reading
Memorization	CCM Unit 29 Prayer Lumen Christi Hymn Assembly Prayers		

All Grades ~ SCOPE & SEQUENCE

Unit 30

	K – 1st Grade	2nd – 3rd Grade	4th – 6th Grade
Activities	n/a	*Greek Primer* (SF), Unit 30 Transliteration	*Reading Greek* (SF), Unit 30 Vocabulary Review
Memorization	CCM Unit 30 Prayer Lumen Christi Hymn Assembly Prayers		

Primary Arithmetic Mastery Chart and Record

Student Name:

Lesson #	Date Started	Date Mastered

Primary Arithmetic Mastery Chart and Record

Intellectual Arithmetic Mastery Chart and Record

Student Name:

Lesson #	Date Started	Date Mastered

Intellectual Arithmetic Mastery Chart and Record

Practical Arithmetic Mastery Chart and Record

Student Name:

Lesson #	Date Started	Date Mastered

Practical Arithmetic Mastery Chart and Record

Music

❖ Below you will find a list of the books, skills, and songs for each unit.

Unit 1	Skill ~ Stretches & Posture New Song ~ Agnus Dei
Unit 2	Skill ~ Breathing & Low-High Voices Song ~ Agnus Dei
Unit 3	Skill ~ Voice Level & Sirens New Songs ~ Merrily We Roll Along and Sanctus
Unit 4	Review
Unit 5	Skill ~ Primary Vowels New Songs ~ n/a
Unit 6	Skill ~ Primary Vowels Continued New Songs ~ n/a
Unit 7	Skill ~ Tongue, Mouth, and Throat Posture New Songs ~ Oats, Peas, Beans, & Barley Grow and the Kyrie
Unit 8	Review
Unit 9	Skill ~ Skips & Thirds New Songs ~ Ite missa est and Lightly Row
Unit 10	Skill ~ Fourths New Songs ~ Aura Lee and first half of the Gloria
Unit 11	Skill ~ Tone Building New Songs ~ Gloria
Units 12-18	Review
Unit 19	Skill ~ Fifths New Songs ~ Lavender's Blue
Unit 20	Skill ~ Sixths New Songs ~ Home on the Range
Unit 21	Skill ~ Consonants New Songs ~ first third of the Credo
Unit 22	Review
Unit 23	Skill ~ Sevenths and Octaves New Songs ~ second third of the Credo
Unit 24	Skill ~ Legato New Songs ~ last third of the Credo
Unit 25	Skill ~ Half-Steps New Songs ~ n/a
Unit 26	Review
Units 27-30	Skill ~ Performance Skills New Songs ~ Performance Songs

SCOPE & SEQUENCE

Reader Mastery Chart and Record

Student Name: _____

Lesson #	Date Started	Date Mastered

Reader Mastery Chart and Record

All Grades ~ SCOPE & SEQUENCE

Religion

- ❖ Below you will find a list of the books and lesson topics for each unit per grade range.
- ❖ See Unit Handbooks for schedule of daily lessons and activities and their locations.

Unit 1

	K – 1st Grade	2nd – 3rd Grade	4th – 6th Grade
Reading	Our Holy Faith, Book 1 (DL) Our Holy Faith, Book 1 Teacher's Manual (DL)	Our Holy Faith, Book 2 (DL)	Our Holy Faith, Book 4 (DL)
Themes	The Home of Jesus on Earth The Presence of God in All Catholic Churches Jesus Comes to Live with Us through the Mass	Our Heavenly Father Takes Care of Us	God the Father: Creation and Fall of Man

Unit 2

	K – 1st Grade	2nd – 3rd Grade	4th – 6th Grade
Reading	Our Holy Faith, Book 1 (DL) Our Holy Faith, Book 1 Teacher's Manual (DL)	Our Holy Faith, Book 2 (DL)	Our Holy Faith, Book 4 (DL)
Themes	Reverence in Church Prayer ~ Sign of the Cross The Priest	God's Greatness	God's Plan for Fallen Man

Unit 3

	K – 1st Grade	2nd – 3rd Grade	4th – 6th Grade
Reading	Our Holy Faith, Book 1 (DL) Our Holy Faith, Book 1 Teacher's Manual (DL)	Our Holy Faith, Book 2 (DL)	Our Holy Faith, Book 4 (DL)
Themes	The Objects in the Church Love and Care of an Earthly Father Love and Care of our Heavenly Father	The Angels	The Holy Spirit and the Church

All Grades ~ SCOPE & SEQUENCE

Unit 4

	K – 1st Grade	2nd – 3rd Grade	4th – 6th Grade
Reading	Our Holy Faith, Book 1 (DL) Our Holy Faith, Book 1 Teacher's Manual (DL)	Our Holy Faith, Book 2 (DL)	Our Holy Faith, Book 4 (DL)
Themes	Why God Created Us Presence of God	God our Creator and Savior, Part I	The Church Leads us to Live Everlasting

Unit 5

	K – 1st Grade	2nd – 3rd Grade	4th – 6th Grade
Reading	Our Holy Faith, Book 1 (DL) Our Holy Faith, Book 1 Teacher's Manual (DL)	Our Holy Faith, Book 2 (DL)	Our Holy Faith, Book 4 (DL)
Themes	God Sees, Hears, and Knows All We Do, Say, and Think God is Present All Through Baptism Three Persons in God	God Our Creator and Savior, Part II	Jesus Christ Founds the Church

Unit 6

	K – 1st Grade	2nd – 3rd Grade	4th – 6th Grade
Reading	Our Holy Faith, Book 1 (DL) Our Holy Faith, Book 1 Teacher's Manual (DL)	Our Holy Faith, Book 2 (DL)	Our Holy Faith, Book 4 (DL)
Themes	God the Creator Creation and Fall of Angels What the Good and Bad Angels Do	The Obedience of Noah	The Members of the Mystical Body of Christ

All Grades ~ SCOPE & SEQUENCE

Unit 7

	K – 1st Grade	2nd – 3rd Grade	4th – 6th Grade
Reading	Our Holy Faith, Book 1 (DL) Our Holy Faith, Book 1 Teacher's Manual (DL)	Our Holy Faith, Book 2 (DL)	Our Holy Faith, Book 4 (DL)
Themes	Prayer ~ Angel of God Creation of the World Adam and Eve	The Obedience of Abraham	The Liturgy as Christ Continuing His Priestly Work in His Mystical Body, the Church

Unit 8

	K – 1st Grade	2nd – 3rd Grade	4th – 6th Grade
Reading	Our Holy Faith, Book 1 (DL) Our Holy Faith, Book 1 Teacher's Manual (DL)	Our Holy Faith, Book 2 (DL)	Our Holy Faith, Book 4 (DL)
Themes	The Fall of Man God's Love and Mercy in Promising the Redeemer	The Obedience of Moses	The Mass as Sacrifice

Unit 9

	K – 1st Grade	2nd – 3rd Grade	4th – 6th Grade
Reading	Our Holy Faith, Book 1 (DL) Our Holy Faith, Book 1 Teacher's Manual (DL)	Our Holy Faith, Book 2 (DL)	Our Holy Faith, Book 4 (DL)
Themes	Gratitude to God for His Gifts Prayer ~ Grace Before Meals Prayer ~ Grace After Meals	The Obedience of Samuel	The Mass as Sacrifice Continued

Unit 10

	K – 1st Grade	2nd – 3rd Grade	4th – 6th Grade
Reading	Our Holy Faith, Book 1 (DL) Our Holy Faith, Book 1 Teacher's Manual (DL)	Our Holy Faith, Book 2 (DL)	Our Holy Faith, Book 4 (DL)
Themes	The Meaning of Prayer Why We Pray How We Should Pray	Obedience of the Holy Family, Part I	The Divine Office

Unit 11

	K – 1st Grade	2nd – 3rd Grade	4th – 6th Grade
Reading	Our Holy Faith, Book 1 (DL) Our Holy Faith, Book 1 Teacher's Manual (DL)	Our Holy Faith, Book 2 (DL)	Our Holy Faith, Book 4 (DL)
Themes	The Lord's Prayer Petition One ~ Hallowed by Thy Name Petition Two ~ Thy Kingdom Come	Obedience of the Holy Family, Part II	The Sacraments

Unit 12

	K – 1st Grade	2nd – 3rd Grade	4th – 6th Grade
Reading	Our Holy Faith, Book 1 (DL) Our Holy Faith, Book 1 Teacher's Manual (DL)	Our Holy Faith, Book 2 (DL)	Our Holy Faith, Book 4 (DL)
Themes	Petition Three ~ Thy Will Be Done on Earth as it is in Heaven Petition Four ~ Give us this day our Daily Bread Petition Five ~ Forgive us our Trespasses and Forgive those who Trespass against us	Obedience of the Holy Family, Part III	The Sacraments Continued

All Grades ~ SCOPE & SEQUENCE

Unit 13

	K – 1st Grade	2nd – 3rd Grade	4th – 6th Grade
Reading	Our Holy Faith, Book 1 (DL) Our Holy Faith, Book 1 Teacher's Manual (DL)	Our Holy Faith, Book 2 (DL)	Our Holy Faith, Book 4 (DL)
Themes	Petition Six ~ Lead Us Not into Temptation Petition Seven ~ But Deliver us from Evil Coming of the Christ Child	Review	Sacramentals

Unit 14

	K – 1st Grade	2nd – 3rd Grade	4th – 6th Grade
Reading	Our Holy Faith, Book 1 (DL) Our Holy Faith, Book 1 Teacher's Manual (DL)	Our Holy Faith, Book 2 (DL)	Our Holy Faith, Book 4 (DL)
Themes	Mary - God's Mother The Annunciation The Visitation	Review	The Liturgical Year

Units 15-18

	K – 1st Grade	2nd – 3rd Grade	4th – 6th Grade
Reading	Our Holy Faith, Book 4 (DL)		
Themes	Christmas Season Activities and Readings		

Unit 19

	K – 1st Grade	2nd – 3rd Grade	4th – 6th Grade
Reading	Our Holy Faith, Book 1 (DL) Our Holy Faith, Book 1 Teacher's Manual (DL)	Our Holy Faith, Book 2 (DL)	Our Holy Faith, Book 4 (DL)
Themes	The Holy Family at Nazareth The Home of the Holy Family	The First Commandment The Second Commandment	The Pre-Lenten Time of Preparation

All Grades ~ SCOPE & SEQUENCE

Unit 20

	K – 1st Grade	2nd – 3rd Grade	4th – 6th Grade
Reading	Our Holy Faith, Book 1 (DL) Our Holy Faith, Book 1 Teacher's Manual (DL)	Our Holy Faith, Book 2 (DL)	Our Holy Faith, Book 4 (DL)
Themes	Joseph, the Head of the Holy Family Mary, the Mother of the Holy Family	The Third Commandment The Fourth Commandment	The Meaning of Lent & Ash Wednesday

Unit 21

	K – 1st Grade	2nd – 3rd Grade	4th – 6th Grade
Reading	Our Holy Faith, Book 1 (DL) Our Holy Faith, Book 1 Teacher's Manual (DL)	Our Holy Faith, Book 2 (DL)	Our Holy Faith, Book 4 (DL)
Themes	Jesus at Play Jesus at Prayer	The Fifth Commandment	The First Sunday of Lent

Unit 22

	K – 1st Grade	2nd – 3rd Grade	4th – 6th Grade
Reading	Our Holy Faith, Book 1 (DL) Our Holy Faith, Book 1 Teacher's Manual (DL)	Our Holy Faith, Book 2 (DL)	Our Holy Faith, Book 4 (DL)
Themes	Jesus Leaves His Home in Nazareth to do His Father's Work Jesus Chooses His Apostles	The Sixth & Ninth Commandments	The Second Sunday of Lent - Transfiguration

All Grades ~ SCOPE & SEQUENCE

Unit 23

	K – 1st Grade	2nd – 3rd Grade	4th – 6th Grade
Reading	Our Holy Faith, Book 1 (DL) Our Holy Faith, Book 1 Teacher's Manual (DL)	Our Holy Faith, Book 2 (DL)	Our Holy Faith, Book 4 (DL)
Themes	Meaning of Lent – Ash Wednesday The Meaning and Spirit of Lent	The Seventh & Tenth Commandments	The Third Sunday of Lent – Joseph Sold into Slavery

Unit 24

	K – 1st Grade	2nd – 3rd Grade	4th – 6th Grade
Reading	Our Holy Faith, Book 1 (DL) Our Holy Faith, Book 1 Teacher's Manual (DL)	Our Holy Faith, Book 2 (DL)	Our Holy Faith, Book 4 (DL)
Themes	Meaning of Lent – Palm Sunday The Meaning and Spirit of Lent	The Eighth Commandment	Rejoice!

Unit 25

	K – 1st Grade	2nd – 3rd Grade	4th – 6th Grade
Reading	Our Holy Faith, Book 1 (DL) Our Holy Faith, Book 1 Teacher's Manual (DL)	Our Holy Faith, Book 2 (DL)	Our Holy Faith, Book 4 (DL)
Themes	Meaning of Lent – Institution of the Eucharist	The Laws of the Church	Passiontide & Passion Week

All Grades ~ SCOPE & SEQUENCE

Unit 26

	K – 1st Grade	2nd – 3rd Grade	4th – 6th Grade
Reading	Our Holy Faith, Book 1 (DL) Our Holy Faith, Book 1 Teacher's Manual (DL)	Our Holy Faith, Book 2 (DL)	Our Holy Faith, Book 4 (DL)
Themes	Meaning of Lent – Institution of the Eucharist	Baptism & Sin	Holy Week

Unit 27

	K – 1st Grade	2nd – 3rd Grade	4th – 6th Grade
Reading	Our Holy Faith, Book 1 (DL) Our Holy Faith, Book 1 Teacher's Manual (DL)	Our Holy Faith, Book 2 (DL)	Our Holy Faith, Book 4 (DL)
Themes	Jesus Christ's Resurrection Things to Do	Sacrament of Penance	Jesus Christ as Sacrifice

Unit 28

	K – 1st Grade	2nd – 3rd Grade	4th – 6th Grade
Reading	Our Holy Faith, Book 1 (DL) Our Holy Faith, Book 1 Teacher's Manual (DL)	Our Holy Faith, Book 2 (DL)	Our Holy Faith, Book 4 (DL)
Themes	Appearance to the Disciples on the Way to Emmaus Appearance to the Apostles	The Holy Eucharist	Jesus Christ as Good Shepherd

All Grades ~ SCOPE & SEQUENCE

Unit 29

	K – 1st Grade	2nd – 3rd Grade	4th – 6th Grade
Reading	Our Holy Faith, Book 1 (DL) Our Holy Faith, Book 1 Teacher's Manual (DL)	Our Holy Faith, Book 2 (DL)	Our Holy Faith, Book 4 (DL)
Themes	Resurrection of the Body The Work of Our Lord during the 40 Days after Easter	The Mass	Christ's Ascension

Unit 30

	K – 1st Grade	2nd – 3rd Grade	4th – 6th Grade
Reading	Our Holy Faith, Book 1 (DL) Our Holy Faith, Book 1 Teacher's Manual (DL)	Our Holy Faith, Book 2 (DL)	Our Holy Faith, Book 4 (DL)
Themes	The Ascension of Our Lord The Holy Spirit	Holy Communion & Review	The Holy Spirit

All Grades ~ SCOPE & SEQUENCE

Science

❖ Below is a list of the topics, books, lessons, and activities for each unit per grade range.
❖ DL = in the digital library; HC = purchase hardcopy edition
❖ See Unit Handbooks for schedule of daily lessons and activities and their location

Unit 1

	K – 1st Grade	2nd – 3rd Grade	4th – 6th Grade
Theme	Atoms		
Read-Aloud	*The Wonder Book of Chemistry* (DL)	*The Wonder Book of Chemistry* (DL)	RS4K *Elementary Chemistry Grades K-4*, Chapter 1.1-5
Foundation Lesson	Edible Atom Model	Edible Atom Model	Edible Atom Model
Activities	Linked Worksheets Nature Walk Drawing from Observation	Linked Worksheets Nature Walk Drawing from Observation	Linked Worksheets RS4K Experiment 1 Nature Walk Nature Journal Video

Unit 2

	K – 1st Grade	2nd – 3rd Grade	4th – 6th Grade
Theme	Elements		
Read-Aloud	*The Wonder Book of Chemistry* (DL)	*The Wonder Book of Chemistry* (DL)	*The Wonder Book of Chemistry* (DL)
Foundation Lesson	Edible Atom Model & Balloons	Edible Atom Model & Balloons	Edible Atom Model & Balloons
Activities	Linked Worksheets Nature Walk Drawing from Observation	Linked Worksheets Nature Walk Drawing from Observation	Linked Worksheets RS4K Experiment 1 Nature Walk Nature Journal Video

All Grades ~ SCOPE & SEQUENCE

Unit 3

	K – 1st Grade	2nd – 3rd Grade	4th – 6th Grade
Theme	Atomic Number and Atomic Weight		
Read-Aloud	"Hydrogen" and "A Drop of Water" in *The Wonder Book of Chemistry* (DL)	"Hydrogen" and "A Drop of Water" in *The Wonder Book of Chemistry* (DL)	RS4K *Elementary Chemistry Grades K-4*, Chapter 2.1-4
Foundation Lesson	Edible Molecules	Edible Molecules	Edible Molecules
Activities	Linked Worksheets Nature Walk Drawing from Observation	Linked Worksheets Nature Walk Drawing from Observation	Linked Worksheets RS4K Experiment 2 Nature Walk Nature Journal Video

Unit 4

	K – 1st Grade	2nd – 3rd Grade	4th – 6th Grade
Theme	Review		
Read-Aloud	n/a	n/a	n/a
Foundation Lesson	Master CCM Memory Work, Units 1-3	Master CCM Memory Work, Units 1-3	Master CCM Memory Work, Units 1-3
Activities	n/a	n/a	n/a

Unit 5

	K – 1st Grade	2nd – 3rd Grade	4th – 6th Grade
Theme	Endothermic vs. Exothermic Chemical Reactions		
Read-Aloud	"The Slice of Toast" and "Burning Phosphorous" in *The Wonder Book of Chemistry* (DL)	"The Slice of Toast" and "Burning Phosphorous" in *The Wonder Book of Chemistry* (DL)	RS4K *Elementary Chemistry Grades K-4*, Chapter 3.1-5 (HC)
Foundation Lesson	Chemical Reaction Experiments	Chemical Reaction Experiments	Chemical Reaction Experiments
Activities	Linked Worksheets Nature Walk Drawing from Observation	Linked Worksheets Nature Walk Drawing from Observation	Linked Worksheets Nature Walk Nature Journal Video

All Grades ~ SCOPE & SEQUENCE

Unit 6

	K – 1st Grade	2nd – 3rd Grade	4th – 6th Grade
Theme	Kinds of Chemical Reactions		
Read-Aloud	*The Wonder Book of Chemistry* (DL)	*The Wonder Book of Chemistry* (DL)	*The Wonder Book of Chemistry* (DL)
Foundation Lesson	Chemical Reaction Experiments	Chemical Reaction Experiments	Chemical Reaction Experiments
Activities	Draw the Experiment Drawing from Observation	Draw the Experiment Drawing from Observation	Linked Worksheets Library Research

Unit 7

	K – 1st Grade	2nd – 3rd Grade	4th – 6th Grade
Theme	Acids and Bases		
Read-Aloud	*The Wonder Book of Chemistry* (DL)	*The Wonder Book of Chemistry* (DL)	RS4K *Elementary Chemistry Grades K-4*, Chapter 4.1-5 (HC)
Foundation Lesson	Acids and Bases Experiment	Acids and Bases Experiment	Acids and Bases Experiment
Activities	Draw the Experiment Drawing from Observation	Draw the Experiment Drawing from Observation	RS4K Experiment 4 Library Research

Unit 8

	K – 1st Grade	2nd – 3rd Grade	4th – 6th Grade
Theme	Review		
Read-Aloud	n/a	n/a	RS4K *Elementary Chemistry Grades K-4*, Chapter 5 (HC)
Foundation Lesson	Master CCM Memory Work, Units 1-7	Master CCM Memory Work, Units 1-7	Master CCM Memory Work, Units 1-7
Activities	n/a	n/a	RS4K Experiment 5

All Grades ~ SCOPE & SEQUENCE

Unit 9

	K – 1st Grade	2nd – 3rd Grade	4th – 6th Grade
Theme	Separating Mixtures		
Read-Aloud	*The Wonder Book of Chemistry* (DL)	*The Wonder Book of Chemistry* (DL)	RS4K *Elementary Chemistry Grades K-4*, Chapter 6 (HC)
Foundation Lesson	Separating Mixtures Experiments	Separating Mixtures Experiments	Separating Mixtures Experiments
Activities	Draw the Experiment Drawing from Observation	Draw the Experiment Drawing from Observation	RS4K Experiment 6 Library Research

Unit 10

	K – 1st Grade	2nd – 3rd Grade	4th – 6th Grade
Theme	States of Matter		
Read-Aloud	*The Wonder Book of Chemistry* (DL)	*The Wonder Book of Chemistry* (DL)	RS4K *Elementary Chemistry Grades K-4*, Chapter 7 (HC)
Foundation Lesson	Transitions Between Solid and Liquid Experiments	Transitions Between Solid and Liquid Experiments	Transitions Between Solid and Liquid Experiments
Activities	Linked Activities Drawing from Observation	Linked Activities Drawing from Observation	RS4K Experiment 7 Linked Activities Library Research

Unit 11

	K – 1st Grade	2nd – 3rd Grade	4th – 6th Grade
Theme	Law of Conservation of Energy & Types of Energy		
Read-Aloud	*The Wonder Book of Chemistry* (DL)	*The Wonder Book of Chemistry* (DL)	RS4K *Elementary Chemistry Grades K-4*, Chapter 8 (HC)
Foundation Lesson	Kinetic Energy	Kinetic Energy	Kinetic Energy
Activities	Linked Activities Drawing from Observation	Linked Activities Drawing from Observation	RS4K Experiment 8 Linked Activities Library Research

All Grades ~ SCOPE & SEQUENCE

Unit 12

	K – 1st Grade	2nd – 3rd Grade	4th – 6th Grade
Theme	Review		
Read-Aloud	n/a	n/a	n/a
Foundation Lesson	Master CCM Memory Work, Units 1-11	Master CCM Memory Work, Units 1-11	Master CCM Memory Work, Units 1-11
Activities	n/a	n/a	n/a

Unit 13

	K – 1st Grade	2nd – 3rd Grade	4th – 6th Grade
Theme	Chemistry Investigation ~ Baking!		
Read-Aloud	King Arthur Flour Website (Linked in SF)	King Arthur Flour Website (Linked in SF)	King Arthur Flour Website (Linked in SF)
Foundation Lesson	Baking	Baking	Baking
Activities	n/a	n/a	n/a

Unit 14

	K – 1st Grade	2nd – 3rd Grade	4th – 6th Grade
Theme	Review		
Read-Aloud	n/a	n/a	n/a
Foundation Lesson	Master CCM Memory Work, Units 1-11	Master CCM Memory Work, Units 1-11	Master CCM Memory Work, Units 1-11
Activities	n/a	n/a	n/a

All Grades ~ SCOPE & SEQUENCE

Unit 15

	K – 1st Grade	2nd – 3rd Grade	4th – 6th Grade
Theme	Magnetism		
Read-Aloud	*n/a*	*n/a*	n/a
Foundation Lesson	Introduction to Magnetism	Introduction to Magnetism	Introduction to Magnetism
Activities	Linked Activities Drawing the Experiment Free-Time Experiment	Linked Activities Drawing the Experiment Free-Time Experiment	Linked Activities Drawing the Experiment Library Research

Unit 16

	K – 1st Grade	2nd – 3rd Grade	4th – 6th Grade
Theme	Magnetism		
Read-Aloud	*n/a*	*n/a*	n/a
Foundation Lesson	The Power of Magnetism	The Power of Magnetism	The Power of Magnetism
Activities	Linked Activities Drawing the Experiment Free-Time Experiment	Linked Activities Drawing the Experiment Free-Time Experiment	Linked Activities Drawing the Experiment Library Research

Unit 17

	K – 1st Grade	2nd – 3rd Grade	4th – 6th Grade
Theme	Magnetism		
Read-Aloud	*n/a*	*n/a*	n/a
Foundation Lesson	A Magnet's Poles	A Magnet's Poles	A Magnet's Poles
Activities	Linked Activities Drawing the Experiment Free-Time Experiment	Linked Activities Drawing the Experiment Free-Time Experiment	Linked Activities Drawing the Experiment Library Research

All Grades ~ SCOPE & SEQUENCE

Unit 18

	K – 1st Grade	2nd – 3rd Grade	4th – 6th Grade
Theme	Review		
Read-Aloud	*Story Book of Science* (DL)	*Story Book of Science* (DL)	*Story Book of Science* (DL)
Foundation Lesson	n/a	n/a	n/a
Activities	Free-Time Experiment	Free-Time Experiment	Free-Time Experiment

Unit 19

	K – 1st Grade	2nd – 3rd Grade	4th – 6th Grade
Theme	Thermal Energy		
Read-Aloud	"Heat Conduction" in *Secrets of Everyday Things* (DL)	"Heat Conduction" in *Secrets of Everyday Things* (DL)	"Heat Conduction" in *Secrets of Everyday Things* (DL) *RS4K Focus on Elementary Physics*, Chapter 5 (HC)
Foundation Lesson	Transferring Thermal Energy	Transferring Thermal Energy	Transferring Thermal Energy and Hypothesis
Activities	Linked Activities Drawing the Experiment	Linked Activities Drawing the Experiment	RS4K Experiment 5 Drawing the Experiment Library Research

Unit 20

	K – 1st Grade	2nd – 3rd Grade	4th – 6th Grade
Theme	Static and Current Electricity		
Read-Aloud	*The Storybook of Science*, Ch. 35-39 (DL)	*The Storybook of Science*, Ch. 35-39 (DL)	*The Storybook of Science*, Ch. 35-39 (DL) *RS4K Focus on Elementary Physics*, Chapter 6 (HC)
Foundation Lesson	Static & Current Electricity Experiment	Static & Current Electricity Experiment	Static & Current Electricity Experiment
Activities	Linked Activities Drawing the Experiment	Linked Activities Drawing the Experiment	RS4K Experiment 6 Drawing the Experiment Library Research

All Grades ~ SCOPE & SEQUENCE

Unit 21

	K – 1st Grade	2nd – 3rd Grade	4th – 6th Grade
Theme	Electricity and Magnetism		
Read-Aloud	*The Storybook of Science* (DL)	*The Storybook of Science* (DL)	*The Storybook of Science* (DL) *RS4K Focus on Elementary Physics,* Chapter 7 (HC)
Foundation Lesson	Electricity and Magnetism Experiment	Electricity and Magnetism Experiment	Electricity and Magnetism Experiment
Activities	Linked Activities Drawing the Experiment	Linked Activities Drawing the Experiment	RS4K Experiment 7 Drawing the Experiment Library Research

Unit 22

	K – 1st Grade	2nd – 3rd Grade	4th – 6th Grade
Theme	Review		
Read-Aloud	*The Storybook of Science* (DL)	*The Storybook of Science* (DL)	*The Storybook of Science* (DL)
Foundation Lesson	Master CCM Memory Work, Units 1-22	Master CCM Memory Work, Units 1-22	Master CCM Memory Work, Units 1-22
Activities	Linked Activities	Linked Activities	Linked Activities

Unit 23

	K – 1st Grade	2nd – 3rd Grade	4th – 6th Grade
Theme	Sound		
Read-Aloud	"Sound" and "Sound Continued" in *Secrets of Everyday Things* (DL)	"Sound" and "Sound Continued" in *Secrets of Everyday Things* (DL)	"Sound" and "Sound Continued" in *Secrets of Everyday Things* (DL) "Velocity of Sound" in *Storybook of Science* (DL)
Foundation Lesson	Sound Observation and Discussion	Sound Observation and Discussion	Sound Observation and Discussion
Activities	Linked Activities Drawing the Experiment	Linked Activities Drawing the Experiment	Linked Activities Drawing the Experiment Library Research

Unit 24

	K – 1st Grade	2nd – 3rd Grade	4th – 6th Grade
Theme	Light and Matter		
Read-Aloud	"Light" in *Secrets of Everyday Things* (DL)	"Light" in *Secrets of Everyday Things* (DL)	"Light" in *Secrets of Everyday Things* (DL) *RS4K Focus on Elementary Physics*, Chapter 9 (HC)
Foundation Lesson	Light and Matter Observation and Discussion	Light and Matter Observation and Discussion	Light and Matter Observation and Discussion
Activities	Linked Activities Drawing the Experiment	Linked Activities Drawing the Experiment	RS4K Experiment 9 Linked Activities Drawing the Experiment Library Research

Unit 25

	K – 1st Grade	2nd – 3rd Grade	4th – 6th Grade
Theme	Newton's First Law of Motion		
Read-Aloud	"Locomotive" in *Storybook of Science* (DL)	"Locomotive" in *Storybook of Science* (DL)	"Locomotive" in *Storybook of Science* (DL) *RS4K Focus on Elementary Physics*, Chapter 1 (HC)
Foundation Lesson	First Law of Motion Observation and Discussion	First Law of Motion Observation and Discussion	First Law of Motion Observation and Discussion
Activities	Linked Activities Drawing the Experiment	Linked Activities Drawing the Experiment	RS4K Experiment 1 Linked Activities Drawing the Experiment Library Research Video

Unit 26

	K – 1st Grade	2nd – 3rd Grade	4th – 6th Grade
Theme	Review		
Read-Aloud	*The Secrets of Everyday Things* (DL)	*The Secrets of Everyday Things* (DL)	*The Secrets of Everyday Things* (DL)
Foundation Lesson	Master CCM Memory Work, Units 1-25	Master CCM Memory Work, Units 1-25	Master CCM Memory Work, Units 1-25
Activities	Newton Rocket Car Craft	Newton Rocket Car Craft	Newton Rocket Car Craft

All Grades ~ SCOPE & SEQUENCE

Unit 27

	K – 1st Grade	2nd – 3rd Grade	4th – 6th Grade
Theme	Newton's Second Law of Motion		
Read-Aloud	*n/a*	*n/a*	*RS4K Focus on Elementary Physics,* Chapter 2 (HC)
Foundation Lesson	Second Law of Motion Observation and Discussion	Second Law of Motion Observation and Discussion	Second Law of Motion Observation and Discussion
Activities	Linked Activity Drawing the Experiment	Linked Activity Drawing the Experiment	RS4K Experiment 2 Linked Activity Drawing the Experiment Library Research

Unit 28

	K – 1st Grade	2nd – 3rd Grade	4th – 6th Grade
Theme	Newton's Third Law of Motion		
Read-Aloud	*n/a*	*n/a*	*RS4K Focus on Elementary Physics,* Chapter 3 (HC)
Foundation Lesson	Third Law of Motion Observation and Discussion	Third Law of Motion Observation and Discussion	Third Law of Motion Observation and Discussion
Activities	Linked Activity Drawing the Experiment	Linked Activity Drawing the Experiment	RS4K Experiment 3 Linked Activity Drawing the Experiment Library Research

Unit 29

	K – 1st Grade	2nd – 3rd Grade	4th – 6th Grade
Theme	Six Simple Machines		
Read-Aloud	*n/a*	*n/a*	*RS4K Focus on Elementary Physics,* Chapter 4 (HC)
Foundation Lesson	Simple Machines Observation and Discussion	Simple Machines Observation and Discussion	Simple Machines Observation and Discussion
Activities	Linked Activity Drawing the Experiment	Linked Activity Drawing the Experiment	RS4K Experiment 4 Linked Activity Drawing the Experiment Library Research Video

All Grades ~ SCOPE & SEQUENCE

Unit 30

	K – 1st Grade	2nd – 3rd Grade	4th – 6th Grade
Theme	Review		
Read-Aloud	*n/a*	*n/a*	*n/a*
Foundation Lesson	Master CCM Memory Work, Units 1-29	Master CCM Memory Work, Units 1-29	Master CCM Memory Work, Units 1-29
Activities	Organize Notebooks from the year.	Organize Notebooks from the year.	Organize Notebooks from the year.

Virtue

❖ Below you will find a list of the virtues studied for each unit.

Unit 1	Love
Unit 2	Hope and Courage
Unit 3	Purity and Modesty
Unit 4	Faith
Unit 5	Discipline
Unit 6	Obedience
Unit 7	Justice
Unit 8	Temperance
Unit 9	Charity – Love of Neighbor
Unit 10	Moderation
Unit 11	Prudence
Unit 12	Gratitude
Unit 13	Humility
Unit 14	Review
Unit 15	Piety
Unit 16	Patriotism
Unit 17	Honesty
Unit 18	Self-Discipline
Unit 19	Forgiveness
Unit 20	Compassion
Unit 21	Cheerfulness
Unit 22	Steadfastness
Unit 23	Dependability
Unit 24	Fear of God
Unit 25	Orderliness
Unit 26	Perseverance
Unit 27	Responsibility
Unit 28	Temperance
Unit 29	Generosity
Unit 30	Review

Preschool ~ Materials Usage Schedule

Introduction

Welcome to the Materials Usage Schedule for Preschool. The schedule is provides a timeline of when materials will be used. The Preschool Materials Usage Schedule is divided into unit lists. Each unit list is divided by subject and by days.

In the Materials Usage Schedule, Day 1 is listed as either a "Co-op Day" or "Field Trip Day." If Day 1 does not have a label, it is a Home Day. Days 2-4 are always considered Home Days in each unit. If you are a "Just Home" Family (those who are not in a local co-op), every day is a home day, so you should plan accordingly.

Important Notices:

- Materials listed under a Co-op Day are provided **at co-op**.

- Materials listed under a Field Trip or Home Day must be provided **at home and do not come from co-op.**

- The following items are **NOT** included on this list:
  - **Books**: See the booklists under Step 2 of "Getting Started" in your online suite.
  - **Linked Lesson Materials**: Items required for lessons and activities in the curriculum that link to outside websites. You will need to follow the links in the Subject Folders (SF) in order to gather materials needed week-to-week.
  - **Extras**: Items needed to complete activities found in the "Extras" section of subjects.
  - **Printed Items**: Documents in the online suite that must be printed for use (handouts, coloring pages, copy work, worksheets, etc.)

- Items listed as "Optional" are not required purchases; they are merely suggestions for enhancing the activity or lesson.

- Please note the following vocabulary:
  - The *water jar* is a container for washing out paintbrushes.
  - A *drawing utensil* is any tool of your choice--marker, pen, or pencil—used for writing or drawing.

For the list of materials to be purchased, see the "Materials Purchase List" located in the "Getting Started" section of the online suite.

Please contact us if you have any questions or concerns.

ABBREVIATION KEY	
DL	Digital Library (in course suite)
SF	Subject Folder (in course suite)
HC	Hard Copy
PLL	*Primary Language Lessons* (book)
ILL	*Intermediate Language Lessons* (book)
RS4K	*Real Science 4 Kids* (book)
I-CAT	*Illustrated Catechism* (book)
OHF-1	*Our Holy Faith, Book 1* (book)
OHF-2	*Our Holy Faith, Book 2* (book)
OHF-4	*Our Holy Faith, Book 4* (book)
OHF-1-TM	*Our Holy Faith, Book 1, Teacher's Manual* (book)

Preschool ~ Materials Usage Schedule

UNIT 1

SUBJECT	DAY 1 (Co-op Day)		DAYS 2 – 4	
MUSIC	N/A		N/A	
ART READING RELIGION	1	Smock or large T-shirt per student	1	Printed Letter/Number Book per student
	1	White crayon per student	1	Piece of construction paper per student
	1	Printed Handout per student	2	Printed Coloring Page Handouts per student
	1	Paint brush per student		
	1	Watercolor set per student		
	1	Paper cup per student		
	1	Water pitcher with water		
	1	Paper towel Roll		
	1	Bottle of Cleaning spray		
	1	Piece of construction paper per		
	1	student		
		Glue stick per student		
VIRTUE	See Linked Lesson		See Linked Lesson	

UNIT 2

SUBJECT	DAY 1 (Co-op Day)		DAYS 2 – 4	
MUSIC	N/A		N/A	
ART READING RELIGION	1	Smock or large T-shirt per student	1	Printed Letter/Number Book per student
	1	Golf ball sized piece of air-dry clay per student	1	Piece of construction paper per student
	1	Pre-made "Corpus Christi Mold" per student	2	Printed Coloring Page Handouts per student
	1	Unblessed Plastic Crucifix		
	1	Plastic knife per student		
	1	Paper plate per student		
	1	12" x 12" piece of plastic wrap per student		
	1	Paper towel Roll		
	1	Bottle of Cleaning spray		
VIRTUE	See Linked Lesson		See Linked Lesson	

Preschool ~ Materials Usage Schedule

UNIT 3

SUBJECT	DAY 1 (Co-op Day)	DAYS 2 – 4
MUSIC	N/A	N/A

ART
READING
RELIGION
	1 Smock or large T-shirt per student
	1 Paper or cardboard sword per
	1 student
	1 Paper Towel Roll
	8 Bottle of Cleaning spray
	    Crayons per student
		1 Printed Letter/Number Book
		    per student
		1 Piece of construction paper per
		    student
		2 Printed Coloring Page
		    Handouts per student

VIRTUE	See Linked Lesson	See Linked Lesson

UNIT 4

SUBJECT	DAY 1 (Field Trip Day)	DAYS 2 – 4
MUSIC	N/A	N/A

ART
READING
RELIGION
	1 Smock or large T-shirt per student
	1 Bottle of Red Finger Paint
	1 Sheet of white paper per student
	1 Paper plate per student
	1 Napkin per student
	1 Preschool ABC Flashcards
	1 Set of Printed Pictures of Red
	    objects per student
		1 Printed Letter/Number Book
		    per student

VIRTUE	See Linked Lesson	See Linked Lesson

Preschool ~ Materials Usage Schedule

UNIT 5

SUBJECT	DAY 1 (Co-op Day)		DAYS 2 – 4	
MUSIC	N/A		N/A	
ART READING RELIGION	1	Smock or large T-shirt per student	1	Printed Letter/Number Book per student
	1	White crayon per student		
	1	Printed Handout per student	1	Piece of construction paper per student
	1	Paint brush per student		
	1	Paint brush per student	2	Printed Coloring Page Handouts per student
	1	Watercolor set per student		
	1	Paper cup per student		
	1	Water pitcher with water		
	1	Piece of construction paper per student		
	1	Glue stick per student		
	1	Paper towel Roll		
		Bottle of Cleaning spray		
VIRTUE	See Linked Lesson		See Linked Lesson	

UNIT 6

SUBJECT	DAY 1 (Co-op Day)		DAYS 2 – 4	
MUSIC	N/A		N/A	
ART READING RELIGION	1	Smock or large T-shirt per student	1	Printed Letter/Number Book per student
	1	Wooden bird house per student		
	1	Paint brush per student	1	Piece of construction paper per student
	1	Bottles of Yellow Acrylic Paints		
	1	Bottles of Blue Acrylic Paints	2	Printed Coloring Page Handouts per student
	1	Bottles of Red Acrylic Paints		
	1	Paper plate per student		
	1	Paper cup per student		
	1	Water pitcher with water		
	1	Portable fan		
	1	Newspaper or large paper bag per student		
	1	Paper towel Roll		
	1	Bottle of Cleaning spray		
VIRTUE	See Linked Lesson		See Linked Lesson	

UNIT 7

SUBJECT	DAY 1 (Co-op Day)	DAYS 2 – 4
MUSIC	N/A	N/A

ART READING RELIGION	1 Completely Finished paper bag Rosary book for example
	1 Prepped paper Rosary booklet per student
	
	Rosary Book Prep
	4 Paper lunch sacks per book
	1 Stapler and Staples
	
	3-4 Pieces of 4″ long ribbon per
	3-4 student
	     Pieces of 5″x5″ squares cardstock
	4-5 per student
	     Pieces of 5″x5″ Assorted colors/
	1 themed stationary paper squares
	1 per student
	1 Pair of scissors per student
	     Glue sticks per student
	     Set of 3-4 Rosary mysteries
	1 pictures per student. (Make sure
	1 that are small enough to fit all on a 5″x5″ square.
	     Paper towel Roll
	     Bottle of Cleaning spray
		1 Printed Letter/Number Book per student
		1 Piece of construction paper per student
		2 Printed Coloring Page Handouts per student

VIRTUE	See Linked Lesson	See Linked Lesson

Preschool ~ Materials Usage Schedule

UNIT 8

SUBJECT	DAY 1 (Field Trip Day)		DAYS 2 – 4	
MUSIC	N/A		N/A	
ART READING RELIGION	1 1 1 1 1 1 1 1 1 1	Smock or large T-shirt per student Bottle of Red Finger Paint Bottle of Blue Finger Paint Sheet of white paper per student Paper plate per student Napkin per student Preschool ABC Flashcards Set of Printed Pictures of Red objects per student Set of Printed Pictures of Blue objects per student Set of Printed Pictures of Purple objects per student	1	Printed Letter/Number Book per student
VIRTUE	See Linked Lesson		See Linked Lesson	

UNIT 9

SUBJECT	DAY 1 (Co-op Day)		DAYS 2 – 4	
MUSIC	N/A		N/A	
ART READING RELIGION	1 1 1 1 1 1 1	Smock or large T-shirt per student 11" X 17" Piece of poster board cut into the shape of a cloud per student Large bags of white cotton balls Bottle of liquid glue per student Saints prayer cards per student or Multiple saint printouts. Marker Paper towel Roll Bottle of Cleaning spray	1 1 2	Printed Letter/Number Book per student Piece of construction paper per student Printed Coloring Page Handouts per student
VIRTUE	See Linked Lesson		See Linked Lesson	

UNIT 10

SUBJECT	DAY 1 (Co-op Day)		DAYS 2 – 4	
MUSIC	N/A		N/A	
ART READING RELIGION	1	Smock or large T-shirt per student	1	Printed Letter/Number Book per student
	1	Ball of bread dough baseball-sized per child	1	Piece of construction paper per student
	1	12" Square of parchment paper per child	2	Printed Coloring Page Handouts per student
	1	Small paper cup per student		
	1/	Cup of flour per student		
	4	Plastic knife per student		
	1	Paper towel Roll		
	1	Bottle of Cleaning spray		
	1			
VIRTUE	See Linked Lesson		See Linked Lesson	

UNIT 11

SUBJECT	DAY 1 (Co-op Day)		DAYS 2 – 4	
MUSIC	N/A		N/A	
ART READING RELIGION	1	Paper towel roll painted white per student	1	Printed Letter/Number Book per student
	3	Toilet paper rolls painted purple per student	1	Piece of construction paper per Letter/Number Book
	1	Toilet paper roll painted rose per student	2	Printed Coloring Page Handouts per student
	5	Yellow pieces of tissue paper per student		
	1	Piece of light green tissue paper per student		
	1	Piece of dark green construction paper cut in the shape of a wreath per student		
	1	Pieces of light green construction paper cut in the shape of leaves per student		
	1	Small pieces of red tissue paper per student		
	1	Paper plate per student		
	1	Glue stick per child		
	1	Bottle of liquid glue per child		
	1	Bottle of Cleaning spray		
VIRTUE	See Linked Lesson		See Linked Lesson	

Preschool ~ Materials Usage Schedule

UNIT 12

SUBJECT		DAY 1		DAYS 2 – 4
MUSIC		N/A		N/A
ART **READING** **RELIGION**	1 1 1 1 1 1 1 1 1 1	Smock or large T-shirt per student Bottle of Red Finger Paint Bottle of Yellow Finger Paint Sheet of white paper per student Paper plate per student Napkin per student Preschool ABC Flashcards Set of Printed Pictures of Red objects per student Set of Printed Pictures of Yellow objects per student Set of Printed Pictures of Orange objects per student	1	Printed Letter/Number Book per student
VIRTUE		See Linked Lesson		See Linked Lesson

UNIT 13

SUBJECT		DAY 1		DAYS 2 – 4
MUSIC		N/A		N/A
ART **READING** **RELIGION**	1 1 1 1 1 1 1 1 1 1	Smock or large T-shirt per student Bottle of Blue Finger Paint Bottle of Yellow Finger Paint Sheet of white paper per student Paper plate per student Napkin per student Preschool ABC Flashcards Set of Printed Pictures of Blue objects per student Set of Printed Pictures of Yellow objects per student Set of Printed Pictures of Green objects per student Preschool ABC Flashcards (DL)	1	Printed Letter/Number Book per student
VIRTUE		See Linked Lesson		See Linked Lesson

338

UNIT 14

SUBJECT	DAY 1		DAYS 2 – 4	
MUSIC	N/A		N/A	
ART READING RELIGION	1	Smock or large T-shirt per student	1	Printed Letter/Number Book per student
	1	Bottle of Red Finger Paint		
	1	Bottle of Blue Finger Paint		
	1	Bottle of Yellow Finger Paint		
	1	Sheet of white paper per student		
	1	Paper plate per student		
	1	Napkin per student		
	1	Preschool ABC Flashcards		
	1	Set of Printed Pictures of Red objects per student		
	1	Set of Printed Pictures of Blue objects per student		
		Set of Printed Pictures of Yellow objects per student		
		Preschool ABC Flashcards		
VIRTUE	See Linked Lesson		See Linked Lesson	

UNIT 15

SUBJECT	DAY 1		DAYS 2 – 4	
MUSIC	N/A		N/A	
ART READING RELIGION	2	1 3/4" to 2" clay pots	1	Printed Letter/Number Book per student
	2	Round wood balls (1 1/2")		
	1	Round wood ball (5/8")		
	1	Fabric scraps (3" long x 2" wide		
	1	Permanent marker		
	1	Small dowel		
	1	Bottle of Blue acrylic paint		
	1	Bottle of Black acrylic paint		
	1	Bottle of Flesh color acrylic paint		
	1	Foam brush per student		
	1	6" pieces of Jute or yarn		
	1	Hot glue gun and glue		
	1	Smock or oversized T-shirt per student		
	1	Sheet Plastic to protect the table or floor		
	1	Paper plate per color per student		
		Napkin per students		
		Printed Picture of the Holy Family		
VIRTUE	See Linked Lesson		See Linked Lesson	

UNIT 16

SUBJECT	DAY 1		DAYS 2 – 4	
MUSIC	N/A		N/A	
ART READING RELIGION	2 1-2 1 1 1 1 1 1 1 1	Clothes pins per student Bottles of acrylic paint (black or color of your choice) 3″ Piece of cardboard (Optional) Hair drier Pair of Scissors Foam brush per student Small ball of yarn - color of your choice Smock or oversized T-shirt per student Sheet of plastic to protect the table or floor Paper plate per color per student Napkin per students	1	Printed Letter/Number Book per student
VIRTUE	See Linked Lesson		See Linked Lesson	

UNIT 17

SUBJECT	DAY 1		DAYS 2 – 4	
MUSIC	N/A		N/A	
ART READING RELIGION	1 1 5- 10 1 1 1	Box Set of 24 crayons per student Printed Handout page of "St. Paul's Conversion Pictures" per student Popsicle sticks per student Glue stick per student or Roll of tape Napkin per students Sheet of plastic to protect the table or floor	1	Printed Letter/Number Book per student
VIRTUE	See Linked Lesson		See Linked Lesson	

Preschool ~ Materials Usage Schedule

UNIT 18

SUBJECT	DAY 1 (Field Trip Day)		DAYS 2 – 4	
MUSIC	N/A		N/A	
ART READING RELIGION	1	Set of watercolor paint set per student	1	Printed Letter/Number Book per student
	1	Paint brush per student		
	1	Printed Coloring Page Handout of		
	1	"The Presentation of Our Lord"		
	1	per student		
	1	Sheet of any colored construction paper		
	1	Smock or oversized T-shirt per		
	1	student		
		Sheet of plastic to protect the table or floor		
		Cup of water per student		
		Napkin per students		
VIRTUE	See Linked Lesson		See Linked Lesson	

UNIT 19

SUBJECT	DAY 1 (Co-op Day)		DAYS 2 – 4	
MUSIC	N/A		N/A	
ART READING RELIGION	1	Smock or oversized T-shirt per student	1	Printed Letter/Number Book per student
	1	Sheet of Bees Wax per student Candle Wick per student	1	Piece of construction paper per student
		(For optional stain glass candle jar. Activity see SF~ Lesson A)	2	Printed Coloring Page Handouts per student
VIRTUE	See Linked Lesson		See Linked Lesson	

UNIT 20

SUBJECT	DAY 1 (Co-op Day)		DAYS 2 – 4	
MUSIC	N/A		N/A	
ART READING RELIGION	1	Pre-cut piece of white card stock with holes per student	1	Printed Letter/Number Book per student
	1	Printed and pre-cut picture of Our Lady of Lourdes	1	Piece of construction paper per Letter/Number Book
	1	Set of colored pencils per student or a set of 24 crayons per student	2	Printed Coloring Page Handouts per student
	1	Pair of Scissors		
	1	Medium-sized bags of rocks		
	1	Liquid Glue bottle per student		
	1	Q-Tip per student		
	1	6" Piece of yarn or ribbon per student		
	1	Smock or oversized T-shirt per student		
	1	Paper cup per student		
		Napkin per student		
VIRTUE	See Linked Lesson		See Linked Lesson	

UNIT 21

SUBJECT	DAY 1 (Co-op Day)		DAYS 2 – 4	
MUSIC	N/A		N/A	
ART READING RELIGION	3	Yellow Chenille Stems / pipe cleaners per child	1	Printed Letter/Number Book per student
	9	Green Chenille Stems / pipe cleaners per child	1	Piece of construction paper per student
	1	Roll of Tape	2	Printed Coloring Page Handouts per student
	1	Pair of scissors per child		
	1	Sheets of white paper		
	1	Printed and pre-cut St. Joseph prayer card per student		
	1	Crayon, pencil or marker per child		
VIRTUE	See Linked Lesson		See Linked Lesson	

UNIT 22

SUBJECT		DAY 1 (Field Trip Day)		DAYS 2 – 4
MUSIC		N/A		N/A
ART READING RELIGION	1	Smock or oversized T-shirt per	1	Printed Letter/Number Book per student
	1	student		
	1	Bottle of Blue Finger Paint		
	1	Bottle of Red Finger Paint		
	1	Bottle of Yellow Finger Paint		
		Sheet of white sturdy weight		
	6	paper like poster board per		
	1	student		
		Small paper plates per student		
	1	Napkin per students		
		Paper towel roll cut into 3rds		
		Print off Circle Handout pattern		
VIRTUE		See Linked Lesson		See Linked Lesson

UNIT 23

SUBJECT		DAY 1 (Co-op Day)		DAYS 2 – 4
MUSIC		N/A		N/A
ART READING RELIGION	1	Set of 14 stations of the cross cards per student	1	Printed Letter/Number Book per student
	1	Glue stick per student	1	Piece of construction paper per student
	1	Hole punch		
	1	3 "Piece of twine, or ribbon per	2	Printed Coloring Page Handouts per student
	1	student		
	1	White box container per student		
		Set of Crayons or Markers per		
	1	student		
	1	Piece of Twine per student		
	1	1" Wooden Cross per student		
		Band-Aid with a #1 written on it per		
	1	student		
	1	Blue ribbon per student		
	1	Small 1" Heart per student		
		Piece of cloth with face of Jesus		
	1	drawn on it per student		
	1	Band-Aid with the #2 written on it		
	1	2" piece of tissue		
	1	Band-Aid with the #3 written on it		
	1	2" Piece of Purple Felt		
	1	2"-3" Nails per student		
	1	Small Crucifix per student		
	1	Picture of The Pieta per student		
		1" Rock per student		
		(Optional) cross stickers		
VIRTUE		See Linked Lesson		See Linked Lesson

UNIT 24

SUBJECT	DAY 1 (Co-op Day)		DAYS 2 – 4	
MUSIC	N/A		N/A	
ART READING RELIGION	1	½ of a small potato heart stamp per student	1	Printed Letter/Number Book per student
	1	Large bottle of green acyclic paint	1	Piece of construction paper per student
	1	White sheet of construction paper per student	2	Printed Coloring Page Handouts per student
	2	¼ Sheets of white construction paper per student		
	1	Paper plate per student		
	1	Smock per student		
	1	Black marker		
	1	Sheet of plastic to protect the floor		
	1	Optional - green piece of construction paper per student		
VIRTUE	See Linked Lesson		See Linked Lesson	

UNIT 25

SUBJECT	DAY 1 (Co-op Day)		DAYS 2 – 4	
MUSIC	N/A		N/A	
ART READING RELIGION	1	Printed Handout Seven Sorrows craft sheet per student	1	Printed Letter/Number Book per student
	2	Pieces of card stock	1	Piece of construction paper per student
	1	Pair of Scissors per student	2	Printed Coloring Page Handouts per student
	1	Exact-o-knife		
	14	Pieces of clear tape per student		
	8	1' long pieces of yarn or string per student		
	1	Hole punch		
VIRTUE	See Linked Lesson		See Linked Lesson	

UNIT 26

SUBJECT	DAY 1 (Field Trip Day)		DAYS 2 – 4	
MUSIC	N/A		N/A	
ART READING RELIGION	1 1 1 1 1 1 1 1	1' x 1' square piece of ½" thick wood Hammer Box of 1" nails Pencil Ruler Package of multi-colored rubber bands Box of 24 crayons per student (Optional) – bottle of black paint	1	Printed Letter/Number Book per student
VIRTUE	See Linked Lesson		See Linked Lesson	

UNIT 27

SUBJECT	DAY 1 (Co-op Day)		DAYS 2 – 4	
MUSIC	N/A		N/A	
ART READING RELIGION	7 10 1 1 1 1 1	Pintables Handout Easter Wreath Scripture Eggs per student Pintables Easter Wreath Pictures Glue stick per student Cardstock wreath circle (approx. 11 ½ " in diameter) Set of 24 crayons per student Pairs of scissors per student Pair of scissors per adults	1 1 2	Printed Letter/Number Book per student Piece of construction paper per Letter/Number Book Printed Coloring Page Handouts per student
VIRTUE	See Linked Lesson		See Linked Lesson	

Preschool ~ Materials Usage Schedule

UNIT 28

SUBJECT	DAY 1 (Co-op Day)		DAYS 2 – 4	
MUSIC	N/A		N/A	
ART READING RELIGION	1	1/2 piece of black poster board	1	Printed Letter/Number Book per student
	1	Yellow piece of paper per		
	1	student	1	Piece of construction paper per student
	1	Pencil per student		
	1	Clamp on light	2	Printed Coloring Page Handouts per student
	1	Pair of Scissors per adult		
	3	Glue stick per student		
		Different color glitter glue tubes		
	1	per student		
		Jesus sticker or printed Jesus		
	1	picture per student		
	1	1" White circle paper per student		
	1	Box of 12- 24 crayons per		
	1	students		
	1	White piece of paper per student		
		Smock or oversized T-shirt per		
	1	student		
		Sheet of plastic to protect the		
		table or floor		
		Napkin per students		
VIRTUE	See Linked Lesson		See Linked Lesson	

UNIT 29

SUBJECT	DAY 1 (Co-op Day)		DAYS 2 – 4	
MUSIC	N/A		N/A	
ART READING RELIGION	20-25	Pieces of Rotini (spiral pasta) per student	1	Printed Letter/Number Book per student
	1	Plain white paper plate per student	1	Piece of construction paper per student
	1	Set Yellow, Orange Brown, Tan, and Black crayons per student	2	Printed Coloring Page Handouts per student
	1	Bottle of Liquid Glue		
	1	Small cup per student		
	1	Q-Tip per student		
	1	Black marker		
	1	Google eyes per student		
	1	Pair of Scissors		
	1	Napkin per students		
VIRTUE	See Linked Lesson		See Linked Lesson	

UNIT 30

SUBJECT	DAY 1		DAYS 2 – 4	
MUSIC	N/A		N/A	
ART READING RELIGION	1 1 1 1 1 1	12″ x 6″ piece of Cardboard Pair of scissors Bag of different colored plastic pony beads Ball of yarn Pencil Embroidery needle (plastic or metal)	1	Printed Letter/Number Book per student
VIRTUE	See Linked Lesson		See Linked Lesson	

Preschool ~ Materials Usage Schedule

K – 1st Grade ~ Materials Usage Schedule

Introduction

Welcome to the Materials Usage Schedule for K – 1st Grade. The schedule is provides a timeline of when materials will be used. The K – 1st Grade Materials Usage Schedule is divided into unit lists. Each unit list is divided by subject and by days.

In the Materials Usage Schedule, Day 1 is listed as either a "Co-op Day" or "Field Trip Day." If Day 1 does not have a label, it is a Home Day. Days 2-4 are always considered Home Days in each unit. If you are a "Just Home" Family (those who are not in a local co-op), every day is a home day, so you should plan accordingly.

Important Notices:

- Materials listed under a Co-op Day are provided **at co-op**.

- Materials listed under a Field Trip or Home Day must be provided **at home and do not come from co-op.**

- The following items are **NOT** included on this list:
  - **Books**: See the booklists under Step 2 of "Getting Started" in your online suite.
  - **Linked Lesson Materials**: Items required for lessons and activities in the curriculum that link to outside websites. You will need to follow the links in the Subject Folders (SF) in order to gather materials needed week-to-week.
  - **Extras**: Items needed to complete activities found in the "Extras" section of subjects.
  - **Printed Items**: Documents in the online suite that must be printed for use (handouts, coloring pages, copy work, worksheets, etc.)

- Items listed as "Optional" are not required purchases; they are merely suggestions for enhancing the activity or lesson.

- Please note the following vocabulary:
  - The *water jar* is a container for washing out paintbrushes.
  - A *drawing utensil* is any tool of your choice--marker, pen, or pencil—used for writing or drawing.

For the list of materials to be purchased, see the "Materials Purchase List" located in the "Getting Started" section of the online suite.

Please contact us if you have any questions or concerns.

ABBREVIATION KEY	
DL	Digital Library (in course suite)
SF	Subject Folder (in course suite)
HC	Hard Copy
PLL	*Primary Language Lessons* (book)
ILL	*Intermediate Language Lessons* (book)
RS4K	*Real Science 4 Kids* (book)
I-CAT	*Illustrated Catechism* (book)
OHF-1	*Our Holy Faith, Book 1* (book)
OHF-2	*Our Holy Faith, Book 2* (book)
OHF-4	*Our Holy Faith, Book 4* (book)
OHF-1-TM	*Our Holy Faith, Book 1, Teacher's Manual* (book)

UNIT 1

SUBJECT	DAY 1 (Co-op Day)	DAYS 2 – 4
ART	1 Handout on paper, in color per student 1 3" x 3" sheet of paper per K-3rd Grade student 1 3" x 3" sheet of 5 mil Copper Sheets per K-3rd Grade student (FILE THE SHARP EDGES) ½ A Plastic Placemat per student – cut large mat in ½ 1 Pencil per student 2 Leather Working Tools per student 1 *(Optional)* Set of Visual Aids on paper 1 Smock or large T-shirt per student 1 Paper towel Roll 1 Bottle of Cleaning spray	1 Handout on paper, in color per student (or per family) 1 3" X 3" sheet of paper per K-3rd Grade student (cut to size and FILE THE SHARP EDGES) 1 3" X 3" sheet of 5 mil Copper Sheets per K-3rd Grade student (purchase a roll to save money) 1 Plastic Placemat per student 1 Pencil per student 2-3 Basic Leather Working Tools per student
CCM	Map 1 Timeline Cards Printed Unit Summary	Map 1 Timeline Cards Printed Unit Summary
HISTORY	1 Printed Handouts "Renaissance Art Images" per student 1 Pair of scissors per student 1 Glue stick per student 1 Stapler per classroom 1 Box of Staples per classroom 1 8 ½ x 11 sheets of colored paper per TWO students 1 8 ½ x 11 sheets of white paper per 1 student 1 Colored Pencils set per student	1 Drawing Utensils per student 2 Paper per student 1 Printed coloring page 5-10 Colored Pencils and/or Crayons per student See Extras
LANGUAGE ARTS	2 Printed Handout per student 1 Drawing Utensils per student	1 Printed Copy work per student 1 Drawing Utensils per student 1 Printed Handout per student
LATIN/ GREEK	1 Printed Hymn of the week per student	1 Printed Hymn of the week per student
MATH	1 Pencil per student 1 Paper per student	1 Pencil per student 1 Paper per student
MUSIC	1 *(Optional)* Pitch instrument	N/A
READING	N/A	N/A
RELIGION	N/A	N/A
SCIENCE	2 Red Jelly Gumdrops per student 2 Blue Jelly Gumdrops per student 2 Yellow Jelly Gumdrops per student 2 7 "pieces of craft wire per student	1 Printed Handout per student 1 Drawing Utensils per student 5-10 Colored Pencils and/or Crayons per student 1 Paper or Journal per student See Linked Lesson (SF)
VIRTUE	N/A	N/A

K – 1st Grade ~ Materials Usage Schedule

UNIT 2

SUBJECT	DAY 1 (Co-op Day)		DAYS 2 – 4	
ART	1	Handout on paper, in color per student (or per family)	1	Drawing Utensils per student
	1	8" x 11" sheet of white printer paper per student	1	Paper per student
	1	8" x 11" sheet of charcoal paper per student	1	Printed Handout per student
	1	Charcoal / willow stick per		
	1	student		
	1	Pencil per student		
		Pencil sharpener per student		
		(Optional) Set of Visual Aids on		
	1	paper, in color		
	1	Smock or large T-shirt per student		
	1	Paper towel roll		
		Bottle of Cleaning spray		
		Sheets of plastic for tables and floors		
CCM		Map 2		Map 2
		Timeline Cards		Timeline Cards
		Printed Unit Summary		Printed Unit Summary
HISTORY	1	See Linked Lesson (SF)	1	Drawing Utensils per student
			1	Paper per student
			1	Printed coloring page
			5-10	Colored Pencils and/or Crayons per student
				See Extras
LANGUAGE ARTS	2	Printed Handout per student	1	Drawing Utensils per student
	1	Drawing Utensils per student	1	Printed Copy work per student
			1	Paper per student
			1	Printed Handout per student
LATIN / GREEK	1	Printed Hymn of the week per student	1	Printed Hymn of the week per student
MATH	1	Pencil per student	1	Pencil per student
	1	Paper per student	1	Paper per student
MUSIC	1	(Optional) Pitch instrument		N/A
READING		N/A		N/A
RELIGION		N/A		N/A
SCIENCE	8	Red Jelly Gumdrops per student		See Linked Lesson (SF)
	8	Blue Jelly Gumdrops per student	1	Printed Handout or Journal per student
	8	Yellow Jelly Gumdrops per student		
	3	7 "pieces of craft wire per student	1	Drawing Utensils per student
		Helium balloons		
VIRTUE		N/A		N/A

UNIT 3

SUBJECT	DAY 1 (Co-op Day)		DAYS 2 – 4	
ART	1	Handout on paper, in color per student (or per family)	1	Unfinished Cross-stitching Kit (from Day 1) per student
	1	4" X 4" piece of paper per student	1	Pair of scissors per student
	1	Quart-sized zip-lock bag per student		
	1			
		Permanent marker		
	1	Pair of scissors per student		
	1	Cross-stitching kit per student (See Link - SF)		
	1	(Optional) Set of Visual Aids on paper, in color		
	1	Paper Towel Roll		
		Bottle of Cleaning spray		
CCM		Map 3		Map 3
		Timeline Cards		Timeline Cards
		Printed Unit Summary		Printed Unit Summary
HISTORY	1	Printed Handout of "Classroom Visual Aids"	1	Drawing Utensils per student
	1	2-3" (H) x 2-3" (W) x 2-3" (D) block of Clay per student	1	Paper per student
			1	Printed coloring page
	¼	Piece of Sponges per student (cut from larger sponge)	5-10	Colored Pencils and/or Crayons per student
	1	Piece of 4"x 4" wax paper per student		See Extras
	1	Small cup for water per student		
	1	Bottle of Cleaning spray		
	1	Newspaper or Plastic Sheet to cover tables and floor		
LANGUAGE ARTS	1	Printed Handout per student	1	Drawing Utensils per student
			1	Printed Copy work per student
			1	Paper per student
			1	Printed Handout per student
LATIN / GREEK	1	Printed Hymn of the week per student	1	Printed Hymn of the week per student
MATH	1	Pencil per student	1	Pencil per student
	1	Paper per student	1	Paper per student
MUSIC	1	(Optional) Pitch instrument		N/A
READING		N/A		N/A
RELIGION		N/A		N/A
SCIENCE	2	Large Marshmallows (of one color) per student.		See Linked Lesson (SF)
	2	Large Marshmallow (of a different color) per student	1	Drawing Utensils per student
			1	Paper or Journal per student
	2	Toothpicks per student	1	Printed Handout per student
VIRTUE		N/A		N/A

K – 1st Grade ~ Materials Usage Schedule

UNIT 4

SUBJECT	DAY 1 (Field Trip Day)		DAYS 2 – 4	
ART	N/A		See "Extras"	
CCM	Maps 1 & 2 Timeline Cards Printed Unit Summary		Maps 1 & 2 Timeline Cards Printed Unit Summary	
HISTORY	N/A		1 2 1 1 5-10	Drawing Utensils per student Paper per student Printed Handout per student Printed coloring page Colored Pencils and/or Crayons per student See Extras
LANGUAGE ARTS	1	Printed Handout per student	1 1 1 1	Drawing Utensils per student Printed Copy work per student Paper per student Printed Handout per student
LATIN / GREEK	1	Printed Hymn of the week per student	1	Printed Hymn of the week per student
MATH	1 1	Pencil per student Paper per student	1 1	Pencil per student Paper per student
MUSIC	1	(Optional) Pitch instrument	N/A	
READING	N/A		N/A	
RELIGION	N/A		N/A	
SCIENCE	N/A		1 1	Drawing Utensils per student Paper or Journal per student
VIRTUE	N/A		N/A	

K – 1st Grade ~ Materials Usage Schedule

UNIT 5

SUBJECT	DAY 1 (Co-op Day)		DAYS 2 – 4	
ART	1	Handout on paper per student	1	Drawing Utensils per student
	1	8" X 12" piece of water color paper per student	1	Paper per student
	1	Paint brush per student	1	Paint brush per student
	1	Paper or plastic cup per student	1	Paper or plastic water cup per student
	1	Paper towel per student	1	Water color pencil set per student
	1	Water pitcher for filling cups with water		
	1	Water color pencil set per student (See Link in SF)		
	1	Pencil sharpener per student		
	1	(Optional) Set of Visual Aids on paper, in color		
	1	Roll of paper towels		
	1	Bottle of cleaning spray		
		Sheets of plastic for floor		
CCM		Maps 3		Maps 3
		Timeline Cards		Timeline Cards
		Printed Unit Summary		Printed Unit Summary
HISTORY	1	Set of Visual Aids on paper, in color	1	Drawing Utensils per student
	1	Printed Handout on "Conquistador Helmet Templates" per student	1	Paper per student
	1		5-10	Colored Pencils and/or Crayons per student
	2	Premade helmet parts templates per every 2 students	1	Printed coloring page per student
	1	Piece of white construction paper per student		See Extras
	1-2			
	1	Pair of scissors per student		
	1	Staplers per classroom		
		Box of staples per classroom		
		Colored Pencil set per student		
LANGUAGE ARTS	1	Printed Handout per student	1	Printed Copy work per student
			1	Drawing Utensils per student
			1	Paper per student
			1	Printed Handout per student
LATIN/ GREEK	1	Printed Hymn of the week per student	1	Printed Hymn of the week per student
MATH	1	Pencil per student	1	Pencil per student
	1	Paper per student	1	Paper per student
MUSIC	1	(Optional) Pitch instrument		N/A
READING		N/A		N/A
RELIGION		N/A		N/A
SCIENCE		See Linked Lesson (SF)	1	See Linked Lessons (SF)
			1	Drawing Utensils per student
				Paper or Journal per student
VIRTUE		N/A		N/A

UNIT 6

SUBJECT	DAY 1 (Co-op Day)		DAYS 2 – 4	
ART	1	(Optional) Set of Visual Aids in color per classroom	1	Drawing Utensils per student
	1	Handout in color per student	1	Drawing paper per student or small oil paint canvas
	1	8″ X 12″ oil paint canvas per	1	Oil paint set or Oil pastel set per student
	1	student Paint brush per student		
	1	Paper or plastic cup per student		
	1	Paper or plastic plate per student		
	1	Paper towel per student		
	1	Water pitcher for filling cups with water		
	1	Pre-painted dark oil painted piece of paper from the "Before the Lesson" section per student		
	1	Oil collection art set per student: (See Link SF)		
	1	Smock or T-shirt per student		
	1	Roll of paper towels		
	1	Bottle of cleaning spray		
CCM		Maps 3		Maps 3
		Timeline Cards		Timeline Cards
		Printed Unit Summary		Printed Unit Summary
HISTORY	5-6	Props or craft items to create simple props.	1	Drawing Utensils per student
			1	Paper per student
			5-10	Colored Pencils and/or Crayons per student
			1	Printed coloring page See Extras
LANGUAGE ARTS	1	Printed Handout per student	1	Drawing Utensils per student
			1	Printed Copy work per student
			1	Paper per student
			1	Printed Handout per student
LATIN / GREEK	1	Printed Hymn of the week per student	1	Printed Hymn of the week per student
MATH	1	Pencil per student	1	Pencil per student
	1	Paper per student	1	Paper per student
MUSIC	1	(Optional) Pitch instrument		N/A
READING		N/A		N/A
RELIGION		N/A		N/A
SCIENCE		See Linked Lesson (SF)		See Linked Lessons (SF)
			1	Drawing Utensils per student
			1	Paper or Nature Journal per student
VIRTUE		N/A		N/A

UNIT 7

SUBJECT		DAY 1 (Co-op Day)		DAYS 2 – 4
ART	1	(Optional) Set of Visual Aids in color per classroom		Drawing Utensils per student
	1	Handout from last week in color per student		Drawing paper per student or small oil paint canvas
	1	(For students who were absent last week) 8″ X 12″ oil paint canvas per student		Oil paint set or Oil pastel set per student
	1	Paint brush per student		
	1	Paper or plastic cup per student		
	1	Paper or plastic plate per student		
	1	Paper towel per student		
	1	Water pitcher of water		
	1	Pre-painted dark oil painted piece of paper		
	1	Oil Paint collection art set per		
	1	student:		
		(See Link SF)		
	1	Smock or T-shirt per student		
	1	Roll of paper towels		
	1	Bottle of cleaning spray		
CCM		Maps 3		Maps 3
		Timeline Cards		Timeline Cards
		Printed Unit Summary		Printed Unit Summary
HISTORY	1	Printed Handout per student	1	Drawing Utensils per student
	1	Drawing Utensils per student	1	Paper per student
	1	(Optional) Paper per student	5-10	Colored Pencils and/or Crayons per student
	5-10	(Optional) Colored Pencils and/or Crayons per student	1	Printed coloring page
				See Extras
LANGUAGE ARTS	1	Printed Handout per student	1	Drawing Utensils per student
			1	Printed Copy work per student
			1	Paper per student
			1	Printed Handout per student
LATIN/ GREEK	1	Printed Hymn of the week per student	1	Printed Hymn of the week per student
MATH	1	Pencil per student	1	Pencil per student
	1	Paper per student	1	Paper per student
MUSIC	1	(Optional) Pitch instrument		N/A
READING		N/A		N/A
RELIGION		N/A		N/A
SCIENCE		See Linked Lesson (SF)		See Linked Lessons (SF)
			1	Drawing Utensils per student
			1	Paper or Nature Journal per student
VIRTUE		N/A		N/A

UNIT 8

SUBJECT	DAY 1 (Field Trip Day)		DAYS 2 – 4	
ART	N/A		See "Extras"	
CCM	Maps 1,2,3 Timeline Cards Printed Unit Summary		Maps 1,2,3 Timeline Cards Printed Unit Summary	
HISTORY	N/A		1	Drawing Utensils per student
			1	Paper per student
			1	Printed Handout per student
			5-10	Colored Pencils and/or Crayons per student
				Printed coloring page
			1	See Extras
LANGUAGE ARTS	1	Printed Handout per student	1	Drawing Utensils per student
			1	Printed Copy work per student
			1	Paper per student
			1	Printed Handout per student
LATIN/ GREEK	1	Printed Hymn of the week per student	1	Printed Hymn of the week per student
MATH	1	Pencil per student	1	Pencil per student
	1	Paper per student	1	Paper per student
MUSIC	1	(Optional) Pitch instrument		N/A
READING	N/A			N/A
RELIGION	N/A			N/A
SCIENCE	N/A		1	Drawing Utensils per student
			1	Paper per student or Nature Journal
VIRTUE	N/A			N/A

UNIT 9

SUBJECT	DAY 1 (Co-op Day)		DAYS 2 – 4	
ART	1	(Optional) Set of Visual Aids Handout on paper, in color per student (or per family)	1	8" X 12" piece of sketch paper per student
	1	8" X 12" piece of sketch paper per student	1	Colored pencils set per student
	1	Colored pencils set per student		Pencil sharpener per student
	1	Pencil sharpener per student		
	1	Roll of paper towels		
	1	Bottle of cleaning spray		
CCM		Maps 4		Maps 4
		Timeline Cards		Timeline Cards
		Printed Unit Summary		Printed Unit Summary
HISTORY	2	Cups of Plain Popped Popcorn per student	1	Drawing Utensils per student
	1	Thread for necklaces	1	Paper per student
	1	Needle per student (embroidery needles may be used)	5-10	Colored Pencils and/or Crayons per student
	1	Paper towels		Printed coloring page
	1	Cleaning spray	1	See Extras
LANGUAGE ARTS	1	Printed Handout per student	1	Drawing Utensils per student
			1	Printed Copy work per student
			1	Paper per student
			1	Printed Handouts per student
LATIN/GREEK	1	Printed Hymn of the week per student	1	Printed Hymn of the week per student
MATH	1	Pencil per student	1	Pencil per student
	1	Paper per student	1	Paper per student
MUSIC	1	(Optional) Pitch instrument		N/A
READING		N/A		N/A
RELIGION		N/A		N/A
SCIENCE		See Linked Lessons (SF)	1	Drawing Utensils per student
			1	Paper per student or Nature Journal
				See Linked Lessons (SF)
VIRTUE		N/A		N/A

UNIT 10

SUBJECT	DAY 1 (Co-op Day)		DAYS 2 – 4	
ART	1	(Optional) Set of Visual Aids Handout in color per student (or per family)	1	8" X 12" piece of sketch paper per student
	1	Drawing started last week per student	1	Colored pencils set per student
	1	8" X 12" piece of sketch paper per student for students who where absent last week		Pencil sharpener per student
	1	Colored pencils set per student		
	1	Pencil sharpener per student		
	1	Roll of paper towels		
	1	Bottle of cleaning spray		
CCM		Maps 5		Maps 5
		Timeline Cards		Timeline Cards
		Printed Unit Summary		Printed Unit Summary
HISTORY	1	Drawing Utensils per student	1	Drawing Utensils per student
	1	Piece of paper per student	1	Paper per student
	5-10	Colored Pencils and/or Crayons for students per student	1	Printed coloring page
			5-10	Colored Pencils and/or Crayons per student
				See Extras
LANGUAGE ARTS	1	Printed Handout per student	1	Drawing Utensils per student
			1	Printed Copy work per student
			1	Paper per student
				Printed Handout per student
LATIN/ GREEK	1	Printed Hymn of the week per student	1	Printed Hymn of the week per student
MATH	1	Pencil per student	1	Pencil per student
	1	Paper per student	1	Paper per student
MUSIC	1	(Optional) Pitch instrument		N/A
READING		N/A		N/A
RELIGION		N/A		N/A
SCIENCE		See Linked Lesson (SF)	1	Drawing Utensils per student
			1	Paper per student or Nature Journal
				See Linked Lessons (SF)
VIRTUE		N/A		N/A

UNIT 11

SUBJECT	DAY 1 (Co-op Day)		DAYS 2 – 4	
ART	1	(Optional) Set of Visual Aids on paper, in color (from Unit 9)	N/A	
	1	Handout on paper, in color per student (or per family) (See Unit 9)		
	1-2	Large tubes of putty (depending on class size)		
	20	Toothpicks per K-3rd Grader		
	1	Foam paper plate per student		
	1	Golf ball sized piece of air-dry clay per student		
	1	Roll of paper towels		
		Bottle of cleaning spray		
	1	Sheet of plastic for floor		
	1	Smock per student		
CCM		Maps 3		Maps 3
		Timeline Cards		Timeline Cards
		Printed Unit Summary		Printed Unit Summary
HISTORY	5-6	Gather props or craft items to create simple props.	1	Drawing Utensils per student
			1	Paper per student
			1	Printed Handout per student
			1	Printed coloring page
				See Extras
LANGUAGE ARTS	1	Printed Handout per student	1	Drawing Utensils per student
			1	Printed Copy work per student
			1	Paper per student
				Printed Handout per student
LATIN/ GREEK	1	Printed Hymn of the week per student	1	Printed Hymn of the week per student
MATH	1	Pencil per student	1	Pencil per student
	1	Paper per student	1	Paper per student
MUSIC	1	(Optional) Pitch instrument		N/A
READING		N/A		N/A
RELIGION		N/A		N/A
SCIENCE		See Linked Lesson (SF)	1	Drawing Utensils per student
			1	Paper per student or Nature Journal
				See Linked Lessons (SF)
VIRTUE		N/A		N/A

UNIT 12

SUBJECT	DAY 1		DAYS 2 – 4	
ART	N/A		See Extras	
CCM	Maps 1,2,3,4,5 Timeline Cards Printed Unit Summary		Maps 1,2,3,4,5 Timeline Cards Printed Unit Summary	
HISTORY	N/A		5-10	Colored Pencils and/or Crayons per student
			1	Printed coloring page
			1	Drawing Utensils per student
			1	Paper per student
			1	Printed coloring page See Extras
LANGUAGE ARTS	1	Printed Handout per student	1	Drawing Utensils per student
			1	Printed Copy work per student
			1	Paper per student
			1	Printed Handout per student
LATIN / GREEK	1	Printed Hymn of the week per student	1	Printed Hymn of the week per student
MATH	1	Pencil per student	1	Pencil per student
	1	Paper per student	1	Paper per student
MUSIC	1	(Optional) Pitch instrument	N/A	
READING	N/A		N/A	
RELIGION	N/A		N/A	
SCIENCE	N/A		1	Drawing Utensils per student
			1	Paper per student or Nature Journal
VIRTUE	N/A		N/A	

UNIT 13

SUBJECT	DAY 1		DAYS 2 – 4	
ART	N/A		N/A	
CCM	Maps 1,2,3,4,5 Timeline Cards Printed Unit Summary		Maps 1,2,3,4,5 Timeline Cards Printed Unit Summary	
HISTORY	N/A		5-10	Colored Pencils and/or Crayons per student Printed coloring page
			1	Drawing Utensils per student
			1	Paper per student
			3	See Extras
LANGUAGE ARTS	1	Printed Handout per student	1	Drawing Utensils per student
			1	Printed Copy work per student
			1	Paper per student
			1	Printed Handout per student
LATIN/ GREEK	1	Printed Hymn of the week per student	1	Printed Hymn of the week per student
MATH	1	Drawing Utensils per student	1	Pencil per student
	1	Paper per student	1	Paper per student
MUSIC	1	(Optional) Pitch instrument	N/A	
READING	N/A		N/A	
RELIGION	N/A		N/A	
SCIENCE	See Linked Lessons (SF)		1	Drawing Utensils per student
			1	Paper per student or Nature Journal See Linked Lessons (SF)
VIRTUE	N/A		N/A	

UNIT 14

SUBJECT	DAY 1		DAYS 2 – 4	
ART	N/A		N/A	
CCM	Maps 1,2,3,4,5 Timeline Cards Printed Unit Summary		Maps 1,2,3,4,5 Timeline Cards Printed Unit Summary	
HISTORY	N/A		5-10	Colored Pencils and/or Crayons per student
				Printed coloring page
			1	Drawing Utensils per student
			1	Paper per student
			1	See Extras
LANGUAGE ARTS	N/A		N/A	
LATIN/ GREEK	1	Printed Hymn of the week per student	1	Printed Hymn of the week per student
MATH	1	Pencil per student	1	Pencil per student
	1	Paper per student	1	Paper per student
MUSIC	1	(Optional) Pitch instrument		N/A
READING	N/A		N/A	
RELIGION	N/A		N/A	
SCIENCE	N/A		1	Drawing Utensils per student
			1	Paper per student or Nature Journal
VIRTUE	N/A		N/A	

UNIT 15

SUBJECT	DAY 1		DAYS 2 – 4	
ART	N/A		N/A	
CCM	Maps 1,2,3,4,5 Timeline Cards Printed Unit Summary		Maps 1,2,3,4,5 Timeline Cards Printed Unit Summary	
HISTORY	N/A		1 1 1 5-6	Drawing Utensils per student Printed coloring page Paper per student Props and materials needed for acting out the story See Extras
LANGUAGE ARTS	1	Printed Handout per student	1 1 1 1	Printed Copy work per student Drawing Utensils per student Paper per student Printed Handout per student See Extras
LATIN/ GREEK	1	Printed Hymn of the week per student	1	Printed Hymn of the week per student
MATH	1 1	Pencil per student Paper per student	1 1	Pencil per student Paper per student
MUSIC	1	(Optional) Pitch instrument	N/A	
READING	N/A		N/A	
RELIGION	N/A		N/A	
SCIENCE	10-12 1 1 2 1 1	Small objects (nails, pennies, paper clips, plastic balls, etc.) per student Shoe box or other container to hold the small objects per student U-shaped magnet Magnets from your refrigerator per student Piece of paper or Nature Journal per student Drawing Utensils per student	1	See Linked Lessons (SF) Piece of paper or Nature Journal per student
VIRTUE	N/A		N/A	

UNIT 16

SUBJECT	DAY 1		DAYS 2 – 4	
ART	N/A		N/A	
CCM	Maps 1,2,3,4,5 Timeline Cards Printed Unit Summary		Maps 1,2,3,4,5 Timeline Cards Printed Unit Summary	
HISTORY	N/A		1	Paper per student
			5-10	Colored Pencils and/or Crayons per student
			1	Pair of Scissors per student
			1	Liquid Glue Bottle per student or Clear Tape Roll per classroom
			5-6	Popsicle sticks per student See Extras
LANGUAGE ARTS	1	Printed Handout per student	1	Printed Copy work per student
			1	Drawing Utensils per student
			1	Paper per student
			1	Printed Handout per student
LATIN/ GREEK	1	Printed Hymn of the week per student	1	Printed Hymn of the week per student
MATH	1	Pencil per student	1	Pencil per student
	1	Paper per student	1	Paper per student
MUSIC	1	(Optional) Pitch instrument	N/A	
READING	N/A		N/A	
RELIGION	N/A		N/A	
SCIENCE	10-12	Small objects (nails, pennies, paper clips, plastic balls, etc.) per student	1	Drawing Utensils per student
	1	Shoe box or other container to hold the small objects per student	1	Piece of paper or Nature Journal per student See Linked Lessons (SF)
	1	U-shaped magnet per student		
	3	Magnets from your refrigerator per student		
	1	Sheet of paper per student		
	1	Piece of metal (e.g. pie or cake pan) per student		
	1	Piece of plastic (e.g. placemat or plastic cutting board) per student		
	1	Piece of cardboard (5 x 7 or 4x6) per student		
	1	Piece of wood (5 x 7 or 4x6 e.g. sheet of thin plywood) per student		
	1	Piece of paper or Nature Journal per student		
	1	Drawing Utensils per student		
VIRTUE	N/A		N/A	

UNIT 17

SUBJECT	DAY 1		DAYS 2 – 4	
ART	N/A		N/A	
CCM	Maps 1,2,3,4,5 Timeline Cards Printed Unit Summary		Maps 1,2,3,4,5 Timeline Cards Printed Unit Summary	
HISTORY	N/A		1	Drawing Utensils per student
			1	Paper per student
			1	Printed Coloring Page per
			5-	student
			10	Colored Pencils and/or Crayons per student
			5-6	Props and materials needed for acting out the story See Extras
LANGUAGE ARTS	1	Printed Handout per student	1	Drawing Utensils per student
			1	Printed Copy work per student
			1	Paper per student
			1	Printed Handout per student
LATIN/ GREEK	1	Printed Hymn of the week per student	1	Printed Hymn of the week per student
MATH	1	Pencil per student	1	Pencil per student
	1	Paper per student	1	Paper per student
MUSIC	1	(Optional) Pitch instrument	N/A	
READING	N/A		N/A	
RELIGION	N/A		N/A	
SCIENCE	10-12	Small objects (nails, pennies, paper clips, plastic balls, etc.) per student	1	Drawing Utensils per student
	1	Shoe box or other container to hold the small objects per student	1	Piece of paper or Nature Journal per student
	3	U-shaped magnet per student		
	1	Magnets from your refrigerator per student		
	1	Sheet of paper per student Printed Handout per student		
VIRTUE	N/A		N/A	

UNIT 18

SUBJECT		DAY 1 (Field Trip Day)		DAYS 2 – 4
ART		N/A		See "Extras"
CCM		Maps 1,2,3,4,5 Timeline Cards Printed Unit Summary		Maps 1,2,3,4,5 Timeline Cards Printed Unit Summary
HISTORY		N/A	1 1 1 5- 10	Drawing Utensils per student Paper per student Printed Coloring Page per student Colored Pencils and/or Crayons per student See Extras See Linked Lesson (SF)
LANGUAGE ARTS	1 1	Printed Handout per student Drawing Utensils per student	1 1 1	Drawing Utensils per student Printed Copy work per student Paper per student per student
LATIN/GREEK	1	Printed Hymn of the week per student	1	Printed Hymn of the week per student
MATH	1 1	Pencil per student Paper per student	1 1	Pencil per student Paper per student
MUSIC	1	(Optional) Pitch instrument		N/A
READING		N/A		N/A
RELIGION		N/A		N/A
SCIENCE	1 3 10- 12 1 1	U-shaped magnet per student Magnets from your refrigerator per student Small objects (nails, pennies, paper clips, plastic balls, etc.) per student (Choose new object) Shoe box or other container to hold the small objects per student Paper per student or Nature Journal per student (Optional) "My First Magnet Kit" (See Link in SF)	1 1	Drawing Utensils per student Paper per student Nature Journal per student See Linked Lessons
VIRTUE		N/A		N/A

UNIT 19

SUBJECT	DAY 1 (Co-op Day)		DAYS 2 – 4	
ART	1	Handout on paper, in color per student (or per family)	N/A	
	9	3" X 3" pieces of square, cotton fabric (assorted colors and patterns) per student		
	1	Sewing needle per student		
	1	Spool of thread per student		
	1	Plastic baggy per student		
	1	marked with permanent marker with the student's name		
	1	(Optional) Set of Visual Aids on paper, in color		
	1	Bottle of cleaning spray		
	1	Paper Towel Roll		
CCM	Maps 1		Maps 1	
	Timeline Cards		Timeline Cards	
	Printed Unit Summary		Printed Unit Summary	
HISTORY	See Linked Lesson (SF)		1	Printed Coloring Pages per student
			5-10	Colored Pencils and/or Crayons per student
			1	
			1	Drawing Utensils per student
				Papers per student
				See Extras
LANGUAGE ARTS	1	Printed Handout per student	1	Printed Copy work per student
			1	Drawing Utensils per student
			1	Paper per student
			1	Printed Handout per student
LATIN/ GREEK	1	Printed Hymn of the week per student	1	Printed Hymn of the week per student
MATH	1	Pencil per student	1	Pencil per student
	1	Paper per student	1	Paper per student
MUSIC	1	(Optional) Pitch instrument	N/A	
READING	N/A		N/A	
RELIGION	N/A (SF)		N/A (SF)	
SCIENCE	See Linked Lesson(SF)		1	Drawing Utensils per student
			1	Paper per student or Nature Journal per student
				See Linked Lessons (SF)
VIRTUE	N/A		N/A	

UNIT 20

SUBJECT	DAY 1 (Co-op Day)		DAYS 2 – 4	
ART	1	Handout on paper, in color per student (or per family) (Unit 19)	N/A	
	1	Baggie of quilt squares from Unit 19 per student		
	1	Sewing needle per student		
	1	Spool of thread per student (For students who were absent)		
	9	3" X 3" pieces of square, cotton fabric (assorted colors and patterns) per student		
	1	Plastic baggy per student marked with permanent marker with the student's name		
	1	(Optional) Set of Visual Aids on paper, in color		
	1	Bottle of cleaning spray		
	1	Paper Towel Roll		
CCM		Maps 2 Timeline Cards Printed Unit Summary		Maps 2 Timeline Cards Printed Unit Summary
HISTORY		See Linked Lesson (SF)	2	Printed Handout per student
			5-10	Colored Pencils and/or Crayons per student
			1	Printed coloring page
			1	Drawing Utensils per student See Linked Lesson (SF) See Extras
LANGUAGE ARTS	1	Printed Handout per student	1	Printed Copy work per student
	1	Drawing Utensils per student	1	Drawing Utensils per student
			1	Paper per student
			1	Printed Handout per student
LATIN/ GREEK	1	Printed Hymn of the week per student	1	Printed Hymn of the week per student
MATH	1	Pencil per student	1	Pencil per student
	1	Paper per student	1	Paper per student
MUSIC	1	(Optional) Pitch instrument		N/A
READING		N/A		N/A
RELIGION		N/A		N/A
SCIENCE		See Linked Lesson (SF)	1	Drawing Utensils per student
			1	Paper per student Nature Journal per student See Linked Lessons (SF)
VIRTUE		N/A		N/A

UNIT 21

SUBJECT	DAY 1 (Co-op Day)		DAYS 2 – 4	
ART	1	Handout on paper, in color per student (or per family)	N/A	
	1	(Optional) Set of Visual Aids on paper, in color		
	1	Disposable camera per student		
	2	L-shaped pieces of cardboard (5" at the bottom and 7" for side) per student		
CCM		Maps 2 Timeline Cards Printed Unit Summary		Maps 2 Timeline Cards Printed Unit Summary
HISTORY		See Linked Lesson (SF)	1	Printed Handout
			5-10	Colored Pencils and/or Crayons per student
			1	Printed coloring page
			1	Drawing Utensils per student Paper per student See Linked Lesson (SF) See Extras
LANGUAGE ARTS	1	Printed Handout per student	1	Drawing Utensils per student
			1	Printed Copy work per student
			1	Paper per student Printed Handout per student
LATIN/ GREEK	1	Printed Hymn of the week per student	1	Printed Hymn of the week per student
MATH	1	Pencil per student	1	Pencil per student
	1	Paper per student	1	Paper per student
MUSIC	1	(Optional) Pitch instrument	N/A	
READING		N/A	N/A	
RELIGION		N/A	N/A	
SCIENCE		See Referenced Resource (SF)	1	Drawing Utensils per student
	1	Drawing Utensils per student	1	Paper per student or Nature Journal per student
	1	Paper per student or Nature Journal per student		See Linked Lessons (SF)
VIRTUE		N/A	N/A	

UNIT 22

SUBJECT	DAY 1 (Field Trip Day)		DAYS 2 – 4	
ART	N/A		See "Extras"	
CCM	Maps 1,2,3,4,5 Timeline Cards Printed Unit Summary		Maps 1,2,3,4,5 Timeline Cards Printed Unit Summary	
HISTORY	N/A		1	Drawing Utensils per student
			1	Paper per student
			5-10	Colored Pencils and/or Crayons per student
			2	Printed Handout per student
			1	See Linked Lesson (SF) See Extras
LANGUAGE ARTS	1	Printed Handout per student	1	Drawing Utensils per student
			1	Printed Copy work per student
			1	Paper per student Printed Handout per student
LATIN / GREEK	1	Printed Hymn of the week per student	1	Printed Hymn of the week per student
MATH	1	Pencil per student	1	Pencil per student
	1	Paper per student	1	Paper per student
MUSIC	1	(Optional) Pitch instrument		N/A
READING	N/A		N/A	
RELIGION	N/A		N/A	
SCIENCE	N/A		1	Drawing Utensils per student
			1	Paper per student or Nature Journal per student See Linked Lesson (SF)
VIRTUE	N/A		N/A	

UNIT 23

SUBJECT	DAY 1 (Co-op Day)		DAYS 2 – 4	
ART	1	Handout on paper, in color per student (or per family)	N/A	
	1	(Optional) Set of Visual Aids on paper, in color		
	1	Disposable camera per student (See Unit 21)		
	2	L-shaped pieces of cardboard (5" at the bottom and 7" for side) per student		
CCM		Maps 2		Maps 2
		Timeline Cards		Timeline Cards
		Printed Unit Summary		Printed Unit Summary
HISTORY	5	Piece of 8x11 Cardstock paper (for puppets) per student	5-10	Colored Pencils and/or Crayons per student
	1	Pencils Colored pencils per	1	Printed coloring page
	1	student	1	Drawing Utensils per student
		Glue sticks per student	2	Paper per student
				Printed Handout per student
				See Extras
LANGUAGE ARTS		N/A	1	Printed Copy work per student
			1	Drawing Utensils per student
			1	Paper per student
			1	Printed Handout per student
LATIN/ GREEK	1	Printed Hymn of the week per student	1	Printed Hymn of the week per student
MATH	1	Pencil per student	1	Pencil per student
	1	Paper per student	1	Paper per student
MUSIC	1	(Optional) Pitch instrument	N/A	
READING		N/A		N/A
RELIGION		N/A		N/A
SCIENCE		See Referenced Resource (SF)	1	Drawing Utensils per student
	1	Drawing Utensils per student	1	Paper per student or Nature Journal per student
	1	Paper per student or Nature Journal per student		See Linked Lessons (SF)
VIRTUE		N/A		N/A

UNIT 24

SUBJECT		DAY 1 (Co-op Day)		DAYS 2 – 4
ART	1	Printed Handout per student (or per family)		N/A
	1	Calligraphy pens set per student (K-3rd)		
	1	12" X 12" piece of Multi-media paper per student		
	1	(Optional) Set of Visual Aids on paper, in color		
	1	Roll of paper towels Bottle of cleaning spray		
CCM		Maps 3 Timeline Cards Printed Unit Summary		Maps 3 Timeline Cards Printed Unit Summary
HISTORY		See Linked Lesson (SF)	5-10	Colored Pencils and/or Crayons per student
			1	Printed coloring page
			1	Drawing Utensils per student
			2	Paper per student See Linked Lesson(SF) See Extras
LANGUAGE ARTS	1	Printed Handout per student	1	Drawing Utensils per student
			1	Printed Copy work per student
			1	Paper per student Printed Handout per student
LATIN/GREEK	1	Printed Hymn of the week per student	1	Printed Hymn of the week per student
MATH	1	Pencil per student	1	Pencil per student
	1	Paper per student	1	Paper per student
MUSIC	1	(Optional) Pitch instrument		N/A
READING		N/A		N/A
RELIGION		N/A		N/A
SCIENCE		See Linked Lessons (SF)	1	Drawing Utensils per student
	1	Drawing Utensils per student	1	Paper per student
	1	Paper per student or Nature Journal per student		See Linked Lessons (SF)
VIRTUE		N/A		N/A

UNIT 25

SUBJECT	DAY 1 (Co-op Day)		DAYS 2 – 4	
ART	1	Printed Handout per student (or per family)	N/A	
	1	HB pencil per student		
	1	Pen and ink set per student (see unit 24)		
	1	12" X 12" piece of Multi-media paper per student		
	1	(Optional) Set of Visual Aids on paper, in color		
	1	Roll of paper towels		
	1	Bottle of cleaning spray		
CCM		Maps 3		Maps 3
		Timeline Cards		Timeline Cards
		Printed Unit Summary		Printed Unit Summary
HISTORY	1	Paper per student	1	Printed Coloring Pages per student
	1	Drawing Utensils per student	5-10	Colored Pencils and/or Crayons per student
	5-10	Colored Pencils and/or Crayons or Colored pencils per student	1	Drawing Utensils per student
			1	Paper per student
				See Linked Lesson (SF)
				See Extras
LANGUAGE ARTS	1	Printed Handout per student	1	Drawing Utensils per student
			1	Paper per student
			1	Printed Handout per student
LATIN/ GREEK	1	Printed Hymn of the week per student	1	Printed Hymn of the week per student
MATH	1	Pencil per student	1	Pencil per student
	1	Paper per student	1	Paper per student
MUSIC	1	(Optional) Pitch instrument	N/A	
READING	N/A		N/A	
RELIGION	N/A		N/A	
SCIENCE		See Linked Lessons (SF)	1	Drawing Utensils per student
	1	Drawing Utensils per student	1	Paper per student Nature Journal per student
	1	Paper per student or Nature Journal per student		See Linked Lessons (SF)
VIRTUE	N/A		N/A	

UNIT 26

SUBJECT	DAY 1 (Field Trip Day)		DAYS 2 – 4	
ART	N/A		See "Extras"	
CCM	Maps 1,2,3,4,5 Timeline Cards Printed Unit Summary		Maps 1,2,3,4,5 Timeline Cards Printed Unit Summary	
HISTORY	N/A		1 1 5-10 1	Drawing Utensils per student Paper per student Colored Pencils and/or Crayons per student Printed coloring page See Extras
LANGUAGE ARTS	1	Printed Handout per student	1 1 1 1	Drawing Utensils per student Printed Copy work per student Paper per student Printed Handout per student
LATIN/ GREEK	1	Printed Hymn of the week per student	1	Printed Hymn of the week per student
MATH	1 1	Pencil per student Paper per student	1 1	Pencil per student Paper per student
MUSIC	1	(Optional) Pitch instrument	N/A	
READING	N/A		N/A	
RELIGION	N/A		N/A	
SCIENCE	N/A		1 1	Drawing Utensils per student Paper per student or Nature Journals See Linked Lesson (SF)
VIRTUE	N/A		N/A	

UNIT 27

SUBJECT		DAY 1 (Co-op Day)		DAYS 2 – 4
ART	1 1 1 1 2 1 1 1 1 1	(Optional) Set of Visual Aids in color HB pencil per student Black ink and pen per student Pair of scissors per student 3″ pieces of yarn per student Hole-punchers per every 2 students Sheet of white paper per student Printed Art Handout per student Roll of paper towels Bottle of cleaning spray	1 1 1 1 1 1 1	HB pencil per student Black ink and pen per student Pair of scissors per student 3″ pieces of yarn per student Hole-punchers per every 2 students Sheet of white paper per student Printed Art Handout per student
CCM		Maps 4 Timeline Cards Printed Unit Summary		Maps 4 Timeline Cards Printed Unit Summary
HISTORY	1 5-10 1	Drawing Utensils per student Colored Pencils and/or Crayons per student Paper per student	5-10 1 1 1 2	Colored Pencils and/or Crayons per student Printed coloring page Drawing Utensils per student Paper per student Printed Handout per student
LANGUAGE ARTS	1	Printed Handout per student	1 1 1	Drawing Utensils per student Printed Copy work per student Paper per student Printed Handout per student
LATIN/ GREEK	1	Printed Hymn of the week per student	1	Printed Hymn of the week per student
MATH	1 1	Pencil per student Paper per student	1 1	Pencil per student Paper per student
MUSIC	1	(Optional) Pitch instrument		N/A
READING		N/A		N/A
RELIGION		N/A		N/A
SCIENCE	 1 1	See Referenced Resource (SF) Drawing Utensils per student Paper per student or Nature Journal per student	1 1	Drawing Utensils per student Paper per student or Nature Journal per student See Linked Lessons (SF)
VIRTUE		N/A		N/A

UNIT 28

SUBJECT	DAY 1 (Co-op Day)		DAYS 2 – 4	
ART	1	(Optional) Set of Visual Aids in color	N/A	
	1	Handout on paper, in color per student (or per family)		
	1	HB pencil per student		
	1	Pair of Scissors per student		
	2-3	Staplers per classroom		
		Sheets of white paper per student or one sticky note pad per student		
CCM		Maps 5		Maps 5
		Timeline Cards		Timeline Cards
		Printed Unit Summary		Printed Unit Summary
HISTORY	5-6	Props or craft items to create simple props.	5-10	Colored Pencils and/or Crayons per student
	1	CD player for classroom		Printed coloring page
	1	Peter and the Wolf CD	1	Drawing Utensils per student
			1	Paper per student
			1	Pair of scissors per student
			1	Paper per student
			1	Popsicle sticks per student
			5-10	
LANGUAGE ARTS	1	Printed Handout per student	1	Drawing Utensils per student
	1	Drawing Utensils per student	1	Printed Copy work per student
			1	Paper per student
			1	Printed Handout per student
LATIN/ GREEK	1	Printed Hymn of the week per student	1	Printed Hymn of the week per student
MATH	1	Pencil per student	1	Pencil per student
	1	Paper per student	1	Paper per student
MUSIC	1	(Optional) Pitch instrument	N/A	
	1	Printed Handout		
READING		N/A		N/A
RELIGION		N/A		N/A
SCIENCE		See Referenced Resource (SF)	1	Drawing Utensils per student
	1	Drawing Utensils per student	1	Paper per student or Nature Journal per student
	1	Paper per student or Nature Journal per student		See Linked Lessons (SF)
VIRTUE		N/A		N/A

UNIT 29

SUBJECT	DAY 1 (Co-op Day)		DAYS 2 – 4	
ART	1	(Optional) Set of Visual Aids in color	N/A	
	1	Handout on paper, in color per student (or per family)		
	1	HB pencil per student		
	1	Pair of Scissors per student		
	1	Staplers per classroom		
	1	Pen & Ink kit per student		
	10-12	Markers or Colored Pencils		
	4-5	Sheets of white paper per student or sticky note pad		
CCM		Maps 5 Timeline Cards Printed Unit Summary		Maps 5 Timeline Cards Printed Unit Summary
HISTORY	5-6	Props or craft items to create simple props.	5-10 1 1	Colored Pencils and/or Colored Pencils and/or Crayons per student Printed coloring page Drawing Utensils per student See Extras
LANGUAGE ARTS	1 1	Printed Handout per student Drawing Utensils per student	1 1 1 1	Drawing Utensils per student Printed copy work per student Paper per student Printed Handout per student
LATIN/ GREEK	1	Printed Hymn of the week per student	1	Printed Hymn of the week per student
MATH	1 1	Pencil per student Paper per student	1 1	Pencil per student Paper per student
MUSIC	1	(Optional) Pitch instrument	N/A	
READING		N/A	N/A	
RELIGION		N/A	N/A	
SCIENCE		See Referenced Resource (SF)	1 1	Drawing Utensils per student Paper per student or Natural Journal See Linked Lessons (SF)
VIRTUE		N/A	N/A	

UNIT 30

SUBJECT	DAY 1		DAYS 2 – 4	
ART	N/A		See "Extras"	
CCM	Maps 1,2,3,4,5 Timeline Cards Printed Unit Summary		Maps 1,2,3,4,5 Timeline Cards Printed Unit Summary	
HISTORY	N/A		N/A	
LANGUAGE ARTS	N/A		1 1	Drawing Utensils per student Paper per student
LATIN / GREEK	1	Printed Hymn of the week per student	1	Printed Hymn of the week per student
MATH	1 1	Pencil per student Paper per student	1 1	Pencil per student Paper per student
MUSIC	1	(Optional) Pitch instrument	N/A	
READING	N/A		N/A	
RELIGION	N/A		N/A	
SCIENCE	N/A		N/A	
VIRTUE	N/A		N/A	

2ⁿᵈ – 3ʳᵈ Grade ~ Materials Usage Schedule

Introduction

Welcome to the Materials Usage Schedule for 2ⁿᵈ – 3ʳᵈ Grade. The schedule is provides a timeline of when materials will be used. The 2ⁿᵈ – 3ʳᵈ Grade Materials Usage Schedule is divided into unit lists. Each unit list is divided by subject and by days.

In the Materials Usage Schedule, Day 1 is listed as either a "Co-op Day" or "Field Trip Day." If Day 1 does not have a label, it is a Home Day. Days 2-4 are always considered Home Days in each unit. If you are a "Just Home" Family (those who are not in a local co-op), every day is a home day, so you should plan accordingly.

Important Notices:

- Materials listed under a Co-op Day are provided **at co-op**.

- Materials listed under a Field Trip or Home Day must be provided **at home and do not come from co-op.**

- The following items are **NOT** included on this list:
  - **Books**: See the booklists under Step 2 of "Getting Started" in your online suite.
  - **Linked Lesson Materials**: Items required for lessons and activities in the curriculum that link to outside websites. You will need to follow the links in the Subject Folders (SF) in order to gather materials needed week-to-week.
  - **Extras**: Items needed to complete activities found in the "Extras" section of subjects.
  - **Printed Items**: Documents in the online suite that must be printed for use (handouts, coloring pages, copy work, worksheets, etc.)

- Items listed as "Optional" are not required purchases; they are merely suggestions for enhancing the activity or lesson.

- Please note the following vocabulary:
  - The *water jar* is a container for washing out paintbrushes.
  - A *drawing utensil* is any tool of your choice--marker, pen, or pencil—used for writing or drawing.

For the list of materials to be purchased, see the "Materials Purchase List" located in the "Getting Started" section of the online suite.

Please contact us if you have any questions or concerns.

ABBREVIATION KEY	
DL	Digital Library (in course suite)
SF	Subject Folder (in course suite)
HC	Hard Copy
PLL	*Primary Language Lessons* (book)
ILL	*Intermediate Language Lessons* (book)
RS4K	*Real Science 4 Kids* (book)
I-CAT	*Illustrated Catechism* (book)
OHF-1	*Our Holy Faith, Book 1* (book)
OHF-2	*Our Holy Faith, Book 2* (book)
OHF-4	*Our Holy Faith, Book 4* (book)
OHF-1-TM	*Our Holy Faith, Book 1, Teacher's Manual* (book)

UNIT 1

SUBJECT	DAY 1 (Co-op Day)		DAYS 2 – 4	
ART	1	Handout on paper, in color per student (or per family)	1	Handout on paper, in color per student (or per family)
	1	3" X 3" sheet of paper per K-3rd Grade student (FILE THE SHARP EDGES)	1	3" X 3" sheet of paper per K-3rd
	1	3" X 3" sheet of 5 mil Copper Sheets per K-3rd Grade student (purchase a roll to save money)	1	Grade student (cut to size and FILE THE SHARP EDGES)
	1	Plastic Placemat per student	1	3" X 3" sheet of 5 mil Copper Sheets per K-3rd Grade student (purchase a roll to save money)
	1	Pencil per student	1	Plastic Placemat per student
	2-3	Leather Working Tools per student	1	Pencil per student
	1	(Optional) Set of Visual Aids, in color	2-3	Basic Leather Working Tools per student
	1	Smock or large T-shirt per student		
	1	Paper towel Roll		
	1	Bottle of Cleaning spray		
	1			
CCM		Map 1		Map 1
		Timeline Cards		Timeline Cards
		Printed Unit Summary		Printed Unit Summary
HISTORY	1	Printed Handout per student	1	Printed coloring page
	1	Pair of Scissors per student	5-10	Colored pencils and/or Crayons per student
	1	Glue stick per student	1	Drawing Utensils per student
	1	Stapler per classrooms	1	Paper per student
	1	Box Staples per classroom	1	Printed Handouts per student
	1	8 ½ x 11 sheets of colored paper per TWO students	1	Pink Drawing Utensils per student
	1-2	8 ½ x 11 sheets of white paper per student	1	Orange Drawing Utensils per student
		Colored Pencil per student	1	Yellow Drawing Utensils per student
	12	A computer or tablet the music (SF)		See Extras
	1			
LANGUAGE ARTS	1	Printed Handout per student	1	Printed Copy work per student
	1	Drawing Utensils per student	1	Drawing Utensils per student
			1	Paper per student
			1	Printed Handout per student
LATIN/ GREEK	1	Printed Hymn of the week per student	1	Printed Hymn of the week per student
MATH	1	Pencil per student	1	Pencil per student
	1	Paper per student	1	Paper per student
MUSIC	1	(Optional) Pitch instrument		N/A
READING		N/A		N/A
RELIGION		N/A		N/A
SCIENCE	2	Red Jelly Gumdrops per student	1	Printed Worksheet
	2	Blue Jelly Gumdrops per student	1	Drawing Utensils per student
	2	Yellow Jelly Gumdrops per student	5-10	Colored pencils and/or Crayons per student
	2	7 "pieces of craft wire per student		See Linked Lesson (SF)
VIRTUE		N/A		N/A

UNIT 2

SUBJECT	DAY 1 (Co-op Day)		DAYS 2 – 4	
ART	1	Handout on paper, in color per student (or per family)	1	Drawing Utensils per student
	1	8" x 11" sheet of white printer paper per student	1	Paper per student
	1	8" x 11" sheet of charcoal paper per student	1	Printed Handout per student
	1	Charcoal / willow stick per student		
	1			
	1	Pencil per student		
		Pencil sharpener per student		
		(Optional) Set of Visual Aids on paper, in color		
	1			
	1	Smock or large T-shirt per student		
	1	Paper towel roll		
		Bottle of Cleaning spray		
		Sheets of plastic for tables and floors		
CCM		Map 1		Map 1
		Timeline Cards		Timeline Cards
		Printed Unit Summary		Printed Unit Summary
HISTORY	1	Drawing Utensils per student	1	Drawing Utensils per student
		See History Pocket 1 (SF)	1	Paper per student
			1	Printed coloring page
			5-10	Colored pencils and/or Crayons per student
			1	See Extras
				Printed Handout per student
LANGUAGE ARTS	1	Printed Handout per student	1	Drawing Utensils per student
	1	Drawing Utensils per student	1	Printed Copy work per student
			1	Paper per student
			1	Printed Handout per student
LATIN / GREEK	1	Printed Hymn of the week per student	1	Printed Hymn of the week per student
MATH	1	Pencil per student	1	Pencil per student
	1	Paper per student	1	Paper per student
MUSIC	1	(Optional) Pitch instrument		N/A
READING		N/A		N/A
RELIGION		N/A		N/A
SCIENCE	8	Red Jelly Gumdrops per student		See Linked Lesson (SF)
	8	Blue Jelly Gumdrops per student	1	Printed Handout or Journal per student
	8	Yellow Jelly Gumdrops per student		
	3	7 "pieces of craft wire per student	1	Drawing Utensils per student
		Helium balloons		
VIRTUE		N/A		N/A

UNIT 3

SUBJECT		DAY 1 (Co-op Day)		DAYS 2 – 4
ART	1	Handout on paper, in color per student (or per family)	1	Unfinished Cross-stitching Kit (from Day 1) per student
	1	4" X 4" piece of paper per student	1	Pair of scissors per student
	1	Quart-sized zip-lock bag per student		
	1			
	1	Permanent marker per classroom		
	1	Pair of scissors per student		
		Cross-stitching kit per student (See Link)		
	1	(Optional) Set of Visual Aid, in color		
	1	Paper Towel Roll		
		Bottle of Cleaning spray		
CCM		Map 2		Map 2
		Timeline Cards		Timeline Cards
		Printed Unit Summary		Printed Unit Summary
HISTORY	1	Printed Handout of "Classroom Visual Aids"	1	Drawing Utensils per student
			1	Paper per student
	1	2-3 inch (H) x 2-3 inch (W) x 2-3 inch (D) block of Clay per student	1	Printed coloring page
	¼	Piece of Sponges per student (cut from larger sponge)	5-10	Colored pencils and/or Crayons per student
	1	Piece of 4"x 4" wax paper per student	1	Printed Handout per student
	1	Small cup for water per student		See Extras
	1	Bottle of Cleaning spray		
	1	Plastic Sheet to cover tables and floor		
	1	Plastic knife per student or clay carving tool		
		Pen per student (or clay carving tools)		
LANGUAGE ARTS	1	Printed Handout per student	1	Drawing Utensils per student
	1	Drawing Utensils per student	1	Printed Copy work per student
			1	Paper per student
			1	Printed Handout per student
LATIN/ GREEK	1	Printed Hymn of the week per student	1	Printed Hymn of the week per student
MATH	1	Pencil per student	1	Pencil per student
	1	Paper per student	1	Paper per student
MUSIC	1	(Optional) Pitch instrument		N/A
READING		N/A		N/A
RELIGION		N/A		N/A
SCIENCE	2	Large Marshmallows (of one color) per student.		See Linked Lesson (SF)
	2	Large Marshmallow (of a different color) per student	1	Drawing Utensils per student
			1	Paper or Journal per student
	2	Toothpicks per student	1	Printed Handout per student
VIRTUE		N/A		N/A

UNIT 4

SUBJECT	DAY 1 (Field Trip Day)		DAYS 2 – 4	
ART	N/A		See "Extras"	
CCM	Maps 1 & 2 Timeline Cards Printed Unit Summary		Maps 1 & 2 Timeline Cards Printed Unit Summary	
HISTORY	N/A		1 2 1 5-10	Drawing Utensils per student Paper per student Printed coloring page Colored pencils and/or Crayons per student See Extras
LANGUAGE ARTS	1 1	Printed Handout per student Drawing Utensils per student	1 1 1 1	Drawing Utensils per student Printed Copy work per student Paper per student Printed Handout per student
LATIN / GREEK	1	Printed Hymn of the week per student	1	Printed Hymn of the week per student
MATH	1 1	Pencil per student Paper per student	1 1	Pencil per student Paper per student
MUSIC	1	(Optional) Pitch instrument		N/A
READING	N/A		N/A	
RELIGION	N/A		N/A	
SCIENCE	N/A		1 1	Drawing Utensils per student Paper or Journal per student
VIRTUE	N/A		N/A	

UNIT 5

SUBJECT	DAY 1 (Co-op Day)		DAYS 2 – 4	
ART	1	Handout on paper, in color per student (or per family)	1	Drawing Utensils per student
	1	8" X 12" piece of water color paper per student	1	Paper per student
	1	Paint brush per student	1	Paint brush per student
	1	Paper or plastic cup per student	1	Paper or plastic water cup per student
	1	Paper towel per student	1	Water color pencil set per student
	1	Water pitcher for filling cups with water		
	1	Water color pencil set per student (See Link in SF)		
	1	Pencil sharpener per student		
	1	(Optional) Set of Visual Aids on paper, in color		
	1	Roll of paper towels		
	1	Bottle of cleaning spray		
	1	Sheets of plastic for floor		
CCM		Maps 2		Maps 2
		Timeline Cards		Timeline Cards
		Printed Unit Summary		Printed Unit Summary
HISTORY	1	Printed Handout	1	Drawing Utensils per student
	1	Drawing Utensils per student	1	Paper per student
		See History Pocket 1 (SF)	1	Printed coloring page
			5-10	Colored pencils and/or Crayons per student
			1	See Extras
				Printed Handout per student
LANGUAGE ARTS	1	Printed Handout per student	1	Printed Copy work per student
	1	Drawing Utensils per student	1	Drawing Utensils per student
			1	Paper per student
			1	Printed Handout per student
LATIN/ GREEK	1	Printed Hymn of the week per student	1	Printed Hymn of the week per student
MATH	1	Pencil per student	1	Pencil per student
	1	Paper per student	1	Paper per student
MUSIC	1	(Optional) Pitch instrument		N/A
READING		N/A		N/A
RELIGION		N/A		N/A
SCIENCE		See Linked Lesson (SF)		See Linked Lessons (SF)
			1	Drawing Utensils per student
			1	Paper or Nature Journal per student
VIRTUE		N/A		N/A

UNIT 6

SUBJECT	DAY 1 (Co-op Day)		DAYS 2 – 4	
ART	1	(Optional) Set of Visual Aids in color per classroom	1	Drawing Utensils per student
	1	Handout in color per student	1	Drawing paper per student or small oil paint canvas
	1	8" X 12" oil paint canvas per student Paint brush per student	1	Oil paint set or Oil pastel set per student
	1	Paper or plastic cup per student		
	1	Paper or plastic plate per student		
	1			
	1	Paper towel per student		
		Water pitcher for filling cups with water		
	1	Pre-painted dark oil painted piece of paper from the "Before the Lesson" section per student		
	1	Oil collection art set per student: (See Link SF)		
	1	Smock or T-shirt per student		
	1	Roll of paper towels		
	1	Bottle of cleaning spray		
CCM		Maps 2		Maps 2
		Timeline Cards		Timeline Cards
		Printed Unit Summary		Printed Unit Summary
HISTORY	1	Gather props or craft items to create simple props.	1	Drawing Utensils per student
	1	Printed Handout per student	1	Paper per student
			5-10	Colored pencils and/or Crayons per student
				Printed coloring page
			1	See Extras
LANGUAGE ARTS	1	Printed Handout per student	1	Drawing Utensils per student
	1	Drawing Utensils per student	1	Printed Copy work per student
			1	Paper per student
			1	Printed Handout per student
LATIN/ GREEK	1	Printed Hymn of the week per student	1	Printed Hymn of the week per student
MATH	1	Pencil per student	1	Pencil per student
	1	Paper per student	1	Paper per student
MUSIC	1	(Optional) Pitch instrument		N/A
READING		N/A		N/A
RELIGION		N/A		N/A
SCIENCE		See Linked Lesson (SF)		See Linked Lessons (SF)
			1	Drawing Utensils per student
			1	Paper or Nature Journal per student
VIRTUE		N/A		N/A

UNIT 7

SUBJECT	DAY 1 (Co-op Day)	DAYS 2 – 4
ART	1 (Optional) Set of Visual Aids in color per classroom 1 Handout from last week in color per student 1 (Student Paintings from last week) 8" X 12" oil paint canvas per student 1 Paint brush per student 1 Paper or plastic cup per student 1 Paper or plastic plate per student 1 Paper towel per student 1 Water pitcher for filling cups with water 1 Pre-painted dark oil painted piece of paper from the "Before the Lesson" section 1 Oil collection art set per student: (See Link SF) 1 Smock or T-shirt per student 1 Roll of paper towels 1 Bottle of cleaning spray	1 Drawing Utensils per student 1 Drawing paper per student or small oil paint canvas 1 Oil paint set or Oil pastel set per student
CCM	Maps 3 Timeline Cards Printed Unit Summary	Maps 3 Timeline Cards Printed Unit Summary
HISTORY	See Linked Lesson (SF)	1 Printed Handouts per student 1 Drawing Utensils per student 1 Paper per student 5-10 Colored pencils and/or Crayons per student Printed coloring page 1 See Extras
LANGUAGE ARTS	1 Printed Handout per student 1 Drawing Utensils per student	1 Drawing Utensils per student 1 Printed Copy work per student 1 Paper per student 1 Printed Handout per student
LATIN/ GREEK	1 Printed Hymn of the week per student	1 Printed Hymn of the week per student
MATH	1 Pencil per student 1 Paper per student	1 Pencil per student 1 Paper per student
MUSIC	1 (Optional) Pitch instrument	N/A
READING	N/A	N/A
RELIGION	N/A	N/A
SCIENCE	See Linked Lesson (SF)	See Linked Lessons (SF) 1 Drawing Utensils per student 1 Paper or Nature Journal per student
VIRTUE	N/A	N/A

UNIT 8

SUBJECT		DAY 1 (Field Trip Day)		DAYS 2 – 4
ART		N/A		See "Extras"
CCM		Maps 1,2,3 Timeline Cards Printed Unit Summary		Maps 1,2,3 Timeline Cards Printed Unit Summary
HISTORY		N/A	1 1 1 5-10 1	Drawing Utensils per student Paper per student Printed Handout per student Colored pencils and/or Crayons per student Printed coloring page See Extras
LANGUAGE ARTS	1 1	Printed Handout per student Drawing Utensils per student	1 1 1 1	Drawing Utensils per student Printed Copy work per student Paper per student Printed Handout per student
LATIN/ GREEK	1	Printed Hymn of the week per student	1	Printed Hymn of the week per student
MATH	1 1	Pencil per student Paper per student	1 1	Pencil per student Paper per student
MUSIC	1	(Optional) Pitch instrument		N/A
READING		N/A		N/A
RELIGION		N/A		N/A
SCIENCE		N/A	1 1 1	Drawing Utensils per student Paper per student Printed Handout or Nature Journal
VIRTUE		N/A		N/A

UNIT 9

SUBJECT	DAY 1 (Co-op Day)		DAYS 2 – 4	
ART	1	(Optional) Set of Visual Aids Handout on paper, in color per student (or per family)	1	8" X 12" piece of sketch paper per student
	1	8" X 12" piece of sketch paper per student	1	Colored pencils set per student
	1	Colored pencils set per student	1	Pencil sharpener per student
	1	Pencil sharpener per student		
	1	Roll of paper towels		
	1	Bottle of cleaning spray		
CCM		Maps 3 Timeline Cards Printed Unit Summary		Maps 3 Timeline Cards Printed Unit Summary
HISTORY	1	Drawing Utensils per student See History Pocket 2 (SF)	1	Drawing Utensils per student
			1	Paper per student
			1	Printed Handouts per student
			5-10	Colored pencils and/or Crayons per student Printed coloring page
			1	See Extras
LANGUAGE ARTS	1	Printed Handout per student	1	Drawing Utensils per student
	1	Drawing Utensils per student	1	Printed Copy work per student
			1	Paper per student
			1	Printed Handouts per student
LATIN/ GREEK	1	Printed Hymn of the week per student	1	Printed Hymn of the week per student
MATH	1	Pencil per student	1	Pencil per student
	1	Paper per student	1	Paper per student
MUSIC	1	(Optional) Pitch instrument		N/A
READING		N/A		N/A
RELIGION		N/A		N/A
SCIENCE		See Linked Lessons (SF)	1	Drawing Utensils per student
			1	Paper or Journal per student See Linked Lessons (SF)
VIRTUE		N/A		N/A

UNIT 10

SUBJECT	DAY 1 (Co-op Day)		DAYS 2 – 4	
ART	1	(Optional) Set of Visual Aids Handout on paper, in color per student (or per family)	1	8″ X 12″ piece of sketch paper per student
	1	Drawing started last week per student	1	Colored pencils set per student
	1	8″ X 12″ piece of sketch paper per student for students who were absent last week		Pencil sharpener per student
	1	Colored pencils set per student		
	1	Pencil sharpener per student		
	1	Roll of paper towels		
	1	Bottle of cleaning spray		
CCM		Maps 3		Maps 3
		Timeline Cards		Timeline Cards
		Printed Unit Summary		Printed Unit Summary
HISTORY	1	Drawing Utensils per student	1	Drawing Utensils per student
		See History Pocket 2 (SF)	1	Paper per student
			1	Printed Handouts per student
			5-10	Colored pencils and/or Crayons per student
				Printed coloring page
			1	See Extras
LANGUAGE ARTS	1	Printed Handout per student	1	Drawing Utensils per student
	1	Drawing Utensils per student	1	Printed Copy work per student
			1	Paper per student
			1	Printed Handout per student
LATIN/ GREEK	1	Printed Hymn of the week per student	1	Printed Hymn of the week per student
MATH	1	Pencil per student	1	Pencil per student
	1	Paper per student	1	Paper per student
MUSIC	1	(Optional) Pitch instrument		N/A
READING		N/A		N/A
RELIGION		N/A		N/A
SCIENCE		See Linked Lesson (SF)	1	Drawing Utensils per student
			1	Paper or Journal per student
				See Linked Lessons (SF)
VIRTUE		N/A		N/A

UNIT 11

SUBJECT	DAY 1 (Co-op Day)		DAYS 2 – 4	
ART	1	(Optional) Set of Visual Aids on paper, in color (from Unit 9)	N/A	
	1	Handout on paper, in color per student (or per family) (See Unit 9)		
	1-2	Large tubes of putty (depending on class size)		
	20	Toothpicks per K-3rd Grader		
	1	Foam paper plate per student		
	1	Golf ball sized piece of air-dry clay per student		
	1	Roll of paper towels		
	1	Bottle of cleaning spray		
	1	Sheet of plastic for floor		
	1	Smock per student		
CCM		Maps 3		Maps 3
		Timeline Cards		Timeline Cards
		Printed Unit Summary		Printed Unit Summary
HISTORY	1	Printed Handout	1	Drawing Utensils per student
	1	Drawing Utensils per student	1	Paper per student
		See History Pocket 8	1	Printed Handout per student
			5-10	Colored pencils and/or Crayons per student
				Printed coloring page
			1	See Extras
LANGUAGE ARTS	1	Printed Handout per student	1	Drawing Utensils per student
			1	Printed Copy work per student
			1	Paper per student
			1	Printed Handout per student
LATIN/ GREEK	1	Printed Hymn of the week per student	1	Printed Hymn of the week per student
MATH	1	Pencil per student	1	Pencil per student
	1	Paper per student	1	Paper per student
MUSIC	1	(Optional) Pitch instrument	N/A	
READING		N/A	N/A	
RELIGION		N/A	N/A	
SCIENCE		See Linked Lesson (SF)	1	Drawing Utensils per student
			1	Paper or Journal per student
				See Linked Lessons (SF)
VIRTUE		N/A	N/A	

UNIT 12

SUBJECT	DAY 1		DAYS 2 – 4	
ART	N/A		See Extras	
CCM		Maps 1,2,3 Timeline Cards Printed Unit Summary		Maps 1,2,3 Timeline Cards Printed Unit Summary
HISTORY	N/A		5-10 1 1 1 1	Colored pencils and/or Crayons per student Drawing Utensils per student Paper per student Printed Handout per student Printed coloring page See Extras
LANGUAGE ARTS	1 1	Printed Handout per student Drawing Utensils per student	1 1 1 1	Drawing Utensils per student Printed Copy work per student Paper per student Printed Handout per student
LATIN / GREEK	1	Printed Hymn of the week per student	1	Printed Hymn of the week per student
MATH	1 1	Pencil per student Paper per student	1 1	Pencil per student Paper per student
MUSIC	1	(Optional) Pitch instrument	N/A	
READING	N/A		N/A	
RELIGION	N/A		N/A	
SCIENCE	N/A		1 1	Drawing Utensils per student Paper or Journal per student
VIRTUE	N/A		N/A	

UNIT 13

SUBJECT	DAY 1		DAYS 2 – 4	
ART	N/A		N/A	
CCM	Maps 1,2,3 Timeline Cards Printed Unit Summary		Maps 1,2,3 Timeline Cards Printed Unit Summary	
HISTORY	N/A		5-10	Colored pencils and/or Crayons per student
			1	Printed coloring page
			1	Drawing Utensils per student
			1	Paper per student
LANGUAGE ARTS	1	Printed Handout per student	1	Drawing Utensils per student
	1	Drawing Utensils per student	1	Printed Copy work per student
			1	Paper per student Printed Handout per student
LATIN/ GREEK	1	Printed Hymn of the week per student	1	Printed Hymn of the week per student
MATH	1	Pencil per student	1	Pencil per student
	1	Paper per student	1	Paper per student
MUSIC	1	(Optional) Pitch instrument	N/A	
READING	N/A		N/A	
RELIGION	N/A		N/A	
SCIENCE	See Linked Lessons (SF)		1	Drawing Utensils per student
			1	Paper or Journal per student See Linked Lessons (SF)
VIRTUE	N/A		N/A	

UNIT 14

SUBJECT	DAY 1		DAYS 2 – 4	
ART	N/A		N/A	
CCM	Maps 1,2,3 Timeline Cards Printed Unit Summary		Maps 1,2,3 Timeline Cards Printed Unit Summary	
HISTORY	N/A		5-10	Colored pencils and/or Crayons per student
				Drawing Utensils per student
			1	Paper per student
			1	
LANGUAGE ARTS	N/A		N/A	
LATIN/ GREEK	1	Printed Hymn of the week per student	1	Printed Hymn of the week per student
MATH	1	Pencil per student	1	Pencil per student
	1	Paper per student	1	Paper per student
MUSIC	1	(Optional) Pitch instrument	N/A	
READING	N/A		N/A	
RELIGION	N/A		N/A	
SCIENCE	N/A		N/A	
VIRTUE	N/A		N/A	

UNIT 15

SUBJECT	DAY 1		DAYS 2 – 4	
ART	N/A		N/A	
CCM	Maps 1,2,3 Timeline Cards Printed Unit Summary		Maps 1,2,3 Timeline Cards Printed Unit Summary	
HISTORY	N/A		1 1	Drawing Utensils per student Paper per student Props and materials needed for acting out the story See Extras
LANGUAGE ARTS	1 1	Printed Handout per student Drawing Utensils per student	1 1 1 1	Printed Copy work per student Drawing Utensils per student Paper per student Printed Handout per student
LATIN/ GREEK	1	Printed Hymn of the week per student	1	Printed Hymn of the week per student
MATH	1 1	Pencil per student Paper per student	1 1	Pencil per student Paper per student
MUSIC	1	(Optional) Pitch instrument		N/A
READING	N/A		N/A	
RELIGION	N/A		N/A	
SCIENCE	10-12 1 1 3 1 1	Small objects (nails, pennies, paper clips, plastic balls, etc.) per student Shoe box or other container to hold the small objects per student U-shaped magnet per student Magnets from your refrigerator per student Piece of paper or Nature Journal per student Drawing Utensils per student	 1	See Linked Lessons (SF) Piece of paper or Nature Journal per student
VIRTUE	N/A		N/A	

UNIT 16

SUBJECT	DAY 1		DAYS 2 – 4	
ART	N/A		N/A	
CCM		Maps 1,2,3 Timeline Cards Printed Unit Summary		Maps 1,2,3 Timeline Cards Printed Unit Summary
HISTORY		N/A	1	Paper per student
			5-10	Colored pencils and/or Crayons per student
			1	Printed coloring page
			1	Pair of Scissors per student
			1	Liquid Glue Bottle per student
			1	or Clear Tape Roll per classroom
			5-6	Popsicle sticks per student See Extras
LANGUAGE ARTS	1	Printed Handout per student	1	Printed Copy work per student
	1	Drawing Utensils per student	1	Drawing Utensils per student
			1	Paper per student
			1	Printed Handout per student
LATIN/ GREEK	1	Printed Hymn of the week per student	1	Printed Hymn of the week per student
MATH	1	Pencil per student	1	Pencil per student
	1	Paper per student	1	Paper per student
MUSIC	1	(Optional) Pitch instrument		N/A
READING		N/A		N/A
RELIGION		N/A		N/A
SCIENCE	10-12	Small objects (nails, pennies, paper clips, plastic balls, etc.) per student	1	Drawing Utensils per student
	1	Shoe box or other container to hold the small objects per student	1	Paper per student See Linked Lessons (SF)
	3	U-shaped magnet per student		
	1	Magnets from your refrigerator per student		
	1	Sheet of paper per student		
	1	Piece of metal (e.g. pie or cake pan) per student		
	1	Piece of plastic (e.g. placemat or plastic cutting board) per student		
	1	Piece of cardboard (5 x 7 or 4x6) per student		
	1	Piece of wood (5 x 7 or 4x6 e.g. sheet of thin plywood) per student		
	1			

	Piece of paper or Nature Journal per student Drawing Utensils per student	
VIRTUE	N/A	N/A

UNIT 17

SUBJECT	DAY 1		DAYS 2 – 4	
ART		N/A		N/A
CCM		Maps 1,2,3 Timeline Cards Printed Unit Summary		Maps 1,2,3 Timeline Cards Printed Unit Summary
HISTORY		N/A	1 1 1 5-10 1 1 1	Drawing Utensils per student Paper per student Printed Coloring Page per student Colored pencils and/or Crayons per student Drawing Utensils per student Paper per student Props and materials needed for acting out the story See Extras
LANGUAGE ARTS	1 1	Printed Handout per student Drawing Utensils per student	1 1 1	Drawing Utensils per student Printed Copy work per student Paper per student Printed Handout per student
LATIN/ GREEK	1	Printed Hymn of the week per student	1	Printed Hymn of the week per student
MATH	1 1	Pencil per student Paper per student	1 1	Pencil per student Paper per student
MUSIC	1	(Optional) Pitch instrument		N/A
READING		N/A		N/A
RELIGION		N/A		N/A
SCIENCE	10-12 1 1 3 1 1	Small objects (nails, pennies, paper clips, plastic balls, etc.) per student Shoe box or other container to hold the small objects per student U-shaped magnet per student Magnets from your refrigerator per student Sheet of paper per student Printed Handout per student	1 1	Drawing Utensils per student Piece of paper or Nature Journal per student
VIRTUE		N/A		N/A

UNIT 18

SUBJECT	DAY 1 (Field Trip Day)		DAYS 2 – 4	
ART	N/A		See "Extras"	
CCM	Maps 1,2,3 Timeline Cards Printed Unit Summary		Maps 1,2,3 Timeline Cards Printed Unit Summary	
HISTORY	N/A		1 1 1 5- 10	Drawing Utensils per student Paper per student Printed Coloring Page per student Colored pencils and/or Crayons per student See Extras See Linked Lesson (SF)
LANGUAGE ARTS	1 1	Printed Handout per student Drawing Utensils per student	1 1 1 1	Drawing Utensils per student Printed Copy work per student Paper per student Drawing Utensils per student per student
LATIN / GREEK	1	Printed Hymn of the week per student	1	Printed Hymn of the week per student
MATH	1 1	Pencil per student Paper per student	1 1	Pencil per student Paper per student
MUSIC	1	(Optional) Pitch instrument	N/A	
READING	N/A		N/A	
RELIGION	N/A		N/A	
SCIENCE	1 3 10-12 1 1	U-shaped magnet per student Magnets from your refrigerator per student Small objects (nails, pennies, paper clips, plastic balls, etc.) per student (Choose new object) Shoe box or other container to hold the small objects per student Paper per student or Nature Journal per student Or (Optional) "My First Magnet Kit" (See Link in SF)	1 1	Drawing Utensils per student Paper per student See Linked Lessons
VIRTUE	N/A		N/A	

UNIT 19

SUBJECT	DAY 1 (Co-op Day)		DAYS 2 – 4	
ART	1	Handout on paper, in color per student (or per family)	N/A	
	9	3" X 3" pieces of square, cotton fabric (assorted colors and patterns) per student		
	1	Sewing needle per student		
	1	Spool of thread per student		
	1	Plastic baggy per student		
	1	marked with permanent marker with the student's name		
	1	(Optional) Set of Visual Aids on paper, in color		
	1	Bottle of cleaning spray		
	1	Paper Towel Roll		
CCM	Maps 1 Timeline Cards Printed Unit Summary		Maps 1 Timeline Cards Printed Unit Summary	
HISTORY	See Linked Lesson (SF)		1	Printed Coloring Pages per student
			5-10	Colored pencils and/or Crayons per student
			1	Drawing Utensils per student
			1	Papers per student
			1	See Extras
LANGUAGE ARTS	1	Printed Handout per student	1	Printed Copy work per student
			1	Drawing Utensils per student
			1	Paper per student
			1	Printed Handout per student
LATIN/ GREEK	1	Printed Hymn of the week per student	1	Printed Hymn of the week per student
MATH	1	Pencil per student	1	Pencil per student
	1	Paper per student	1	Paper per student
MUSIC	1	(Optional) Pitch instrument	N/A	
READING	N/A		N/A	
RELIGION	N/A		N/A	
SCIENCE	See Linked Lesson (SF)		1	Drawing Utensils per student
			1	Paper or Journal per student See Linked Lessons (SF)
VIRTUE	N/A		N/A	

UNIT 20

SUBJECT	DAY 1 (Co-op Day)		DAYS 2 – 4	
ART	1	Handout on paper, in color per student (or per family) (Unit 19)	N/A	
	1	Baggie of quilt squares from Unit 19 per student		
	1	Sewing needle per student		
	1	Spool of thread per student (For students who were absent)		
	9	3" X 3" pieces of square, cotton fabric (assorted colors and patterns) per student		
	1	Plastic baggy per student marked with permanent marker with the student's name		
	1	(Optional) Set of Visual Aids on paper, in color		
	1	Bottle of cleaning spray		
	1	Paper Towel Roll		
CCM		Maps 2 Timeline Cards Printed Unit Summary		Maps 2 Timeline Cards Printed Unit Summary
HISTORY	1	Drawing Utensils per student See History Pockets (SF)	2	Printed Handout per student
			5-10	Colored pencils and/or Crayons per student
			1	Printed Coloring Pages per student
			1	Drawing Utensils per student See Linked Lesson (SF) See Extras
LANGUAGE ARTS	1	Printed Handout per student	1	Printed Copy work per student
	1	Drawing Utensils per student	1	Drawing Utensils per student
			1	Paper per student
			1	Printed Handout per student
LATIN/ GREEK	1	Printed Hymn of the week per student	1	Printed Hymn of the week per student
MATH	1	Pencil per student	1	Pencil per student
	1	Paper per student	1	Paper per student
MUSIC	1	(Optional) Pitch instrument	N/A	
READING		N/A	N/A	
RELIGION		N/A	N/A	
SCIENCE		See Linked Lesson (SF)	1	Drawing Utensils per student
			1	Paper or Journal per student See Linked Lessons (SF)
VIRTUE		N/A	N/A	

UNIT 21

SUBJECT		DAY 1 (Co-op Day)		DAYS 2 – 4
ART	1	Handout on paper, in color per student (or per family)		N/A
	1	(Optional) Set of Visual Aids on paper, in color		
	1	Disposable camera per child		
	2	L-shaped pieces of cardboard (5" at the bottom and 7" for side) per student		
	1	Black Marker per classroom		
CCM		Maps 2 Timeline Cards Printed Unit Summary		Maps 2 Timeline Cards Printed Unit Summary
HISTORY	1	Drawing Utensils per student See History Pockets (SF)	5-10	Colored pencils and/or Crayons per student
			1	Printed Coloring Pages per student
			1	Drawing Utensils per student
			1	Paper per student See Linked Lesson (SF)
			2	Printed Handout per student See Extras
LANGUAGE ARTS	1	Printed Handout per student	1	Drawing Utensils per student
	1	Drawing Utensils per student	1	Printed Copy work per student
			1	Paper per student
			1	Printed Handout per student
LATIN / GREEK	1	Printed Hymn of the week per student	1	Printed Hymn of the week per student
MATH	1	Pencil per student	1	Pencil per student
	1	Paper per student	1	Paper per student
MUSIC	1	(Optional) Pitch instrument		N/A
READING		N/A		N/A
RELIGION		N/A		N/A
SCIENCE		See Referenced Resource (SF)	1	Drawing Utensils per student
	1	Drawing Utensils per student	1	Paper or Journal per student See Linked Lessons (SF)
	1	Paper per student Journal per student		
VIRTUE		N/A		N/A

UNIT 22

SUBJECT	DAY 1 (Field Trip Day)		DAYS 2 – 4	
ART	N/A		See "Extras"	
CCM	Maps 1,2,3,4 Timeline Cards Printed Unit Summary		Maps 1,2,3,4 Timeline Cards Printed Unit Summary	
HISTORY	N/A		1 1 5-10 2 1 1	Drawing Utensils per student Paper per student Colored pencils and/or Crayons per student Printed Coloring Pages per student Printed Handout per student See Linked Lesson (SF) See Extras
LANGUAGE ARTS	1 1	Printed Handout per student Drawing Utensils per student	1 1 1	Drawing Utensils per student Printed Copy work per student Paper per student Printed Handout per student
LATIN/ GREEK	1	Printed Hymn of the week per student	1	Printed Hymn of the week per student
MATH	1 1	Pencil per student Paper per student	1 1	Pencil per student Paper per student
MUSIC	1	(Optional) Pitch instrument	N/A	
READING	N/A		N/A	
RELIGION	N/A		N/A	
SCIENCE	N/A		1 1	Drawing Utensils per student Paper or Journal per student See Linked Lesson (SF)
VIRTUE	N/A		N/A	

UNIT 23

SUBJECT	DAY 1 (Co-op Day)		DAYS 2 – 4	
ART	1	Handout on paper, in color per student (or per family)	N/A	
	1	(Optional) Set of Visual Aids on paper, in color		
	1	Disposable camera per student (See Unit 21)		
	2	L-shaped pieces of cardboard (5" at the bottom and 7" for side) per student		
CCM		Maps 2		Maps 2
		Timeline Cards		Timeline Cards
		Printed Unit Summary		Printed Unit Summary
HISTORY		See Linked Lesson (SF)	5-10	Colored pencils and/or Crayons per student
			1	Printed Coloring Pages per student
			1	Drawing Utensils per student
			1	Paper per student
			1	Printed Handout per student See Extras
LANGUAGE ARTS		N/A	1	Printed Copy work per student
			1	Drawing Utensils per student
			1	Paper per student
			1	Printed Handout per student
LATIN/ GREEK	1	Printed Hymn of the week per student	1	Printed Hymn of the week per student
MATH	1	Pencil per student	1	Pencil per student
	1	Paper per student	1	Paper per student
MUSIC	1	(Optional) Pitch instrument		N/A
READING		N/A		N/A
RELIGION		N/A		N/A
SCIENCE		See Referenced Resource (SF)	1	Drawing Utensils per student
		Drawing Utensils per student	1	Paper or Journal per student
		Paper or Journal per student		See Linked Lessons (SF)
VIRTUE		N/A		N/A

UNIT 24

SUBJECT		DAY 1 (Co-op Day)		DAYS 2 – 4
ART	1	Printed Handout per student (or per family)		N/A
	1	HB pencil per student		
	1	Pen and ink set per student		
	1	Calligraphy pens set per student (K-3rd)		
	1	12" X 12" piece of Multi-media paper per student		
	1	(Optional) Set of Visual Aids on paper, in color		
	1	Roll of paper towels		
	1	Bottle of cleaning spray		
CCM		Maps 3		Maps 3
		Timeline Cards		Timeline Cards
		Printed Unit Summary		Printed Unit Summary
HISTORY		See Linked Lesson (SF)	5-10	Colored pencils and/or Crayons per student
			1	Printed coloring page
			1	Drawing Utensils per student
			2	Paper per student
				See Linked Lesson(SF)
				See Extras
LANGUAGE ARTS	1	Printed Handout per student	1	Drawing Utensils per student
	1	Drawing Utensils per student	1	Printed Copy work per student
			1	Paper per student
				Printed Handout per student
LATIN/ GREEK	1	Printed Hymn of the week per student	1	Printed Hymn of the week per student
MATH	1	Pencil per student	1	Pencil per student
	1	Paper per student	1	Paper per student
MUSIC	1	(Optional) Pitch instrument		N/A
READING		N/A		N/A
RELIGION		N/A		N/A
SCIENCE		See Linked Lessons (SF)	1	Drawing Utensils per student
	1	Drawing Utensils per student	1	Paper per student
	1	Paper per student or Nature Journal per student		See Linked Lessons (SF)
VIRTUE		N/A		N/A

UNIT 25

SUBJECT	DAY 1 (Co-op Day)		DAYS 2 – 4	
ART	1	Printed Handout per student (or per family)	N/A	
	1	HB pencil per student		
	1	Pen and ink set per student (See Unit 24)		
	1	12" X 12" piece of Multi-media paper per student		
	1	(Optional) Set of Visual Aids on paper, in color		
	1	Roll of paper towels		
	1	Bottle of cleaning spray		
CCM		Maps 3		Maps 3
		Timeline Cards		Timeline Cards
		Printed Unit Summary		Printed Unit Summary
HISTORY	1	Paper per student	1	Printed coloring page per student
	1	Drawing Utensils per student	5-10	
	5-10	Colored pencils and/or Colored pencils and/or Crayons per student		Colored pencils and/or Colored pencils and/or Crayons per student
			1	Drawing Utensils per student
			1	Papers per student
				See Linked Lesson (SF)
				See Extras
LANGUAGE ARTS	1	Printed Handout per student	1	Drawing Utensils per student
	1	Drawing Utensils per student	1	Printed Copy work per student
			1	Paper per student
				Printed Handout per student
LATIN/ GREEK	1	Printed Hymn of the week per student	1	Printed Hymn of the week per student
MATH	1	Pencil per student	1	Pencil per student
	1	Paper per student	1	Paper per student
MUSIC	1	(Optional) Pitch instrument	N/A	
READING		N/A	N/A	
RELIGION		N/A	N/A	
SCIENCE		See Linked Lessons (SF)	1	Drawing Utensils per student
	1	Drawing Utensils per student	1	Paper per student or Nature Journal per student
	1	Paper per student or Nature Journal per student		See Linked Lessons (SF)
VIRTUE		N/A	N/A	

UNIT 26

SUBJECT	DAY 1 (Field Trip Day)		DAYS 2 – 4	
ART		N/A		See "Extras"
CCM		Maps 1,2,3,4 Timeline Cards Printed Unit Summary		Maps 1,2,3,4 Timeline Cards Printed Unit Summary
HISTORY		N/A	1 1 5-10 1	Drawing Utensils per student Paper per student Colored pencils and/or Colored pencils and/or Crayons per student Printed coloring page per student See Extras See Linked Lesson (SF)
LANGUAGE ARTS	1 1	Printed Handout per student Drawing Utensils per student	1 1 1	Drawing Utensils per student Printed Copy work per student Paper per student Printed Handout per student
LATIN / GREEK	1	Printed Hymn of the week per student	1	Printed Hymn of the week per student
MATH	1 1	Pencil per student Paper per student	1 1	Pencil per student Paper per student
MUSIC	1	(Optional) Pitch instrument		N/A
READING		N/A		N/A
RELIGION		N/A		N/A
SCIENCE		N/A	1 1	Drawing Utensils per student Paper or Journal per student See Linked Lesson (SF)
VIRTUE		N/A		N/A

UNIT 27

SUBJECT	DAY 1 (Co-op Day)		DAYS 2 – 4	
ART	1 1 1 1 2 1 1 1 1 1	(Optional) Set of Visual Aids in color HB pencil per student Black ink and pen per student Pair of scissors per student 3″ pieces of yarn per student Hole-punchers per every 2 students Sheet of white paper per student Printed Art Handout per student Roll of paper towels Bottle of cleaning spray	1 1 1 1 1 1 1	HB pencil per student Black ink and pen per student Pair of scissors per student 3″ pieces of yarn per student Hole-punchers per every 2 students Sheet of white paper per student Printed Art Handout per student
CCM	Maps 4 Timeline Cards Printed Unit Summary		Maps 4 Timeline Cards Printed Unit Summary	
HISTORY	1 5-10 1	Drawing Utensils per student Colored pencils and/or Colored pencils and/or Crayons per student Paper per student	5-10 1 1 1 1	Colored pencils and/or Crayons per student Printed coloring page Drawing Utensils per student Paper per student Printed Handout per student See Extras
LANGUAGE ARTS	1	Printed Handout per student	1 1 1 1	Drawing Utensils per student Printed Copy work per student Paper per student Printed Handout per student
LATIN/ GREEK	1	Printed Hymn of the week per student	1	Printed Hymn of the week per student
MATH	1 1	Pencil per student Paper per student	1 1	Pencil per student Paper per student
MUSIC	1	(Optional) Pitch instrument		N/A
READING		N/A		N/A
RELIGION		N/A		N/A
SCIENCE		See Lesson in (SF) Drawing Utensils per student Paper or Journal per student	1 1	Drawing Utensils per student Paper or Journal per student See Linked Lessons (SF)
VIRTUE		N/A		N/A

UNIT 28

SUBJECT		DAY 1 (Co-op Day)		DAYS 2 – 4
ART	1 1 1 1 2-3	(Optional) Set of Visual Aids in color Handout on paper, in color per student (or per family) HB pencil per student Pair of Scissors per student Staplers per classroom Sheets of white paper per student or one sticky note pad per student		N/A
CCM		Maps 5 Timeline Cards Printed Unit Summary		Maps 5 Timeline Cards Printed Unit Summary
HISTORY	5-6 1 1	Props or craft items to create simple props. CD player for classroom Peter and the Wolf CD	5-10 1 1 1 1 1 5-10 1	Colored pencils and/or Crayons per student Printed coloring page Drawing Utensils per student Paper per student Pair of scissors per student Paper per student Popsicle sticks per student Printed Handout per student See Extras
LANGUAGE ARTS	1 1	Printed Handout per student Drawing Utensils per student	1 1 1 1	Drawing Utensils per student Printed Copy work per student Paper per student Printed Handout per student
LATIN / GREEK	1	Printed Hymn of the week per student	1	Printed Hymn of the week per student
MATH	1 1	Pencil per student Paper per student	1 1	Pencil per student Paper per student
MUSIC	1	(Optional) Pitch instrument		N/A
READING		N/A		N/A
RELIGION		N/A		N/A
SCIENCE	 1 1	See Referenced Resource (SF) Drawing Utensils per student Paper or Journal per student	1 1	Drawing Utensils per student Paper or Journal per student See Linked Lessons (SF)
VIRTUE		N/A		N/A

UNIT 29

SUBJECT	DAY 1 (Co-op Day)		DAYS 2 – 4	
ART	1 1 1 1 1 10-12 4-5	(Optional) Set of Visual Aids in color Handout on paper, in color per student (or per family) HB pencil per student Pair of Scissors per student Stapler per classroom Pen & ink kit per student Markers ☐ Colored Pencils Sheets of white paper per student or sticky note pad		N/A
CCM		Maps 5 Timeline Cards Printed Unit Summary		Maps 5 Timeline Cards Printed Unit Summary
HISTORY	5-6	Props or craft items to create simple props.	5-10 1 1 1 1	Colored pencils and/or Crayons per student Printed coloring page Drawing Utensils per student Paper per student Pair of scissors per student See Extras
LANGUAGE ARTS	1 1	Printed Handout per student Drawing Utensils per student	1 1 1	Drawing Utensils per student Printed Copy work per student Paper per student Printed Handout per student
LATIN/ GREEK	1	Printed Hymn of the week per student	1	Printed Hymn of the week per student
MATH	1 1	Pencil per student Paper per student	1 1	Pencil per student Paper per student
MUSIC	1	(Optional) Pitch instrument		N/A
READING		N/A		N/A
RELIGION		N/A		N/A
SCIENCE		See Referenced Resource (SF)	1 1	Drawing Utensils per student Paper or Journal per student See Linked Lessons (SF)
VIRTUE		N/A		N/A

UNIT 30

SUBJECT	DAY 1		DAYS 2 – 4	
ART	N/A		See "Extras"	
CCM	Maps 1,2,3,4,5 Timeline Cards Printed Unit Summary		Maps 1,2,3,4,5 Timeline Cards Printed Unit Summary	
HISTORY	N/A		1 5-10 1	Drawing Utensils per student Colored pencils and/or Crayons per student Printed Handout per student
LANGUAGE ARTS	N/A		N/A	
LATIN/ GREEK	1	Printed Hymn of the week per student	1	Printed Hymn of the week per student
MATH	1 1	Pencil per student Paper per student	1 1	Pencil per student Paper per student
MUSIC	1	(Optional) Pitch instrument	N/A	
READING	N/A		N/A	
RELIGION	N/A		N/A	
SCIENCE	N/A		N/A	
VIRTUE	N/A		N/A	

4th – 6th Grade ~ Materials Usage Schedule

Introduction

Welcome to the Materials Usage Schedule for 4th – 6th Grade. The schedule is provides a timeline of when materials will be used. The 4th – 6th Grade Materials Usage Schedule is divided into unit lists. Each unit list is divided by subject and by days.

In the Materials Usage Schedule, Day 1 is listed as either a "Co-op Day" or "Field Trip Day." If Day 1 does not have a label, it is a Home Day. Days 2-4 are always considered Home Days in each unit. If you are a "Just Home" Family (those who are not in a local co-op), every day is a home day, so you should plan accordingly.

Important Notices:

- Materials listed under a Co-op Day are provided **at co-op**.

- Materials listed under a Field Trip or Home Day must be provided **at home and do not come from co-op.**

- The following items are **NOT** included on this list:
  - **Books**: See the booklists under Step 2 of "Getting Started" in your online suite.
  - **Linked Lesson Materials**: Items required for lessons and activities in the curriculum that link to outside websites. You will need to follow the links in the Subject Folders (SF) in order to gather materials needed week-to-week.
  - **Extras**: Items needed to complete activities found in the "Extras" section of subjects.
  - **Printed Items**: Documents in the online suite that must be printed for use (handouts, coloring pages, copy work, worksheets, etc.)

- Items listed as "Optional" are not required purchases; they are merely suggestions for enhancing the activity or lesson.

- Please note the following vocabulary:
  - The *water jar* is a container for washing out paintbrushes.
  - A *drawing utensil* is any tool of your choice--marker, pen, or pencil—used for writing or drawing.

ABBREVIATION KEY	
DL	Digital Library (in course suite)
SF	Subject Folder (in course suite)
HC	Hard Copy
PLL	*Primary Language Lessons* (book)
ILL	*Intermediate Language Lessons* (book)
RS4K	*Real Science 4 Kids* (book)
I-CAT	*Illustrated Catechism* (book)
OHF-1	*Our Holy Faith, Book 1* (book)
OHF-2	*Our Holy Faith, Book 2* (book)
OHF-4	*Our Holy Faith, Book 4* (book)
OHF-1-TM	*Our Holy Faith, Book 1, Teacher's Manual* (book)

For the list of materials to be purchased, see the "Materials Purchase List" located in the "Getting Started" section of the online suite.

Please contact us if you have any questions or concerns.

UNIT 1

SUBJECT	DAY 1 (Co-op Day)		DAYS 2 – 4	
ART	1	Handout on paper, in color per student (or per family)	1	Handout on paper, in color per student (or per family)
	1	6"X 6" sheet of paper per 4th-6th Grade student (cut to size and FILE THE SHARP EDGES)	1 1	6"X 6" sheet of paper per 4th-6th Grade student (cut to size and FILE THE SHARP EDGES)
	1	6" X 6" sheet of 5 mil Copper Sheets per 4th-6th Grade student (purchase a roll to save money)	1	6" X 6" sheet of 5 mil Copper Sheets per 4th-6th Grade student (purchase a roll to save money)
	1	Plastic Placemat per student	1	Plastic Placemat per student
	1	Pencil per student	1	Pencil per student
	2 -	Basic Leather Working Tools per student	2-3	Basic Leather Working Tools per student
	3	(Optional) Set of Visual Aids on paper, in color		
	1	Smock or large T-shirt per student Paper towel Roll		
	1 1	Bottle of Cleaning spray		
CCM		Map 1 Timeline Cards Printed Unit Summary		Map 1 Timeline Cards Printed Unit Summary
HISTORY	1	Printed Handouts per student	1	Drawing Utensils per student
			1	Paper per student
			3	Printed Handouts per student
			1	Blue Drawing Utensils per student
			1	Pink Drawing Utensils per student
			1	Orange Drawing Utensils per student
				See Extras
LANGUAGE ARTS	2	Printed Handout per student	1	Printed Copy work per student
	1	Drawing Utensils per student	1	Drawing Utensils per student
			1	Paper per student
			1	Printed Handout per student
LATIN/ GREEK	1	Printed Hymn of the week per student	1	Printed Hymn of the week per student
MATH	1	Pencil per student	1	Pencil per student
	1	Paper per student	1	Paper per student
MUSIC	1	(Optional) Pitch instrument		N/A
READING		N/A		N/A
RELIGION		See OHF-4 (SF)		See OHF-4 (SF)
SCIENCE	2	Red Jelly Gumdrops per student	1	Printed Worksheet
	2	Blue Jelly Gumdrops per student	1	Drawing Utensils per student
	2	Yellow Jelly Gumdrops per student	5-10	Crayons/colored pencils per student
	2	7 "pieces of craft wire per student		See Linked Lesson (SF)
VIRTUE		N/A		N/A

UNIT 2

SUBJECT	DAY 1 (Co-op Day)		DAYS 2 – 4	
ART	1	Handout on paper, in color per student (or per family)	1	Drawing Utensils per student
	1	8" x 11" sheet of white printer paper per student	1	Paper per student
	1	8" x 11" sheet of charcoal paper per student	1	Printed Handout per student
	1	Charcoal / willow stick per student		
	1	Pencil per student		
	1	Pencil sharpener per student		
		(Optional) Set of Visual Aids on paper, in color		
	1	Smock or large T-shirt per student		
	1	Paper towel roll		
	1	Bottle of Cleaning spray		
		Sheets of plastic for tables and floors		
CCM		Map 1		Map 1
		Timeline Cards		Timeline Cards
		Printed Unit Summary		Printed Unit Summary
HISTORY	1	Printed Handout per student	4	Printed Handout per student
	1	Drawing Utensils per student	5-10	Drawing Utensils per student
LANGUAGE ARTS	1	Printed Handout per student	1	Drawing Utensils per student
	1	Drawing Utensils per student	1	Paper per student
			1	Printed Handout per student
LATIN / GREEK	1	Printed Hymn of the week per student	1	Printed Hymn of the week per student
MATH	1	Pencil per student	1	Pencil per student
	1	Paper per student	1	Paper per student
MUSIC	1	(Optional) Pitch instrument		N/A
READING		N/A		N/A
RELIGION		See OHF-4 (SF)		See OHF-4 (SF)
SCIENCE	8	Red Jelly Gumdrops per student		See Linked Lesson (SF)
	8	Blue Jelly Gumdrops per student	1	Printed Handout or Science Journal per student
	8	Yellow Jelly Gumdrops per student		
	3	7 "pieces of craft wire per student	1	Drawing Utensils per student
		Helium balloons		
	1	Printed Handout per student		
VIRTUE		N/A		N/A

UNIT 3

SUBJECT	DAY 1 (Co-op Day)		DAYS 2 – 4	
ART	1	Handout on paper, in color per student (or per family)	1	Unfinished Cross-stitching Kit (from Day 1) per student
	1	4" X 4" piece of paper per student	1	Pair of scissors per student
	1	Quart-sized zip-lock bag per student		
	1			
		Permanent marker		
	1	Pair of scissors per student		
	1	Cross-stitching kit per student (See Link)		
	1	(Optional) Set of Visual Aids in color		
	1	Paper Towel Roll		
		Bottle of Cleaning spray		
CCM		Map 2		Map 2
		Timeline Cards		Timeline Cards
		Printed Unit Summary		Printed Unit Summary
HISTORY	1	Printed Handout of "Classroom Visual Aids"	1	Drawing Utensils per student
	1	2-3 inch (H) x 2-3 inch (W) x 2-3 inch (D) block of Clay per student	1	Paper per student
	¼	Piece of Sponges per student	5-10	Crayons/colored pencils per student
		Piece of 4"x 4" wax paper per student	3	Printed Handout per student
	1	Small cup for water per student		See Extras
	1	Bottle of Cleaning spray		
	1	Newspaper or Plastic Sheet to cover tables and floor		
	1	Plastic knife per student (or clay carving tools)		
	1	Pen per student (or clay carving tools)		
LANGUAGE ARTS	1	Printed Handout per student	1	Drawing Utensils per student
	1	Drawing Utensils per student	1	Paper per student
	1	Printed Handout	1	Printed Handout per student
LATIN/ GREEK	1	Printed Hymn of the week per student	1	Printed Hymn of the week per student
MATH	1	Pencil per student	1	Pencil per student
	1	Paper per student	1	Paper per student
MUSIC	1	(Optional) Pitch instrument		N/A
READING		N/A		N/A
RELIGION		See OHF-4 (SF)		See OHF-4 (SF)
SCIENCE	2	Large Marshmallows (of one color) per student.		See Linked Lesson (SF)
	2	Large Marshmallow (of a different color) per student		
	2	Toothpicks per student		
VIRTUE		N/A		N/A

4th – 6th Grade ~ Materials Usage Schedule

UNIT 4

SUBJECT	DAY 1 (Field Trip Day)		DAYS 2 – 4	
ART	N/A		See "Extras"	
CCM	Maps 1 & 2 Timeline Cards Printed Unit Summary		Maps 1 & 2 Timeline Cards Printed Unit Summary	
HISTORY	N/A		1 1 1 5-10	Drawing Utensils per student Paper per student Printed Handout per student Crayons/colored pencils per student See Extras
LANGUAGE ARTS	1 1	Printed Handout per student Drawing Utensils per student	1 1 1	Drawing Utensils per student Paper per student Printed Handout per student
LATIN/ GREEK	1	Printed Hymn of the week per student	1	Printed Hymn of the week per student
MATH	1 1	Pencil per student Paper per student	1 1	Pencil per student Paper per student
MUSIC	1	(Optional) Pitch instrument		N/A
READING	N/A		N/A	
RELIGION	See OHF-4 (SF)		See OHF-4 (SF)	
SCIENCE	N/A		1 1	Drawing Utensils per student Paper or Journal per student
VIRTUE	N/A		N/A	

UNIT 5

SUBJECT	DAY 1 (Co-op Day)		DAYS 2 – 4	
ART	1	Handout on paper, in color per student (or per family)	1	Drawing Utensils per student
	1	8" X 12" piece of water color paper per student	1	Paper per student
	1	Paint brush per student	1	Paint brush per student
	1	Paper or plastic cup per student	1	Paper or plastic water cup per student
	1	Paper towel per student	1	Water color pencil set per student
	1	Water pitcher for filling cups with water		
	1	Water color pencil set per student (See Link in SF)		
	1	Pencil sharpener per student		
	1	(Optional) Set of Visual Aids on paper, in color		
	1	Roll of paper towels		
	1	Bottle of cleaning spray		
		Sheets of plastic for floor		
CCM		Maps 2		Maps 2
		Timeline Cards		Timeline Cards
		Printed Unit Summary		Printed Unit Summary
HISTORY	1	Printed Handouts per student	3	Printed Handouts per student
			1	Drawing Utensils per student
			1	Paper per student
			5-10	Crayons/colored pencils student
LANGUAGE ARTS	1	Printed Handout per student	1	Drawing Utensils per student
	1	Drawing Utensils per student	1	Paper per student
	1	Printed Handout	1	Printed Handout per student
LATIN/ GREEK	1	Printed Hymn of the week per student	1	Printed Hymn of the week per student
MATH	1	Pencil per student	1	Pencil per student
	1	Paper per student	1	Paper per student
MUSIC	1	(Optional) Pitch instrument		N/A
READING		N/A		N/A
RELIGION		See OHF-4 (SF)		See OHF-4 (SF)
SCIENCE		See Linked Lesson		See Linked Lessons (SF)
			1	Drawing Utensils per student
			1	Paper or Nature Journal per student
VIRTUE		N/A		N/A

UNIT 6

SUBJECT		DAY 1 (Co-op Day)		DAYS 2 – 4
ART	1	(Optional) Set of Visual Aids in color per classroom	1	Drawing Utensils per student
	1	Handout in color per student	1	Drawing paper per student or small oil paint canvas
	1	8" X 12" oil paint canvas per student Paint brush per student	1	Oil paint set or Oil pastel set per student
	1	Paper or plastic cup per student		
	1	Paper or plastic plate per student		
	1	Paper towel per student		
	1	Water pitcher for filling cups with water		
	1	Pre-painted dark oil painted piece of paper from the "Before the Lesson" section per student		
		Oil collection art set per student: (See Link SF)		
		Smock or T-shirt per student		
		Roll of paper towels		
		Bottle of cleaning spray		
CCM		Maps 2		Maps 2
		Timeline Cards		Timeline Cards
		Printed Unit Summary		Printed Unit Summary
HISTORY	1	Printed Handout per student	1	Printed Handouts per student
	1	Drawing Utensils per student	1	Drawing Utensils per student
			1	Paper per student
			5-10	Crayons/colored pencils per student
LANGUAGE ARTS	1	Printed Handout per student	1	Drawing Utensils per student
	1	Drawing Utensils per student	1	Paper per student
			1	Printed Handout per student
LATIN / GREEK	1	Printed Hymn of the week per student	1	Printed Hymn of the week per student
MATH	1	Pencil per student	1	Pencil per student
	1	Paper per student	1	Paper per student
MUSIC	1	(Optional) Pitch instrument		N/A
READING		N/A		N/A
RELIGION		See OHF-4 (SF)		See OHF-4 (SF)
SCIENCE		See Linked Lesson		See Linked Lessons (SF)
			1	Drawing Utensils per student
			1	Paper or Nature Journal per student
VIRTUE		N/A		N/A

4th – 6th Grade ~ Materials Usage Schedule

UNIT 7

SUBJECT	DAY 1 (Co-op Day)	DAYS 2 – 4
ART	1 (Optional) Set of Visual Aids in color per classroom 1 Handout from last week in color per student 1 (Student Paintings from last week) 8" X 12" oil paint canvas per student 1 Paint brush per student 1 Paper or plastic cup per student 1 Paper or plastic plate per student 1 Paper towel per student 1 Water pitcher for filling cups with water 1 Pre-painted dark oil painted piece of paper from the "Before the Lesson" section 1 Oil collection art set per student: (See Link SF) 1 Smock or T-shirt per student 1 Roll of paper towels 1 Bottle of cleaning spray	Drawing Utensils per student Drawing paper per student or small oil paint canvas Oil paint set or Oil pastel set per student
CCM	Maps 3 Timeline Cards Printed Unit Summary	Maps 3 Timeline Cards Printed Unit Summary
HISTORY	1 Printed Handout per student 1 Drawing Utensils per student	1 Printed Handouts per student 1 Drawing Utensils per student 1 Paper per student 5-10 Crayons/colored pencils per student See Extras
LANGUAGE ARTS	1 Printed Handout per student 1 Drawing Utensils per student	1 Drawing Utensils per student 1 Paper per student 1 Printed Handout per student
LATIN/ GREEK	1 Printed Hymn of the week per student	1 Printed Hymn of the week per student
MATH	1 Pencil per student 1 Paper per student	1 Pencil per student 1 Paper per student
MUSIC	1 (Optional) Pitch instrument	N/A
READING	N/A	N/A
RELIGION	See OHF-4 (SF)	See OHF-4 (SF)
SCIENCE	See Linked Lesson (SF)	See Linked Lessons (SF) 1 Drawing Utensils per student 1 Paper or Nature Journal per student
VIRTUE	N/A	N/A

UNIT 8

SUBJECT	DAY 1 (Field Trip Day)		DAYS 2 – 4	
ART	N/A		See "Extras"	
CCM	Maps 1,2,3 Timeline Cards Printed Unit Summary		Maps 1,2,3 Timeline Cards Printed Unit Summary	
HISTORY	N/A		1 1 3	Drawing Utensils per student Paper per student Printed Handout per student
LANGUAGE ARTS	1 1	Printed Handout per student Drawing Utensils per student	1 1 1	Drawing Utensils per student Paper per student Printed Handout per student
LATIN / GREEK	1	Printed Hymn of the week per student	1	Printed Hymn of the week per student
MATH	1 1	Pencil per student Paper per student	1 1	Pencil per student Paper per student
MUSIC	1	(Optional) Pitch instrument	N/A	
READING	N/A		N/A	
RELIGION	See OHF-4 (SF)		See OHF-4 (SF)	
SCIENCE	N/A		1 1 1	Drawing Utensils per student Paper per student Printed Handout or Nature Journal
VIRTUE	N/A		N/A	

UNIT 9

SUBJECT	DAY 1 (Co-op Day)		DAYS 2 – 4	
ART	1	(Optional) Set of Visual Aids Handout on paper, in color per student (or per family)	1	8" X 12" piece of sketch paper per student
	1	8" X 12" piece of sketch paper per student	1	Colored pencils set per student
	1	Colored pencils set per student		Pencil sharpener per student
	1	Pencil sharpener per student		
	1	Roll of paper towels		
	1	Bottle of cleaning spray		
CCM		Maps 3		Maps 3
		Timeline Cards		Timeline Cards
		Printed Unit Summary		Printed Unit Summary
HISTORY	1	Printed Handout per student	1	Drawing Utensils per student
			1	Paper per student
			3	Printed Handout per student
LANGUAGE ARTS	1	Printed Handout per student	1	Drawing Utensils per student
	1	Drawing Utensils per student	1	Paper per student
			2	Printed Handouts per student
LATIN/ GREEK	1	Printed Hymn of the week per student	1	Printed Hymn of the week per student
MATH	1	Pencil per student	1	Pencil per student
	1	Paper per student	1	Paper per student
MUSIC	1	(Optional) Pitch instrument		N/A
READING		N/A		N/A
RELIGION		See OHF-4 (SF)		See OHF-4 (SF)
SCIENCE		See Linked Lessons (SF)	1	Drawing Utensils per student
			1	Paper per student
				See Linked Lessons (SF)
VIRTUE		N/A		N/A

UNIT 10

SUBJECT	DAY 1 (Co-op Day)	DAYS 2 – 4
ART	1 (Optional) Set of Visual Aids Handout on paper, in color per student (or per family) 1 Drawing started last week per student 1 8" X 12" piece of sketch paper per student for students who were absent last week 1 Colored pencils set per student 1 Pencil sharpener per student 1 Roll of paper towels 1 Bottle of cleaning spray	1 8" X 12" piece of sketch paper per student 1 Colored pencils set per student Pencil sharpener per student
CCM	Maps 3 Timeline Cards Printed Unit Summary	Maps 3 Timeline Cards Printed Unit Summary
HISTORY	N/A	1 Drawing Utensils per student 1 Paper per student 3 Printed Handout per student
LANGUAGE ARTS	1 Printed Handout per student 1 Drawing Utensils per student	1 Drawing Utensils per student 1 Paper per student 1 Printed Handout per student
LATIN / GREEK	1 Printed Hymn of the week per student	1 Printed Hymn of the week per student
MATH	1 Pencil per student 1 Paper per student	1 Pencil per student 1 Paper per student
MUSIC	1 (Optional) Pitch instrument	N/A
READING	N/A	N/A
RELIGION	See OHF-4 (SF)	See OHF-4 (SF)
SCIENCE	See Linked Lesson (SF)	1 Drawing Utensils per student 1 Paper per student See Linked Lessons (SF)
VIRTUE	N/A	N/A

UNIT 11

SUBJECT	DAY 1 (Co-op Day)		DAYS 2 – 4	
ART	1	(Optional) Set of Visual Aids on paper, in color (from Unit 9)	N/A	
	1	Handout on paper, in color per student (or per family) (See Unit 9)		
	1-2	Large tubes of putty (depending on class size)		
	50	Toothpicks per 4th-6th Grader		
	1	Foam paper plate per student		
	1	Golf ball sized piece of air-dry clay per student		
	1	Roll of paper towels		
	1	Bottle of cleaning spray		
	1	Sheet of plastic for floor		
		Smock per student		
CCM		Maps 3		Maps 3
		Timeline Cards		Timeline Cards
		Printed Unit Summary		Printed Unit Summary
HISTORY	1	Paper per student	1	Drawing Utensils per student
			1	Paper per student
			3	Printed Handout per student
LANGUAGE ARTS	1	Printed Handout per student	1	Drawing Utensils per student
			1	Paper per student
			1	Printed Handout per student
LATIN/ GREEK	1	Printed Hymn of the week per student	1	Printed Hymn of the week per student
MATH	1	Pencil per student	1	Pencil per student
	1	Paper per student	1	Paper per student
MUSIC	1	(Optional) Pitch instrument	N/A	
READING		N/A	N/A	
RELIGION		See OHF-4 (SF)		See OHF-4 (SF)
SCIENCE		See Linked Lesson	1	Drawing Utensils per student
			1	Paper per student
				See Linked Lessons (SF)
VIRTUE		N/A	N/A	

UNIT 12

SUBJECT	DAY 1		DAYS 2 – 4	
ART	N/A		See Extras	
CCM	Maps 1,2,3 Timeline Cards Printed Unit Summary		Maps 1,2,3 Timeline Cards Printed Unit Summary	
HISTORY	N/A		5-10	Crayons/colored pencils per student
			1	Drawing Utensils per student
			2	Printed Handout per student
LANGUAGE ARTS	1	Printed Handout per student	1	Drawing Utensils per student
	1	Drawing Utensils per student	1	Paper per student
			1	Printed Handout per student
LATIN / GREEK	1	Printed Hymn of the week per student	1	Printed Hymn of the week per student
MATH	1	Pencil per student	1	Pencil per student
	1	Paper per student	1	Paper per student
MUSIC	1	(Optional) Pitch instrument	N/A	
READING	N/A		N/A	
RELIGION	See OHF-4 (SF)		See OHF-4 (SF)	
SCIENCE	N/A		1	Drawing Utensils per student
			1	Paper per student
VIRTUE	N/A		N/A	

UNIT 13

SUBJECT	DAY 1		DAYS 2 – 4	
ART	N/A		N/A	
CCM	Maps 1,2,3 Timeline Cards Printed Unit Summary		Maps 1,2,3 Timeline Cards Printed Unit Summary	
HISTORY	N/A		5-10 1 1 3	Crayons/colored pencils per student Drawing Utensils per student Paper per student Printed Handout per student
LANGUAGE ARTS	1 1	Printed Handout per student Drawing Utensils per student	1 1 1	Drawing Utensils per student Paper per student Printed Handout per student
LATIN/ GREEK	1	Printed Hymn of the week per student	1	Printed Hymn of the week per student
MATH	1 1	Pencil per student Paper per student	1 1	Pencil per student Paper per student
MUSIC	1	(Optional) Pitch instrument	N/A	
READING	N/A		N/A	
RELIGION	See OHF-4 (SF)		See OHF-4 (SF)	
SCIENCE	See Linked Lessons (SF)		1 1	Drawing Utensils per student Paper per student See Linked Lessons (SF)
VIRTUE	N/A		N/A	

UNIT 14

SUBJECT	DAY 1		DAYS 2 – 4	
ART	N/A		N/A	
CCM		Maps 1,2,3 Timeline Cards Printed Unit Summary		Maps 1,2,3 Timeline Cards Printed Unit Summary
HISTORY		N/A	5-10 1 1 2	Crayons/colored pencils per student Drawing Utensils per student Paper per student Printed Handout per student
LANGUAGE ARTS		N/A		N/A
LATIN/ GREEK	1	Printed Hymn of the week per student	1	Printed Hymn of the week per student
MATH	1 1	Pencil per student Paper per student	1 1	Pencil per student Paper per student
MUSIC	1	(Optional) Pitch instrument		N/A
READING		N/A		N/A
RELIGION		See OHF-4 (SF)		See OHF-4 (SF)
SCIENCE		N/A		N/A
VIRTUE		N/A		N/A

UNIT 15

SUBJECT	DAY 1		DAYS 2 – 4	
ART	N/A		N/A	
CCM	Maps 1,2,3 Timeline Cards Printed Unit Summary		Maps 1,2,3 Timeline Cards Printed Unit Summary	
HISTORY	N/A		1 1	Drawing Utensils per student Paper per student Props and materials needed for acting out the story
LANGUAGE ARTS	1	Printed Handout per student Drawing Utensils per student Paper per student	1 1 1	Drawing Utensils per student Paper per student Printed Handout per student
LATIN/ GREEK	1	Printed Hymn of the week per student	1	Printed Hymn of the week per student
MATH	1 1	Pencil per student Paper per student	1 1	Pencil per student Paper per student
MUSIC	1	(Optional) Pitch instrument	N/A	
READING	N/A		N/A	
RELIGION	See OHF-4 (SF)		See OHF-4 (SF)	
SCIENCE	10-12 1 2 1 1	Small objects (nails, pennies, paper clips, plastic balls, etc.) per student Shoe box or other container to hold the small objects per student U-shaped magnet Magnets from your refrigerator per student Piece of paper or Nature Journal per student Drawing Utensils per student	 1 1	See Linked Lessons (SF) Piece of paper or Nature Journal per student Printed Handout per student
VIRTUE	N/A		N/A	

UNIT 16

SUBJECT	DAY 1		DAYS 2 – 4	
ART	N/A		N/A	
CCM	Maps 1,2,3 Timeline Cards Printed Unit Summary		Maps 1,2,3 Timeline Cards Printed Unit Summary	
HISTORY	N/A		1 5-10 1 1 1	Paper per student Crayons/colored pencils per student Printed Handout per student Paper per student Drawing Utensils per student
LANGUAGE ARTS	1 1	Printed Handout per student Drawing Utensils per student	1 1 1 1	Printed Copy work per student Drawing Utensils per student Paper per student Printed Handout per student
LATIN / GREEK	1	Printed Hymn of the week per student	1	Printed Hymn of the week per student
MATH	1 1	Pencil per student Paper per student	1 1	Pencil per student Paper per student
MUSIC	1	(Optional) Pitch instrument	N/A	
READING	N/A		N/A	
RELIGION		See OHF-4 (SF)		See OHF-4 (SF)
SCIENCE	10-12 1 1 3 1 1 1 1 1 1 1	Small objects (nails, pennies, paper clips, plastic balls, etc.) per student Shoe box or other container to hold the small objects per student U-shaped magnet per student Magnets from your refrigerator per student Sheet of paper per student Piece of metal (e.g. pie or cake pan) per student Piece of plastic (e.g. placemat or plastic cutting board) per student Piece of cardboard (5 x 7 or 4x6) per student Piece of wood (5 x 7 or 4x6 e.g. sheet of thin plywood) per student Piece of paper or Nature Journal per student Drawing Utensils per student	1 1	Drawing Utensils per student Paper per student See Linked Lessons (SF)
VIRTUE	N/A		N/A	

UNIT 17

SUBJECT	DAY 1		DAYS 2 – 4	
ART	N/A		N/A	
CCM	Maps 1,2,3 Timeline Cards Printed Unit Summary		Maps 1,2,3 Timeline Cards Printed Unit Summary	
HISTORY	N/A		1 1 5-10 2	Drawing Utensils per student Paper per student Crayons/colored pencils per student Printed Handout per student
LANGUAGE ARTS	1 1	Printed Handout per student Drawing Utensils per student	1 1 1	Drawing Utensils per student Paper per student Printed Handout per student
LATIN/ GREEK	1	Printed Hymn of the week per student	1	Printed Hymn of the week per student
MATH	1 1	Pencil per student Paper per student	1 1	Pencil per student Paper per student
MUSIC	1	(Optional) Pitch instrument	N/A	
READING	N/A		N/A	
RELIGION	See OHF-4 (SF)		See OHF-4 (SF)	
SCIENCE	10-12 1 1 3 1 1	Small objects (nails, pennies, paper clips, plastic balls, etc.) per student Shoe box or other container to hold the small objects per student U-shaped magnet per student Magnets from your refrigerator per student Sheet of paper per student Printed Handout per student	1 1	Drawing Utensils per student Piece of paper or Nature Journal per student
VIRTUE	N/A		N/A	

UNIT 18

SUBJECT	DAY 1 (Field Trip Day)		DAYS 2 – 4	
ART	N/A		See "Extras"	
CCM	Maps 1,2,3 Timeline Cards Printed Unit Summary		Maps 1,2,3 Timeline Cards Printed Unit Summary	
HISTORY	N/A		1 1 5- 10	Drawing Utensils per student Paper per student Crayons/colored pencils per student See Extras See Linked Lesson (SF)
LANGUAGE ARTS	1 1	Printed Handout per student Drawing Utensils per student	1 1 1	Drawing Utensils per student Paper per student Printed Handout per student
LATIN/ GREEK	1	Printed Hymn of the week per student	1	Printed Hymn of the week per student
MATH	1 1	Pencil per student Paper per student	1 1	Pencil per student Paper per student
MUSIC	1	(Optional) Pitch instrument	N/A	
READING	N/A		N/A	
RELIGION	See OHF-4 (SF)		See OHF-4 (SF)	
SCIENCE	1 3 10- 12 1 1	U-shaped magnet per student Magnets from your refrigerator per student Small objects (nails, pennies, paper clips, plastic balls, etc.) per student (Choose new object) Shoe box or other container to hold the small objects per student Paper per student or Nature Journal per student Or (Optional) "My First Magnet Kit" (See link SF)	1 1	Drawing Utensils per student Paper per student or Nature Journal per student See Linked Lessons
VIRTUE	N/A		N/A	

UNIT 19

SUBJECT	DAY 1 (Co-op Day)		DAYS 2 – 4	
ART	1	Handout on paper, in color per student (or per family)	N/A	
	9	3" X 3" pieces of square, cotton fabric (assorted colors and patterns) per student		
	1	Sewing needle per student		
	1	Spool of thread per student		
	1	Plastic baggy per student		
	1	marked with permanent marker with the student's name		
	1	(Optional) Set of Visual Aids on paper, in color		
	1	Bottle of cleaning spray		
	1	Paper Towel Roll		
CCM	Maps 1		Maps 1	
	Timeline Cards		Timeline Cards	
	Printed Unit Summary		Printed Unit Summary	
HISTORY	See Linked Lesson (SF)		1	Crayons/colored pencils per student
			5-10	
			1	Drawing Utensils per student
			1	Papers per student
			1	See Linked Lesson (SF)
			1	Printed Handout per student
				See Extras
LANGUAGE ARTS	1	Printed Handout per student	1	Drawing Utensils per student
			1	Paper per student
			1	Printed Handout per student
LATIN/ GREEK	1	Printed Hymn of the week per student	1	Printed Hymn of the week per student
MATH	1	Pencil per student	1	Pencil per student
	1	Paper per student	1	Paper per student
MUSIC	1	(Optional) Pitch instrument	N/A	
READING	N/A		N/A	
RELIGION	See OHF-4 (SF)		See OHF-4 (SF)	
SCIENCE	See Linked Lesson		1	Drawing Utensils per student
			1	Paper per student or Nature Journal per student
				See Linked Lessons (SF)
VIRTUE	N/A		N/A	

UNIT 20

SUBJECT	DAY 1 (Co-op Day)		DAYS 2 – 4	
ART	1	Handout on paper, in color per student (or per family) (Unit 19)	N/A	
	1	Baggie of quilt squares from Unit 19 per student		
	1	Sewing needle per student		
	1	Spool of thread per student (For students who were absent)		
	9	3" X 3" pieces of square, cotton fabric (assorted colors and patterns) per student		
	1	Plastic baggy per student marked with permanent marker with the student's name		
	1	(Optional) Set of Visual Aids on paper, in color		
	1	Bottle of cleaning spray		
	1	Paper Towel Roll		
CCM		Maps 2 Timeline Cards Printed Unit Summary		Maps 2 Timeline Cards Printed Unit Summary
HISTORY		See Linked Lesson (SF)	2	Printed Handout per student
			5-10	Crayons/colored pencils per student
			1	Drawing Utensils per student See Linked Lesson (SF)
LANGUAGE ARTS	1	Printed Handout per student	1	Printed Copy work per student
	1	Drawing Utensils per student	1	Drawing Utensils per student
			1	Paper per student
			1	Printed Handout per student
LATIN / GREEK	1	Printed Hymn of the week per student	1	Printed Hymn of the week per student
MATH	1	Pencil per student	1	Pencil per student
	1	Paper per student	1	Paper per student
MUSIC	1	(Optional) Pitch instrument		N/A
READING		N/A		N/A
RELIGION		See OHF-4 (SF)		See OHF-4 (SF)
SCIENCE		See Linked Lesson (SF)	1	Drawing Utensils per student
			1	Paper per student or Nature Journal per student See Linked Lessons (SF)
VIRTUE		N/A		N/A

UNIT 21

SUBJECT	DAY 1 (Co-op Day)		DAYS 2 – 4	
ART	1	Handout on paper, in color per student (or per family)	N/A	
	1	(Optional) Set of Visual Aids on paper, in color		
	1	Disposable camera per child		
	2	L-shaped pieces of cardboard (5" at the bottom and 7" for side) per student		
CCM		Maps 2		Maps 2
		Timeline Cards		Timeline Cards
		Printed Unit Summary		Printed Unit Summary
HISTORY	1	Printed Handout per student	5-10	Crayons/colored pencils per student
	1	Drawing Utensils per student	1	Drawing Utensils per student
			1	See Linked Lesson (SF)
				Printed Handout per student
				See Extras
LANGUAGE ARTS	1	Printed Handout per student	1	Drawing Utensils per student
	1	Drawing Utensils per student	1	Paper per student
			1	Printed Handout per student
LATIN/ GREEK	1	Printed Hymn of the week per student	1	Printed Hymn of the week per student
MATH	1	Pencil per student	1	Pencil per student
	1	Paper per student	1	Paper per student
MUSIC	1	(Optional) Pitch instrument	N/A	
READING		N/A	N/A	
RELIGION		See OHF-4 (SF)		See OHF-4 (SF)
SCIENCE		See Linked Lesson (SF)	1	Drawing Utensils per student
	1	Drawing Utensils per student	1	Paper per student
	1	Paper per student Nature Journal per student		See Linked Lessons (SF)
VIRTUE		N/A		N/A

UNIT 22

SUBJECT	DAY 1 (Field Trip Day)		DAYS 2 – 4	
ART	N/A		See "Extras"	
CCM	Maps 1,2,3,4 Timeline Cards Printed Unit Summary		Maps 1,2,3,4 Timeline Cards Printed Unit Summary	
HISTORY	N/A		1 1 5-10 2 1	Drawing Utensils per student Paper per student Crayons/colored pencils per student Printed Handout per student See Linked Lesson (SF) See Extras
LANGUAGE ARTS	1 1	Printed Handout per student Drawing Utensils per student	1 1 1	Drawing Utensils per student Paper per student Printed Handout per student
LATIN/ GREEK	1	Printed Hymn of the week per student	1	Printed Hymn of the week per student
MATH	1 1	Pencil per student Paper per student	1 1	Pencil per student Paper per student
MUSIC	1	(Optional) Pitch instrument	N/A	
READING	N/A		N/A	
RELIGION	See OHF-4 (SF)		See OHF-4 (SF)	
SCIENCE	N/A		1 1	Drawing Utensils per student Paper per student or Nature Journal per student See Linked Lesson (SF)
VIRTUE	N/A		N/A	

UNIT 23

SUBJECT	DAY 1 (Co-op Day)		DAYS 2 – 4	
ART	1	Handout on paper, in color per student (or per family)	N/A	
	1	(Optional) Set of Visual Aids on paper, in color		
	2	Disposable camera per child(Unit 21) L-shaped pieces of cardboard (5" at the bottom and 7" for side) per student		
CCM		Maps 2 Timeline Cards Printed Unit Summary		Maps 2 Timeline Cards Printed Unit Summary
HISTORY	1	Printed Handout per student	5-10	Crayons/colored pencils per student
	1	Drawing Utensils per student	1	Drawing Utensils per student
			1	Paper per student
			2	Printed Handout per student
LANGUAGE ARTS	1	Printed Handout per student	1	Printed Copy work per student
	1	Drawing Utensils per student	1	Drawing Utensils per student
			1	Paper per student
			1	Printed Handout per student
LATIN/ GREEK	1	Printed Hymn of the week per student	1	Printed Hymn of the week per student
MATH	1	Pencil per student	1	Pencil per student
	1	Paper per student	1	Paper per student
MUSIC	1	(Optional) Pitch instrument		N/A
READING		N/A		N/A
RELIGION		See OHF-4 (SF)		See OHF-4 (SF)
SCIENCE		See Lesson in (SF) Drawing Utensils per student Paper per student or Nature Journal per student	1 1	Drawing Utensils per student Paper per student or Nature Journal per student See Linked Lessons (SF)
VIRTUE		N/A		N/A

UNIT 24

SUBJECT	DAY 1 (Co-op Day)		DAYS 2 – 4	
ART	1	Printed Handout per student (or per family)	N/A	
	1	HB pencil per student		
	1	Pen and ink set per student		
	1	Bottle black ink set per student (4th- 6th Grade)		
	1	Nib Holder per student (4th- 6th Grade)		
	1	Set of pen nibs per student (4th- 6th Grade)		
	1	12" X 12" piece of Multi-media paper per student		
	1	(Optional) Set of Visual Aids on paper, in color		
	1	Roll of paper towels		
	1	Bottle of cleaning spray		
CCM		Maps 3 Timeline Cards Printed Unit Summary		Maps 3 Timeline Cards Printed Unit Summary
HISTORY	1	Printed Handout per student	5-10	Crayons/colored pencils per student
	1	Drawing Utensils per student	1	Drawing Utensils per student
	1	Paper per student	1	Paper per student
			2	Printed Handout per student
LANGUAGE ARTS	1	Printed Handout per student	1	Drawing Utensils per student
	1	Drawing Utensils per student	1	Paper per student
			1	Printed Handout per student
LATIN/ GREEK	1	Printed Hymn of the week per student	1	Printed Hymn of the week per student
MATH	1	Pencil per student	1	Pencil per student
	1	Paper per student	1	Paper per student
MUSIC	1	(Optional) Pitch instrument		N/A
READING		N/A		N/A
RELIGION		See OHF-4 (SF)		See OHF-4 (SF)
SCIENCE		See Linked Lessons (SF)	1	Drawing Utensils per student
	1	Drawing Utensils per student	1	Paper per student
	1	Paper per student or Nature Journal per student		See Linked Lessons (SF)
VIRTUE		N/A		N/A

UNIT 25

SUBJECT	DAY 1 (Co-op Day)		DAYS 2 – 4	
ART	1	Printed Handout per student (or per family)	N/A	
	1	HB pencil per student		
	1	Pen and ink set per student (see unit 24)		
	1	12″ X 12″ piece of Multi-media paper per student		
	1	(Optional) Set of Visual Aids on paper, in color		
	1	Roll of paper towels		
	1	Bottle of cleaning spray		
CCM		Maps 3		Maps 3
		Timeline Cards		Timeline Cards
		Printed Unit Summary		Printed Unit Summary
HISTORY	1	Paper per student	1	Printed Coloring Pages per student
	1	Drawing Utensils per student	5-10	
	5-10	Crayons/colored pencils or Colored pencils per student	1	Crayons/colored pencils per student
			1	Drawing Utensils per student
				Papers per student
				See Linked Lesson (SF)
				See Extras
LANGUAGE ARTS	1	Printed Handout per student	1	Drawing Utensils per student
	1	Drawing Utensils per student	1	Printed Copy work per student
			1	Paper per student
			1	Printed Handout per student
LATIN/ GREEK	1	Printed Hymn of the week per student	1	Printed Hymn of the week per student
MATH	1	Pencil per student	1	Pencil per student
	1	Paper per student	1	Paper per student
MUSIC	1	(Optional) Pitch instrument	N/A	
READING		N/A	N/A	
RELIGION		See OHF-4 (SF)	See OHF-4 (SF)	
SCIENCE		See Linked Lessons (SF)	1	Drawing Utensils per student
	1	Drawing Utensils per student	1	Paper per student or Nature Journal per student
	1	Paper per student or Nature Journal per student		See Linked Lessons (SF)
VIRTUE		N/A	N/A	

UNIT 26

SUBJECT	DAY 1 (Field Trip Day)		DAYS 2 – 4	
ART	N/A		See "Extras"	
CCM	Maps 1,2,3,4 Timeline Cards Printed Unit Summary		Maps 1,2,3,4 Timeline Cards Printed Unit Summary	
HISTORY	N/A		1 1 5-10	Drawing Utensils per student Paper per student Crayons/colored pencils per student See Extras
LANGUAGE ARTS	1 1	Printed Handout per student Drawing Utensils per student	1 1 1	Drawing Utensils per student Paper per student Printed Handout per student
LATIN/ GREEK	1	Printed Hymn of the week per student	1	Printed Hymn of the week per student
MATH	1 1	Pencil per student Paper per student	1 1	Pencil per student Paper per student
MUSIC	1	(Optional) Pitch instrument		N/A
READING	N/A		N/A	
RELIGION	See OHF-4 (SF)		See OHF-4 (SF)	
SCIENCE	N/A		1 1	Drawing Utensils per student Paper per student or Nature Journals See Linked Lesson (SF)
VIRTUE	N/A		N/A	

4th – 6th Grade ~ Materials Usage Schedule

UNIT 27

SUBJECT	DAY 1 (Co-op Day)		DAYS 2 – 4	
ART	1	(Optional) Set of Visual Aids in	1	HB pencil per student
	1	color	1	Black ink and pen per student
	1	HB pencil per student	1	Pair of scissors per student
	1	Black ink and pen per student	1	3″ pieces of yarn per student
	2	Pair of scissors per student	1	Hole-punchers per every 2
	1	3″ pieces of yarn per student		students
	1	Hole-punchers per every 2	1	Sheet of white paper per
	1	students	1	student
	1	Sheet of white paper per student		Printed Art Handout per
	1	Printed Art Handout per student		student
		Roll of paper towels		
		Bottle of cleaning spray		
CCM		Maps 4		Maps 4
		Timeline Cards		Timeline Cards
		Printed Unit Summary		Printed Unit Summary
HISTORY	1	Drawing Utensils per student	5-10	Crayons/colored pencils per student
		See Linked Lesson (SF)	1	Drawing Utensils per student
			1	Paper per student
			2	Printed Handout per student
				See Extras
LANGUAGE ARTS	1	Printed Handout per student	1	Drawing Utensils per student
			1	Paper per student
			1	Printed Handout per student
LATIN/ GREEK	1	Printed Hymn of the week per student	1	Printed Hymn of the week per student
MATH	1	Pencil per student	1	Pencil per student
	1	Paper per student	1	Paper per student
MUSIC	1	(Optional) Pitch instrument		N/A
READING		N/A		N/A
RELIGION		See OHF-4 (SF)		See OHF-4 (SF)
SCIENCE		See Lesson in (SF)	1	Drawing Utensils per student
		Drawing Utensils per student	1	Paper per student or Nature
		Paper per student or Nature		Journal per student
		Journal per student		See Linked Lessons (SF)
VIRTUE		N/A		N/A

4th – 6th Grade ~ Materials Usage Schedule

UNIT 28

SUBJECT	DAY 1 (Co-op Day)		DAYS 2 – 4	
ART	1	(Optional) Set of Visual Aids in color	N/A	
	1	Handout on paper, in color per student (or per family)		
	1	HB pencil per student		
	1	Pair of Scissors per student		
	2-3	Staplers per classroom		
		Sheets of white paper per student or one sticky note pad per student		
CCM		Maps 5		Maps 5
		Timeline Cards		Timeline Cards
		Printed Unit Summary		Printed Unit Summary
HISTORY	1	Printed Handout per student	5-10	Crayons/colored pencils per student
			1	Drawing Utensils per student
			1	Paper per student
			3	Printed Handout per student
				See Extras
LANGUAGE ARTS	1	Printed Handout per student	1	Drawing Utensils per student
	1	Drawing Utensils per student	1	Paper per student
			1	Printed Handout per student
LATIN / GREEK	1	Printed Hymn of the week per student	1	Printed Hymn of the week per student
MATH	1	Pencil per student	1	Pencil per student
	1	Paper per student	1	Paper per student
MUSIC	1	(Optional) Pitch instrument	N/A	
READING		N/A	N/A	
RELIGION		See OHF-4 (SF)	See OHF-4 (SF)	
SCIENCE		See Lesson in (SF)	1	Drawing Utensils per student
	1	Drawing Utensils per student	1	Paper per student or Nature Journal per student
	1	Paper per student or Nature Journal per student		See Linked Lessons (SF)
VIRTUE		N/A	N/A	

441

UNIT 29

SUBJECT	DAY 1 (Co-op Day)		DAYS 2 – 4	
ART	1 1 1 1 1 1 10- 12 4-5	(Optional) Set of Visual Aids in color Handout on paper, in color per student (or per family) HB pencil per student Pair of Scissors per student Staplers per classroom Pen & ink kit per student Markers ☐ Colored Pencils Sheets of white paper per student or sticky note pad		N/A
CCM	Maps 5 Timeline Cards Printed Unit Summary		Maps 5 Timeline Cards Printed Unit Summary	
HISTORY	1	Drawing Utensils per student	5- 10 1 1 2	Crayons/colored pencils per student Drawing Utensils per student Paper per student Printed Handout per student See Extras
LANGUAGE ARTS	1 1	Printed Handout per student Drawing Utensils per student	1 1 1	Drawing Utensils per student Paper per student Printed Handout per student
LATIN/ GREEK	1	Printed Hymn of the week per student	1	Printed Hymn of the week per student
MATH	1 1	Pencil per student Paper per student	1 1	Pencil per student Paper per student
MUSIC	1	(Optional) Pitch instrument		N/A
READING	N/A		N/A	
RELIGION	See OHF-4 (SF)		See OHF-4 (SF)	
SCIENCE	See Lessons (SF)		1 1	Drawing Utensils per student Paper per student or Natural Journal See Linked Lessons (SF)
VIRTUE	N/A		N/A	

UNIT 30

SUBJECT	DAY 1		DAYS 2 – 4	
ART	N/A		See "Extras"	
CCM	Maps 1,2,3,4,5 Timeline Cards Printed Unit Summary		Maps 1,2,3,4,5 Timeline Cards Printed Unit Summary	
HISTORY	N/A		1 1 5-10 1	Drawing Utensils per student Paper per student Crayons/colored pencils per student Printed Handout per student
LANGUAGE ARTS	N/A		N/A	
LATIN/ GREEK	1	Printed Hymn of the week per student	1	Printed Hymn of the week per student
MATH	1 1	Pencil per student Paper per student	1 1	Pencil per student Paper per student
MUSIC	1	(Optional) Pitch instrument	N/A	
READING	N/A		N/A	
RELIGION	See OHF-4 (SF)		See OHF-4 (SF)	
SCIENCE	N/A		N/A	
VIRTUE	N/A		N/A	

Made in the USA
Middletown, DE
03 August 2020

13469213R00252